KARAOKE and COLD LAZARUS

Dennis Potter is Britain's most acclaimed television dramatist. His plays for TV include *Blue Remembered Hills* (1979), *Brimstone and Treacle* (commissioned in 1975 but banned until 1987), the series *Pennies from Heaven* (1978), *The Singing Detective* (1986), *Blackeyes* (1989) and *Lipstick on Your Collar* (1993). He also wrote novels, stage plays and screenplays. He died in June 1994. *Seeing the Blossom*, his final television interview, was published in 1994.

by the same author

fiction

BLACKEYES
HIDE AND SEEK
TICKET TO RIDE
PENNIES FROM HEAVEN

screenplays

PENNIES FROM HEAVEN
THE SINGING DETECTIVE
BLUE REMEMBERED HILLS AND OTHER PLAYS
(also includes *Joe's Ark* and *Cream in My Coffee*)

plays

BRIMSTONE AND TREACLE
SUFFICIENT CARBOHYDRATE

also available

SEEING THE BLOSSOM

DENNIS POTTER

Karaoke
and
Cold Lazarus

with an Introduction
by the author

faber and faber
LONDON · BOSTON

First published in 1996 by Faber and Faber Limited
3 Queen Square London WC1N 3AU

Photoset by Parker Typesetting Service, Leicester
Printed in England by Clays Ltd, St Ives Plc

A CIP record of this book
is available from the British Library
ISBN 0-571-17478-7

2 4 6 8 10 9 7 5 3 1

CONTENTS

INTRODUCTION

We all know that we are going to die, and so the bleak clinical statement that the event is indeed about to happen to me in rather shorter order than I might have expected should not in itself make all that difference to the way I live, work and feel: that is, the way I *write*. But let me rush to assure you, in what may turn out to be an importunate gabble, that *everything* feels different. Sometimes, too, in modes that are almost perversely serene or emancipating, thus making the whole experience far less dread-filled and ceiling-contemplative than I could ever have dared to imagine.

Every word written by me in this book has been composed under the matter-of-fact death sentence given to me in the middle of 'February, fill ditch black or white'. Let this go some way, therefore, to excusing the odd shape of this little piece I am now writing to serve duty both as an introduction to my last two productions for television, as well as a glancing valediction to all the previous works as well.

The prognoses have jumped about a little disconcertingly, varying in these last couple of months between 'certainly a few weeks more' to 'three to five months', and one passing, pinky-blue sort of haze that implied life deep into high summer and the first tinges of the leaves beyond. These variants appear to have as much to do with the temperament of the doctor in question as with the well-charted histology of the disease.

But perhaps (and importantly) it is the other way around, and they are reacting to the manner of my own assertions. It almost seems to me as though it is *me* who has to make up his own mind about how and where and when on the limited scale I should pack up my bags and go. It depends, so to speak, on the pen in my hands.

My first thoughts upon hearing that I had cancer of the pancreas, with secondaries already on the liver, were that 'my affairs' were in one hell of a muddle – and I'm not just talking about a lost premium bond. No, they'd been worsened by recent and seemingly endless pain which had made me push things aside or abandon them altogether, by my wife Margaret's illness, and further jammed up by some bad risks I had taken with the business side of my working life.

Like most husbands and fathers I had assumed it to be a paramount duty of mine to leave my family as much as I fairly could in terms of their financial security, and with as few tangled-up administrative problems regarding my by now quite sizeable assets and their future earning powers.

I totted up all I *thought* I had, and began the coldly fascinating process of 'the time he has to put his affairs in order', a phrase which had always intrigued me since I first read it as a child in, I think, a Biggles book. In other words, I had to concoct some sort of Family Trust to take care of all my works and their licences, and I had to make a will, the one document in which one cannot literally afford to be pusillanimous.

This took me several long days of mind-crunching paperwork. The great complication was the fact that I had not long before badly broken one of the cardinal rules of the biz there's no other biz like (or the biz all other businesses are getting to be like) by investing fat sums of my own present and presumed future resources in my own work – only to find it not very well received.

A year before, thanks in part to my legally permissible borrowing powers over my own self-regulated Pension Fund (started off by MGM money, and swiftly swollen by decades of other ready American booty for projects that rarely passed the start line, as well as all the others which, mostly elsewhere, did), I was able to put in more than half a million pounds of my 'own' money into the ailing budget of a BBC film I had called *Midnight Movie* without any intention of ironic foreboding. By becoming the Corporation's sole if minority partner, the movie was able to begin shooting.

'The film has been completed but has not yet found a distributor': the most common epitaph in the sprawl of chipped, tarnished, sloping memorial slabs to an independent British film industry which by now must be as big as that enormous sprawl of the dead at Kensal Green Cemetery.

Writing, producing and hustling for the as yet still unseen *Midnight Movie* had already wrenched out large chunks of my working year. I'd not taken any fees for these combined full-time jobs (not even, oh whisper it low, for the script itself). Worse, I had helped finance our normal and by no means spartan living standards by airily taking on two rich commissions that had been dangling so sweetly in front of me for some time. These were for a six-part original series for the BBC, and another six-parter for Channel 4, the latter spun out on nothing much more than what had felt like an inspired lunch-time burble where I thought I suddenly saw the myriad glistenings of a 'great story' about half-way down my wine glass.

The common perception behind all this, of course, was that *time* was not at issue. Time was something one had, a physicist's T, in plenty, ever available, waiting for use. And it was the great shock of finding out that this was not the case which has provided me with the only genuine moment of panic about my imminent death I have so far experienced: a feeling as swiftly and brutally done with by the time it takes to fall down a flight of stairs.

My account books were so much less healthy than I had been blithely assuming. I had a four-to-five year overhang of debts-plus-interest to my own Pension Fund, and – if this were indeed to be the point of crumble and collapse – I would have to pay back £60,000 in upfront advances to the BBC and £100,000 to Channel 4 – as well as forego all the delivery-and-acceptance payments, production fees, sales and 'associated residual rights' connected with the original commissions.

I have for a long period now been exceptionally fortunate with my earning powers in what is a very frail trade, so much so that I tended to walk along certain circular corridors at, say, Shepherd's Bush with something of the exaggeratedly furtive air taken by a pantomime villain tiptoeing away from a scene of his own particular dastardy. Now, maybe, the game was up at last.

When the cancer was so belatedly diagnosed, and thereupon found too advanced to be treated either by surgery or by chemotherapy, I was led deep into the drowsing valleys of morphine and heroin where hobgoblins wait to chatter. This had to be the landscape of *WhatamIgoingtodo?*, where the first signposts indicate how to curl yourself up into a ball and weep away what is left.

Journey past those, though, and the choices soon became very simple for me, especially as the truly ravaging pain became more under control.

By chance, I had also just been offered a first stab at a remake of an old but not very good movie, and the whacking great upfront fee the Americans guaranteed would soon take the sting out of those pay-the-money-back issues at the two British television stations. Did I therefore go flat out at my most now-hear-*this* pitch for the Hollywood number, and duly deliver the first draft of whatever quality they would have guaranteed to buy, so long as I hid the news of the lethal diagnosis until the contract had been signed? Worse things have happened, after all. But no, I didn't want to squander my last energies on work of this nature, where the better you make it the less chance there is of the film actually being shot. 'No' went back down the transatlantic telephone line, and with it a few shards of saved dignity as well.

The issue was, then, did I work on and on with the muddle *Karaoke* had become through the months of pain that had followed the earlier neglect, trying to rescue a complicated play and its central metaphors from the disaster I think I had made of it? Or did I dive in, hell or glory, and find in *Cold Lazarus* something like 'the story' I had glimpsed deep down in the Gevrey Chambertin?

Time was again the leading question, followed hard upon by some doubt about what making words would be *like* when making them under such duress. Would they become too careless without the restraints of their future reception, critical or otherwise, being of little or no consequence? Or would they warp and buckle, would I lose control of them, so that things yukky, maudlin and sanctimonious could come slinking and nudging across the ready-laid duckboards?

In the end – and it was the struggle of just one day and one night – I decided that I would cast adrift all I had so far written of *Karaoke*, and start as from new, scene one, page one. And that then, oh, if there were time, that then I would plunge headlong into *Cold Lazarus*. Even if strength and spirit gave out during the progressive degradations of the growing tumours, and even if I ran smack into the most blank-eyed of writers' blocks, there would surely be enough pages of any kind of quality – gibberish, even – for my redoubtable literary executor, my agent Judy Daish, to resist any 'please pay back' affronts or solicitations.

'Putting my affairs in order', plus some hospital business and a few other attendant nasties, meant that I could take the first day of March as my start-up day. 'A pinch and a punch, the first of the month!' There was a pleasing symmetry to that, of the same nice kind I used to get when starting a shiny new exercise book at school.

When writing flat-out, seriously no-nonsensing with anything else whatsoever, I always set myself certain targets per day in terms of page numbers, and if a page or two are lost in one day's difficulties or interruptions, they have to be made up during the next twelve-or-so-hour session. I also reckon on the basis of a minute a page when calculating the length of a script, and lay the work out accordingly in longhand on an A4 writing book. In a sort of print costive enough to drive its first reader (my daughter Sarah) mad, not on the basis of illegibility but in anxieties about the true nature of the person who has composed it in so appallingly neat, clear and orderly a fashion.

The combination of ten pages a day, every day, to make from the first day of the month also had its charms in terms of simple mental arithmetic. I realized from the beginning that the 360-pages a six-hour serial needed would be too much to leave space for the other 360 pages that the waiting *Cold Lazarus* would also need – especially if there were to be no gap in between to catch a new breath let alone a violently new subject. Such a schedule demanded seventy-two days without break from 1 March, and that would take me to close of play on the evening of 11 May.

Mind you, this date was on the right side of the fifty-ninth birthday (17 May) I had somehow privately resolved to reach in the midst of all the prognoses. A draconian stint in further deliberations might not yet be totally out of the question after all. So I mentioned the 11 May target-for-work to one of the more tacit of the doctors who were suddenly drifting in and out of my attention, and asked whether it was likely that I could work properly for such a span. A sharp intake of incredulity was sufficient answer. I then enquired of another in the deliberately more sardonic terms I was ready to use in my own dialogue. 'Tick one box,' I invited. 'Possible, Probable.' The hesitation was long enough to make the answer real enough, and it wasn't the gentler of the two.

But . . . *if* I tried *two four-parters* . . .?

Well, this still kept the kind of lengths each of the two themes needed in a form natural to the television schedules. I could think, then, in terms of 480 pages in fifty days, allowing at least a full day for the turn-around of mood, theme and subject. I would have until the end of the working day on 15 April, which was far more safely tucked into the stretches I had been given. All I wanted was a path through all the opiates and analgesics, all the clutches and the humiliations, that would show up sufficient patches of calm or clear landscape where I could genuinely 'write my all'.

I made myself sit at my desk at five o'clock in the morning of Tuesday, 1 March, twelve hours before I was due to see my accountant, Stanley Rosenthal, a co-trustee of the Family Trust for my work. I sat down and wrote the word KARAOKE in big bright capitals, and almost immediately ignited. As soon as I began to write I began to live again. Within hours I knew I was writing freely, within days I felt I was writing well, and I knew by the time the week was out that I was writing truthfully.

Already, as I sat down on that first darkly early hour of the first morning, I had been unable to avoid the strange and rather disturbing feeling that things directly in front of me were somehow *presenting* themselves to me. Everything was demanding look, look, look at me; and all the dignity of everything was in the present tense, the one that breaks at the tip of your tongue or your pen, the tense that is itself a sense, like a taste. On that morning, as in some wholly new experience not at all mystical or dream-like but flint-hard and clean, I submerged a great part of myself to the now-ness of that self, where everything was both trivial and significant, including the differences between the two.

The rim of the coffee cup, the faint seagull-wing cusp made by a slant of light on top of the coffee, and the pleasurable surprise in finding the fold of the bedsheet should be just like that. The hard edge of the continent that was my desk, the emptiness of the paper, the wonderful slithers and curls to make with the ups and downs of letters and punctuation marks, and, above all, the curious little bite as the fine-tipped pen I work with made contact with the crisply waiting paper! I could of course go on and on, multiplying to distraction, but it didn't come out as promiscuous multiplication at all, rather as division. A paring down to what was precisely here precisely now in the very present tense itself full stop.

Present tense. First person. I decided, as I have often in the past, to use the outward *forms* of autobiography to give the engine-power *Karaoke* needed. My man had to walk alongside me in this adventure. He had to be ill, and in pain, and with an impending and intractable death sentence. He had to be more than a little withdrawn, a little sardonic and a little lost. And he had to be a proud writer. None of which, I hope it goes without further saying, means that he had to be *me*. Indeed, in many crucial ways (especially in terms of his isolation) precisely the opposite. No more like me, in fact, than the singing detective who had shared my natal patch and peeling skin. But like me enough to understand one of the minor aberrations I sometimes have felt about the scenes going on in front of me.

I have sometimes caught myself thinking, or half-thinking, that the world going on out there right at the brink of one's self has somehow been momentarily prearranged so that even the present tense has been turned in upon itself and there is no point of equilibrium to be found anywhere in anything. A sort of horizontal vertigo. It is only a passing fancy, or the mildest form of lunacy, easily understandable as one of a writer's plausible derangements as he so regularly patterns his thoughts and emotions into acceptable shapes and forms. I simply wanted to make the gap widen, or the unease spread and spread until, under the force of purely physical pain and sickness, plus plenty of alcohol, that old whole background murmur of writerly anxiety could become the long tunnel through which My Hero would have to crawl.

Daniel Feeld, the central character, is already in physical crisis at the start, and he begins by more than half-imagining that something he has recently written has *escaped* into the world outside, almost as a contagion might. He thinks he is being fed back bits of his old dialogue. Things keep arranging themselves to fit an old storyline. He keeps stumbling into the debris of styles and contents that belong on other pages, pages that should have been abandoned and are dangerous to use.

In this extremity, he has to struggle back towards relationships and understandings he thought he had managed to do without. He has to find out about his own work, and so he has, without knowing it or without consciously going through the experience of it, to *find out* about *himself* and thereby expose himself to himself in order to discover where the constant prewritten Karaoke stops and his own song might survive a line or two.

Such a process means, I hope, that you will not be too surprised to come across many a sly nod back to my own working styles, as well as a few deft gleanings from some of my other pieces; not remotely in any sense of self-plagiarism or self-pleading, but as the one genuinely autobiographical strand in the piece, part of the truth of Daniel's own present-tense experiences and the physical burdens which go with them.

I had no idea how the story was going to unfold, nor whom he would meet along the way, except that I was sure the use of pictures in a cutting room was going to be something that both reverberated and explained, threatened and unravelled. I also had no idea how it would all end, except that he had to know that he was going to die and had to make appropriate arrangements with his affairs and himself.

Getting to know Daniel Feeld made me wonder a lot about what kind of thing he was now writing, because he was obviously the sort to have something on the boil. And during this time, of course, in the physical effort and sheer joy of writing the eccentricities and styles of *Karaoke*, I too had lurking somewhere the original thoughts about *Cold Lazarus* which had made me put it up so eagerly to Channel 4 in the first place.

It came to me as strongly as the taste of the moistly raw shallot dipped in salt that Daniel was writing *Cold Lazarus* partly out of fear of death, partly as a way of pushing the world back into an utter otherly place, and partly as a means of smuggling in a few memories or events or patterns that he needed to face down once more in his remaining, guttering-candle stump of life.

Once that link had been made in my own head, I had no fear of the transition between the two plays. Daniel and I could jump across from one heaving boat to the other. Moreover, by knowing this, I had a richness of emotional detail denied to everyone but myself until the time came to let it explode. The two works, so called, were actually *one*. The reverberations or even merely the syncopations between the two would also be far more than retrospective; they would cast forward too, and be there under the surface, all the time, and growing.

Twice I severely had to resist the almost overwhelming temptation to break into the latter part of *Cold Lazarus* with a scene of Daniel Feeld actually writing it at his own cluttered desk in the time between his murder of 'Pig' Mailion and his own death, which would have meant that he would have to have written his own deathbed scene at the start of *Cold Lazarus*, something not too far removed from what I was actually doing myself.

Fortunately, the temptations were finally scourged and driven off, otherwise the whole edifice would have been twisted into the kind of game, or cheat, that it had so far resisted becoming. Certainly, it is in ludic mode, and walks along that perilous line all the time, for it has to if it is to work at all.

Whether or not the two – or the one, as I now see it – 'work at all' is not, of course, something for me to decide. You will understand that there are now ways in which in my present situation that cannot be of the slightest consequence to me. You will also understand that, again in my present situation, there are now ways in which on this matter *only* my opinion has consequence. As for that I simply wish to say that *Karaoke* and *Cold Lazarus* are as fitting a summation as they are a testament both to my character and my career as I should ever want.

There is one other thing that must be said. Throughout this hurried description of work, of page numbers, day numbers and draconian schedules, there had to be an answering measure of great emotional and physical effort as my condition necessarily deteriorated. All of which means that, almost exhausted now, almost extinct, I had to that self-same degree to neglect those in front of me who were suffering as well, particularly my own sick and struggling wife, Margaret, the steadfast green-eyed one ever.

All vocations tend towards the self-mutilating as well as the cannibalistic of the nearest and dearest, but I don't think I would have had the stomach for the possible brutality if Margaret and all the others so close to me had not all immediately seen that doing what I did in the way that I did meant that I was able to live by the means of this work – and to live with the dignity they too needed for me and from me. I offer up the pieces in my love and my life.

Dennis Potter,
28 April 1994

KARAOKE

Karaoke was first broadcast by the BBC in April 1996. The cast was as follows:

DANIEL FEELD	Albert Finney
NICK BALMER	Richard E. Grant
LADY RUTH BALMER	Julie Christie
MRS HAYNES	Alison Steadman
ARTHUR ('PIG') MAILION	Hywell Bennett
ANNA GRIFFITHS	Anna Chancellor
BEN BAGLIN	Roy Hudd
SANDRA SOLLARS	Saffron Burrows
OLIVER MORSE	Ian McDiarmid
LINDA LANGER	Keeley Hawes
MRS BAGLIN	Liz Smith
PETER BEASLEY	Ralph Brown
IAN	Simon Donald
PETER	Neil Stuke
BRASSERIE WAITER	Steven Mackintosh
ANGIE (THIRD HOSTESS)	Natascha McElhone
IMPATIENT PATIENT	Matthew Scurfield
CONSULTANT	Stephen Boxer
STAFF NURSE	Katherine O'Toole
SEAN	Clive Mendus
DEAN	Tom Fisher
HOSPITAL DOCTOR	Matthew Cottle
TOM (DRIVER)	Paul Raffield
WINE BAR BUSINESSMAN	Tony Bluto
BARMAID	Fay Ripley
DR NIGEL BARKER	Grant Russell
WOMAN ON PHONE	Beth Goddard
YOUNG MAN	Ewan McGregor
WINE BAR SECRETARY	Siobhan Flynn
FIRST OCCUPANT	Martin Malone
SECOND OCCUPANT	Chris Larkin
THIRD OCCUPANT	Sam Halpenny

FIRST YUPPIE DRINKER	Charley Boorman
SECOND YUPPIE DRINKER	Giles Taylor
FOREIGN WAITER	Christopher Glover
FIRST NURSE	Viviana Verveen
SECOND NURSE	Cathy Murphy
FIRST JAPANESE MAN	Yashinori Yamamoto
SECOND JAPANESE MAN	Takahashi Sudo
THIRD JAPANESE MAN	Togo Igawa
FIRST HOSTESS	Jody Saron
SECOND HOSTESS (Pt 1) & TOUTING HOSTESS (Pt 4)	Katy Carmichael
FIRST PORTER	David Norman
SECOND PORTER	Stewart Howson
CLIVE (THE SCRATCHER)	Arthur Whybrow
WAITRESS (Pt 3)	Miranda Pleasence
HOSPITAL RECEPTIONIST	Lucy Cohu
ARAB SON	Eddy Lemare
LUIGI	Arturo Venegas
ARTHUR ('PIG') MAILION	G. B. (Zoot) Money
BUSINESSMAN (Pt 1)	Niven Boyd
CABBIE (Pt 1)	Robert Putt

Written by	Dennis Potter
Production company	Whistling Gypsy
Producers	Kenith Trodd
	Rosemarie Whitman
Executive Producers	Michael Wearing
	Peter Ansorge
Director	Renny Rye
Editor	Clare Douglas
Production Designer	Gary Williamson
Director of Photography	Ashley Rowe
Costume Designer	Janty Yates

PART ONE

KARAOKE SCREEN
*Against montages of images with some relevance to the music
(teenagers kiss, jive, drive chrome-fendered-and-finned cars, etc) the
words of the song come up on the lower half of the screen, in English,
sandwiched by Japanese.*
> **Why must I be**
> **A teenager in love?**

*At the same time, from the start, a male voice is singing, badly, with
an East End accent, the same words as they march across the screen,
darkening on cue.*
Pull out and pan across.

INT. WEST END KARAOKE AND HOSTESS CLUB. NIGHT
*Panning past other karaoke screens showing the same pictures and
text, past a big table of grinning Japanese businessmen, to find the
singer,* ARTHUR ('PIG') MAILION, *a bald, bull-necked heavy in his
late forties, bellowing ludicrously inappropriate words with no sign of
irony or any hint of loss of an obviously high self-regard. He wears a
gaudily striped tie, in bad taste.*
MAILION: (*Singing*)
> **Each time we have a quarrel**
> **It almost breaks my heart**
> **'Cos I am so afraid**
> **That we will have to part –**

INT. A TABLE. THE CLUB. NIGHT
As MAILION *continues to bellow, a middle-aged (English)
businessman pulls a comic face, addressing* SANDRA, *a young
and sexily clad* HOSTESS. *They have champagne.*
BUSINESSMAN: God in heaven. Must be *yonks* since he was a
teenager. In or out of love.
(SANDRA *is either bored or unwell.*)
SANDRA: (*Flat*) Yeah. Well. There you go.
BUSINESSMAN: If he keeps this up, he'll empty the place.
SANDRA: (*Same tones*) He can do what he likes, can't he?

(*The* BUSINESSMAN *looks at her, not satisfied on many counts.*)

BUSINESSMAN: Oh. Can he?

(*But she suddenly flashes* MAILION *a look of the fiercest possible hatred, only momentarily, before recomposing her face into its previous 'deadness', and her voice into its former flatness.*)

SANDRA: He's only the bloody owner, enn'e? I mean, it's his place, darling.

CLOSE-UP – MAILION. KARAOKE CLUB

Holding the microphone as though it were a weapon, and oblivious of the now increasingly evident dismay of the group of (as yet unhostessed) Japanese –

MAILION:

The stars up above –
I cry a tear
For nobody but you –

(*Dissolve into –*)

EXT. A LONDON HOSPITAL. DAY

Like the Princess Grace, the King Edward VII or the London Clinic, rather than an old institutional pile or new tower mediblock. The 'Ambulances Only' space is all but empty. It feels a little alienating, and is cloudily lit.

The song goes through the dissolve, but unsettlingly fading out Mailion's bellow, and, pari passu, *fading in the voice of Craig Douglas (one of the original singers), but so steadily that there are a few seconds where the two voices are disturbingly in the balance of a duet.*

– I'll be the lonely one
If you should say
We're through
I shall go on –

INT. WAITING ROOM. RADIATION DEPARTMENT. HOSPITAL. DAY

A comfortable if institutionalized oblong of chairs, tables with newspapers, inaudible CNN on Cable TV, and a staffed reception desk. Most of those waiting seem Arab or Asiatic, except for one man

6

buried under a wide-spread Financial Times. *The song continues –*
  – go on loving you
  Each night I ask –

CLOSE-UP – FACE UNDER *FINANCIAL TIMES*
*As the newspaper lowers, in virtually a theatrical cue, the face is
revealed of* BEN BAGLIN, *a crumpled, rather pot-bellied, balding and
bespectacled literary agent of narrow tastes but limitless shrewdness,
and he is 'singing' the Craig Douglas voice – with a definite, self-
parodic twinkle.*
BEN: (*'Sings', i.e. lip-syncs*)
  – the stars up above
  Why must I be-e-e
  A teenager in –

INT. X-RAY ROOM BEYOND RECEPTION. DAY
Where a smock-wearing patient, DANIEL FEELD, *about fifty, is flat
out with raised knees on an X-ray table under and alongside
formidable machinery, with a* NURSE *near his head and a* DOCTOR
at his feet, looking across and down at him.
*But 'Why Must I Be A Teenager in Love?' continues at full pitch,
dominating any other sounds.*
  – love?
  I cry a tear
  For nobody but you
  I'll be the –

EXTREME CLOSE-UP – DANIEL FEELD ON X-RAY TABLE
*Looking, feeling a little desolate, eyes fixed on something like one who
doesn't want to know what's going on elsewhere – but the music
seems to sing in his head, and something about his expression shows
that he knows that it is 'there', and he is listening –*
  – the lonely one
  If you should say –

FLASH: CLOSE-UP – MAILION AT KARAOKE CLUB
*A swift visitation in Daniel's mind – dropping Craig Douglas for the
awful Mailion version.*
MAILION: (*Bellows*)

**– we're through
I shall go on –**

CLOSE-UP – DANIEL ON X-RAY TABLE
*And he mutters the conclusion of the line in the lyric, almost without
realizing it –*
DANIEL: (*Mutters*) – on loving you.

INT. X-RAY ROOM. DAY
DOCTOR: (*Puzzled*) On what?
DANIEL: Sorry? (*Then, embarrassed*) Oh. Nothing. I – This is all
    a bit undignified, isn't it? I *think* I was thinking about
    something else. At least, I *hope* I was thinking about
    thinking about something else.
DOCTOR: Well, Mr Feeld. I'm now going to insert this soft tube
    into your rectum.
DANIEL: I'm now *definitely* thinking about something else.
    Spare me the guided tour. *Please.*
DOCTOR: Oh, it's not too uncomfortable I assure you. But –
    you'll feel as though you want to defecate. Needless to say,
    I'd be extremely grateful if you didn't.
DANIEL: God, no. I've been well and truly purged anyway, and
    – (*Helplessly belches.*) Oops. Sorry.
DOCTOR: I don't mind it coming out *that* end. But if you could
    resist the urge to – um – OK? Here goes –

CLOSE-UP – DANIEL ON TABLE
Face showing tension then half-surprised relief.
DOCTOR: (*Off-screen, continuous*) The liquid barium is going in –
    comfortable? All right? – You'll be able to see what's going
    on in your intestines by looking at that little monitor there
    to your right . . .
DANIEL: (*Tight-voiced*) Not my sort of drama, doctor. And I
    didn't play with frog spawn when I was a lad, either. (*But
    he does sneak a sidelong look.*)

X-RAY MONITOR SCREEN
An intestinal digestive system at work. Watch a while . . .

EXTREME CLOSE-UP – DANIEL ON TABLE
His half-sidelong, almost half-furtive expression changes as he tensely half-watches his own intestines at work. He suddenly sucks in his breath, for –

X-RAY MONITOR SCREEN
Words come up on the lower half of the intestinal drama, in English, sandwiched by Japanese, marching across the screen and darkening as though on cue –
> **Each time we have a quarrel**
> **It almost breaks my heart**

SUDDEN CLOSE-UP – NURSE. X-RAY ROOM
Looming as though from nowhere between DANIEL *and the monitor, with a gentle smile – but flat tones.*
NURSE: He can do what he likes, can't he? (*But her lips are clearly saying something else, as in a very bad dub from a foreign-language film*)

INT. WAITING ROOM. RADIATION DEPARTMENT. DAY
BEN BAGLIN, *newspaper untidily thrust aside, looks at his watch, and taps or jigs his foot in irritation, but then his impatient attention is momentarily caught by activity at –*

INT. RECEPTION DESK. WAITING ROOM. DAY
An extraordinarily old ARAB WOMAN, *half-shrouded but bent, stooped and myriadly wrinkled, stands clutching the forearm of her Westernized but accented* SON *– who must be at least sixty – as a young, severe-looking medical* RECEPTIONIST *tries to make sense of the son's replies to her form-filling, it being clear that the ancient mother (or even grandmother) speaks no English at all.*
SON: (*As though he has said it twice before*) *Cla* Rijjis.
RECEPTIONIST: No, no. (*Speaks slowly.*) Her address here in the United Kingdom. Her *home* here.
SON: What?
RECEPTIONIST: (*Slowly*) In *England*. Where does she live?
SON: (*Angrily*) I said. I said! *Cla* Rijjis.
RECEPTIONIST: Cla – Rijjis. How do you – Oh. (*Suddenly.*) Claridge's? The hotel?

SON: (*Gesticulates, more angrily*) I said! I said! Cla Rijjis!
(*The very, very old woman clings to his arm, immobile, impassive, out of it.*)

RECEPTIONIST: Sorry, sir. I'm sorry. And – if I could just have your – um – your mother's date of birth.

SON: (*Oddly furious*) What? What? What you say?

RECEPTIONIST: (*Again, slowly*) Her age, sir. Please. How old is she? When was she born?
(*The* SON, *who seems to be more and more strangely maddened by this whole process, spurts out a voluble stream of ill-tempered Arabic at the frail, withered nonagenarian hanging on to his expensively clothed forearm as though for dear life. She stares back at him through rheumy eyes, expressionless.*)

INT. WAITING ROOM. DAY
Ben's mild amusement at this diversion is no longer strong enough to hold back his obvious impatience. He tuts and looks at his watch again, as –

SON: (*Off*) Sixty-one. She sixty-one.

RECEPTIONIST: (*Off, incredulous*) Sixty-one? Oh, but –
(*Ben – no longer listening, so that it is deflected comedy – stands with a sigh of relief. His point of view –*)

INT. X-RAY AREA/RECEPTION DESK. DAY
DANIEL, *fully clothed, is coming through from the X-ray area beyond. He has to pass in front of the reception desk, where –*

SON: (*Near-scream*) Six. One. Six! One! Sixty bloody one!
(DANIEL *sees how flustered the unfortunate* RECEPTIONIST *is, and – passing close – gives her a swift wink of sardonic complicity.*)

DANIEL: (*To* RECEPTIONIST) That was a great year for St Emilion – but it should be drunk now, OK?

SON: (*Furious*) Who in charge here? Eh? Eh? Who not bloody idiot? Eh?
(*But* DANIEL *has gone on, towards* BEN, *who is clearly eager to go.*)

INT. WAITING ROOM AND PASSAGES TO EXIT BEYOND. DAY
DANIEL: (*To* BEN) Well, Ben. That wasn't as bad as my

thoughts had made it out to be. My dignity does not, after all, reside in my bum-hole.

(BEN *is too pointedly looking at his watch as they walk* – BEN *very duck-footed.*)

BEN: Good. Good. But it took longer than *my* thoughts, Daniel. And I think I'm going to be date for my late.

(BEN *has a peculiar problem for a literary agent of lapsing into unknowing spoonerisms when at all flustered: that is, he reverses the opening consonants of consecutive letters, especially at the end of a sentence.*)

DANIEL: (*Cutting in*) It was the second bit I didn't like very much. The barium was fine – well, *ish* – but then they go and pump *air* up your arse –

BEN: Air? What do you mean, air? (*But he looks distractedly at his watch again.*)

DANIEL: It's to extend the lower bowel or something – Puff, puff. Christ, I thought I was going to float out of here like the Graf Zepplin! *Slow down*, Ben. I've got the guts ache!

(BEN *is racing on ahead.*)

EXT. THE HOSPITAL. DAY

BEN, *in the lead, comes out of the Harley Street-type street, followed by Daniel, who seems to be in some discomfort but is already lighting a cigarette. They are moving past the 'Ambulances Only' section to where* BEN's *smart* BMW *is at a meter.*

BEN: Wish you *had* been able to float, Daniel. Why the heck don't you finally *finally* learn to drive? Surely it'd make a sot of lense.

DANIEL: Now, now. Your spoonerisms are showing, Ben! (*Half-stops, holds stomach.*) Look – if I can't call on you, as my agent, for the *occasional* if demeaning bit of comfort and chauffeuring, then I'm pretty damned sure that there are a few other grand literary agents in this town who would be quite willing to oblige. And *without* getting their words back to front!

(BEN *stops, half-turns, surprised – and sees* DANIEL *taking his hands away from his stomach, his cigarette tossed away.*)

BEN: Dan. Are you all right?

DANIEL: (*Severely*) How much did I earn last year, Ben?
(*They look at each other. A small challenge.*)

BEN: (*Half-laughs*) Hey, now. What's all this? You know very
well I don't mind driving you to something like this – but I
moo have a deeting.

DANIEL: (*Glint*) No. Come on. How much? Last year?
(BEN *is almost comically, and revealingly, quick.*)

BEN: Four hundred and eighty-eight thousand, seven hundred
and twenty-four pounds, eighty pence. Gross.

DANIEL: (*Shocked*) Jesus Christ on a bike! (*Blink, double shock.*)
And you know it (*Clicks fingers*) *just like that.*

BEN: (*Morosely*)To the pearest nenny. (*Tuts.*) Nearest p-penny!
(DANIEL *is still – surprisingly – shaken, and puts a hand out to
the railings at the side of the pavement.* BEN *looks at his watch.*)

DANIEL: You know, I had no idea it would be as much as –
(*Half-laugh.*) When are they going to catch on, those studios
paying for drafts they never actually make –? (*An amused,
accusing glint at impatient* BEN.) So – let's see – you yourself,
Ben Baglin, you make forty-eight – no, nearly forty-nine
thousand pounds yourself in twelve months from my
scratchy old pen, eh? And then you kick up a fuss about –
(*A young couple have been walking towards them, and, exactly
as they pass, talking to each other, the half-amused, half-
exasperated* YOUNG MAN *can be heard.*)

YOUNG MAN: I mean, heavens – I mean, it's not as though you
haven't done it often enough before, now is it?

CLOSE-UP – DANIEL. STREET
*A spasm of shock seems to pass through him. He stands dead still,
looking oddly haunted.*

DANIEL: (*Half-whisper*) But – but they're speaking my –
(*Crash out into* –)

INT. A BRASSERIE TABLE. NIGHT
A pouty, pretty young woman in a scene from one of DANIEL
FEELD's *scripts, played by an actress called* LINDA, *and a thug
called* PETER.

LINDA: (*Sullen*) Don't want to do it with him at all, fanks very
much.

PETER: I mean, Christ – I *mean*, it's not as though you ain't
done it often enough before –

INT./EXT. BEN'S CAR. WI STREETS. DAY
Ben, driving, is also looking sidelong at DANIEL *next to him, as one
not sure whether to be incredulous or amused.*
BEN: Daniel. Daniel, what are you saying here? Come on.
You're *joking*, right?
(DANIEL *looks out of the passenger window, considering, then
looks at* BEN.)
DANIEL: They were speaking my lines.
BEN: No, no, no.
DANIEL: (*Steadily*) It's been happening to me all morning, Ben.
This man burbling on the radio when I woke up – OK,
OK, it was in a different context, yes, all that – but
suddenly he comes out with an exact same sentence from
my *Karaoke* script. And then –
BEN: (*Trying to interrupt*) But that's cure poincidence –
DANIEL: (*Insistent, overriding*) And then when I was about to
have the barium enema, I *distinctly heard* the song that
begins the whole story – you know, 'Why Must I Be a . . .'
BEN: (*Snort*) What you mean, *heard*? Like Joan of Arc, do you
mean – ?
DANIEL: (*Ignoring this*) And then afterwards, the nurse. She – or
I thought she – (*Stops.*) Oh. What's the point. (*Looks out of
the window again.*) All I know is – All I know is – *something
very strange is* –
(*But he stops speaking, staring out at the street, self-absorbed.*
BEN *looks at him, a little more concerned.*)
BEN: You've just been feeling a bit low, Daniel. That stomach
ache, and – forgive me, but I'll say it just *once* more, I
promise. Don't you think you're drinking just a bit too
much?
(DANIEL *doesn't reply, or turn. But then, suddenly, urgently –*)
DANIEL: Drop me here. Stop!
BEN: (*Misunderstanding*) Aw, Daniel, come on –
DANIEL: No, no, it's just that – No. I've decided not to go to
the cutting room. This bloody tummy-ache, it's – No. If
you put me down here, I can beat that one-way system and

cut through to my flat. I think I need to lie down a bit. Or
walk a bit. Or *something*.

BEN: Oh. Sure. OK. You want me to call the cutting room? Or
anybody?

(DANIEL *is getting out of the car.*)

DANIEL: I'm seeing flap, flap, rush, rush Anna for dinner
tonight, anyway. We're going to that brasserie where they
filmed the opening. Yuk.

EXT. STREET. DAY

DANIEL *watches Ben's car drive off with a tentative twist of a smile,
goes to cross the wide road, then suddenly stops with a sharp intake of
breath and clutches at his stomach. The pain is obviously severe, and
too regular.*

*Then he swiftly controls it, or himself, with a near-comical ferocity,
and strides on across the road with something like a hummed 'Heigh-
Ho! Heigh-Ho!' of the Seven Dwarfs going to work.*

EXT. A BRASSERIE. WEST END. NIGHT

*Big windows splash light across the wide, wet pavement as some
pedestrians scurry past, umbrellas tilting against the direction of what
seems to be a sudden rainstorm. The traffic slushes and swishes, and
all the reflected lights slither and slide.*

*Music comes driving in hard and twangy and somehow (hear it!)
rain-like from the opening of the scene, guitars to the fore. Hank
Williams's 'Your Cheatin' Heart'.*

HANK WILLIAMS: (*Over*)

Your cheatin' heart
Will make you weep
You'll cry and cry
And try to sleep –

CLOSE-UP – FACE UNDER UMBRELLA

*As a front-on, tilted, head-masking big black umbrella lifts, as on a
theatrical cue not unlike 'singing' Ben with the* Financial Times, *to
reveal the face of* OLIVER MORSE, *an elderly, held-in, ascetic or
vaguely military and distinctly patrician gentleman, utterly
inappropriately 'singing' in the Hank Williams voice, but with a
certain cruel relish in his expression.*

OLIVER: (*'Sings', i.e. lip-syncs*)
But sleep won't come
The whole night through
Your cheatin' heart
Will tell on you –

INT. BRASSERIE. NIGHT
Big, pseudo-French, fairly full, with large ceiling fans torpidly
rotating. Most of the customers are at the long, curving bar and the
bare tables set aside for drinks, but half a dozen or so at the bright-
clothed tables for 'Diners Only'.
Above the buzz and chatter, 'Your Cheatin' Heart' continues, full
blast, on the brasserie sound system.
When tears come down
Like falling rain
You'll toss around
And call my name –

CLOSE-UP – OLIVER MORSE AT TABLE
OLIVER *is alone at a table, eating a steak with half a bottle of red*
wine and a salad, self-absorbed, so that the continuing music on the
brasserie speakers seems not to impinge on him at all.
– you'll walk the floor
The way I do
Your cheatin' heart
Will tell on you!
(*But then the vocal gives way to a twangy interlude, and as the*
music sinks down into the general brasserie background sounds,
Oliver's jaws suddenly stop moving in mid-chew, oddly so. He
stares down into his wine glass with a disturbing intensity –)

CLOSE-UP – WINE GLASS. OLIVER'S POINT OF VIEW
Something apparently strange slowly revolves and flickers darkly on
the surface of the red wine.

CLOSE-UP – OLIVER AT TABLE
A frown – and then, with sudden relief, out loud –
OLIVER: Oh. It's the fan. Of course.

INT. BRASSERIE. DINING AREA. NIGHT.
As Oliver looks up at the ceiling and the big, torpid fan to check, he meets instead the eyes of a hovering waiter who clearly (if warily) knows him as a regular here.
WAITER: Sorry, Mr Morse – ?
OLIVER: (*Blinks*) What?
WAITER: I thought you spoke –
(OLIVER *raises his brows, rather chillingly patrician.*)
OLIVER: I?
WAITER: (*Oddly nervous*) No, no. My mistake. I –
(*Oliver seems to study him for a fraction of a second, then –*)
OLIVER: Ah. I see. You think that I talk to myself, do you?
WAITER: No, Mr Morse. Of course not.
OLIVER: (*Snapping*) Then why are you *hovering*?
(*They look at each other, then* OLIVER *smiles, almost apologetically. They both laugh.*)
WAITER: (*With relief*) I just thought you wanted something –
OLIVER: Oh, but I do. All old men want to call back yesterday. But I don't imagine for one moment that *this* establishment could offer up –
(*But looking around dismissively as he says this, Oliver's eyes suddenly fix, as though on the road to Damascus, and he seems to see some sort of revelation, way across the large brasserie, at –*)

INT. BRASSERIE. BAR AND DRINKS TABLES. NIGHT
The already identified actress LINDA *– playing a girl called 'Sandra' – is about to sit at one of the drinks tables with* PETER, *an actor bearing the same forename as the person he plays, very much the Essex Man type.*
Peter thumps down an opened bottle of wine in front of tackily or tartily attractive LINDA *(or 'Sandra') as though killing a chicken by its neck, his every gesture seemingly overtly macho.*
PETER: Now look, Sandra.
LINDA: No. *You* look.
PETER: I *mean* – it's not as though you got to keep on doing it wiv him, now is it?
(*During which latter dialogue the picture is diminishing in size to –*)

STEENBECK SCREEN. A CUTTING ROOM. DAY
*The above scene is now on the small but sharply defined screen of a
Steenbeck Editing Machine, viewed by two male and one female
figures, very still, with their backs to the camera.
The Steenbeck picture soon gives way and widens to –*

INT. BRASSERIE. BAR SECTION. NIGHT
LINDA: Don't want to do it with him at all, fanks very bleed'n
   much!
   (*The camera seems to be overly favouring* LINDA.)
PETER: I mean, Christ – I mean, it's not as though you haven't
   done it often enough before.
LINDA: (*Flashing*) Whatchewmean?
   (*Picture diminishing to –*)

STEENBECK SCREEN
Showing big close-up of LINDA *even though* PETER *is speaking.*
PETER: (*Off screen.*) Oh, come on, angel. You've had more
   bonks wiv more blokes than –

INT. SOHO CUTTING ROOM. DAY
*Linda's face in still filling the Steenbeck screen as, wider, a usual,
cluttered, wholly functional cutting-room oblong is revealed, its half-
blinded windows looking out on to rooftops and down into a Soho
alley.*
PETER: (*Off-screen, continuous*) – I've had bleed'n Weetabix.
   (*The telephone in the cutting room starts to ring, irritatingly,
   and 'that sharp Anna', the woman of the three in the room,
   answers it, and stoops close to it, in a very low (virtually
   inaudible) voice.*)
LINDA: (*On screen*) Now look! I've hardly ever never done it for
   the – No! Not for money! I'd want a thousand down on the
   table before I even – You've got a bloody cheek, Peter. Sod
   off!
PETER: (*Still off screen*) Hey. *Hey.* Watch that lip.
   (IAN, *the editor, a young Scot who pretends to be a dour Scot,
   suddenly stops the reel. He is seated square on at the controls,
   and he doesn't look pleased. Next to him, restless, moving about
   is* NICK BALMER, *a febrile, public-school type, constantly*

flirting with charlatanry, genuinely rich, always hungry to engage in power games.)

LINDA, *who has been much too much in close-up on the Steenbeck screen, is left with her pouty reaction to Peter's out-of-shot remarks, a provocative still.*

NICK *seems to know (defensively) why* IAN *has stopped the reel and just as the Scot is about to speak, he quickly gets in first – at virtually the same time as* ANNA, *alertly watching both of them, finishes on the phone with an audible 'OK, Ben. Thanks.'*)

NICK: (*To* IAN) No, no, no. I know what you're – No. It's very definitely *her* we want to see, Ian.

IAN: Is it?

NICK: I know it is.

IAN: You sure?

NICK: (*Abrupt*) I-know-it-is. Full stop.

(IAN *looks at him, with a well-known dry Scottishness. Then –*)

IAN: Fine. Period.

(ANNA, *worriedly looking at both, has been hovering by the phone. She is a producer more in title than in deed on this particular show, in a worryingly anomalous position.*)

ANNA: I'm not saying I disagree, Nick. But I think Ian has *something* of a point when he –

NICK: (*Cuts in*) Who was that?

ANNA: Sorry?

NICK: (*Bad-tempered*) On the phone.

ANNA: Oh. Ben Baglin. 'Back-to-front-Ben'. (*At his blankness*) Daniel Feeld's agent.

(NICK *half-turns away with something of a snort. He is feeling insecure and therefore aggressive.*)

NICK: Daniel Feeld. Words *never* back to front. In his scripts they are supposedly in a perfect sequence pre-ordained by Almighty God himself. (*Then, pacing, as though to himself.*) Daniel Fucking Feeld. The precious bastard.

ANNA: I – It seems he can't come to the cutting room until tomorrow. He's not very –

NICK: (*Interrupting*) Thank God for that. Perhaps we can get on a bit at last.

(ANNA *and* IAN *look at each other.* NICK, *increasing his pacing, is unaware of the exchange. But then* IAN *speaks, with dour satisfaction.*)

IAN: But he'll have his say, you know. Especially about the music. (*Glint.*) Och, now – he *will!* And his funny old agent will tell you to take a junning rump.

EXT. BLOCK OF FLATS. WI. DAY
Rather elegant in a now slightly worn Edwardian manner, off a quiet street. This is where Daniel lives. Music comes in, smart, on the cut, 'Smoke Gets in Your Eyes', in a swingy, non-vocal, 'orchestral' version.

INT. LIVING ROOM. DANIEL'S FLAT. DAY
The music is issuing from Daniel's CD part of his expensive 'music centre' in a large but untidily book-and-paper-strewn room with a big, old desk and creaky swivel chair.
DANIEL *is pacing, dragging hard on a cigarette, as though it were oxygen, but obviously in some physical distress. Stomach ache. Music continuing.*
Suddenly, almost savagely, he crosses to the CD, clicks it off, goes to put out his cigarette in an ashtray near it, and sees another cigarette still alight, nearly burnt down to its filter, already in the ashtray.

EXTREME CLOSE-UP – DANIEL
Close enough to see that there are small beads of sweat on his forehead and at his hairline. He tuts self-disgust as he stubs out both cigarettes.
DANIEL: (*Morosely, to self*) EEC Council Directive 89 stroke 622. You pig. You indulgent pig. (*Snort*) Obey the EEC! Obey!

INT. OPEN-PLAN DINER/KITCHEN OFF AND PART OF LIVING ROOM. DAY
In another sudden movement, as though in response to another swift spasm of stomach pain, DANIEL *rushes to one of the overhead cupboards, opens a third-full bottle of Glenfiddich Scotch and takes a heavy, double glug-glug of a swig straight from the bottle, with the air of a man who often does it.*
As he shudders slightly from the raw smack of it, his phone rings.
DANIEL: (*Pretend melodrama*) Aaaaaagh! The Health Police!

INT. DOCTOR'S ROOMS. LONDON. DAY
A rather too-long-haired, slightly unlikely GP figure, DR BARKER, *is the one telephoning* DANIEL. *His desk seems like a computer workstation, and the office a mass of greenery, plus a stylish aquarium of vivid fish.*

DR BARKER: (*Phone*) Daniel. Good afternoon. Nigel here. I've had the plates biked around to me, and I think I can safely tell you what's wrong with you.

INT. DANIEL'S LIVING ROOM. DAY
DANIEL: (*Phone*) Well. Join the queue, Doc, It's like a Harrods Sale.

INT. BARKER'S ROOM. DAY
DR BARKER: (*Phone*) You are suffering from sigmoid spastic colon, Daniel. It's these spasms which give you the pain. You can actually *see* one going on when you look at the plates. Anyway, I've got your prescription ready. I'll have it biked round to Ben's office and someone there will file it and bring you the pills. They're called Spasmonal. Stop the spasms, OK? And then let's see. (*All the time he speaks he is clicking his posh ballpoint pen in, out, in, out, in.*)

INT. DANIEL'S LIVING ROOM. DAY
DANIEL *lighting a cigarette and blowing out a discontented column of smoke.*
DANIEL: (*Phone*) Spastic colon? Yeah? Is that what you're calling it? Sounds sweet.

INT. BARKER'S ROOM. DAY
DR BARKER: (*Phone*) Or what is popularly known as IBS – Irritable Bowel Syndrome. Use whichever diagnosis impresses whomsoever the most. I'm sorry it's not a little more *dramatic*.

INT. DANIEL'S LIVING ROOM. DAY
While he is on the phone, Daniel's eye settles on a pile of books about virtual reality, cyberspace and 'The Media Lab', stacked on the floor at the edge of the desk. He is pushing at them with his foot as he speaks.

DANIEL: (*Phone*) Well, I've known for a long time that I've got an irritable *head* syndrome – but is that all it is? And what causes it?

DR BARKER: (*Off, on phone*) In a word, stress.

(DANIEL *sucks in smoke, angrily.*)

DANIEL: Fucking nonsense. *Stress. Me?* (*Comic yell.*) I'm as gentle as the beat of an angel's wings. (*He puts the phone down. And then he laughs. Then he draws in smoke again, pondering. He rifles through untidy heaps of papers on his big desk, and with a tiny 'Ah!' of triumph locates the bound typescript of a filmscript.*)

CLOSE-UP – TYPESCRIPT
The title Karaoke: Original Screenplay by Daniel Feeld.

CLOSE-UP – DANIEL READING TYPESCRIPT
He starts at the beginning and, after a little while, begins to speak out loud what he is reading:

DANIEL: (*Eventually*) '– come up on the lower half of the screen, in English, sandwiched by Japanese. At the same time, a male voice is singing, badly, with an East End accent, the same words as they march across the screen, darkening on cue –'

(*Fading in, as his voice drops below the music, the bellowing voice of* ARTHUR MAILION. *Slow dissolve.*)

EXT. WEST END STREET. NIGHT
Rain falling, making lights slither and passing traffic swish and slush, vaguely melancholy.
The 'Why Must I be a Teenager' song goes through the slow dissolve, losing Mailion's bellow in the process, in favour of the original singer, Craig Douglas.

> **I cry a tear**
> **For nobody but you**
> **I'll be a lonely one –**

EXT. BRASSERIE. THE STREET. NIGHT
Windows splashing light, as a few pedestrians pass, umbrellas tilted.

> **– if you should say we're through**

I shall go on –

INT. BRASSERIE. NIGHT
*The same place as seen before, but differently dressed, with
many French posters around the walls. The ceiling fans are also
the same, and the song continues just above the buzz and
chatter, though by no means as loudly as in the previous
transition – i.e. just as on the normal background music speaker
system.*
– loving you
Each night I ask –

CLOSE–UP – DANIEL FEELD. BRASSERIE TABLE
*The background music (continuing) is making him look around and
about in a troubled, half-scared manner – and he looks over to the
big windows and the wet street beyond, almost as though expecting a
fictive presence to be outside. Even though he has food, a cigarette
smoulders in the ashtray, possessively near to him.*
– the stars up above
Why must I be-e-
A teenager in love?
DANIEL: (*Suddenly, in time with song, but speaking the lines*)
'I'll be a lonely one
If you should say –'
(*Widening –*)

INT. DANIEL AND ANNA'S TABLE. BRASSERIE. NIGHT
*Daniel's lines have been said so unexpectedly, it seems, that his
companion (the woman from the cutting room) looks up startled
from her own food. She is thirtyish – and 'sort of attractive' but
willing to take ideological issue about such a revealing phrase.*
ANNA: What – ? Oh, yes. That song –
(*The Craig Douglas song is continuing on the speaker system,
but now even less noticeably.*)
DANIEL: The song at the start of *Karaoke*. The baptismal bounce.
(*She is suddenly evasive.*)
ANNA: Well – yes.
DANIEL: What do you mean? (*With an edge.*) Aren't you sure,
Ms Producer?

ANNA: Sure?

DANIEL: (*Nastily*) Hey, babe. What's that steak made of? Asbestos. Cork. What?
(*And he also sounds as though he has been drinking.*)

ANNA: Maybe. Or my brain.

DANIEL: (*Too sharply*) Your what?
(*Anna looks at him steadily.*)

ANNA: You live alone, don't you, Dan?
(*Daniel returns the look, equally steadily.*)

DANIEL: No wife, no mistress. The occasional sleazy and all but commercial sneeze-like bonk, preferably with someone who has more to lose than I have. No children. No commitments. *No cleaner.* And, please note, *and* a capacity for minding my own business.
(*He slurps down a lot of wine, with an almost childish air of triumph and challenge, and then – eating or not – drags down a quick puff of cigarette smoke.*)

ANNA: Well, that's all very nice.

DANIEL: Except?

ANNA: Except it makes you forget how to talk to people. And how to treat your colleagues. Or even how to be even half-way polite.
(*Edgy, tipsy, he makes what might be a slight gesture of apology.*)

DANIEL: But it was a crucial, comic opening song in my script, Anna. Where we first see that sleaze place, and Arthur Mailion bellowing the words so badly. 'Pig' Mailion, the blackmailer, the real, foul-mouthed heavy.
(*The tune in the background music has changed tinkle-tinkle to something else, now barely audible.* ANNA *seems evasive again.*)

ANNA: Why do they do it, restaurants? Muzak, or whatever?

DANIEL: To fill the empty and divert the bored. What else? Showbiz. Essence of.

ANNA: I usually manage to shut it out. I mean, if you let background music get to you, you'd hardly ever be able to eat out at all. They even do it in funeral parlours nowadays.

DANIEL: (*Drinks*) 'On the Sunny Side of the Street' or – um – 'Life is Just a Bowl of Cherries'. Eh?

23

(*She laughs, a little. But* DANIEL, *though tipsy, can see she is uncomfortable about something. And he guesses.*)

DANIEL: (*Slowly, deliberately*) Each night I ask the stars up above, why must I be teenager in love?

(*Tiny pause. She drinks, eyes fixed on him, then –*)

ANNA: Too on the nose.

DANIEL: That's the point. *Smack* on the schnoz, my love.

ANNA: No, I mean to be *really* funny, or – And it just sort of lies there, that song. Nick isn't – well, you know what Nick's like – but he isn't happy with it.

DANIEL: (*Mock, jeering sympathy*) Aaa, poor lickle ting!

ANNA: And he wants to change it.

DANIEL: Well, he can't. And in any case he's already shot it. It was on one of those bloody awful cassettes you sent me.

ANNA: He shot an alternative version.

DANIEL: (*Splutter*) he *what?*

ANNA: (*Nervously*) He's – Daniel, it's not a bad choice as such – same sort of – He's used 'Your Cheatin' Heart'. The Hank Williams number. And it –

(*She stops as Daniel rises very noisily, clattering down knife and fork, all but trembling with excessive and near-alcoholic rage, jabbing a finger out at her.*)

DANIEL: Wait there. Don't *move!*

(*In fact, she is too startled to do anything else as Daniel plunges away from the table, striding across the brasserie in a manner that attracts a few curious glances.*)

INT. BRASSERIE. END OF BAR. DAY

There is an open payphone against the wall and by the cigarette machines at the far end of the bar, nearest the glass-doored exit to the wet streets. But an unkempt YOUNG WOMAN *is using the phone as an enraged* DANIEL *almost skids to an affronted halt, wanting the phone.*

WOMAN ON PHONE: – and that's what he said. God, I was in stiches! –

DANIEL: (*Between his teeth*) Hurry up.

(*The* WOMAN *imitates a man's would-be comical voice, with what must be a shared derision with whomever she is telephoning.*)

24

WOMAN ON PHONE: 'Wot? Wo'?' he said. 'All bloody right then,'
    he said. 'What do *you* call a fish that hasn't got an eye –?'
DANIEL: (*Gratingly*) Are you going to be long?
    (*She pointedly turns her back on him.*)
WOMAN ON PHONE: 'It's a – 'oh, God, Annie – wait for it –
DANIEL: I said are you –
WOMAN ON PHONE: 'It's a fsh. Get it? A fsh. No "i", see.
    (*As she cackles, inordinately, Daniel has already rushed on out
    through the exit doors into the wet streets, glaring angrily back
    at her.*)

INT. BRASSERIE. NIGHT
At her table, ANNA *can see – at a distance –* DANIEL *hurtling
through the glass exit doors and running, just a little way along in
the wet before going out of her view. She looks utterly bemused. Anna
half-rises, looks at Daniel's plate, glass etc., then sits down again.*
ANNA: (*Very quietly*) Oh, shit. (*She puts out the remnants of one of
    his cigarettes with a look of great disgust.*)

CLOSE-UP – ELABORATE MATCHSTICK EDIFICE
*Made entirely of Swan Vesta matches (or so it seems) is an
elaborate, strictly to scale construct: tower, palace, bridge, Big Ben,
cathedral, or any such marvel. It is not yet complete – and a hand is
laboriously or carefully placing one more matchstick into its proper
position, with consummate delicacy.*
Then off, the phone rings. And rings and rings.
INT. BEN BAGLIN'S STUDY. NIGHT
*This is Ben's unexpected (indeed, obsessive) hobby. (He never reads
scripts, but is great at selling them.) He is dismayed by the interruption,
crossing to the insistent ringing phone with a hiss of disapproval.*

EXT. TELEPHONE BOOTHS. STREET. NIGHT
Three new-style booths, two occupied, one by DANIEL. *The rain has
become heavier and is bouncing on the pavement. Daniel's body-
irritation is palpable from almost any distance.*

INT./EXT. DANIEL'S TELEPHONE BOOTH. NIGHT
DANIEL: (*Phone*) At last! Ben – what the – Ben, this is Daniel –
    What the hell are you doing, man?

INT. BEN'S STUDY. NIGHT

BEN: (*Phone, angrily*) Doing? Doing? I'm up to my neck in scripts as usual, what do you think I'm ducking fooing?

INT./EXT. BOOTH. NIGHT

DANIEL: (*Phone, not mollified*) Well, you certainly take half a decade to answer! The point is this – that snotty, chinless bastard Nick Balmer has taken it into his puffed-up apology for a head to tamper with *Karaoke*, and I want you – *straight away* – at once! Ben! I want you –

INT. BRASSERIE. NIGHT

WAITER: (*To* ANNA) Is everything all right, madam?

ANNA: Oh, yes. Splendid, thank you. Dinner with a lunatic. It's part of the community care programme.
(*The* WAITER, *foreign, doesn't quite understand and doesn't quite know whether to smile, and withdraws rather awkwardly.* ANNA, *in fact, finds it all deeply embarrassing. She sighs and pushes away her plate, unfinished, as though to go. But then, suddenly,* DANIEL *is back, looking as though he has not behaved in any odd way at all. He is soaking wet.*)

DANIEL: Well, we'll soon have that sorted out. I hope.

ANNA: (*Fed up*) Daniel. For Christ's sake.

DANIEL: (*Shaking off rain*) Oh. You haven't finished eating, have you? Didn't you like it, or – Hey. And your glass is empty! Oh, I'm *sorry*.
(*Sitting at his place, he sploshes the last of the bottle into her glass and holds up the empty bottle, immediately catching the eye of the previously unsure* WAITER.)

ANNA: (*Weary acceptance*) Oh, God. Haven't you had enough already?

DANIEL: (*Beaming*) I knew you'd say that. (*Looks at her.*) Anna, I'm sorry. I'm not the sort of writer who thinks that his words on the page are some kind of holy writ in tablets of stone.

ANNA: (*Glinting*) No? Well, then – put down your chisel.
(*He looks at her, and then laughs, and spreads his hands apologetically. But then – the loop of tape being irritatingly short – 'Why Must I be a Teenager' coincidentally begins*

again, and each registers it at the same time. And then each genuinely laughs. She takes a sip of wine, signalling some sort of restored 'normality'. DANIEL *half-hums the background tune, and smiles, with just a touch of anxiety.*)

DANIEL: This is – weird. Sort of creepy.

ANNA: How do you mean?

DANIEL: Well, I felt a bit unsettled eating here in the first place.

ANNA: *Your* choice, fella.

(DANIEL *is looking about again as the fresh wine arrives and his glass is filled. He lights a cigarette.*)

DANIEL: I mean, the place where you lot filmed on that Sunday all those months ago. The self-same place. And here they are playing the first song in the script. And it *will* be, Anna. *Will* be! I don't *like* the song, of course, but I hate the other one – and it doesn't have the same resona –

(*He stops mid-word, strangely, and stares down into his newly filled wine glass with an odd intensity.*)

ANNA: What's the matter?

CLOSE-UP – WINE GLASS, DANIEL'S POINT OF VIEW
The shadow of the big ceiling fan, torpidly revolving above, flickers on the surface of the red wine.

INT. DANIEL AND ANNA'S TABLE. BRASSERIE. NIGHT
She stares at him. He recovers, speaking with sudden relief.

DANIEL: Oh. It's the fan. Of course!

(*She stays staring at him.*)

ANNA: Daniel –

DANIEL: (*Cuts in*) The fan – reflected on the top of the – For a moment there I thought I was getting a message from somewhere else – or – or – the way the – on the surface of the – (*He tails off into sudden embarrassment, and then registers a wince of pain from his stomach.*)

ANNA: (*Steadily*) Daniel. Why are you repeating your own lines?

DANIEL: Am I? (*Gulp*) Yes. I – (*Sudden change of tone.*) Oh, this stomach. God in heaven. (*Another change of tone.*) Speaking my own lines? Well – isn't that rather the point? Isn't that what my script's *about*? Karaoke! As a metaphor, I mean. The music's written and performed by someone else, and

27

there's this piddling little space left for you to sing yourself, but only to *their* lyrics, *their* timing. It's that feeling that – (*He winces again. This time, she notices it more. With concern.*)

ANNA: Dan? Are you all right?

DANIEL: (*Not answering*) The way we hear – see – *think* that what is so–say *out there.* (*Gestures around.*) In front of us – the way we feel it's somehow or other been *arranged* in advance by – by – Oh, I don't know what to call it –

ANNA: Paranoia?

(*He half-glares, then nods, and* drinks – *and laughs.*)

DANIEL: (*Half-hiccup*) I've always longed to be an artsy–fartsy arsehole, Anna, which is why I want to work for the Arts Council or that magazine, what's it? *Sight and Sound?* I'd make a – (*Again, he stops in mid-word. His face changes. He stares across the brasserie –*)

INT. BAR/DRINKS TABLES. BRASSERIE. NIGHT

Just about to sit, an attractive (if slightly tarty) young woman SANDRA *– i.e. the girl who was the Karaoke Club hostess in the opening location,* NOT *the actress* LINDA *– and a much older, distinctly Essex man* PETER *– i.e. a real thug who simply happens by chance to have the same Christian name as the actor* PETER, *but is only a little like him in physical appearance.* PETER *is thumping down an opened bottle of wine by its neck, rather as though it were a chicken being strangled.*

They are too far away from Daniel's table to be distinctly heard by either DANIEL *or* ANNA.

INT. DANIEL AND ANNA'S TABLE. BRASSERIE. NIGHT

Over at the dining section of the large brasserie, ANNA *– puzzled by a dramatic change in Daniel's expression – turns to see what he can see.*

DANIEL: (*Hiss*) It's straight out of – it's the second page of my – (*Almost a shudder.*) *What's happening here?*

INT. BAR SECTION. THE NEWCOMERS' TABLE. NIGHT

PETER: (*Snarls as he sits*) Just – look, hang about a sec. If you'll just hold your bleed'n horses a minute.

INT. DANIEL AND ANNA'S TABLE. DINING SECTION. NIGHT
Turning her eyes back to DANIEL, ANNA *is about to speak, but –*
ANNA: I don't –
DANIEL: (*Awed*) 'If you'll just hold your bleed'n horses a minute –'
ANNA: (*Blinks*) What?
DANIEL: Look – is this some sort of set-up – Are you lot trying
    out a joke on me, or what? (*Small beads of sweat are suddenly
    glistening on his forehead. It seems he is genuinely frightened: a
    metaphysical terror, so to speak.*)
ANNA: Daniel? What on earth are you on about?
    (*He looks are her, haunted. A beat.*)
DANIEL: (*Awed*) *They are speaking my lines.*

INT. BAR AREA. BRASSERIE. NIGHT
PETER: Now look, Sandra!
SANDRA: No! *You* look.
PETER: I mean, it's not as though you got to –

CLOSE-UP – DANIEL AT HIS TABLE
Eyes clamped on the distant couple, with fearful intensity.
PETER: (*Over*) – keep on doing it wiv him, now is it?
SANDRA: (*Over*) Don't want to do it wiv him at all, fanks very
    bleed'n much!
    (*Worryingly,* DANIEL *is half-moving his lips to the dialogue –
    and the voices have a disturbing half-resonance of voices-in-the-
    head. The two newcomers are actually too far away from his
    table for him to hear what they are really saying: a crucial
    ambiguity or doubt that must remain.*)

INT. BAR AREA. NIGHT
*Peter's thuggish streak is showing. (You will notice small changes,
shifts in dialogue, too.) And there is often some* slight *doubt, via
position or distance or playing to off-lines, about whether this
actually is* their dialogue.
PETER: I mean, Christ – I *me-e-en* it's not as though you ain't
    done it often enough before, honey.
SANDRA: What you mean?
PETER: (*Snorts*) What do I mean? Blimey. Wake up! You've had
    more blokes than I've had bleed'n –

EXTREME CLOSE-UP – DANIEL
*Face loomingly filling the screen as he stares across at the newcomers,
concluding (out loud) Peter's line, precisely on cue.*
PETER: Weetabix.

CLOSE-UP – ANNA AT THEIR TABLE
*Blank incomprehension, swift but comical in its degree of
bewilderment.*

INT. BAR AREA. NIGHT
SANDRA: (*Indignant*) I've never hardly *ever* never done it for the
    – No! Not for money! What do you think I am? I'd want a
    thousand down on the table before I even – You've got a
    bloody cheek, Peter. Sod off!
PETER: Hey. *Hey.* Watch that lip!

INT. DANIEL AND ANNA'S TABLE. NIGHT
DANIEL *tries to push all this away, or to explain, with a helpless
little gesture which almost knocks over his glass, in a way that a
drunk might. He steadies the glass, then gulps down the rest of its
contents.*
DANIEL: I'm sorry, love – I – (*nervous laugh*) For a minute there
    I thought those two – over there – you see? – (*Darts another
    look.*) They're too far away, aren't they? Can *you* hear what
    they're saying? (*Urgently, all but reaching across to clutch her
    hand.*) Anna? *Can* you?
ANNA: Your speech is getting slurred. Do you know that?
DANIEL: Anna! Can you hear what they're saying!
ANNA: Of course I can't. And why would I even want to, for
    heaven's sakes?
    (*She looks at him, as he pours yet more wine.*)
    Daniel. Please. Surely you've had enough. And it can't be
    doing that stomach of yours much good. Haven't they told
    you that, the doctors?
    (*But Daniel doesn't seem to hear her. His eyes are fixed on the
    other two.*)

INT. PETER AND SANDRA'S TABLE. NIGHT
PETER: Why don't you look at me when I'm talking to you?

What the hell's going on in that pretty little head? Eh?

SANDRA: That guy. Keeps staring at me.

(*Instantly alert,* PETER *half-twists to look at* DANIEL, *like someone regularly on his guard. He satisfies himself before speaking.*)

PETER: What, him? He's nothing. And you ought to be used to all that by now. You're something you are, Sandra. Real special.

SANDRA: No, all the time – eyes sticking out of his head.

(*A small unease returns to* PETER.)

PETER: So long as he's not from your actual Customs and Excise – (*Studies Daniel.*) Nah. Nah. Looks too intelligent.

SANDRA: You'd think I was in the bleed'n Top Shop window or something. I've had enough of this!

(*She suddenly pokes out her tongue towards distant* DANIEL, *aggressively. And keeps it stuck out.*)

PETER: Hey! None of that! You dragged up in a pigsty or what?

INT. DANIEL AND ANNA'S TABLE. NIGHT

Hugely embarrassed by the stuck-out tongue so clearly meant for him, DANIEL *drags his eyes from the distant couple with a flinch.* ANNA, *tight-faced, utterly fed up, is signing the credit card slip for the bill.*

DANIEL: Oh, but – but – (*Then, with a slight hiccup.*) Anna. That was my invite –

ANNA: You're not here, Daniel. You're off on some other planet. The one you can only see through the bottom of a bottle. Come on! Eh? Get yourself home and sleep it off. You're due in the cutting room tomorrow, and I'd like your head *clear*.

DANIEL: (*Recovering, ill-willed*) Yeah. To assess the mess.

ANNA: (*Tight*) What mess?

DANIEL: Hah!

ANNA: No. What mess?

WAITER: Thank you ver' much. I hope you enjoy. Come again please.

(*The hapless* WAITER *takes the credit slip. Anna takes her card, standing as she does so.*)

ANNA: We all know what Nick's like – but I think he's done a pretty good job on your script, Daniel.

DANIEL: (*Still seated*) He's too arrogant! It's that twit-twit bray! That uppah uppah class thing, cousin-or-something of the Queen thing. A trenchful of blue shite.

ANNA: Must go, Daniel.

DANIEL: (*Still seated*) It's *my* work, *my* sweat, he's fucking up! *I'm* not going to be knocked down by his bloody Rolls-Royce!

ANNA: There's a long way to go yet. Lots of things happen in the cutting room, as you well know. You didn't bother to come on location *once*, and you've only seen a few rushes on cassette, so why don't you wait and – (*Sighs, turning away.*) And anyway you don't mean half of this. You're *drunk*, Dan. It's gibberish.

(DANIEL *darts yet one more troubled look at the far table, goes to stand, but staggers a little.*)

DANIEL: It's more *tiredness* than the – (*Then, nasty edge*) And deep disappointment, I'm sorry to say . . . deep, deep disapp –

(*But she is already walking away through the big, noisy brasserie towards the glass double-doors of the far side exit.*)

– Aey – Hang on! I'm trying to say, to say, shum – something important here about –

(*Going after her, with the slight, disguised sway of an alcoholic,* DANIEL *has to pass almost directly in front of Peter and Sandra's table. Reaching it, just behind fast-walking* ANNA, *he half-stops. And stares at* SANDRA, *helplessly, blatantly.*)

CLOSE-UP – SANDRA

A feisty 'girl', she again registers Daniel's stare, and flashes back an electric, very definite 'Up you!' glare, with a tilt of the nose.

INT. BRASSERIE. NIGHT

DANIEL *is compelled to slide his eyes away. He goes to say something to* ANNA – *presuming her to be just ahead* – *only to find that she has already gone on out into the wet street. Moving on, he knocks into the back of someone's chair.*

EXT. PAVEMENT AND BRASSERIE. NIGHT
ANNA *is looking for a taxi with the body-language of one who knows you do not easily get a cab when it is raining.*
DANIEL *comes out, with a slight lurch, quickly controlled. But even now his head is half-turned to look back at the brasserie, as though to see the particular table which worries him so much. Then, to* ANNA –
DANIEL: The girl in my *Karaoke* – God. She has such a horrible death, doesn't she? Will I see any of that in the cutting room tomorrow? The killing.
    (*She keeps her eyes skinned, looking for a taxi, flapping in vain at a full one.*)
ANNA: We're still on the first reel. Of course not.
DANIEL: (*Bleak*) The poor girl. *It's such a horrible way to die.*
    (*What he says, and the way he says it, make her look at him. She goes to say something, then says something else instead.*)
ANNA: Why can you never get a taxi when it's raining?
    (*His eyes have flicked back uneasily to the brasserie doors, but he recovers his attention, almost, with a half-laugh.*)
DANIEL: Oh, but you can if you've got an umbrella – Rucking fain, as Ben'd say – (*Stops.*) Half a mo' – didn't I have an umbrella? When 'Why Must I be a Teen – ' (*Stops.*) Oh, no. That was the old man in my – um – my –
ANNA: (*With huge relief*) Here's one! Do you want a lift – ? Daniel?
    (*But his eyes have slid yet again back to the brasserie windows, compulsively.*)

INT./EXT. DANIEL'S POINT OF VIEW. BRASSERIE. NIGHT
PETER *and* SANDRA *just about glimpsed through the slightly steamy glass.*

EXT. WET STREET. NIGHT
Anna's taxi is pulling away, swishing in the wet. The pale blob of her face is looking blankly back at DANIEL *through the rain-splattered rear window.*

CLOSE-UP – DANIEL. PAVEMENT
His face changing to a small moment of mysterious panic.
DANIEL: (*To self*) No. Don't go!

EXT. WET STREET. NIGHT
Suddenly, and pointlessly, DANIEL is running after the fast-departing cab, waving his arms, heedless of any other traffic.
DANIEL: (*Yelling*) Anna! Wait! Wait – !

INT./EXT. ANNA'S TAXI. STREET. NIGHT
The CAB DRIVER can see the running, gesticulating man in his mirror.
CABBIE: Shall I stop?
ANNA: (*Crisply*) No, thank you. Not on your life!

INT. BRASSERIE. AT WINDOWS. NIGHT
A table of three young YUPPIES, drinkers not diners, right up against one of the street windows, with one of them holding forth –
DRINKER: And this guy – (*Chuckles, puts on terrible American accent*) – 'Listen,' he says. 'He's got one hell of a serious condition. Fat-al!' And I'm thinking, God, no, do you mean Aids or the Big C or – 'Worse,' he said. 'He's *undercapitalized*!'
(*The others laugh, a little, but then stop laughing because Daniel's face is looming up at and then all but pressed against their window, peering in, as a child might at a sweetshop window.*)

INT./EXT. BRASSERIE. NIGHT
A strange figure in the rain peering in far too close to the glass, with utterly fixed intensity. He is attempting to look across the width of the room to SANDRA.
Then DANIEL too slowly realizes in comic embarrassment that someone has stretched his mouth with his fingers and is flap-flapping his tongue, pulling a hideous face at him. One of the YUPPIE DRINKERS, objecting to (as they see it) being stared at.

INT. YUPPIE TABLE. BRASSERIE. NIGHT
The three roar with laughter at the way in which DANIEL is discomfited.
SECOND DRINKER: He should press his conk up against a *drug store* window.
(*And they laugh again.*)

EXT. STREET. NIGHT
*Having retreated awkwardly from embarrassment. Daniel looks lost
in the rain, hovering now at the edge of the puddled pavement, like
one chewing on his own brain. He takes one decidedly furtive look
back at the glimmering brasserie, and then – seemingly decisive –
swiftly crosses the wide, wet street to the traffic island at its middle.
Where he stops.*

CLOSE-UP – DANIEL. TRAFFIC ISLAND
*He stops dead still on the island as increasing traffic swish-slushes
past on either side. He broods – broods.*
Slow half-dissolve.

INT. A BEDROOM. NIGHT
*Apparently naked except for some frothy frills of explicitly
provocative underwear, a tumble of loose hair reaching towards her
shoulderblades, a shapely* YOUNG WOMAN, *who could from this
angle be either* SANDRA *or the actress* LINDA, *has the palms of her
hands flat against a rather peculiarly patterned wall, bending
forward almost at a right angle, and (it seems) being penetrated with
grunting satisfaction by some heavy man who is otherwise more or
less out of shot.*
But the slowness of the dissolve keeps the brooding presence of
DANIEL *on the traffic island somehow 'present' within the scene, –
like a deeply unhappy spectre. Then – clear –*

EXTREME CLOSE-UP – DANIEL. TRAFFIC ISLAND
He sucks in his breath, and then in sepulchral tones –
DANIEL: (*To self*) 'And then the gaudily striped tie comes over
    his head and around her throat. She thinks at first that it
    is –'

INT. BEDROOM. NIGHT
DANIEL: (*Over, same tones*) some other kind of game in the
    manner she had come to expect from him. But then the
    choking begins.'
    (*And so it is, on screen, as a killing begins. Initially, there is a
    gurgling scream –*)

35

CLOSE-UP – DANIEL (TRAFFIC ISLAND)
*The nasty sound reverberates or resonates in his head, and he
clenches his face in disgust and – suddenly – as the sound turns into
something else.*

EXT. TRAFFIC ISLAND. STREET. NIGHT
DANIEL *steps out all but in front of a fast, wildly honking Rolls-
Royce, which misses him by an inch, if that, throwing up muddy
spray and making* DANIEL *gasp with shock and fear. Literally, the
nearest of near misses.*

CLOSE-UP – REAR WINDOW OF THE ROLLS
A startled face looks back. It is posh NICK BALMER, *the director of
Daniel Feeld's* Karaoke, *in his posh car, with his own peak-capped
regular* DRIVER.

INT./EXT. THE ROLLS-ROYCE. NIGHT
There is no divider between driver and passenger, but NICK *always
sits in the back.*
DRIVER: (*Badly shaken*) My God. There's some bloody lunatics
    about, Mr Balmer.
NICK: (*Turning back from rear window*) You don't know how
    exactly right you are, for once.
DRIVER: Sorry – ?
NICK: (*Amused*) Well, it so happens that *that* particular lunatic
    was My Writer. I would have given you a bonus if you'd
    flattened the cocky little bugger – (*Laughs.*) And I'd have
    doubled it had you reversed back over whatever was left of
    him! Squishy guts. A great sound.
DRIVER: (*Amused*) Sounds good to me. Will I get another go at
    it, sir?
NICK: (*Grimly*) I'll make sure you do, Tom.

EXT. TRAFFIC ISLAND. STREET. NIGHT
*Still reacting in shock to the perilously near miss that had made him
leap back on to the island,* DANIEL *gropes with a shaking hand to
hold on to the bollard. A moment. Then –*
DANIEL: (*Tremble, mutter*) Come on. Come on. It's only a story.
    A – *story.*

(*The rain seems to be coming down more heavily than ever, flattening his hair, soaking his clothes. He seems unaware of it.*)

EXT. RESIDENTIAL STREET. NOTTING HILL'S 'HILLGATE'. NIGHT
A taxi pulls up, in the same rain, at about the same time, outside a neat, narrow, desirable little house on a steep, narrow street.

INT./EXT. TAXI. NIGHT
It is Anna's cab from the brasserie. Leaning forward, ready to get out, she instructs the CABBIE.
ANNA: (*Half-apologetic*) I know this is the second time I've changed my mind –
CABBIE: Don't matter a bit to me, miss.
ANNA: But if you could wait here. I shouldn't be longer than fifteen minutes at the most.
CABBIE: As long as you like, love.
ANNA: And then take me on to where I first said, Muswell Hill.
CABBIE: (*Beaming*) Couldn't be better. That's my neck of the woods, and then I'm done.

INT. BEN BAGLIN'S STUDY. NIGHT
Seen initially through the beautifully complex (if bizarre) hundreds of thousands of matchsticks which make up the structure of what I will from now on, for convenience, call Notre-Dame in Paris, through which criss-cross half-completions the happy, bespectacled face of Ben looms, a schoolboy in heaven.
Reflecting what must have been his earlier (and irritating) telephone call from DANIEL, BEN *is – virtually without knowing it – half-humming, half-singing scraps of 'Your Cheatin' Heart' as he so-o-o carefully trims down and tentatively positions one more small matchstick.*
BEN: (*To self, humming/singing*)
When tears dum dee
Like talling fain
You'll dum dee dum
And tall my came – !
(*Knock! Knock! somehow tentatively on his door. He reacts like one shot. Quiveringly –*)
No!

INT. LANDING/UPPER HALL AT BEN'S DOOR. NIGHT
An immediately odd-looking octogenarian – BEN'S MOTHER *– with chemically vivid red hair, long false red fingernails and a kimono, smiles quaveringly at* ANNA *outside the door.*

BEN'S MOTHER: He'll be very, very cross with me, my dear. I shall be made to go to bed early.

ANNA: (*Swallows*) Oh, but I'm sure –

(BEN'S MOTHER *is opening the door, so slowly that it is like a door creaking open in an old thriller.*)

INT. BEN'S STUDY. NIGHT
BEN *has scuttled as far away as he can from his wondrous Notre-Dame, and stands with his back to it facing the opening door, as though* (*comically*) *trying to hide the edifice with his own rotund figure – which is impossible. And he still has a matchstick in his fingers.*

BEN: (*Splutters*) Mother! No! What have I always said! Mother! How could – (*He flaps his arms helplessly.*) Anna! You really, really –

ANNA: (*Quickly*) Ben. I'm terribly sorry to –

BEN'S MOTHER: (*Shouting*) She's a nice girl, Ben!

BEN: (*Screaming to* MOTHER) Bo to ged!

BEN'S MOTHER: (*Retreating*) I'm going. I'm going. (*Voice coming from beyond door now, off.*) A nice girl. Nice, nice girl. That's what you should be thinking of, Ben! Ben – !
(*And the voice, the near-apparition, has gone, leaving embarrassed* ANNA *and twitching* BEN *looking at each other. Then –*)

ANNA: (*Quietly, humbly*) Oh, dear. I –

BEN: (*With dignity*) This is my leisure hour. My *private* time.

ANNA: Yes, I'm – Oh, God. I'm sorry to barge in on you like this, but I've just been with your client Daniel Feeld, and I –
(*Her eyes, shifting about in varying degrees of embarrassment, have now fallen upon the fabulous matchstick cathedral. Her words dry for a moment.* BEN *sees the reason.*

BEN: My, my nephew – what? – Ah! My youngest sister's youngest boy. She won't let him – so I – well – during the day, you know – I'm *out*, after all – So I –

ANNA: (*Genuinely*) But isn't it *wonderful*.

(*Tiniest pause. A momentary quiver on Ben's flustered cheek.*)

BEN: Is it?

(ANNA *cannot help but advance nearer to the intricate edifice, which must surely have taken a decade to construct.*)

ANNA: (*In a gurgle*) The boy must be a *genius*, it's so – (*Then it dawns on her and her tone changes.*) Really, Ben. This is something I am very glad to have seen. I thought all these sort of things, all those sort of skills had – gone with the wind!

(BEN, *who is so obscurely ashamed of what is so much more than his 'hobby', is watching her carefully to see if there is any hint of condescension or of amusement. For the moment, he seems satisfied, warily, that there are no such responses.*)

BEN: Well. Yes. I know what you – (*At last he sees the match in his hand.*) I must admit I'm sometimes tempted to hend a land on it myself –

ANNA: Pardon?

(BEN *slaps his own cheek, quite hard, and very comically.*)

BEN: Lend a hand! Lend a hand! (*Looks at her.*) You know I have this pittle troblem now and then? Usually when agitated.

ANNA: I – (*Gentle smile*) Yes, Ben. But everyone thinks it's rather endearing, if you'll forgive me saying so. I – and I'm truly sorry to have caused you any – um – agitation by barging in like this –

(BEN *deflects his residual 'shame' on to his weird old* MOTHER.)

BEN: She's been fine up until about eighteen months ago, my dear old Ma. Eighty-seven years old, been all around the world in all sorts of conditions, and never once been in hospital. My father was a colonel, y'see. Army. No – fit as a fiddle, old Ma. Didn't even go into hospital when I came along. I was born on the lack of a borry. (*Half-pause, but then deems himself to have said 'back of a lorry' properly.*) But nowadays, I'm afraid, the old head has sort of packed in a bit. Well, there you are, there you are. What did you want to see me about, Anna? Kucking *Faraoke*, I suppose.

EXT. SHOP DOORWAY OPPOSITE BRASSERIE. NIGHT
DANIEL – *the wide road successfully crossed at last – waits in half-shelter, staring across the wet street at the bright-windowed brasserie, waiting, obsessively waiting, and chainsmoking. Cigarette butts litter the pavement at his feet.*

INT. BEN'S STUDY. NIGHT
ANNA: – and I was just so worried. He's obviously not very well, and there's going to be such a terrible blow-up when he finally *does* come to the cutting room. I dread it. And I think it's going to threaten the show, Ben. *Really.*
BEN: Nick Balmer is not *my* client, thank God – but I've had previous dealings, my girl, and he can be a very, very pifficult derson. Dear old Dan, whom I dearly love, in case you doubt it – well, he's only half your problem, if that. You'll have to be the boxing referee who gets a right hook from one and an upper-cut from t'other. (*Looks at her, twinkles.*) Be strong. And wear metal underwear, eh?
(ANNA, *clearly worried, tries a rueful smile; and an admission.*)
ANNA: The trouble is, I'm not in a very strong position on this project, to be absolutely honest.
BEN: (*Gently*) Yes. I know that, my dear. Very awkward for you. It's not easy to step up from being a line producer –
ANNA: You see, Nick has invested nearly three-quarters of a million pounds of his own loot in the film. He *owns* the script –
BEN: (*Quickly*) With certain contractual restraints.
ANNA: Of course. But what I'm saying is –
BEN: (*Cutting in*)What you're saying is that Nick Balmer appointed you and will make damned sure that in the last resort you – do – what – he – wants. He who fays the piddler.
(*Tiny pause. She wants to be indignant, but can't be. She feels stripped. He smiles, and touches her arm.*)
ANNA: (*Near to tears*) Oh, what a – Yes. You're dead right, of course. I may well have to resign – throw it all up. Walk off into what won't be a sunset.
(*He continues to pat her arm, twinklingly avuncular.*)
BEN: No, no, no. Hang on in there. Do what you can. Come

40

on. You know this business almost as well as I do. It's as tightly packed as a bolf gall (*smacks his face but does not correct it to 'golf ball'*) with idiots, charlatans, strutting egoists flundering bools!

EXT. SHOP DOORWAY. STREET. NIGHT
Sheltering in the still heavy rain, DANIEL *is still staring across at the brasserie on the other side of the wet street. Then his expression changes. His body tenses. He throws down his last cigarette.*

EXT. DANIEL'S POINT OF VIEW. BRASSERIE. NIGHT
SANDRA *and* PETER *are coming out into the pouring rain, and seem dismayed by it.*

EXT. PAVEMENT AT BRASSERIE. NIGHT
Closing in on PETER *and* SANDRA, *front on, as they walk away, so that there is no doubt that this is genuinely their own dialogue, whereas before some ambiguity of angle or of distance has almost always left open the* possibility *that their speech has been 'written for them' by the pen or the mind of* DANIEL FEELD.
SANDRA: It was only drizzling when we came into that dump. Now look at it! Pissing down.
PETER: You got a real nice way of putting things, I'll give you that.
SANDRA: (*Flat*) Up you.
PETER: I mean, a bloke could take you anywhere.
SANDRA: Well, I just had me hair done, enn' I?
PETER: Moan, moan. Christ, you've only got to walk a few yards.
SANDRA: You haven't got enough up top to worry about, haveya? Outside or in.
PETER: Hey!
SANDRA: Well, it's right.
PETER: Here. Have my bloody coat, willya! Put it over your head and shut up
SANDRA: (*Graceless*) Ta.

EXT. STREET. NIGHT
DANIEL *has crossed over from the other side of the road and is now*

*on their trail like an awkward and distinctly damp bloodhound, at
sufficiently discreet a distance to make us wonder whether he actually
can overhear their real words – which in the above scene are
unquestionably genuine – or whether he is making up voices that are
really in his head or from his old script.*
*Getting cautiously nearer to the two, their apparently continuing
speech has a slightly different resonance: the voices-in-the-head one.*
PETER: So.
SANDRA: So?

EXTREME CLOSE-UP – DANIEL
*Grim-faced and his collar turned up, almost as though for disguise as
much as for protection from the still slanting rain –*
PETER: (*Off screen, added resonance*) So – you'll meet him?
　　Yeah? At least *meet* him. Won'tya! And it's a real nice
　　hotel, love.

EXT. STREET. FRONT-ON PETER AND SANDRA. NIGHT
PETER *and* SANDRA *continue to walk in the rain, doggedly
followed, with* PETER *looking sidelong at her with a kind of angry
solicitation, and her teeteringly high heels go click-clack-click on the
puddled pavement. A few moments with no speech, but obvious
irritation between both of them, his jacket held by her over her hair-
do.*

EXT. STREET. BEHIND PETER AND SANDRA. NIGHT
As from sodden Daniel's perspective.
PETER: (*At last, angrily tugging at her*) Sandra!
SANDRA: (*Fierce*) What?
PETER: You're a bitch. A real bitch!

CLOSE-UP – SANDRA
*And no reason at all why her words should not be 'real', the
consequence of a whole host of alternative possibilities.*
SANDRA: But what do *I* get out of it? You tell me that!

EXT. STREET. BEHIND PETER AND SANDRA. NIGHT
Shot to include trailing DANIEL, *who may just be within hearing
range, but probably isn't!*

PETER: (*Up ahead*) It's not what you get, angel. It's what you *don't* get!

CLOSE-UP – SANDRA
Again no reason why her line should not be utterly authentic.
SANDRA: (*Hostile*) Whatchewmean?

EXT. STREET UP AHEAD. DANIEL'S POINT OF VIEW. NIGHT
Clean point of view, not including DANIEL *in shot. But that slight, barely detectable in-the-head resonance again.*
PETER: (*Back to camera, up ahead*) You don't get that clip round the ear'ole for a start, my girl. And you won't be needing no work off of no plastic surgeon, willya?

EXT. STREET. NIGHT
All three in shot, but DANIEL *suddenly stops walking.*

CLOSE-UP – DANIEL. STREET
Appalled by what he thinks he can hear, which is what he also rather feverishly imagines he has already composed, Daniel stands stock still, dripping with wet.
SANDRA's *swaying figure has gone out of his sight and the tchick-tchack-tchick of her very high heels recedes evocatively from earshot. Then softly, ludicrously, with a little tremble in the voice –*
DANIEL: (*Whisper to self*) Got to save her. Got to – *rewrite*, or – or – (*And then, jaw suddenly setting in determination, he moves again, to follow the departing couple, for all the world like a would-be hero in a thriller. Then again, determined*) New lines!

EXT. KARAOKE/HOSTESS CLUB. NIGHT
Carefully observed by DANIEL, *who has caught up with them,* PETER *and* SANDRA *stop outside a would-be 'discreet' West End club, clearly only a few streets away from the brasserie.*
At the distance from which DANIEL *is observing them, it is obvious only that* PETER *and* SANDRA *are still having what seems to be an ill-willed or even potentially violent discussion.*

EXTREME CLOSE-UP – DANIEL
Carefully watching, but indisputably loitering, his jacket collar turned

up, the slight, fictive resonance of voices-in-the-head comes again.
SANDRA: (*Over, angry*) No. I've got my own reason for working
    here. And it's a very special one.

EXT. CLUB. NIGHT
*Closer, much closer, to the arguing two, and Peter's and Sandra's
lines are very audible, and (again) with no good reason why they
should not make sense or fit into a hundred other possible sequences of
ill-willed conversation.*
PETER: What is it, then? Come on! What?
SANDRA: Never you mind!

EXT. CLUB FROM OPPOSITE PAVEMENT. NIGHT
Aware of being watched by another, umbrella-carrying pedestrian,
DANIEL *has prudently moved to the other side of the narrow little
street off the wide main road where the brasserie was. He is peering
across at* PETER *and* SANDRA, *relentlessly.*
They seem to be parting now, and badly, for SANDRA *is giving
Peter's jacket back to him with an angry-looking thrust.*

EXT. CLUB. PAVEMENT. NIGHT
Close, and genuine.
PETER: (*Angrily*) I know what goes on in there. God Almighty!
    You know damned well it's just a posh sort of knocking-
    shop!
SANDRA: (*Angry laugh*) Ha! That's what *you* think! And you've
    got no bloody idea at all!

CLOSE-UP – DANIEL (STREET)
His eyes full of hatred as he watches PETER *go in a hiss of hatred.*
DANIEL: (*To self, just audible*) Bastard. (*But then he clenches
    with a sudden pain, and clutches at his stomach with a small
    gasp.*)

EXT. CLUB. STREET. NIGHT
From Daniel's pained but still stubbornly attentive point of view,
PETER *leaves, carrying his jacket as though he doesn't care about
rain, makes a dismissive gesture, and goes toward a big Mercedes,
parked a little way down the narrow street, off the wide road.*

SANDRA *turns away, indifferent, and goes into the karaoke club.*

KARAOKE SCREEN
Against montages of images with some relevance to the music (alas, including a pair of copulating dogs) the words of the song come up on the lower half of the screen, in English, sandwiched by Japanese –
> **How much is that doggie**
> **In the window?**

At the same time, from the start of the screen, a pair of male voices are singing, off screen, the same words as they march across the screen, darkening on cue. But this time the words are being sung in Japanese, whose (to us) alien falsetto and strange consonants make the ridiculous lyric even weirder and funnier.
Pull out and pan across –

INT. KARAOKE/HOSTESS CLUB. NIGHT
Panning past several karaoke screens showing the same advancing words and pictures, as the double-Japanese singing continues, off.
SECOND SCREEN: (*Including piddling dog*)
> **The one with the waggly tail**
> **How much is that –**

THIRD SCREEN: (*Including dog on hind-legs*)
> **– doggie in the window**
> **I do hope that doggie's for sale**

FOURTH SCREEN: (*Including dancing circus dog*)
> **I must take a trip to California**
> **And leave my –**

FIFTH SCREEN: (*Including dog fight*)
> **– poor sweetheart alone**
> **If he has a dog –**

FINAL SCREEN: (*Back to copulating dogs*)
> **– he won't be lonely**
> **And the doggie will have**
> > **a good home**

(*Reaching – at the end of the slow, comic pan –*)

INT. AT THE STAND. KARAOKE CLUB. NIGHT
Two small, natty JAPANESE BUSINESSMEN *have a mike each, singing happily away to the evident approval of their compatriot*

colleagues, who are clustered together at a long table, or tables, shunted together, with a scatter of half-clad HOSTESSES.
One of the neat pair, unfortunately, looks very like the wartime Emperor Hirohito.

TWO JAPANESE: (*In Japanese*)
How much is that doggie
In the window?
The one with the waggly tail
How much is that doggie
In the window?
I do hope that doggie's for sale!

INT. KARAOKE CLUB. NIGHT

DANIEL *enters through a beaded curtain from some sort of reception area, very damp and unsure of himself. He looks around, surprised by the largeness of the space, the technology of it, and momentarily bemused by the singing Japanese duo. His face shows that it fits and yet also doesn't fit whatever he had once described in his screenplay. He is looking for* SANDRA, *who is nowhere to be seen. But in alcoves to one side, parallel with the long bar at which he stands, several provocatively underdressed* HOSTESSES *sit, mostly chatting to each other, but also – here and there – a few such with five/six middle-aged* BUSINESSMEN *in suits, drinking – as well as the few at the Japanese tables.*

INT. BAR. NIGHT

A BARMAID-*cum-procuress, probably – not quite so brazenly dressed as the others – is quick to pounce, all smiling teeth.*

BARMAID: Well, hi! It's still raining, then! Hows about a nice dry champagne?

DANIEL: (*Eyes flicking about*) Um. Well, OK. Yes.

BARMAID: Would you like it brought over to one of the alcoves over there? It's more comfy and one of the young ladies –

DANIEL: No.

BARMAID: No? Oh, but you'll be so much –

DANIEL: (*Cutting in*) I'll just stand here, thanks. I'm not going to stay very long. I presume I'm allowed to do that. And I'm very fond of dogs.

BARMAID: You can do what you like here. That's the whole

46

point darling. So just relax, OK?

DANIEL: (*Unsmiling, lighting cigarette*) Thanks. I'll just crack my
knuckles from time to time.

(*There is already an edge to the barmaid's false smile, and now
she loses it altogether.*)

INT. AN ALCOVE. NIGHT

Three HOSTESSES, *drinking, smoking, look across to the far end of
the bar, where* DANIEL *sips, smokes, shifts like one very uneasy.
Music continuing.*

FIRST HOSTESS: They all somehow sort of look the bloody
same, don't they?

SECOND HOSTESS: Yeah. Scumbags.

(*But each face is set in a comically smouldering smile of
invitation, each turned to* DANIEL *at the end of the bar.*)

THIRD HOSTESS (ANGIE): It's wet – might not be many in, that's
the trouble. And he looks too pissed to try a poke.

INT. CLUB. NIGHT

*The singing Japanese have just done, to a scatter of cheers and claps
from their compatriots and, dutifully, from the* HOSTESSES *already
at that particular table.*

Music of a different kind resumes and a HOSTESS, *differently garbed
from the others, is going around with a portable mike and a book listing
tunes and lyrics, trying to cajole others into going up to the stand.*

INT. BAR. CLUB. NIGHT

ANGIE *has come over to simper and present herself to* DANIEL, *alone
at the bar.*

ANGIE: Hi! My name is Angie. I was looking at –

DANIEL: (*Dully, morose*) No.

(*She blinks, and like a wound-up doll mechanically starts again.*)

ANGIE: Hi! I'm Angie. I was looking at you when you came in
and I fought, he's –

DANIEL: (*Cutting in*) Who?

ANGIE: Sorry?

DANIEL: Who did you fight?

(*They look at each other, as though mutually surprised. Then
he laughs, tipsily.*)

ANGIE: What are you laughing at, then?

DANIEL: I've used that line before.

ANGIE: Pardon?

DANIEL: But so have you.

ANGIE: (*Confused*) Look – I'm only trying to be –

DANIEL: (*Abrupt*) Go away.

ANGIE: What – ?

DANIEL: Please. No. I know you're only doing your – but – (*He winces, and involuntarily touches his stomach.*) I've got this – this – (*Starts to giggle, half-tipsy, half-desperate.*) Don't know whether my head's in my belly or my belly's in my head. They're both a fucking mess.

ANGIE: (*Uncertain laugh*) Christ.

DANIEL: (*Laughing still*) So if you'll leave me be.

ANGIE (*Surprisingly cheerful*) Oh, all right then. Cheers.
(*She turns away without more ado. Daniel stops laughing, winces, and follows her retreating, very shapely figure almost wistfully, then inadvertently meets the eye of the hoveringly alert* BARMAID.

BARMAID: Perhaps you'd rather have a nice little chat with one of the others –

DANIEL: No. I only came in for a –
(*But his face changes. The* BARMAID *turns to see why.*)

INT. CLUB. NIGHT
Out of a door beyond the other end of the long bar – obviously, from some kind of changing room – SANDRA *comes, now dressed like one of the* HOSTESSES, *although with a sulky demeanour and no attempt at the standard smile.*
Rising from a table, hitherto unseen, Arthur Mailion – the owner, the 'singer' in the very opening scene – goes towards her, face set, shoulders squaring, like one angry and arrowing in for a row. And we see that she knows it.

INT. BAR. NIGHT
BARMAID: (*To* DANIEL) Lovely. Isn't she.
(DANIEL, *staring, does not speak for a moment.*)

DANIEL: (*Huskily*) I – (*seems to have to clear his throat.*) Yes. Yes she is. Very lovely. Even in that garb.

INT. TOP END OF BAR. NIGHT

MAILION *is in the midst of a nasty, blustering, thuggish tirade, his meaty hands gripping Sandra's shoulders as though to make her face him.*

MAILION: – and with a face like a fucking bent fiddle!
> (*She clearly wants to answer back in kind, but seemingly dares not.*)

SANDRA: I'm sorry, Mr Mailion, really, but I just had this row with my boyfriend *as was* and –

MAILION: (*Cutting in*) I don't give a pint of horse piss for your private life, my gal. *This* is where you get paid, *this* is where you should bring your pretty little arse *on time* and this is where (*Drops hands and with horrible, finger-jabbing punctuation*) you-should-crack–your–fucking–fizzog-in-a-fucking-*smile*. Right?

SANDRA: (*Desperate little smile*) Right.
> (*But she is saved from any further abuse by the arrival at the top end of the bar, near where she is facing* MAILION, *of the* BARMAID.)

BARMAID: Excuse me, Mr Mailion. But the gentleman down there at the other end of the bar would like to have a drink with Sandra.

SANDRA: (*Almost eagerly*) Fine.
> (MAILION *turns and nods and smiles at* DANIEL *as though in benediction, but, at the side of his mouth, to* SANDRA –)

MAILION: Dom fucking Perignon, right?

CLOSE-UP – DANIEL. BAR
Half-closing his eyes in a little shudder of shame and unease, an image lethally flashes up at him.
Flash: The Bedroom Murder. Briefest angled glint of the looping tie coming over what now seems more clearly to be SANDRA's *neck (the 'real'* SANDRA) *and the horrible beginings of her, shocked, starting to choke/scream.*

CLOSE-UP – DANIEL. BAR
DANIEL : (*To self, mutter*) Such a horrible way to – (*But almost at the same moment –*)

49

INT. THE BAR, CLUB. NIGHT

SANDRA: (*Fixed-smile routine*) Hi! I was looking at you when you came in and I fought, he's the kind of –
(*Her voice trails off, her fixed smile half-dies as she looks, really looks, at him, half-sure that he was the 'Brasserie Starer'.*)

DANIEL: You fought?

SANDRA: Beg pardon?

DANIEL: (*Almost wearily*) These lines keep cropping up. The same lines – (*Then, quickly*) I mean you'd – like a drink? Please?
(*She goes to say something accusing, but – Mailion's words still ringing – changes it in mid-expression.*)

SANDRA: Well, thanks very much – yeah! – But, hey, why don't we have a bottle?

DANIEL: (*Grandly, tipsily*) Certainly.

SANDRA: (*Harder*) Dom Perignon.

DANIEL: (*Swaying*) Ab-so-lutely. The best for the best.
(*But she cannot, in the end, hold back.*)

SANDRA: You were staring at me, weren't you? In that café place.

DANIEL: I – yes.

SANDRA: And you followed me in here, didn'tya?

DANIEL: (*Intense*) Yes. I did.
(*She stares at him, troubled by the intensity of his gaze – or his stare.*)

SANDRA: (*Half-scared*) What you want? What you playing at?

DANIEL: (*Urgently*) Please. What is your name?

SANDRA: (*Half-unwilling*) Sandra. (*At the suck of his breath*) What's the matter?

DANIEL: And the man you were with, he was called Peter, wasn't he?

SANDRA: Yeah. But – what's that got to do with you? You know him or what?
(*He looks at her imploringly. He hesitates. Unable to explain the depths of his anxiety to himself, he doesn't know how to tell her. So –*)

DANIEL: (*Almost a stutter*) I – I'm a writer.
(*She just looks at him, waiting.*)

(*Again*) I – put words into other people's mouths. And at
the moment – (*He sways, a terrible spasm of pain.*) At the
moment, I – oh, God! My stomach! (*Gabbles, trying to get it
out in time.*) It's all coming true in front of me. It's all –
Listen. I said I put words into people's mouths. Well, I
also – (*Urgently, wincing with stomach pain.*) Are you getting
any of this? Can you understand *at all?*
(*So urgently that he grabs at her arm. She pulls away, and
looks around.*)

SANDRA: Hey. Steady on, Romeo.

DANIEL: (*Urgently, not stopping*) It's not just marks on a page.
It's not just words in other people's mouths. I make them
do things. I even let them screw each other or lie to each
other or or or or *kill* each other – Yes! Kill! Kill!
(*Under the enormously urgent desperation of what he is
saying, Daniel seems to be crumpling up, sinking down, and
at the same time, for support, and in earnest plea, clutching at
first her arms and then her waist as he crumples – and 'Why
Must I be a Teenager in Love?' starts up on the karaoke
machine.*)

SANDRA: (*Yelling*) Hey! Somebody! Quick!

EXTREME CLOSE-UP – DANIEL
*As he disintegrates, so to speak, physically and emotionally, falling,
clutching now at her legs, he all but screams a sob of the direst
warning.*

DANIEL: And *you* – it's you, you, Sandra! They're going to *kill
you* –
(*At the same time, encouraged by their previous experience it
seems, the two neat* JAPANESE BUSINESSMEN *are singing, off
screen, in their own language. And at the same time, too, she
screams louder for help.* DANIEL *has by now collapsed, flat out
on the floor, seemingly unconscious.*)

INT. KARAOKE CLUB. NIGHT
*Not everyone, and not all at once, but people begin to react to the
strange scene way over in the far corner at the far end of the long bar.
Some stand, some gape, then some come running – including*
MAILION, *looking bullishly indignant.*

MAILION: (*Bellowing*) 'Ere! You can't do that in my place!
(*And the music continues – the Japanese duo, in shot, have not yet noticed anything awry, for they are looking across at the many screens, where pictures and words are as before in the opening scene.*)

INT. KARAOKE STAND. CLUB. NIGHT
TWO JAPANESE: (*Singing in Japanese*)
Each night I ask
The stars up above
Why must I be-e-e
A teenager in love?
(*Fade picture. Fade music.*)

PART TWO

EXT. PARIS SEMI-MONTAGE. DAY
*Swiftly dissolving between sunlit, dream-like images of standard
expectations – Eiffel Tower, Seine, Arc de Triomphe, Tricoleur, etc.
etc. – ideally from aerial perspectives, the most evocatively brochure-
like montage, gradually narrowing down, as though inexorably, to
the plangent rhythms of the standard accordion (heard from the
start) to find –*

EXT. NOTRE-DAME. DAY
*Rearing in all its grandeur above the Seine, getting closer and closer,
so that its clangorous bells gradually impose themselves upon the 'I
Love Paris' or whatever kitsch from the accordion – entering, as from
the flight of a jackdaw – straight into –*

CLOSE-UP – THE BELLS OF NOTRE-DAME
*Swing – clang – swing with what becomes the resonance of dream,
pulling out a little to find, after all –*

CLOSE-UP – MATCHSTICK NOTRE-DAME
*Taking, so to speak, a moment before realizing out of what material
this great and complicated edifice is constructed – and then glimpsing,
through some incomplete part of it (such as the bare-matchstick-
skeleton of a flying buttress), the distant, out-of-focus face of the
agent 'back-to-front'* BEN BAGLIN. *The bells continue to clang.*

INT. BEN'S STUDY. DAY
*It is early morning. Ben is still clothed as when Anna visited
unannounced, which was the previous night. He has fallen asleep on
his tummy in an ungainly sprawl on a sofa between his desk and the
matchstick edifice.*

CLOSE-UP – BEN BAGLIN
*As his eyes half-flutter open in the act of waking, the Notre-Dame
bells reluctantly fade from his head.
Then he sees that he has half a dozen shaved or headless matchsticks*

53

*clutched as though for dear life in one of his clenched hands, taken
from a workbox on the carpet beside the sofa full of modelling paints,
clays, blades and whatnot.*

BEN: (*Sluggish, straightening*) Oooh – not again – ooch – (*Rubs
the small of his back.*) Och! By mack! ('My back!') Time to
met gooving ('get moving').

INT. STAIRS AND LANDING AT BEN'S DOOR. DAY
Strange old BEN'S MOTHER, *kimonoed, vividly red-haired and
nailed, carries up a tray the last few steps on to the landing. The tray
holds a cup, a small pot of coffee, a plate with one poached egg on a
single piece of toast, and – strangely – a pair of tweezers.
She puts the tray down for a moment on an elegant rosewood table in
this upper hall, in front of a large, ornamentally edged mirror.*

CLOSE-UP – BEN'S MOTHER AND MIRROR
*She seems to greatly approve of the apparition which is her own
reflection, and purses together her painted cherry-red lips in her
wrinkled face to throw her own image an admiring kiss.*
BEN'S MOTHER: Koochy-koochy-koo! (*Then her expression
changes to a Macbeth witch, she loosens her loose kimono, lifts
one arm and with the other hand takes the tweezers, and – with a
wince and then a tiny cackle – pulls out a hair from her armpit.*)

CLOSE-UP – TRAY ON ROSEWOOD TABLE
BEN'S MOTHER *carefully lifts the poached egg and slides the long,
grey (she hasn't dyed there) armpit hair under it, and gently places
the egg back into position over the hair.*

INT. BEN'S STUDY. DAY
BEN *is now more or less awake, yawning and stretching now without
discomfort, but unable to avoid a last, yearning look as he hovers
around the matchstick Notre-Dame. He is about to reach out and
tenderly touch it when the door opens, and he jerks away, quickly.*
BEN'S MOTHER: (*Cheerful*) *Good* morning, bright Ben! I could
see you fell asleep on your sofa again – and that's naughty,
naughty, Ben.
BEN: (*Seeing tray*) Ma. You mustn't. You really don't need to
do this –

BEN'S MOTHER: Come, come. Come along. An egg before the bath, as your father always used to say. (*She is putting the tray on Ben's desk in a space between a clutter of scripts – unread – and the telephone.*)

CLOSE-UP – TELEPHONE. HER POINT OF VIEW
A small light on the built-in answer-machine flashes one-two-three, one-two-three, to show that there have been that number of messages since BEN *fell asleep at his 'hobby'.*

INT. BEN'S STUDY. DAY
As BEN *moves to the desk –*
BEN: Well, you're a sweet old dear, Ma, there's no mistaking it. Coffee too, eh! Thank you very –
BEN'S MOTHER: You got some messages, Ben. One. Two. Three. (BEN *sits, picks up knife and fork, ready to attack his poached egg on toast.*)
BEN: Work. Work. Work. They can damned well wait a bit, Ma. I give them my life and soul as it is, these whingeing scribes and greedy producers. My tiny amount of leisure is very precious to me – to *us*, eh?
(*He is already eating. She has moved away a little, but now stops to watch him eat with a glint of excitement flashing out of her wizened and make-up-caked face.*)
BEN'S MOTHER: Nice, is it? Is it nice, Ben?
(BEN, *mouth full, pours himself some coffee, and sips and chews as he speaks.*)
BEN: Last night, Ma – that fretful woman and all that – listen – I'm sorry I made you go to bed early. I'm very sorry.
BEN'S MOTHER: Yes, my boy. You were wrong. *And* she's a nice young woman! I can't upend you and give you a good smack, Ben. (*Sudden cackle, then an immediate straight face again.*) But there are other ways, other ways, boy.

CLOSE-UP – BEN EATING
His jaws stop for a moment, he feels about inside his mostly full mouth with his tongue, then puts his fingers to his lips, pulling out a strand of something (and we know what).
BEN'S MOTHER: (*Off*) Free-range.

INT. BEN'S STUDY. DAY

BEN *still trying to pull out a bit of the hair his teeth must already have chopped in half.*

BEN: What?

BEN'S MOTHER: You can't beat them, dear. Free-range eggs from chickens that are allowed to roam here, there and everywhere.

BEN: (*Dubious*) Yes. I suppose so.

BEN'S MOTHER: Even if they do get the odd bit of hay or farmyard del-i-cac-y in the yolk, eh?

(*And, with another wicked cackle of sheer glee, she is gone, in a swift flap of kimono.* BEN *sort of half-smiles at her departing figure, then his face changes. He seems to consider something for a fraction of a second, then pulls a real or imagined remnant of hair from his mouth and pushes his plate away.*)

BEN: (*Savagely*) Bunning old cugger! (*Then, going to rise, his eye half-catches the flashing light on the telephone, and he presses the right button.*

CLOSE-UP – TELEPHONE AND BUILT-IN ANSWER MACHINE

FIRST MESSAGE: (*American accent*) Hi there, Ben. This is Irwin Wilerwaller. It's – what? Yeah – midnight thirty *your* time. Give me a call. I'm talking about the stop-go animation flyer –

INT. BEN'S STUDY. DAY

BEN *has moved away from the desk, listening, and is starting to shed his clothes in an untidy tumble to go to an* en suite *bathroom or shower room just off the study.*

BEN: (*To self, derisively*) Yeah. Yeah.

FIRST MESSAGE: (*Continuous, over*) – on those whatchacallit fucking woolly things – sheep! – yeah – Working title's *Baa Baa*, would you believe? Anyway, Ben, they've decided to make the old Nanny Goat in the next field – the arthritic one if you've read the script, which I know darned well you won't have –

INT. BATH/SHOWER ROOM OFF STUDY. DAY

BEN, *still listening without too great an interest, examines his* stubbled, sleepy-eyed face in a mirror, with palpable distaste, and puts his tongue out for further, unreassuring examination.

FIRST MESSAGE: (*Continuous, off*) – the Goat is to be *British*, Ben. So there you go. Four, five pages, maybe, for a Pinter, Gray, Whitemore, Stoppard or (*Nasty chuckle*) even one of *your* scripters *if* you move your feet. OK? *Owe me!*
(*It finishes.*)

CLOSE-UP – TELEPHONE AND BUILT-IN ANSWER MACHINE
Bleep! and second message begins.
ANNA'S VOICE: (*On machine*) Anna Griffiths, Ben. Just want to – ah – to apologize once more for crashing in on you earlier this evening – and I and I – yes, I'm showing my neurotic – Oh, Christ, Ben. If you could somehow or other –
(*During which –*)

INT. BATH/SHOWER ROOM OFF STUDY. DAY
BEN: (*To self*) For God in bloody heaven! (*And he continues to discard clothes.*)
ANNA'S VOICE: (*Continuous, off*) – get to Daniel Feeld *before* he comes to the cutting –
BEN: (*Pulling off a sock*) Oh, shut up! Bloody woman.
ANNA'S VOICE: (*Continuous, off*) – room, I'd be very grateful and – (*Abruptly.*) Sorry. Good-night, Ben. Sorry.
(BEN *has now removed the other sock, and stands in order to take off his underpants – Y-Fronts – which is all there is left to remove.*)

INT. BEN'S DESK. THE STUDY. DAY
The answer machine begins to deliver up the third and last message.
THIRD MESSAGE: (*Male voice*) My name is Andrew Mossley, Duty Officer at Hillgate Police Station. It is 1.20 a.m., Wednesday morning. We have your number, sir, from St Christopher's Hospital in Clipstone Street –

INT. BATH/SHOWER ROOM. DAY
Comically alarmed, BEN *is swiftly and yet somehow furtively pulling his Y-Fronts back up, like one denying an indecency charge.*

THIRD MESSAGE: (*Continuous, off*) – and it was obtained from the wallet of a Mr Daniel Feeld, who was at that time, so far as we are –
(BEN *at first sighs relief, but as soon stiffens in alarm again.*)

CLOSE-UP – TELEPHONE/ANSWER MACHINE
THIRD MESSAGE: (*Continuous*) – aware, unconscious and so unable to speak. Mr Feeld was admitted into the –

INT. BEN'S STUDY. DAY
BEN, *gaping, is standing now at the shower-room doorway, staring across at the telephone/answer machine on his desk.*
THIRD MESSAGE: (*Continuous*) – George Ward of St Christopher's Hospital, Clipstone Street, at 11.52 tonight – that's last night as I speak – Tuesday night, the 14th. This does not appear to be a police matter, sir. But the hospital could find no other private number –
(*Dissolving.*)

EXT. SOHO ALLEY. DAY
A wretchedly forlorn, ill-clad down-and-out – almost certainly schizophrenic and alcoholic – rummages with mutteringly angry contempt in a bin of sorts, at the back of a restaurant or café, pulling out various kinds of yuk and dribbling filth. His hands are scratched and bloodied, and he has a badly swollen eye-socket.
THIRD MESSAGE: (*Continuous, over*) and so far as I am aware the gentleman in question is still in a comatose or unconscious condition –
(*Message voice fading as pan up from the narrow little alley, up some crumbly building-backs, to a pair of windows on the fourth or fifth floor, which are –*)

INT. CUTTING ROOM. SOHO. DAY
This time it is only NICK BALMER, *the director, and* IAN, *the editor, who are positioned side by side at the Steenbeck, still on Reel One (and at about the same contentious scenes) and still, to judge by their initial expressions, in fundamental disagreement.*
PETER: (*Off, on Steenbeck*) – all that by now. You're something you are, Sandra. Real special.

58

LINDA: (*Off, on Steenbeck*) No, all the time – eyes sticking out of his head.

(*Obviously, these are the two actors in Daniel's script, not the real* SANDRA *and* PETER.)

CLOSE-UP – STEENBECK SCREEN
Coming to the picture as a small unease returns to PETER.

PETER: So long as he's not from your actual Customs and Excise.

(*But as he is about to turn – as in the 'original' with the real* SANDRA *and* PETER – *to study the distant figure across the brasserie – who is now, of course, the patrician old man* OLIVER MORSE *rather than* DANIEL – *the picture on the Steenbeck closes tighter in on* LINDA.)

IAN: (*Off, while* LINDA *in close-up*) *There!* Him, y'see? On *him!*

PETER: (*On screen*) Nah. Nah. Looks too intelligent.

(*And the picture, so briefly off her, flicks back to* LINDA *again, more sensibly so, at least at the beginning.*)

INT. CUTTING ROOM. DAY
With the Steenbeck screen well in view, and the two watching faces looming – Ian's angrily set, tight-lipped, and NICK *with the well-practised insouciance of allegedly sardonic raised eyebrows – as if to indicate that he is mildly incredulous or even amused by Ian's various 'nonsenses' on this point.*

LINDA: (*On screen*) You'd think I was in the bleed'n Top Shop window or something. I've had enough of this! (*Calls across the brasserie, attracting lots of attention.*) Oo the 'ell you looking at!

(*The real* SANDRA *had not said this last line. But* LINDA *does the same action, more or less, by sticking out her tongue at distant* OLIVER.)

PETER: (*Off, on screen*) Hey! None of that! You dragged up in a pigsty or what?

IAN: (*At same time*) Why *not* on him? What's the sense of it, Nick?

(*But* NICK *keeps his eyes steadily on the Steenbeck screen, despite a half-suppressed tut! of anger from* IAN.)

CLOSE-UP – STEENBECK SCREEN
Almost as the picture cuts to OLIVER MORSE, *close in, in the brasserie.*
His eyes are fixed on LINDA, *across the big room, and they do not*
flicker away in embarrassment, or change in any other way.
Instead –
OLIVER: (*Very softly*) And I've missed you, too, my lost little
    love.
    (*Steenbeck screen widening to –*)

INT. BRASSERIE. NIGHT
Suddenly, LINDA *is standing in front of* OLIVER'*s table, her eyes*
blazing – and the focus, now, of almost everyone's attention in the
brasserie.
LINDA: Hey. You! Keep yer eyes in yer bleed'n head! Right?
    (*But* OLIVER *looks at her, with such a tender smile that she is*
    momentarily nonplussed.)
OLIVER: Oh, my dear, dear one.
LINDA: (*Confused*) Don't you look at *me* like that! You dirty old
    sod!
    (*Her confusion has served to push her existing anger and ill-will*
    into a totally excessive whirl of rage. She picks up his glass and
    throws the contents straight at him. But OLIVER, *amazingly,*
    does not jerk back or react, and keeps on looking at her with the
    gentle smile. The red wine trickles and drips down his face, and
    yet he looks utterly dignified and does not try to dab it off.
    Bewildered by such dignity, and half in shame at her own
    excess, LINDA *stares at him, not sure what to do or say.*
    Everyone is staring.)
OLIVER: (*Quietly*) You always were such a passionate young
    woman. Don't worry about it, my dear. The wine is really
    rather poor. Certainly not up to the Gevrey Chambertin we
    used to enjoy, mmm?
    (LINDA *gapes, incredulous and flummoxed. She turns on her*
    high heels, with a toss of her long hair.)
LINDA: You're a nutter.
    (*Not sure of herself now, she storms back towards her table,*
    watched all the way by OLIVER *with a curiously affectionate*
    little smile – and by everyone else with quite different sets of
    expressions.)

INT. LINDA AND PETER'S TABLE. BRASSERIE. NIGHT
*Where Essex Man is appalled by Essex Girl, so to speak, as she
returns, increasingly self-conscious, all eyes upon her.*
PETER: (*Hiss*) Christ Almighty.
LINDA: (*Sullen undertone*) Shut up.
>   (PETER *looks around at the others still looking at them, and
>   leans forward to her, utterly enraged at such unwanted
>   conspicuousness but trying to keep his voice down. The words
>   virtually come out through his teeth.*)
PETER: You're out of control! You're dis-gust-ing! What the
>   fuck do you fink you're fucking well doing?
>   (*She is still sullen and subdued rather than flashing with anger.*)
LINDA: He asked for it, didn't he?
PETER: I've never seen anything so – It's dis-gust-ing! You're
>   not in a bloody McDonald's, are you? What the fuck are
>   you going to do next? Spit on the floor? What?
>   (*But even as the actor* PETER *very slightly overdoes his
>   spluttering performance, his eyes swivel about the brasserie, as
>   though the character he plays is supposed to keep checking,
>   checking on the people around him.*
>
>   *Linda's own eyes have begun to look back at* OLIVER,
>   *vaguely uneasy. It does not seem as though she is listening.*)

INT. OLIVER'S POINT OF VIEW OF LINDA ACROSS BRASSERIE.
NIGHT
*Her now puzzled eyes and subdued manner, looking back at him
half the length of the large oblong of the brasserie, and – in a very
odd shift, entirely from his mind, and in keeping with his previous
reactions to the first sight of her, as well as to her wine-throwing
attack on him –* OLIVER *seems to invent dialogue for her which
slightly more fits her present subdued condition.*
LINDA: (*Distant*) I see your pain, Oliver dear – (*And it is a
>   middle-class voice.*) But there is –
>   (*Diminishing down to –*)

STEENBECK AND ITS SCREEN
LINDA: (*continuous*) – nothing I can do about it, except endure
>   as *you* have endured.

INT. CUTTING ROOM. DAY
This time, the moody 'Tut!' is from NICK, *and there is a little twist of a pretend-dour-Scot 'smile' from* IAN, *and a single word.*
IAN: Aye.
> (*Meanwhile, the picture on the Steenbeck screen is continuing, adequately in view in this set-up, as the scene's images switch close on* OLIVER.)

CLOSE-UP – STEENBECK SCREEN
OLIVER: (*Again, quietly*) I know, my love. We are trapped in our own yearning. Forgive me. Forgive.
WAITER: (*Into shot*) Are you all right, Mr Morse? That was a – I'm very very –

INT. CUTTING ROOM. DAY
Picture and sound stop dead, leaving a still of a flustered WAITER *in mid-apologetic arm flap on the bright, sharply defined little screen.*
IAN, *at the controls, seated, looks up at* NICK, *who is standing rather twitchily half-alongside and half-behind him.* IAN *waits, knowing full well that* NICK *does not like admitting to any difficulties.*
NICK: (*Eventually*) The narrative is all tangled and knotted here – If we're not careful we shall lose sight of any kind of A-B-C drive in the story.
IAN: (*Drily*) And settle for Q, X and Y.
> (NICK *glares, then decides to smile – for the time being.*)
NICK: In terms of the *story* we have to have what in effect are voice-overs from Linda – I mean, it won't work without them.
IAN: (*Deliberate*) Disnae work wi' them, neitherrr.
NICK: (*Half-aggressive*) No?
IAN: No.
> (NICK *walks up and down a bit, caged, trying to reassure himself.*)
NICK: We can't really tell yet, not definitively. We need to look at the whole sequence – I mean, if the old man doesn't 'hear' in quotes the voice of the utterly different young woman he remembers with such – such *ache* from so long, long ago – if he doesn't think think and think in his odd, obsessive way that this cheap little tart called Sandra is

somehow the living *embodiment* of the other lovely young
woman he once wooed and lost – then – then – well –

IAN: (*Almost with relish*) The whole story goes down the drain.
(NICK *has been quite expressive in his relentless pacing, showing
creativity, or his other side, but at Ian's cold-water comment he
stops moving, and stares at his editor with the icy disdain of an
officer-class type to an ordinary rank.*)

NICK: That's extremely helpful, Ian. I deeply appreciate such a
useful remark. Like so many of your impromptu asides and
comments.

IAN: (*Hunched-up, monosyllabic*) Sorry.
(NICK *looks at him, twists his mouth as though to embark upon
a real tirade – and all the potential disruptions that would cause
– but then seems to think better of it, and leans in abruptly to
restart the Steenbeck picture.*)

NICK: Let's just *look* at the thing, shall we?
(*As –*)

CLOSE-UP – STEENBECK AND SCREEN
The flustered WAITER *is suddenly released from immobility.*
WAITER: – very sorry. I've never seen anything like –
(*The picture widens to –*)

INT. BRASSERIE. NIGHT
As OLIVER, *coming into shot, looks up at the* WAITER.
OLIVER: Artistic temperament. (*Fond smile.*) Oh, we've had
many a – (*Smile stops, face hardens: the bit that Daniel had
quoted near end of first episode.*) What do *you* know about
her? How can *you* possibly understand? These things
happen and they are none of your business.
(*The* WAITER *reacts.*)

WAITER: Fine. Fine.
OLIVER: (*Snaps*) And bring me my bill.
(*A demeanour slightly compromised by the drop of spilled red
wine hovering on the edge of his chin, ready to drop down his
already wine-splashed tie. But* OLIVER, *seemingly unaware and
certainly untroubled by this, looks across the brasserie at the one
particular table again, over in the bar area.*)

INT. LINDA'S TABLE. BRASSERIE. NIGHT

As LINDA *– still vaguely puzzled or uneasy – pulls her eyes away from* OLIVER *to face the continuing, low-voiced tirade from Peter, in mid-flow.*

PETER: – not on Southend Pier picking out your winkles, are you?

    (*She looks at him, almost blank, then – in a change of tone –*)

LINDA: You heard this one? It's a good 'un.

PETER: (*Blinking*) Wha – ?

LINDA: These two bats. In a cave. Right?

PETER: Sandra!

LINDA: 'Anging upside down.

    (*But she darts a swift, almost covert look at Oliver's table.*)

PETER: (*Indignant*) You to'ally round the twist or what? You hearing a word of what I'm saying – ?

    (*The picture diminishing to –*)

STEENBECK AND SCREEN

LINDA: They *do* hang upside down. Bats.

NICK: (*Off*) I *love* the way she says *that* line.

PETER: (*On screen, same time*) I don't want to know!

    (*Widening –*)

INT. CUTTING ROOM. DAY

NICK *and* IAN *watching the continuing reel. It is increasingly obvious that* NICK *is besotted with* LINDA, *the actress playing Daniel Feeld's 'Sandra'.*

LINDA: Anyway. These two bats –

PETER: (*Hissing*) You're getting right up my nose.

LINDA: (*Taking no notice*) They're talking to each other. Right?

    (*On the Steenbeck screen – centrally in our view –* PETER *looks at her, becoming wary. He wonders if she is trying to say something in a roundabout way; and he definitely wants something from her.*)

PETER: We talk, Sandra. You and me. We've always got on, haven't we, chick?

EXTREME CLOSE-UP – NICK. CUTTING ROOM

As LINDA *speaks, off, on the Steenbeck, a sneaky little close-up of*

NICK *shows almost adolescent-like adoration/lust burning out of his watching eyes.*

LINDA: (*Off*) And the one bat says to the other bat – 'Gawd, I'm effin *'ungry! – '*

INT. CUTTING ROOM. DAY
NICK (*same adoring expression*) *and virtually expressionless* IAN *watching the Steenbeck screen,* IAN *sitting,* NICK *standing.*

LINDA: (*On screen, continuous*) – I could do wiv some fresh blood, and I want it *now!'*
(*The telephone in the cutting room starts to ring.*)

PETER: (*On screen, now worried-looking*) Look – this bloke – he's not a bad sort – I mean, you've had worse. All right, all right, so he's got a bit of a beer belly and he wears *glasses* and that –
(*Ring! Ring! irritatingly all through. During which –*)

IAN: (*Nods at phone*) I'd better –

NICK: (*Fierce*) Let it fucking ring!

PETER: (*On screen, continuous*) – but Sandra, love, listen, I need a favour off him real bad, and he'd go for you in a big way. Do this for me! Please!
(*Still ringing.*)

INT. GEORGE WARD, ST CHRISTOPHER'S HOSPITAL. DAY
A smallish ward in a rather run-down hospital – eight patients – and there, at the far end, by a window, is DANIEL, *in bed, in 'borrowed' hospital pyjamas, looking pale and broody.*
BEN *it is who has been trying to telephone the cutting room, holding a paper bag in his other hand.*

BEN: (*Phone*) Come on. Come on. Come on!
(*He is using a portable – wheeled – hospital pay phone that can be plugged into a socket between each pair of beds. And he is also overconscious of an* IMPATIENT PATIENT *hovering in dressing gown at the foot of Daniel's bed, waiting for the phone, and jingling coins in his dressing-gown pocket, all the time.*)

IMPATIENT PATIENT: (*To* DANIEL) Getting no answer, is he?

DANIEL: (*Indifferent*) Doesn't look like it.

IMPATIENT PATIENT: How long's he going to keep trying, then?

(DANIEL *looks at him, with a measure of distaste, and speaks with what appears to be thoughtful precision.*)

DANIEL: Well. Two, or at the most three, hours. It's Buckingham Palace, you see, and they're notorious for keeping you hanging about like a spare flunkey.

IMPATIENT PATIENT: *What?* (*Then, whingeing.*) Only the wife is busy helping with orphans and cripples. She only has half an hour, see, this very half –

BEN: (*Loudly, slamming down phone*) The cazy lunt!
(*The waiting* PATIENT *stops, frowns at* BEN, *rather comically half-sensing bad language, and wheels the phone away with a conqueror's air, back to his own distant bed.*)

DANIEL: (*To* BEN, *amused*) Who are you so tarmingly chalking about, Ben, old bean?

BEN: (*Genuinely puzzled*) 'Tarmingly chalking – ?' (*Then*) Now, now. No call for that, Daniel. I've got enough to put up with, thank you very much. (*Sits on chair beside bed, still holding paper bag.*) In that cutting room – well, it's Ian who should answer, or one of his assistant editors, but – oh, no – if Nick's there and Nick is in one of his God's Gift to the Arts moods, he won't let *anyone* answer!

DANIEL: (*Wearily*) Oh, leave it, Ben.
(BEN *looks at* DAN. *He* does *look extremely wan, and very worn.*)

BEN: (*Changed tone*) You don't look too good, my dear chap. (*Looks around.*) Why did they put you in here? Not up to much, is it?

DANIEL: (*Solemn*) No more drink.

BEN: (*With a half-smile*) No?

DANIEL: That's definite. Not a drop! You've got to help me here. I've crossed over some sort of line. You or somebody should have told me. Held me back!
(BEN *knows the injustice of such an accusation, but adjusts his face, clutching his paper bag.*)

BEN: Yes, Daniel. We should. It wasn't as though we hadn't all noticed.
(*They look at each other, solemnly, and then they each start to laugh at exactly the same time.*)

DANIEL: They put me in here because it was all that was

available and because I was in no position to have any say
in the matter. (*Broods – in slight terror.*) I didn't know where
I was or what I was or who I was. And when I woke up,
here, in this bed, in the middle of last night, I thought –
(*He stops.* BEN *waits, but sees that* DANIEL *cannot finish some
dread sentence.*)

BEN: Have they diven you a gia – (*Checks in time.*) Have you
had any sort of diagnosis yet, Dan?
(DANIEL *is still dead-eyed brooding about the unfinished
sentence that began 'I thought'. He has to force his attention
back to* BEN.)

DANIEL: What? Oh. Well – not really. Just sinister-feeling
suspicions. (*Looks at watch.*) In about half an hour they're
going to give me this endoscopy – I think that's what it's
called – you know, look inside you with a teeny-weeny
camera or something. Sees things that ordinary scans
don't, anyway.

BEN: (*Half-winces*) But which way do they go – I mean – sorry –

DANIEL: Down the throat, so I gather. (*Sniff.*) Bloody hell and
damn it. (*Looks at* BEN, *troubled.*) I don't know what it's all
about. They're sniffing around about *something.* They've
been in touch with Barker, and they know about the
barium enema and the barium meal before that. (*Looks
about, furtively.*) Ben – !

INT. DANIEL'S POINT OF VIEW – THE REST OF THE WARD. DAY
*For virtually the first time, there is no nurse, no orderly, no medic
about. The* IMPATIENT PATIENT *is still using the phone, down at
the other end.*

INT. TOP OF THE WARD. DAY
BEN *is taken by the sudden urgency of Daniel's use of his name.*

BEN: What?

DANIEL: (*In an urgent hiss*) Draw the curtains – the curtains
around the bed – *quickly.*
(*Feeling some unnamed urgency, and rather awkwardly, for he
is an awkward man,* BEN *puts his paper bag down on the
chair, and – too slowly for* DANIEL *– pulls the curtains around
the bed.*

And manages, in the process, to end up outside the now closed-off bed.)

INT. DANIEL'S ENCLOSED BED. DAY
Daniel is comically lightning fast as he bends over to his locker, gropes, pulls out a cigarette and lighter, and instantly drags in smoke as though it were the last elixir of life, with a wondrous 'Aaaaah' of pure satisfaction.

INT. THE OUTSIDE OF DANIEL'S ENCLOSED BED. DAY
BEN, *outside the curtains, feels (however ridiculously) just a momentary twinge of what is a social embarrassment about invading the space of someone now so clearly, privately, set apart.*
BEN: (*Clears his throat*) Daniel?

INT. DANIEL'S ENCLOSED BED. DAY
DANIEL *is practically eating the cigarette, so great is his relief, with a big, silly, beatific smile wreathing his features.*
Ben's head pokes through the curtains, still like one unsure about intruding. The face poking through the curtain like a headless puppet against a cloth backdrop makes DANIEL *jump inside for a micro-second, so odd does it look and so overwhelmingly exclusive had been the hours-deprived satisfaction of nicotine.*
DANIEL: (*Half-chokes on smoke*) Bloody hell, Ben, you – (*Then, urgently*) Ben, please. Stand guard! Just stay out there for a minute or two – Go on! Be alert!
BEN: Sorry – ?
DANIEL: (*Dragging-in smoke*) Keep your eye out for a doctor or a nurse or something! There's *one* of them that looks like a bin-bag liner on its day out. *Go on.* Look!
BEN: (*Affronted*) All right. All right.
(*And his balding, bespectacled, rubbery-muscled face disappears behind the curtain.*)

INT. OUTSIDE ENCLOSED BED. DAY
BEN *removes his head and turns, his back to the curtain, ready to stand guard. Eyes comically switching about, taking the job very seriously, he stage-whispers reassurance over his shoulder.*
BEN: All clear, Dan. All clear. Not a surse in night!

INT. WITHIN CURTAINED BED. DAY

DANIEL *nods happily, and draws in more smoke, dropping the lengthening ash into one of the hospital-issue slippers at the side of the bed, which he has lifted and rested on his chest.*

INT. OUTSIDE ENCLOSED BED. DAY

BEN *dutifully rakes his eyes around the ward, rather unnecessarily. At the far end from him, the* IMPATIENT PATIENT *finishes his hitherto quietish telephone call with an exaggerated good-cheer of farewell which sounds as much for the benefit of the other patients as for his recipient.*

IMPATIENT PATIENT: (*Phone, loudly*) So you see after all What a Friend We Have in Jesus, eh? Eh? –

CLOSE-UP – IMPATIENT PATIENT

IMPATIENT PATIENT: (*Phone, continuous*) All's well that ends well, Betty. So ta-ta-for-now, then, my sweet old pudding! (*He looks across the ward towards* BEN, *then bends to unplug the mobile phone.*)

INT. GEORGE WARD. DAY

BEN *dutifully on guard outside Daniel's curtained-off bed stiffens alertly as a new figure comes through the entrance doors in the middle of the ward, on the far side from Daniel's bed. But it is only* ANNA, *the harassed producer, bearing a large bouquet of flowers. She looks around, then sees* BEN, *waves, and advances towards him. At the same time, from further back, the* IMPATIENT PATIENT *begins wheeling the mobile phone in the same direction.*

CLOSE-UP – ANNA

As she realizes that the curtains are closed around what must be Daniel's bed, she suddenly stops, with a tiny leap of anxiety at her throat.

INT. GEORGE WARD. DAY

BEN *flaps a hand of invitation to* ANNA, *signalling that all is well.*
BEN: (*Calls to her*) No. It's all right – come on.

INT. WITHIN DANIEL'S ENCLOSED BEDSPACE. DAY
DANIEL *is still in his schoolboy-behind-the-pavilion mode about his beloved cigarettes, flicking ash into the slipper, and reacts with half-alarm to Ben's voice beyond the curtain.*
DANIEL: (*Hissing*) What is it? Who is it?
BEN: (*Off*) It's all right. It's Anna come to visit.
DANIEL: (*To self*) Shit. (*He starts to light another cigarette from the burning tip of the first one, which is duly stubbed out in the slipper.*)

INT. OUTSIDE CURTAINED BED. DAY
BEN: (*Furtive whisper to* ANNA) He's just having a cigarette on the sly, Anna.
(*She at first finds herself conspiratorially whispering too, until she realizes what she is doing. The mobile telephone comes up alongside, and the* IMPATIENT PATIENT *waits.*)
ANNA: I thought for a moment there that – (*Stops whispering.*) Why are we whispering, Ben?
BEN: (*Loudly*) I'm on guard, you see.
ANNA: (*Less loudly*) How is he? What happened? And thanks for the message, by the way.
(BEN *looks back over his shoulder, aware that* DANIEL *will probably be able to hear anything said, and motions* ANNA *towards the flower-decked central table and chairs, where patients can have lunch.*)
BEN: Fark your peet for a mo, Anna. We'll have a little word.
IMPATIENT PATIENT: Well, brought it all the way back. Do you want it or no?
BEN: (*Airily*) Later. Later.
(*The* IMPATIENT PATIENT *is jingling coins in his dressing-gown pocket, irritatingly.*)
IMPATIENT PATIENT: Well, I wouldn't have taken all this trouble, then, would I? Is he *smoking* in there? Is he?
ANNA: Is that any of your business?
IMPATIENT PATIENT: Is it *what*? It's *all* our business, lady. And you're only a *visitor*, if you don't mind!
(*But* BEN *and* ANNA *have moved on to the central table, ignoring him.*)

INT. CENTRAL TABLE. GEORGE WARD. DAY

Lots of flowers, and only one OLD MAN *seated at one end of it, reading the* Sun *and intermittently scratching himself, hand sliding into his dressing gown to claw at his armpit.* BEN *and* ANNA *sit, close together, speaking in low tones, at the other end of the table.*

BEN: (*Worried*) There's *something* badly amiss, Anna. First they gave him the barium meal X-ray to see if he had a stomach ulcer. Nothing showed, but it doesn't always apparently, so they treated him for that. He's been in main for ponths! Then the enema thing yesterday morning – well, that showed up spasms in the colon – painful, yes – but now they seem to be on to something else.

ANNA: (*Looks back at the bed*) Like what? (*Then*) Oh. Look at that *creature* –

INT. ANNA AND BEN'S POINT OF VIEW – ENCLOSED BED. DAY

The IMPATIENT PATIENT, *jingling the coins in his dressing-gown pocket, is half-officiously, half-unsure, hovering outside Daniel's curtain, trying to see if he can detect any smoke rising up the top rails.*

INT. CENTRAL TABLE. DAY

BEN *glares across at the* IMPATIENT PATIENT, *but carries on* –

BEN: The pancreas, apparently. That's what they're going to look at this afternoon.

ANNA: What? (*Hesitant.*) For – um – cancer, or –

BEN: (*Hollow-voiced*) I don't know.

INT. DANIEL'S ENCLOSED BEDSPACE. DAY

Rather as Ben's head had poked through, now, suddenly, but with an expression of sniffy, morally superior, God-granted disapproval, the IMPATIENT PATIENT *has penetrated the curtained sanctum.* DANIEL, *of course, is well into another cigarette.*

IMPATIENT PATIENT: I hope you know that this is a No Smoking area and quite right too! Put it out!
   (DANIEL, *imagining himself still guarded, and dreamily focusing his thoughts on some non-material middle distance, jumps at first, in alarm, and then brilliantly and immediately turns it into a look of sickened pity and horror.*)

DANIEL: (*Choking*) Oh, my G – *your face* – !

IMPATIENT PATIENT: (*Startled*) Wha – ?

(DANIEL *averts his eyes and then – as though bravely – forces them back to the head thrust between the curtains.*)

DANIEL: Sorry – (*Shudders.*) Sorry – But it was such a sh – Oh, you poor soul. Have you had it *like that* for very long?

(*The impatient patient's hands fly up to his face, and the movement causes more of him to be revealed behind the curtain.*)

IMPATIENT PATIENT: W-what you mean?

DANIEL: Well, *I* think you're very brave to walk around with a face as bad as that. (*With a little puzzled frown.*) Sorry. What was it you were saying? I was so startled I didn't quite catch it.

(*The other stares at* DANIEL *for a micro-second and, with an odd, almost inaudible little noise in the throat, disappears.*)

EXTREME CLOSE-UP – DANIEL

DANIEL *stubs out the remnants of this last cigarette in the slipper still lying across his chest, with a grin of utterly pleasurable malice.*

INT. GEORGE WARD. DAY

The IMPATIENT PATIENT *strides back down the ward, his hands fluttering up to his face now and then, not at all sure, on his way to the bath/toilet facilities at the bottom end of the ward. He passes the central table, and* BEN *and* ANNA, *whose heads are leaning in close together in what seems earnest conversation. They break off, intrigued, at –*

INT. CENTRAL TABLE. DAY

The flustered (or at least unsure) IMPATIENT PATIENT *has stopped at the opposite end of the table to* BEN *and* ANNA, *where sits the elderly, occasional armpit-scratcher – it looks as though those two patients have struck up one of the temporarily close hospital relationships.*

IMPATIENT PATIENT: (*To scratcher, abruptly*) What's the matter with my face, Clive?

(*Old* CLIVE *clearly imagines that some kind of joke is in the offing, and responds in what he imagines to be an appropriate and amusing way.*)

72

CLIVE: (*In a 'growl'*) Nothing much, mate. It's just bloody ugly, that's all.
(*He is surprised when the* IMPATIENT PATIENT *plunges on his way without a punch-line or indeed any further comment.* ANNA *and* BEN *look at each other, and start to laugh.*)

INT. WASHROOM. END OF WARD. DAY
The IMPATIENT PATIENT, *rushing in, stares and stares at his reflection in the nearest mirror.*

INT. GEORGE WARD. DAY
Two white-booted, white-clad hospital porters with poles and folded linen are coming through the ward entrance doors, making for Daniel's curtained-off bed space.

INT. CENTRAL TABLE. WARD. DAY
With a muttered 'Christ!', somewhat startling ANNA, BEN *moves more quickly than he has done for at least a couple of decades.*

INT. GEORGE WARD. DAY
Fast if flat-footed, belly wobbling, BEN *somehow gets in front of the two* PORTERS – *who exchange amused glances about him – to reach Daniel's bed before they do. But in his desperate haste, he all but trips over his own feet as he reaches the curtains, and –*

INT. WITHIN DANIEL'S ENCLOSED SPACE. DAY
BEN *sprawls through the curtains, already out of breath and in a bit of a panic, practically falling across the bed and a startled* DANIEL.
BEN: (*Gasps*) Put it out! Put it out! Comebody's soming!

INT. GEORGE WARD. DAY
The two PORTERS *are, at almost the same time, pulling open the curtains around Daniel's bed. They look at flustered* BEN, *straightening himself.*
FIRST PORTER: What's up, guv?
BEN: (*Still out of breath*) Nothing. Nothing at all. Just – ah – something I'd sorgotten to fay.
SECOND PORTER: (*Blinking*) Pardon?

73

DANIEL: (*Chuckling*) He was trying to protect me. I've been smoking, you see.

FIRST PORTER: Good on ya!

DANIEL: (*To* BEN) Here, Ben. Get rid of the smoking gun, if you wouldn't mind.

(*He hands* BEN *the now filthy slipper.*)

SECOND PORTER: (*To* DANIEL) Daniel Feeld. That right?

DANIEL: Correct.

SECOND PORTER: We're to take you down for an endoscopy. But you know about that – Yes?

DANIEL: (*Sighs*) I do indeed.

(*One of them is already rolling* DANIEL *over as the other places the linen, stretcher-like material under him.*)

FIRST PORTER: (*To hovering, flustered* BEN) If you wouldn't mind stepping back a bit –

BEN: Sorry. Sorry.

(*He moves back out of the way, quickly, all but colliding backwards with* ANNA, *who has come up to the bed space and is standing off a little, her frequent look of anxiety well and truly in place.*

The PORTERS *are now inserting the poles into the ready-made runners at the sides of the stretcher material, so that they are now able to lift* DANIEL.)

SECOND PORTER: (*To* DANIEL) You all right?

DANIEL: (*Subdued*) Fine.

(*As they lift him, he turns his head to* BEN *and* ANNA, *standing together.*)

FIRST PORTER: As right as rain, eh?

DANIEL: (*To* BEN) They'll only need to keep me in overnight again, so they say. Could you manage to collect me at nine o'clock in the morning, Ben. I'd be very –

BEN: (*Quickly*) Of course, of course!

DANIEL: (*Being moved off*) Hello, Anna.

ANNA: Keep your pecker up, Daniel.

DANIEL: (*Departing*) I'm afraid my pecker's been picked. Or *pickled*, anyway. (*But he is smiling – if rather tightly.*)

INT. EXIT DOORS AND CORRIDOR. GEORGE WARD. DAY
DANIEL *being carried from view, to a big, rubber-wheeled trolley*

waiting at the far side of the ward door. But as he does, he calls back, loud and challengingly to BEN *and* ANNA.

DANIEL: (*Calls*) *No more booze!* It – makes – you – drunk!

INT. GEORGE WARD. DAY
There is a titter around the ward in general appreciation of what is (most correctly) assumed to be a bitter joke. Narrowing down to –

INT. DANIEL'S EMPTY BED. DAY
BEN *and* ANNA *sort of share the general small amusement.*

ANNA: That'll be the day, eh, Ben?

BEN: Well, he wouldn't be the same, would he, without the whatsit sparkling at the brim. (*Notices something.*) God. The bucking fag!

ANNA: (*Confused*) What – ?

BEN: (*Angrily*) The bag. The bag!
(*He swoops on the paper bag, on the chair next to Daniel's bed, which he had been clutching throughout this visit until the moment he drew the bed curtains.*)

ANNA: What is it?
(BEN *opens up the bag and shows her, all crumpled and forlorn.*)

BEN: Grapes. For Daniel.
(ANNA *starts to laugh, then takes* BEN *by the arm.*)

ANNA: Never mind, Ben. It's the thought that counts. And it's a pretty squashed and sorry-looking thought, if you don't mind me saying so.
(BEN *peers into the bag, and then sniffs at it – not too sure.*)

BEN: (*Dubiously*) Maybe. Maybe. (*Looks at watch.*) Christ!

ANNA: (*Mischievously*) Date for a late?

BEN: Yes. Very!

EXT. SOHO ALLEY BELOW CUTTING ROOM. LATE DAY
Seen from above (actually, as though from the cutting-room window) the café or restaurant bin/bins are being raided again. A decrepit old baglady is delving, gathering together (with more signs of satisfaction than the previous down-and-out) various scraps of food or packaging.

EXT. WINDOW. CUTTING ROOM. LATE DAY
Way up, the face of NICK BALMER, *the director, looking down.*

INT. CUTTING ROOM. LATE DAY
NICK, *at the window, has his back to the Steenbeck, at which* IAN
sits. NICK *is in a melancholy mood, of a kind we have not seen from
him before. He turns from the window, pulling down the blind a little
against the slanting rays of the late sun, the sadness of the scene in
the alley below seeming to cling to him. Meanwhile, from the head of
the scene, the Steenbeck voices are continuing, its sharply defined
little screen not yet in view.*

LINDA: (*Steenbeck, off*) 'Gawd, I'm effin 'ungry. I could do wiv
    some fresh blood, and I want it *now*!'
NICK: (*To self*) Me, too.
    (*He more or less just shapes the words with his mouth. It really
    is addressed to no one but himself and his own growing
    melancholy.*)

CLOSE-UP – IAN AND STEENBECK. CUTTING ROOM
IAN *has a habit of hunching up into himself when discontented, and
this is what he is doing now, partly swallowing down a yawn, as he
stares for the hundredth time at a particular, beyond-rough-cut scene.
The Steenbeck screen, from this angle, is only partly in our view.*

PETER: (*Steenbeck, half-off screen*) Look – this bloke – he's not a
    bad sort – I mean, you've had worse.
    (*The half-seen picture on the screen – unlike before, when the
    phone was ringing – flickers now to another image.*)

STEENBECK SCREEN
LINDA *is now in big close-up on the Steenbeck, reacting to Peter's
continuing lines: clearly, a* NICK-*imposed editing decision.*

PETER: (*Off, continuous*) All right, all right, so he's got a bit of a
    beer belly and he wears *glasses* and that – but Sandra,
    love –
    (*The trouble is that, although held in big close-up, Linda is not
    'genuinely' reacting to the sense of what is so demeaningly being
    said to her. It looks phoney, in real acting terms.*)

INT. CUTTING ROOM. LATE DAY

NICK *comes up alongside* IAN *and stares at the little screen with his editor – the screen now well in shot, seemingly stuck on variants of close shots of* LINDA, *with barely a glimpse of* PETER.

PETER: (*Off, continuous*) – listen, I need a favour off him real
  bad, and he'd go for you in a big way. Do –
  (NICK, *suddenly leaning in, moves the Steenbeck lever to stop.*
  Linda's face is left in big close-up on the little screen, motionless
  and silent. IAN *and* NICK *look at each other for a brief moment.*
  Then, in subdued tones –)

NICK: It still hasn't got that – (*Half-stops, restarts, more honestly.*)
  Doesn't work. Does it?

IAN: (*Drily*) Not totally.

NICK: (*Twitching*) And yet I *know* it's all there, waiting to be –
  (*Half-stops again, then*) What you think, Ian?

IAN: It's like, well – (*Cruel mock concern*) Can I say this?

NICK: You can say what you like.
  (*But he turns away at once, and pulls the window blind*
  completely down, so suddenly violent that its plastic ring goes
  tip-tap-tip against the windowsill.)
  Surely you know that, Ian. What the hell is the point of me
  having an editor if you think anything otherwise. Please!
  Speak!

IAN: Thank you.
  (*But then, very disconcertingly, and almost certainly*
  deliberately, IAN *stays silent, eyes fixed expressionless on the*
  stilled image of LINDA.
  NICK, *over by the window, stares at him, then stares harder at*
  him, then comes back towards the Steenbeck. It is a sort of
  defeat, even if a tiny one, and this is always something NICK
  finds hard to handle.)

NICK: (*Eventually, in a tight voice*) Well? What?
  (IAN *simply nods at the Steenbeck screen.*)

IAN: (*Broadening his Scots*) Och. You're fond of the wee lassie,
  the noo.

NICK: (*Coldly*) What does that mean? Take your kilt off!

IAN: (*A beat*) What it means, Nick, is that *it shows.*
  (NICK *swallows, and begins to pace up and down again,*
  disturbed and perhaps even vaguely ashamed.)

NICK: I'm not altogether sure here what it is you're driving at. She's so consistently *good* in this particular . . . (*Stops, and also stands still.*) What are you saying, Ian?

(IAN *takes his time, then lobs the word.*)

IAN: Lingering.

NICK: (*Eyes flash*) Say again?

IAN: *Licking* her. (*Turns in his chair and looks directly at* NICK.) You've made her your lollipop, man.

NICK: (*Explodes*) That's exactly the sort of sly, innuendo-ridden snidery which gets right up my – (*Pulls himself back.*) Look. What you're doing. The way you sit there. You're making comments even when you don't open your mouth. It's all so negative –

IAN: That's because you *will not* listen, Nick. She's fine in this and in that, though the inexperience always shows.

NICK: (*Quivering*) Not in my –

IAN: (*Cutting in*) But you're *demanding* that she takes the weight of almost every single scene she's in. The grammar goes out the window. You seem to have forgotten there's such a thing as a two-shot! Och!

(NICK is *listening, but he does not answer directly to the point.*)

NICK: Obsession. It's obsession I'm after. That old man Oliver Morse. The way he has cradled and cosseted and somehow curdled the failed love of his life. And so it's about *her*. No, not 'about' her, I don't mean quite that – I mean *she* is the focus of the obsession. *She*. And that's why, in editing terms, I want to keep looking at her, examining her, *staring* at her, prowling around her and and – (*Almost laughs.*) OK. Licking her, too.

(*Tiny pause. They look at each other. Ian's dourness seems to have softened a little because of this last explanation – which is also, of course, tangentially, an account of Nick's own feelings for the same young woman.*)

IAN: I know what you're saying.

NICK: (*Brightening*) You do?

IAN: Aye. (*But he pointedly looks at his watch.*)

NICK: Well, before we wend our weary ways – Maybe ten minutes or so in that huggermugger hole opposite – ? I'm meeting my wife there later.

78

IAN: That what?

NICK: The wine bar.

(IAN *switches off the Steenbeck, with relief.*)

IAN: If only the English could speak plain English. But, then, I suppose that would really give the game away, wouldn't it?

INT. GEORGE WARD. ST CHRISTOPHER'S. LATE DAY

Just as a CONSULTANT *or senior-registrar type – bland, middle-aged, at ease with himself – pulls up a chair a little closer to* DANIEL, *in bed, his endoscopy done with. But before he can say anything, 'controlled' anxiety breaks through.*

DANIEL: Can I go now? You've had your peep in and around the swamp. I feel OK. Can't I go *tonight*? Got a lot of work to do.

CONSULTANT: Mmm – better if you stay overnight, Mr Feeld. You've had quite a little trauma. Why take unnecessary risks? Go in the morning – as early as you like.

DANIEL: (*Snorts*) As bright as a lark.

CONSULTANT: Well, I'm not too sure about that little bird –

DANIEL: Is it the one that tells you things?

CONSULTANT: (*Smiles*) Not quite. I was going to say that its allegedly happy little song is as likely to be a sign of hunger, fear or distress as anything else.

DANIEL: Oh, a Des O'Connor sort of bird, you mean. (*Then, quickly*) What did you see down there in my personal pit? What sort of gold nuggets have I got?

(*Slightest beat of tension. The* CONSULTANT *looks at him, choosing his words with skill until he knows what type of man he is dealing with.*)

CONSULTANT: A blockage. In the pancreas.

(*Tiny pause. Daniel's expression does not change.*)

DANIEL: Why don't they let people smoke in here?

(*The* CONSULTANT *spreads his hands and laughs a little.*)

CONSULTANT: They've contracted out the cleaning services.

DANIEL: Blockage?

CONSULTANT: Blockage. Yes.

DANIEL: Is that a euphemism? Don't you mean *growth*?

CONSULTANT: Ah. But we don't know yet whether it's benign or malignant.

DANIEL: And how will you find out?

CONSULTANT: I'd like you to come in the day after tomorrow, Friday, at noon. You'll have a biopsy of the pancreas and a biopsy of the liver – then stay in just that one night for –

DANIEL: Here?

CONSULTANT: Oh, yes. We've the best facilities in that particular –

DANIEL: No. I mean here *in this ward*. It's obviously the one they keep for serial killers, child molesters and (*Melodramatic hiss*) *Anti-Smoking Fanatics*. Look, I'm on BUPA and all that. If I –

CONSULTANT: (*Interrupting*) Then of course you can be put into a room of your own. When you arrived here late last night, apparently, you were pretty much out of things, and did not even manage to mutter the magic initials. I'm afraid it's too late in the day to move you for tonight, but – oh, well, stick it out! As long as you don't set the fucking bed on fire.

DANIEL: (*Gasps*) What did you say?

CONSULTANT: (*Twinkling*) You heard me well enough.

DANIEL: (*Still astounded*) My God. Consultants or whatever you're called have *changed* a lot, haven't they? It's not Mad Cow Disease or something, is it?

CONSULTANT: (*Amused*) Ah. You writers. Always the last to notice. Well, almost. I forgot the critics, didn't I? No – tonight – *in this bed* – you'll be given a suppository, some sleeping pills and something pretty powerful to keep the pain at bay.

DANIEL: Like cigarettes?

(*The* CONSULTANT *smiles and begins to rise.*)

CONSULTANT: Oh, something better than that.

DANIEL: An obstruction. (*Less a question than a sudden, hollow-sounding statement.*)

CONSULTANT: An obstruction.

(*They look at each other for a micro-second, each 99 per cent sure of something dreadful. Then – *)

DANIEL: (*Smiling*) Well. That's what I've always wanted to be. Good-night.

CONSULTANT: (*Smiling*) Good-night.

(DANIEL *watches him leave, and his smile slowly dies as he does so.*)

INT. EXIT DOORS. GEORGE WARD. LATE DAY
As the CONSULTANT *leaves, he is suddenly engulfed on either side by a flood of visitors: it must be exactly on the hour.*

CLOSE-UP – DANIEL'S BED. THE WARD
DANIEL*'s eyes flick about with a writerly interest in the evident varieties of the human animal. He is especially taken with the sight of a matronly woman in Salvation Army uniform, and follows her walk down to the far end of the ward with growing pleasure, completed when he sees –*

INT. FAR END GEORGE WARD. DAY
The matronly Salvation Army lady gives the IMPATIENT PATIENT *a peck on the cheek – and then, after a second or so, both turn to stare down the ward towards* DANIEL, *the* IMPATIENT PATIENT *unknowingly touching his face as he does so.*

CLOSE-UP – DANIEL. HIS BED
A satisfied little chuckle. It dies. Then – very softly –
DANIEL: (*To self*) Blockage. (*Tiny pause.*) Writer's block. (*Tinier pause.*) I remember when I could make a whole ward *sing*. (*The grin starts to creep back, then stops dead. Swoop along his eyeline.*)

INT. EXIT DOORS. GEORGE WARD. LATE DAY
Later than the others, a new visitor arrives, stops, looks around. It is the 'real' SANDRA, *and a* SANDRA *not too sure of herself. Her eyes fall on* DANIEL *at the top of the ward. A momentary pause. Then she moves in his direction, high heels clacking, instantly attracting some wistful attention from a few bed-bound males.*

CLOSE-UP – DANIEL. HIS BED
His look, now, is almost one of sheer terror.

INT. CUTTING ROOM. LATE DAY
The Steenbeck is switched off, the blind is down at the window

overlooking the alley, the room is empty and the light rather dusky.
A widening shaft of brighter light from the corridor as the door opens,
and ANNA *comes in, carrying briefcase. She seems surprised to find*
the place unoccupied, looks at her wrist-watch and tuts in
annoyance. Off, the bass throb-throb of distant music. She puts on a
light, tears off a page from a pad, writes something quickly, and
leaves the note (we can't really read it) propped up on the Steenbeck
where it can't be missed.

INT. SOHO WINE BAR. LATE DAY/DUSK
The distant throb-throb coming, in fact, from the very crowded just-
after-work wine bar, where virtually all the tables are occupied and it
is often shoulder-to-shoulder elsewhere in the low-ceilinged, curiously
shaped room.

CLOSE-UP – IAN IN WINE BAR
IAN *claps his emptied glass down on to a small table, in the style of a*
man rather bored and determined to go.
IAN: Must away.
    (*Wider –*)

INT. CORNER OF WINE BAR. LATE DAY/DUSK
IAN *has not looked at* NICK, *his companion at the little table, as he*
spoke. This is probably because, at immediate glance, the director is
in a withdrawn, discontented, brooding mood, capable of exploding
into worse.
NICK: You what? Are you going?
IAN: Yes. I am.
    (NICK *looks at him, then says something which, unexpectedly,*
    sounds almost imploring.)
NICK: How is it possible to be extremely happy and extremely
    unhappy at one and the same time?
IAN: (*Standing*) Wear a condom.
    (NICK *half-twists a smile, but then –*)
NICK: I'm very glad to know her. But sometimes I wish to God
    I'd never met her.
    (IAN *looks down at him with exasperation, and even the first*
    tinge of affection.)
IAN: Linda?

NICK: Linda.
> (*And* NICK *turns his head away, partly in shame, then gulps some wine.*)

IAN: Nick. Go home, man.

NICK: No, Ian. I'm meeting my wife. Here – she's coming here. She's up for the evening. Why don't you stay a bit? Ruth would love to meet you.

IAN: (*Pretend fawn*) Och, no – you're both too grrrand for me.

NICK: (*Frowning*) What?

IAN: I can't. Honestly. I'm late. And an early start, yes?
> (NICK – *the complicated man – is suddenly unfriendly.*)

NICK: Yes. An early start. Thanks for the drink.
> (*And he half-turns away, dismissive.* IAN *looks down at him, goes to speak, then winds his way out through the throng without a word.*)

CLOSE-UP – NICK

Definitely broody, unsettled, and ping-ping! goes one of his fingernails on the rim of his almost emptied wine glass. Then –

NICK: (*To self*) Linda.
> (*He becomes aware of conversation close to him.*)

BUSINESSMAN: (*Off, near*) – soon see some semblance of order in all the chaos –
> (*He looks up.*)

INT. CORNER OF WINE BAR. DUSK

At the abutting little table to NICK *– a suited* BUSINESSMAN, *trying too hard to pull in a paunch, and a female* SECRETARY, *neat and pretty, easily describable as 'too young for him'.*

BUSINESSMAN: (*Continuous*) Any new job is rather like the first day at school, don't you think?

SECRETARY: Blackboard chalk and hockey sticks. I almost wish.

BUSINESSMAN: (*Laughs*) The thing is not to get hypnotized by the computer gobbledegook. I wouldn't want all those VDUs to spoil your really rather lovely eyes.
> (NICK, *watching now, sees her smile tighten. Her posture clearly signals 'No'.*)

CLOSE-UP – NICK
His eyes flick away from the two with a bleak amusement.
NICK: (*Mutters to self*) Doesn't want him.
  (*His bleak amusement becomes bleakness only. He looks around for something.*)

INT. WINE BAR. DUSK
Nick's point of view settling on a pay phone on the opposite wall, which a woman is just finishing using. He gets up, quickly, and moves towards it, suddenly decisive.

CLOSE-UP – A DOMESTIC TELEPHONE
A female hand with long painted nails and a loose, chinking bracelet on the wrist reaches for a ringing phone – but then hovers above it, waiting, not picking it up.

INT. WINE BAR. DUSK
Quite wide: NICK *at the pay phone, using his body like a shield against any potential eavesdropper. He looks, from any distance, furtive and tense.*

INT. LINDA'S FLAT. LIVING ROOM. DUSK
The hovering hand belongs to LINDA *the actress. She waits, also tense, for her answer machine to click on, complete with its message for filtering calls.*
LINDA'S ANSWERPHONE VOICE: Hi! This is Linda Langer! (*Coy little giggle.*) I'm not sure how these fings work. Am I in or am I out? Say who you are, and leave your love or whatever it is after the funny little bee-ee-p. By-ee!
  (*Beep!*)
NICK: (*On answer machine*) Linda. It's Nick. Nick Balmer at – oh – 6.20 on Wednesday evening. (*Tiny pause.*) I somehow feel that you are there. Please pick up the phone. *Linda? Please!*
  (LINDA, *biting her lip and uneasy as hell, turns to look across the room.*)

CLOSE-UP – ARTHUR MAILION. LINDA'S FLAT
The bull-necked thug at his ease in a big, expensive armchair smacks

his fist into the palm of his other hand with huge satisfaction.
MAILION: You've got him, gal! Got him good and proper!

INT. PAY-PHONE WALL. WINE BAR. DUSK
NICK *slowly replaces the pay phone, his body clenched.*

INT. WINE BAR. ENTRANCE. DUSK
*Pushing through the increasingly noisy throng and on into the wine
bar is a finely strung, genuinely aristocratic, immensely but discreetly
rich woman in her late forties/early fifties,* RUTH, *Nick's wife, at
least fifteen years older than him, and by far the main source of his
wealth. She is* LADY RUTH BALMER, *in fact, being the only child of
the eccentric peer Lord Collingwode.*
RUTH *sees* NICK *at the pay phone. Something inside her makes her
stop. A sense of strain is showing.* NICK *redials, with the same furtive
body-language as before.*

INT. LINDA'S FLAT. DUSK
LINDA *is switching on a table-lamp in the slightly darkening room,
its tassels swaying as she touches it, as though transmitting some of
her tension, as –*
NICK: (*On answer machine*) OK. OK. Maybe you're not there
     after all. You make me feel paranoid! (*Attempted laugh.*)
     You make me feel a million different kind of thing, and –
     (*A rush*) Point is, message is, can you meet for lunch or at
     least a drink tomorrow, Thursday, at half-past twelve in
     that same old place? I'll be there, anyway. Bye.
     (*On the other side of the big and slightly vulgar room,* ARTHUR
     MAILION *is still very pleased.*)
MAILION: Of course you can!

CLOSE-UP – NICK. PAY PHONE
He again replaces the phone, with a resigned sigh.
NICK: (*To self*) 'Am I in or am I out?'
RUTH'S VOICE: (*Off screen*) Wasn't she in?

INT. WINE BAR. DUSK
NICK *turns, startled, guilt swamping his face.*
NICK: What – ?

RUTH: (*Not aggressive tones*) The chirpy little sparrow. Isn't she in her nest? Or is she out fouling someone else's?

NICK: What are you talking about?

RUTH: (*With a sad smile*) Oh, Nick.

NICK: (*Spluttering*) Ruth. For goodness' sake! I was – you want to know what I was doing? – Ruth. What is this? I was trying to find out about Daniel Feeld, the weird bastard.

(RUTH *looks at him evenly. She decides, it seems, to accept the lie.*)

RUTH: Are you and he having another row? Daniel Feeld on the warpath, is he? (*Little laugh.*) I hear he can be *very* tough.

NICK: No. It's just screams and shouts.

RUTH: At you? Is it?

NICK: You won't believe this – but last night, after talking like a genuine psychotic to poor Anna, he carried on boozing in some sleazy clip-joint or other, collapsed stone-cold unconscious, and was carried off to hospital. They're not letting him out until tomorrow, apparently.

CLOSE-UP – RUTH. WINE BAR
A movement into her during NICK's bilious recounting of what we already know, to find the strain and some kind of subdued grief palpable upon her. It is nothing to do with what NICK is saying about DANIEL. She seems to sway a little and, momentarily, half-close her eyes.

INT. WINE BAR. DUSK
NICK *suddenly sees, and clutches at her arm.*

NICK: Ruth. What's the matter – ? Darling! Has something happened?

RUTH: No, Nicholas. Nothing whatsoever.

NICK: (*Concerned*) But you look – (*tries a smile.*) You look as though you need a drink, my love.

RUTH: You mean, I look old.

(NICK *kisses her on the forehead, a trifle too stiffly.*)

NICK: No such thing. Simply, you *do* need a drink. And so do I!

RUTH: Yes. You always do.

NICK: (*Surprised*) Me?

RUTH: When you're with me. (*And she smiles at him, full on.*)

INT. GEORGE WARD. ST CHRISTOPHER'S HOSPITAL. DUSK
*The majority of the visitors seem to be leaving. The uniformed
Salvation Army lady, for instance, is giving the* IMPATIENT
PATIENT *a dry peck of farewell.*

INT. DANIEL'S BEDSPACE. DUSK
DANIEL *is looking at and listening to the seated* SANDRA *with all the
air of a child enchanted by a fairy-story being told by a wizard.
When animated, she is a virtually non-stop gabbler, exploding with
energy.*

SANDRA: What? After you went down, shouting yer bleed'n
head off? Christ. There was hell to pay. Them two bloody
Japs kept on singing – if that's whatchew call it – and their
whole table was joining in. They were right offended, I can
tell you. They didn't want no fuss, no way. But Pig – that's
what we call him, the boss – he –
(*A little twitch of alarm from* DANIEL, *the first time he has
moved a face muscle since she started her account.*)

DANIEL: Pig?

SANDRA: Yeah. That's what we call him. *Anyway,* he was so –

DANIEL: (*Interrupting*) But why *Pig?*

SANDRA: 'Cos that is what he is, enn'e? Christ, a sty's a bleed'n
sight too good for him as a matter of fact. And he was so
mad when you went down like that –

DANIEL: (*Swallowing*) Pig?
(*She doesn't register his anxiety – he has already talked about
'Pig' Mailion in his script, when dining with* ANNA; *the only
time there has appeared to be a real as opposed to misheard or
coincidental crossover – but sweeps on, clutching her little
sequin-clustered bag on her knees.*)

SANDRA: Yeah. And he was so mad wivya I fought for a minute
he was going to stamp on your froat.

DANIEL: Oh. That's nice.

SANDRA: (*Suddenly fierce*) And I wouldn't have minded neither!
I mean – you'd been grabbing 'old of me legs and scarin'
the shit out of me. I fought you was a right nutter and no
mistake.
(DANIEL *makes a little gesture of apology.*)

DANIEL: I'm afraid I was very, very drunk – amongst other things.

(*She smiles at him, warmly.*)

SANDRA: Oh, that's all right. I know different now, don't I? But you didn't half give me a turn, and when them ambulance blokes turned up after God knows how long, I could hear them saying where you was going to – but I couldn't find which ward, not for ages. They're bloody useless down at that desk in the front 'all. And not very polite about it neither.
(DANIEL, *almost despite himself, is being charmed and amused by her.*)

DANIEL: Well, that was very clever of you to find me at all. I was very surprised when you came in through that –

SANDRA: (*Interrupting*) You changed colour. (*Change of tone.*) And I'm not saying that you still don't give me the willies a bit. But I can see you're not off yer 'ead. You know the way I mean. Not like that, anyway. But – (*Looks hard at him, puzzled.*) Bloody *weird* though, ennit?
(*Tiniest pause.* DANIEL *is quite solemn.*)

DANIEL: Yes. It is.

SANDRA: (*With alarm*) But you don't *really* fink I'm –

DANIEL: (*Interrupting*) No. That's silly. It must be. It *has* to be. Look – I'm a –

STAFF NURSE: (*Interrupting*) I'm sorry. Visiting time finished, oh, more than ten minutes ago.

SANDRA: (*To* NURSE) Yeah, but I didn't start on time, did I? That's not fair, is it?

STAFF NURSE: I'm sorry, but there it is – We're starting our busy round now and I'm afraid –
(DANIEL *is swinging his feet to the floor and reaching for his dressing gown.*)

DANIEL: It's OK, Nurse. I'll just walk a little down the corridor with my – guest.

STAFF NURSE: (*Unsure*) Oh, but I don't –

DANIEL: No harm in that. In any case, it's what I intend to do.

STAFF NURSE: Don't be long. (*And she leaves, obviously, and unnecessarily, disapproving.*)

SANDRA: (*Pleased*) That's telling her!
(DANIEL, *standing now, puts his feet into his slippers, amused.*)

DANIEL: I'm out of here in the morning. I can afford to offend whomsoever I choose.

INT. GEORGE WARD AND EXIT. DUSK
*As they move off the ward – her heels clicking and male eyes on her –
the 'funny little girl', as she is proving to be when not in her sullen or
affronted modes, looks sidelong at* DANIEL, *her eyes bright.*

SANDRA: I love the way you talk!

DANIEL: (*Amused*) Do you?

SANDRA: Not 'alf. I could listen to you for hours!

> (*As they go out through the ward doors into the dreary corridor
> beyond* DANIEL *sneaks a puzzled, covert, sidelong look at her
> as she click-clacks along, carrying her little sequinned bag.
> Although he doesn't yet know it, and although it is ridiculous
> and certainly without any point, this is – so to speak – the very
> moment he 'falls in love' with her.*)

EXT. SOHO STREET AND WINE BAR. DUSK
ANNA, *toting her bulging briefcase and looking flustered yet again, is
half-striding, half-running towards the wine bar, but not in the
direction she would have taken had she come straight from the
cutting room, where she has left a note.*

INT. WINE BAR. DUSK
Entering the noisy and even more crowded wine bar, ANNA *looks
around, and puffs a tired disappointment. Most of her view of the
odd-shaped room, however, is blocked by other bodies. She turns
away, obviously deflated, but then, as she leaves, she catches sight
of –*

CLOSE-UP – MIRRORED PANEL OR SUCHLIKE. WALL OF WINE
BAR
*High, mottled, with the gold lettering of an 'antique' Craven-A
cigarette advertisement on it, the mirror reflects back one of the odd
angles of the depth of the bar, over the heads of most of the customers
who had previously been blocking her view. Nick and Ruth's
reflection can just be seen, as he bobs his head forward for some
ordinary reason – such as filling her glass.*

INT. CORNER OF WINE BAR. DUSK
NICK *and* RUTH, *squashed up in a far corner. He'd lost the other
table when going to the pay phone.*

NICK: Well, let's get out of here and hear ourselves think. Somewhere cheerful and inspiring like the YMCA or the Ivy. (*Laugh.*) Including bubble and squeak.

RUTH: (*More relaxed now*) Or shepherd's pie! I'll accept the squeak. But I'm not at all sure about the bubble.

NICK: (*Too smoothly*) Oh, come on, my love, that's the one thing you'll never lose. Your champagne sparkle. (*Breaks off.*) Anna!

ANNA: Nick. (*Less sure.*) R-Ruth – I'm – phew. I'm almost out of breath. I went to every damned pub and wine bar I know you sometimes go after the cutting room – except, of course, the nearest!

(*But* NICK *is already frowning, one eye on the bulging briefcase.*)

NICK: Something's up.

RUTH: (*More thoughtfully*) You need to sit down, Anna. It is Anna, isn't it?

ANNA: How clever of you to remember, we've only met the – No. I can't stay. *Really* can't, I mean – (*To* NICK) Yes. It's a problem. The dopey droop of a lawyer has just come up with some incredible bad luck –

NICK: (*Twitching*) Come on! Out with it!

ANNA: (*Dramatically*) There *is* an Arthur Mailion.

NICK: *What?*

ANNA: And his nickname is 'Pig'.

RUTH: (*Laughing*) 'Pig' Mailion! No – I don't believe it!

(NICK *claps his hand to his forehead and wails.*)

NICK: No! Oh – no-o-o!

ANNA: I'm afraid so. And what's worse – now this really takes the biscuit – what's worse is that this Mailion does actually, really and truly, own or manage a sort of – well, a rather questionable place *where they do play karaoke!*

RUTH: Sit down, Anna. Come on.

(*She indicates the rising drinker at the table just behind them.* ANNA *takes over the vacated chair, so preoccupied that she does it without the slightest by-your-leave to the other* TWO OCCUPANTS *at the particular table.*)

FIRST OCCUPANT: Hoy!

SECOND OCCUPANT: Bloody manners. Bloody disgusting.

INT. NICK/RUTH/ANNA VARIANTS – THREE SHOTS. WINE BAR.
DUSK

NICK: (*Ferociously thinking, numbering with his fingers*) Well,
Mailion is not in the first reel – not in the second, or the –
But, hang on, he's mentioned by name, isn't he? Several
times.

ANNA: Fourteen times.

NICK: Oh, shit. (*Drinks, bangs down glass.*) Oh, *shit – shit – shit!*

FIRST OCCUPANT: (*Off*) And language to match!

(RUTH *does not seem especially interested, but –*)

RUTH: Just call him Tallion or Rallion or something that
sounds a bit like it.

NICK: (*Jeering*) 'Pig' Tallion – oh, yes – great – Don't you see
the little joke? 'Pig' Mailion. Pygmalion – you know –

RUTH: I thought I had just managed to work out such exquisite
subtlety, Nicholas.

(*He looks at her, his swift temper on the boil again, but
manages to pull himself back.*)

NICK: Sorry. Sorry. But –

ANNA: But the real problem is in the scenes where he is actually
playing. I mean, we can lose the joke and sort of get round
most of the rest –

NICK: Oh, this is a bugger. This is a real *bugger.* (*Catches an
eye.*) You! Mind your own business!

INT. CORNER OF WINE BAR. DUSK

NICK, *looking absolutely ferocious, is addressing the* FIRST
OCCUPANT *of the allegedly chair-purloined table next to them.*

FIRST OCCUPANT: You talking to me!

NICK: Yes! You! Attend to your own affairs.

SECOND OCCUPANT: My God.

FIRST OCCUPANT: Now you listen to me, fella – !

(*But aristocratic* RUTH *has more than a complete disdain for
public 'scenes': they actually make her feel physically sick. She
turns her body towards the two strangers, her voice clear and
calm.*)

RUTH: I'm very sorry about this. Do forgive us. I'm afraid we've
just had some rather bad news, and it's upset my husband
so much he's completely forgotten his manners.

NICK: (*Half-choking*) Ruth!

ANNA: (*Quick, to stranger*) Yes. Sorry! My fault.

> (*The* FIRST OCCUPANT, *although on his way to being tipsy, is so taken by the quiet, firm elegance of Ruth's manner – and, maybe, too the sense of vulnerable strain around her like an aura – that he completely capitulates.*)

FIRST OCCUPANT: That's all right, love. I didn't know. It's just a misunderstanding.

> (*But the* SECOND OCCUPANT *stays glaring at* NICK, *who returns the look in kind. Just as the missing* THIRD OCCUPANT *comes back to the one-chair-depleted table, carrying an opened bottle.*)

THIRD OCCUPANT: Hey. Where's my chair?

ANNA: (*Standing*) I'm sorry – I thought you'd gone.

> (*The* THIRD OCCUPANT *grabs the chair back without ceremony.*)

THIRD OCCUPANT: Ta.

> (*And the little contretemps is over.*)

INT. NICK/RUTH/ANNA. WINE BAR. DUSK

ANNA, *of course, is now standing – or, rather, nervously hovering.*

ANNA: Obviously, we can't change what's already been shot. But I've looked it up – there are three scenes where 'Pig' Mailion is sort of central, two of them with Peter and one where he is that other thug – whatsisname?

NICK: (*Gloomily*) Reg.

ANNA: Reg – where he's Reg's guest at the very opening, showing off in the karaoke bar, singing 'Why Must I be a Teen – '

NICK: (*Interrupting*) 'Your Cheatin' Heart', you mean.

ANNA: (*Slightly hesitant*) Or whatever – But there's no problem in *that* scene about the name. We can't afford even half a day's reshoot –

NICK: Who says so?

ANNA: Not unless there's more money forthcoming.

NICK: Well, that can –

RUTH: (*Cutting in, very precise*) Which there isn't.

> (NICK *looks at* RUTH, *his face not sure whether to smile or to frown.*)

NICK: But if it means –

RUTH: (*Still very precise*) No more money.

NICK: (*Held-in-hatred*) Yes. Yes. Point made. Unless we take it off that drunken fool's contract. *He's* the one directly responsible.

ANNA: What do you mean?

NICK: Daniel Feeld! I mean to God! He uses the *real* name of a *real* character in a situation that could easily be represented as from his *real* life – are you telling me that's just coincidence, simply mere chance? No way! It's the most unprofessional, the most –

ANNA: But he can't have done it deliberately, Nick. That simply doesn't make sense.

RUTH: (*Coolly*) Of course it doesn't.

(NICK *glares at* RUTH, *then tries to hide it as she sees it.*)

NICK: Listen. That man is a pretty sick guy!

ANNA: I'm – yes. I'm afraid he is. More than we have realized, I think. But not in the sense *you* mean, Nick.

NICK: So what do we do? As if this film hasn't got problems enough already! (*Violently*) Shit! Shit! I feel like walking away from the whole fucking mess! Right now!

(*Pause. The two women look at him. He is all but trembling with rage and his other, buried frustrations. Widening – *)

INT. CORNER OF WINE BAR. DUSK

FIRST OCCUPANT: (*Rising*) There's a chair here now, if you still want one.

INT. ST CHRISTOPHER'S HOSPITAL. DUSK

Out of earshot, but talking, DANIEL *in his dressing gown and high-heeled* SANDRA *have come into a corner at right angles off the ward entrance corridor, which eventually leads to a balcony and fire escape.*

INT./EXT. CORRIDOR AND BALCONY

Approaching into earshot, DANIEL *and* SANDRA *complete the length of the smaller corridor and open the doors on to the old, mostly iron balcony that overlooks a crabbed, dusty, hidden sort of central garden, surrounded on all sides by the hospital wings.*

SANDRA: – so what sort of fings, then?

DANIEL: Oh. Television for when children have officially gone to bed, movies that hardly ever get made, books with paper covers, obituaries, greeting cards.

SANDRA: Would I have seen anything what you done?

DANIEL: Not unless you had a birthday recently.

SANDRA: Yeah! Me twenty-second.

DANIEL: (*Opening balcony doors*) Twenty-two. (*Wistful*) Oh, my God.

SANDRA: (*Misunderstanding*) Yeah. Getting on a bit, ennit?
(*They walk on to and along –*)

EXT. THE BALCONY. DUSK/NIGHT
Untouched Victoriana from the original building, and the thickening twilight adds to its fading or neglected charms. Daniel looks around, appreciatively, but then –

DANIEL: Places like this – bits left over from other times, other people – (*Wry laugh.*) You see, my life's been given over to *writing*. Words. Words. Fucking words.

SANDRA: (*Comic reproof*) Oooh.

DANIEL: Words. That's all I've ever been any good at, if I'm any good at all. And I've an idea that I'm soon going to find out about that, one way or the other.
(*This sounds a bit grim.*)

SANDRA: Whatchewmean?
(*DANIEL deflects the question, and what preceded it, by pointing out something ahead of them.*)

DANIEL: Look, if we go to the end of this balcony, and if that funny little gate thing opens, we can go all the way down past the other balconies –

SANDRA: To the garden, yeah. You like gardens?

DANIEL: (*Smiles*) I like the *word* 'garden'. It has a – well, the ring of primal innocence.

SANDRA: The what?

DANIEL: Adam and Eve.

SANDRA: Oh, them two. Yeah. But what about the whatsit? The snake.
(*He laughs as they push at the end 'gate', which swings open with an elderly cre-e-eak!*)

EXT. TWO/THREE SIMILAR BALCONIES. DUSK/NIGHT
*Threaded by iron steps down between them, each with a noisy little
'gate', and each gate with its thriller soundtrack creak. During
which –*

DANIEL: Words. Ah, words. 'Snake' is actually quite a nice one,
though not as good as 'elbow', I must admit.

SANDRA: (*Snorts*) Elbow.

DANIEL: What a lovely sound your heels make on this old iron.

SANDRA: (*Pleased*) Do they? Ta.

DANIEL: I have that sound in one of my stage directions in the
last script I finished. (*Small, half-uneasy laugh.*) Just one of
the little things that's been bothering me.

SANDRA: What's it called? Your story.
(*He looks sidelong at her, then pushes open the last little iron
'gate', which proves to be the most awkward one of them all.*)

DANIEL: (*With a puff*) *Karaoke.*

EXT. GRAVEL PATH. HOSPITAL GARDEN. DUSK/NIGHT
*Now she seems uneasy again as they crunch along a narrow gravel
path between dusty and malnourished bushes towards a central,
small, chipped garden statue of stone, once a fountain.*

DANIEL: I called it *Karaoke* because – oh, you know, the song
or the story of our lives is sort of already made up for us.

SANDRA: (*Frowning*) Well – in a way – I mean, yeah. I know the
feeling.

DANIEL: (*Delighted*) Do you? (*Then*) Oh, look! A real old garden
bench!

SANDRA: Bit dirty an' all.

EXT. BENCH. DUSK/NIGHT
*He makes a pantomime show of dusting off a bit of the seat for
Milady, and she laughs, agreeing to sit. The sequins on her little bag
seem to be glowing brighter as the light continues to fade into
something silkier and darker.*

DANIEL: There. Perfectly clean, my dear.

SANDRA: (*Laughs*) Ta! You're a gent.
(*As he sits, he suddenly winces. She notices, but says nothing –
and waits.*)

DANIEL: (*Eventually*) As you can see, I haven't been feeling too great lately.

SANDRA: What's wrong, then?

(*He doesn't answer directly – not knowing for absolutely sure himself – but tries to explicate the inexplicable.*)

DANIEL: (*With a half-laugh*) I've been on the wrong diet. Eating and drinking my own thoughts. And I kept hearing what I thought were my own lines come back at me! (*Another sort of laugh.*) That brasserie. Where I kept staring at you.

SANDRA: Not 'alf!

DANIEL: Well, we filmed in that place a few months ago. It's part of my story, you see. And it's where this girl Sandra has a row with this thuggish bloke called Peter.

(*She is looking at him very closely now. He seems in pain again, with little beads of sweat once more.*)

SANDRA: (*No expression*) Sandra and Peter.

DANIEL: I thought – Christ, how mad can you get! Or how pissed! – I thought you were saying *my* words. I really did. And in my story – (*Wipes his forehead with the back of his hand.*) In the story, she gets murdered.

SANDRA: (*Scared*) Stop it! That's what give me the creeps, ennit! I mean, you might be bloody *psychic* or whatever it's called. (*Looks at him, shifting away a little as though in precaution.*) What's this girl Sandra do? In the story. For a living, I mean?

EXTREME CLOSE-UP – SANDRA. BENCH
From unease into doubt into fear and ultimately into terror as she listens.

DANIEL: (*Off screen*) Oh, she's a kind of model – glamour model, I think they call it – No, this Sandra hasn't really been what you'd call a good girl – but she also works sort of part-time as a hostess, if that's the right word, in this ver-y slea-zy club. It's run by a right villain. The nastiest character I've ever written, by far.

EXT. BENCH. DUSK/NIGHT

DANIEL: Funny thing is – well, they call him Pig too. All the girls who, sort of, work there, keeping the customers happy in ways that aren't always proper, to say the least.

SANDRA: (*Controlled quiver*) Pig?
    (*He looks at her, steadily.*)
DANIEL: Yes. Pig. It started out on the page as a little joke. His
    surname is Mailion, you see. 'Pig' Mailion. Pygmalion.
    Get it? (*Suddenly.*) What's the matter!
    (SANDRA *puts her knuckles to her mouth, stares at him wildly
    for a micro-second, then literally yelps in terror – and simply
    runs.* DANIEL *rises, shaken, calling after her.*)
Sandra! Wait! Sandra!

EXT. HOSPITAL GARDEN. DUSK/NIGHT
So fast, on such high heels that she several times falls, SANDRA *runs
as though for her life, beginning a hysterical scream, heading blindly
for some big ground-floor double doors on the opposite wing of the
hospital to the one they had descended from via the various old
balconies.*

EXT. BENCH. DUSK/NIGHT
Aghast, DANIEL *stops calling after her, sees her clutch, pull at and
eventually wrench open the distant doors, and crumples back down
again on to the old, white, wrought-iron bench, sucking in his
breath.*

CLOSE-UP – DANIEL
*His forehead is now glistening with heavy sweat. The pain is back at
its full, voraciously biting throb. He tries to breathe in and out,
slowly, to regain some measure of control of himself. Then –*
DANIEL: (*In a whisper*) Please. Please God. (*Pause.*) Please
    (*Pause.*) Please don't let any of this be true.

EXT. GARDEN. FROM ABOVE. DUSK/NIGHT
FEMALE VOICE: Mr Feeld. Mr Feeld!

EXT. GARDEN. DUSK/NIGHT
DANIEL, *clenched into himself, looks up and then on up to see a*
STAFF NURSE *on the balcony of the George Ward floor calling down
to him, not pleased.*
STAFF NURSE: (*Way above*) What are you doing! Come back to
    your bed! We're doing the drug round!

EXT. BENCH. DUSK/NIGHT
DANIEL *doesn't answer, doesn't move.*
DANIEL: (*Mutters to self*) Just give me a drink instead.
> (*Then he notices Sandra's glitzy little bag on the bench beside him. He picks it up, feels the sequins for a moment with the tips of his fingers.*)

EXTREME CLOSE-UP – DANIEL
His haggard expression momentarily softens as he fingertip-feels the bright little sequins. There can be no doubt that certain long-buried emotions in him are tenderly sprouting.

EXT. BENCH. DUSK/NIGHT
STAFF NURSE: (*Off, calling*) Mr Feeld! This is very naughty! Please come back at once!
> (*Without a glance in the caller's direction,* DANIEL *suddenly decides to open Sandra's small bag. His expression changes.*)

CLOSE-UP – SANDRA'S BAG
And, clear to see, a small 'silver' pistol, almost ornamental in appearance, but undoubtedly lethal: the real thing.

EXT. BENCH. DUSK/NIGHT
A moment. DANIEL *half-lifts the gun from the bag, then shoves it back in again, quickly, closing the bag. A beat.*
DANIEL: (*Hollowly*) Oh, my God.
> (*As he lifts his eyes, full of alarm, the chipped, stone garden statue – once the centrepiece of a now long-unused fountain – seems to stare directly back at him, person to person.*)

CLOSE-UP – STATUE
The broken, stained and badly chipped face of a time-mildewed Eros, peculiarly bleak and almost leering in the thickening dusk or early darkness. A loud shot rings out, over; but only in the imagination.

PART THREE

CLOSE-UP – OLD STATUE. HOSPITAL GARDEN
The badly chipped and stained face of a mildewed Eros momentarily
brightens as it seems to catch the slanting rays of early morning sun,
rising above the quadrangle of elderly hospital buildings.

EXT. CENTRE OF HOSPITAL GARDEN. DAY
DANIEL FEELD *is staring straight at the soiled Eros, much as though*
it were a living thing he is about to address. Indeed, his lips move for
the smallest moments, as at the brink of actual speech. Then he stops
any possibility of words with a rueful or sardonic little smile.
DANIEL *is now fully clothed – in what he was wearing at dinner*
with ANNA *at his karaoke club collapse on Tuesday night, two nights*
before. He is in the almost secret, central garden of St Christopher's,
waiting to be collected, or released. He is on the same neglected bench
that he had shared with SANDRA *the previous evening.*
He is, of course, smoking. Several crushed cigarette ends are at his
feet, showing that he retreated to this almost private place within the
hospital at least half an hour before. And beside him on the bench,
next to his disposable lighter and almost finished packet of
Rothmans, is Sandra's sequin-dotted little bag.
STAFF NURSE: *(Off, calls)* Mr Feeld! Daniel Feeld!

EXT. ST CHRISTOPHER'S HOSPITAL. DAY
High up on the old building, from Daniel's point of view, above
several of the seemingly no longer used iron balconies, the STAFF
NURSE *calls for Daniel. Next to her, in his business suit, is the*
Notre-Dame of all literary agents, 'back to front' BEN BAGLIN.

EXT. GARDEN FROM ABOVE. DAY
Way down in the dusty garden, DANIEL *stares up for a moment, like*
one startled, then quickly stuffs Sandra's pretty little bag into his
jacket pocket, rises, and carries cigarettes and lighter with him in his
hand.
STAFF NURSE: *(To Ben)* He shouldn't be down there, you know.
    And he was wandering all over the place last night, poking

around in cupboards and corridors.

BEN: (*With a frown*) Pleeping sills?

STAFF NURSE: I beg your pardon?

BEN: Should have given him some. He's a restless fellow. Pills. You know.

STAFF NURSE: Oh – *sleeping* pills. Yes. Sorry – I misheard you. Oh, he had those all right. Indeed, he did! (*Laugh – half-meant.*) We'd have done better to tie him hand and foot to the bed.

BEN: (*Mock surprise*) Oh, don't they do that in hospitals any more?

(*She looks sidelong at him.*)

EXT. ST CHRISTOPHER'S HOSPITAL. DAY

Ben's smart BMW leaving the already car-crowded old buildings, allegedly in Clipstone Street, near the looming Telecom Tower.

INT./EXT. BEN'S CAR. STREETS. DAY

BEN *and* DANIEL. DANIEL *is clutching a small carrier bag on his lap, and not even smoking.* BEN *is sneaking little looks at his client, sitting beside him, checking on his condition. There has obviously been some silence. Then –*

DANIEL: (*Sighing*) Please, Ben. Don't keep sneaking looks at me on the sly –

BEN: Sorry, old chap.

DANIEL: I'm OK, honestly, just a bit sort of – preoccupied –

BEN: But the pain, Dan?

DANIEL: I'm only aware, at this moment, of a dull and distant thunder – No. They gave me morphine this morning. And I've got some in this bag too. That's what worries me.

BEN: Well, if it stops the pain –

DANIEL: Oh, sure, sure – Christ, who in their right mind willingly submits to pain – (*Tiny pause – unexpectedly tender.*) Except Christ himself, of course. Silly bugger. Sweet, silly bugger. (*Tiny pause – different tone.*) No. It's *why*. Why morphine? Eh? And why these effing biopsies tomorrow morning? They've brought it forward to nine a.m. Why? *Why?* Because they're *on to something*, Ben. And it's something really –

(*He doesn't finish. He would have said 'terrible'. He looks out of the side window, giving* BEN *the chance to sneak another quick examination, with a concerned face.*)

EXT. SHOP WINDOW, FROM CAR. DAY
Ben's car has to stop for a moment at a pedestrian crossing. DANIEL, *looking out of passenger window, sees the big plate-glass window of a department store where impossibly elegant and anorexically slender fibreglass mannequins are variously posed, standing, leaning and sitting, in various new fashions, their 'faces' completely cold and oddly eloquent in their deathliness.*

INT./EXT. BEN'S CAR. DAY
DANIEL *turns from the window to speak to* BEN *as the car is about to move off again.*
DANIEL: (*Vaguely pleased*) But after all, Ben, since we are no longer *citizens* nor children of God, but mere *consumers*, there are always enough hints of a grace or even an eternity that can simply be bought and so-o-*old!*
(*The last syllable coming out with a gasp because* BEN, *just moving off, has violently braked, jerking them both forward, hard against their seat belts.* DANIEL *almost lets go of his carrier bag, and clutches it into himself, quickly.*)

EXT. PEDESTRIAN CROSSING. CITY STREET. DAY
By one of the sheerest coincidences occasionally permitted in life, as well as in the laziest of dramatic inventions, the Arab nonagenarian (allegedly sixty-one) seen fraily uncomprehending at the radiation department area reception desk with her irascible son in Part One, has stepped off the pavement at the very last moment, near fatally, for – it being a one-way street – other cars squeal to hurried stops too. And some honk!

INT./EXT. BEN'S CAR. DAY
DANIEL *and* BEN *are forced to watch the hunched, crone-like, creep of a progression of the swathed old woman over the pedestrian crossing.*
BEN: (*Obviously satiric*) She should bo gack to her own country, eh, Daniel?

DANIEL: Ah. But she is. She's going home.

(*As they move off again,* DANIEL *smirks.*)

I strongly suspect, Ben, that I'm very soon going to be
given licence to be unbearably humbuggish and *sickeningly*
sanctimonious. Oh boy, oh boy! (*He chuckles.*) Can't you
line me up for a few *Thought for the Day*s or whatever it is
they call those dreadful interruptions to the normal flow of
flood, quake, war and starvation? Hey! I'd be good at it.
(*Tries out the right, unctuous radio-cleric tones.*) 'Good
Morning. Have you ever noticed why it is . . .?'

EXT. BLOCK OF FLATS. WI. DAY

Ben's car parked in the quiet street at the rather elegant if slightly
worn Edwardian building where DANIEL *has his flat.*

INT. LIFT. THE BLOCK. DAY

Slow, ornate old lift steadily climbing to the fifth and top floor.

BEN: Oh. Nearly forgot. Now, Daniel, don't be insulted. I'm
    assuming you *want* to work. Correct?

DANIEL: Bet your bottom dollar! *And* your ten cents of it.

BEN: Only there's this – oh, it's something from Irwin
    Wilerwaller about –

DANIEL: (*Interrupting*) The thing that worries me about
    Americans. They never even *hint* at a smile when they say
    their own names. And sometimes add 'Junior' at the end of
    it, too.

BEN: What? Oh, well, anyway, he's a helpful little chap. This
    animation thing all those zillions are pouring into – *Baa Baa.*

DANIEL: (*No expression*) Baa Baa.

    (*The lift doors have to be pulled open at the floor by its passengers.*)

BEN: (*Opening doors*) B double A. B double A.

INT. PASSAGE. FIFTH FLOOR. DAY

Quietly musty, not particularly well lit, but good carpet, good
maintenance, as BEN *and* DANIEL *move towards the last door at the*
side opposite the lifts.

BEN: (*Just a little uneasy*) There's quite a bit of dialogue
    English-style – Brit, I mean – for a Ganny Noat.

DANIEL: What the hell are you talking about – ?

(BEN *gives his cheek a token slap as* DANIEL *starts fumbling in his pockets for his door keys, while protectively clutching the carrier bag.*)

BEN: Goat. Goat. It's an arthritic old – (*Forces it out right*) Nanny Goat in a field next door to Our Hero, the Superlamb –

(DANIEL *opening the door.*)

DANIEL: That does it! I was really interested until you brought in the arthritis, Ben. No. Not my cup of camomile.

INT. HALL. DANIEL'S FLAT. DAY

BEN: I didn't think so, but one never –

DANIEL: (*Cuts in, comically*) How much, though?

(*As they go on through to –*)

INT. LIVING ROOM/DINER. THE FLAT. DAY

BEN *is beginning to look around with the air of a man who has, though wanting to, never been here before. As described before, it is comfortable, even elegant, spacious – but untidy, with books and papers, including the pile about virtual reality and cryotechnology on the floor, by the littered desk.*

DANIEL: (*Aware*) Look around as much as you like, Ben – or even open cupboards if you want. It'll be your one and only chance.

BEN: (*Flustered*) No, no. I'm not neing bosy. It's – ah – yes. Very nice. Indeed.

(DANIEL, *during this, has been taking some of the things out of the carrier bag, supplies from the hospital, including strips of pills, strips of bullet-shaped suppositories, and a small packet of Rohypnol sleeping tablets, which he variously distributes on the limitedly available bookshelf space. And then, almost too obviously secretive, he puts the carrier bag – which still contains something: Sandra's bag – behind a chair.*)

DANIEL: Well, it's not very *tidy*, I know. But what the hell – that's the mote in *my* eye, eh? If you know the quote.

BEN: (*Looking puzzled at the positioning of the carrier bag*) No. I don't. Why are you trying to *hide* that –

(DANIEL *pointedly half-collapses on to the deep sofa, like one suddenly very weary, and looks up at awkwardly hovering* BEN *with a twinkle. There is obviously a fairly well-hidden but deep affection between the two men.)*

DANIEL: (*Deflecting the question*) Twice a day every Sunday, and sometimes three times, up the hill to the little stone chapel and its hard benches – and the bloody Gospel alive and bubbling all around you, inside and out.

BEN: Oh. That. Yes.

DANIEL: The Forest of Nead. N-e-a-d. Between the two rivers. And need, e-e-d, too! (*Half-scornful little laugh.*) If you spend a childhood in such a place, Ben, grey and green, stone and tree and – Well, you'd know well enough where Jacob wrestled with the angel or Jesus walked on the water. Where *were* you brought up, Ben? Please don't let me guess.

BEN: Wembley Park.

(*They look at each other, then each begins to laugh, at exactly the same time.*)

DANIEL: I see. The Valley of the Shadow of Death.

(*They laugh again.* BEN *stops.*)

BEN: Are you all right? Are you?

DANIEL: Oh, come, come, Benjamin.

BEN: But you *do* want to work?

DANIEL: Want to!

(*And as though given a sudden shot of adrenalin straight into the vein he all but* springs *up from the deep sofa and goes over to his desk, plumping down into the swivel chair and lifting up from the floor the armful of books, magazines, cuttings, etc., etc., relating to virtual reality and all that.*)

BEN: (*As* DANIEL *moves*) All right. All right. You want to!

DANIEL: I want to join up two things that are sort of in the air at the moment – one is virtual reality, with all the things that *will* go on in so-called cyberspace, and the other is cryogenics.

BEN: (*Blank*) Is what?

DANIEL: Technology at absolute zero temperature.

(BEN *pulls a face, not overwhelmed.*)

BEN: I suppose you could try warming it up a bit?

(*But* DANIEL *is too suddenly enthusiastic to acknowledge even an attempt at a joke.*)

DANIEL: You must have read about those frozen bodies! You
    know, those very rich nerds who arrange that at or as near
    to the very point of their death as can be managed, they are
    deep, deep frozen as rapidly as possible in the hope that
    eventually –
BEN: Oh, yes. I know what –
DANIEL: (*Sweeping on*) – something, someone will be able to
    cure them of what it was that took them off and cell by cell
    bring them back to – Shit. My message light is flashing. I
    didn't notice. Did you?
    (*Since the telephone is half-obscured by a drift of paper, Ben's
    answer is not surprising.*)
BEN: No. Can't say I did.
DANIEL: Oh, well, it can wait, whatever it is – (*Sudden thought.*)
    Unless it's –
    (*He stops saying what he was going to say, and presses the
    playback button.*)

CLOSE-UP – TELEPHONE/ANSWER MACHINE
ANNA'S VOICE: Hello. Daniel. It's Anna here.

FLASH: CLOSE-UP – BEN
A small groan.

FLASH: CLOSE-UP – DANIEL
A tiny hiss.

INT. DANIEL'S LIVING ROOM. DAY
ANNA'S VOICE: (*Continuous*) I know you're out of St
    Christopher's this morning. I *do* hope you're feeling better,
    and I'm sorry to bother you at such a time. I'm calling
    early – well, actually, it's five o'clock in the morning and to
    be honest I haven't had very much sleep, but –
    (*During which* DANIEL *has swiftly dumped the virtual reality
    and cryogenics pile and moves to –*)

INT. KITCHEN/DINER OFF LIVING ROOM. DAY
*Separated mostly by a wide 'breakfast counter' from the big, wide
living room,* DANIEL *opens a top cupboard and holds up the bottle of*

Glenfiddich we have seen before, as signal and invitation to BEN
(*Anna's voice continuing on machine*).

INT. LIVING ROOM. DAY
In response BEN *points a finger of reproof* (*Anna's voice continues,
see below*).
BEN: (*Quoting hospital* DANIEL) '*No more booze!*'

INT. KITCHEN. DAY
DANIEL *makes a near or pretend two-finger gesture, getting two
glasses, then 'freezing' as Anna's voice sinks in at the appropriate
moment.*
ANNA'S VOICE: (*Continuous*) – I simply had to call you about
     this – um – little problem, which I know Nick will be – um
     – well, he'll want to talk to you about it, I'm afraid. The
     point is, Daniel, that by sheer bad luck, there is, there
     really is, somebody called Arthur Mailion, as in your
     script, and he is, really is, nicknamed 'Pig', 'Pig' Mailion
     by some of those who know him –

CLOSE-UP – BEN
*Registering an agent's extreme irritation with a potential contractual
problem rather than anything more profound.*

CLOSE-UP – DANIEL
*A face in genuine shock – and then, almost, a flash of relief, a chink
of revelation that helps make explicable for him what had been
sickeningly inexplicable.*

INT. LIVING ROOM/DINER. DAY
ANNA'S VOICE: (*Continuous*) – and he is apparently in what *could*
     be seen as the same line of business as our 'Pig' Mailion,
     the fictional one, I mean. Now I've gone through the script
     and what we've shot – several times, believe you me –
     (DANIEL *takes a slug of Scotch straight from the bottle, and
     then dashes from the diner section, across the living room to the
     desk, and –*)

CLOSE-UP – ANSWER MACHINE
Daniel's finger plunges down on the appropriate button, clicking the whole thing off.
ANNA'S VOICE: (*Continuous*) – and I think with a little ingenuity
    on all our parts we can basically –
    (*'Basically', the overused adverb, is the last word allowed.*)

INT. LIVING ROOM. DAY
BEN: (*Irritated and therefore haplessly spoonerist*) What a shucking
    fame.
DANIEL: More than that, Ben. (*Ominously*) Much more.
    (*Half-inadvertently, his eyes flick to the near-hidden carrier bag
    under the chair.* BEN *follows the glance, puzzled.*)
BEN: Daniel. What are you –
DANIEL: (*Decisive*) I'm very grateful to you, Ben, picking me up
    from that dump and all that. I know how it eats into your day –
BEN: Not at all. Not at all.
DANIEL: But I need to be alone now for a while, if you don't
    mind. I can already feel Ms Garbo whispering in my left
    ear. (*Walking through to hall.*) I'll talk to you later. On the
    phone. I want to write about cryogenics. Want to write
    about a frozen head, Ben. A deeply frozen brain iced-up
    with frozen memories. Sounds right, huh?
    (BEN *has to follow, with one backward glance at the, what is to
    him now, mysterious carrier bag.*)

INT. HALL. DAY
BEN: Fine. Fine, Dan. It'll be great to get you wack to bork.
    (*And he slaps his own cheek, on the way out, as* DANIEL *nods
    matter-of-fact agreement.*)

INT. LIVING ROOM. DAY
DANIEL: (*Off, from hall*) Oh, and if you've got a parking ticket –
    charge it to me!
BEN: Don't be silly.
    (*Sound of front door shutting.*
    DANIEL *comes back into the room at a lick, with a set
    expression, picks up the carrier, delves into it, and puts Sandra's
    glitzy little bag on his desk.*)

INT. DANIEL'S DESK. LIVING ROOM. DAY
DANIEL *has not had a long enough chance before this, it seems, to examine the contents of Sandra's bag in complete privacy. He shakes out everything that is so tightly stuffed into the bag, carelessly knocking books and papers and oddments off his desk in order to make a clear space.*
First, he holds up the 'silver' pistol, turning it around and about, then suddenly and melodramatically swivelling fast around in his revolving chair to –

ZOOM EYELINE
The gun whirls around and points at the window.
DANIEL: (*Loudly*) Bang!

EXTREME CLOSE-UP – DANIEL AT DESK
No more childlike play. He is suddenly deeply thoughtful. He stays very, very still for a moment. And then a voice from his Karaoke *script resonates in his head.*
PETER: (*Voice-over, actor* PETER) You're aht of control! You're dis-gust-ing! What the fuck do you fink you're fucking well doing?

INT. DANIEL'S DESK. DAY
DANIEL *turns back to the other things from Sandra's bag on his desk, carefully placing the pistol down so that it points away from himself.*
He picks up, examines, a small, decorated powder compact with its little fluffy brush. There is a tenderness about the way he holds this which shows what he now feels about her. He does the same thing in the same revealing way with the other cosmetics in the bag: a lipstick holder.
DANIEL: (*Softly*) Pretty little thing.
(*Then he snorts in total self-derision – and carries on handling or examining the other things. A button. A rather grubby polo mint, just the one. Two ten-pound notes tightly rolled together, almost into a tube. An Access card – is this a promising lead?*)
Ah. Good.

CLOSE-UP – ACCESS CARD
Name and signature: Sandra Sollars.

DANIEL: (*Off screen*) But – it's out of date!

INT. DANIEL'S DESK. DAY
DANIEL *carefully unrolls a small strip of paper which looks as though it has been torn from the bottom of an envelope or something similar. He peers at it, like someone who needs glasses.*
DANIEL: (*Reads*) '2 o'clock. Maninta'. (*Pause.*) Maninta. Maninta? (*Then, triumphant.*) Ah! Thank you!
(*As he opens a small folded card, which has 'Streetwiseviddy' printed on it, rather cheap-looking.*)

CLOSE-UP OPENED CARD
It is a video club membership card with Sandra Sollars, 56 Rednall Terr., Hammersmith W6 on it, plus her signature, the same as on the redundant Access card.

EXT. SOHO RESTAURANT. DAY
A small Italian restaurant, not at all the cheap, cheerful trattoria type, but more the up-market, supposedly discreet, tête-à-tête variety.

INT. ITALIAN RESTAURANT
It's early lunch-time. NICK *had said 'half-past twelve' on Linda's answer machine when calling her from the wine bar the evening before (Wednesday). A small, genuinely old clock on a wall shows twenty past twelve.*
Only two of the reasonably well-spaced tables are occupied, both by waiting males; one is an elderly gent. Go closer to the other.

INT. NICK'S TABLE. RESTAURANT. DAY
NICK, *alone, seems tense, his eyes on the door to the Soho-busy street beyond. He is scarcely aware that he is breaking a long breadstick into small and then smaller pieces. He looks at his watch, knowing full well that it is too early. And then sips some sparkling mineral water.*
ITALIAN WAITER (LUIGI): You would like to order a drink now, signor?
NICK (*With a sigh*) No, Luigi, I said when – (*Another sigh.*) Oh. Yes. All right. Bring me a Scotch, no ice. No! A Campari and soda with – Um. Luigi. I'll have a, a – (*Sudden gush of*

words.) Bring me a Courvoisier with Stone's Green Ginger.
Thank you.

(LUIGI *looks at him, sensing boiling unease, and smiles assent
to the order.* NICK *looks down at the broken pieces of breadstick
with some surprise, puts one fragment in his mouth, and scoops
the rest into a tidier pile with the side of his hand.*)

EXTREME CLOSE-UP – NICK
*So close, in fact, that only the lower two-thirds of his face fills the
screen. And almost like a wildlife or nature documentary on a
particular animal's feeding ritual! Crunch-crunch-crunch-crunch go
Nick's jaws on the hard little tubular piece of breadstick, and his
mouth is moving like a grinding mill. The* tension *in him is
complete, and can feed only on itself.*

EXT. SOHO SQUARE/GOLDEN SQUARE OR SIMILAR. DAY
A properly parked, customized Range Rover, a ridiculous town car.

INT./EXT. RANGE ROVER. DAY
ARTHUR 'PIG' MAILION, *at the driver's position, and the lovely if
vulgar young actress* LINDA LANGER *beside him. She looks sulky,
pouty and on the verge of stronger hostility. His normal, bullish, outa-
my-way manner is at this moment tempered by a tinge of wheedle.*

MAILION: Oh, come on, Linda. Put yer bleed'n lip back where
    it belongs. When you pout like that, darling, 's more like a
    bleed'n cushion.
LINDA: Oh. That's nice.
MAILION: Stop worrying your sweet little wiggle-waggle abaht
    it, willya!
    (*She turns to look at him, with a full glare.*)
LINDA: Arfur – listen! He's done a hell of a lot for me, enne? I
    mean, I wouldn't be nuffink if he –
MAILION: (*Cutting in*) Bollocks.
LINDA: I wouldn't be a – When this comes out, he reckons I'm
    going to be *big*. A star!
MAILION: Well. You will be! You still will be, won'tcha? Christ.
    Can't you think straight or what? Number One. The first
    rule of life, angel. Look after *Unero Numo*, then the rest'll
    look after itself.

(*A beat, as she examines him.*)

LINDA: But who *is* Number One, Arthur?

MAILION: (*Cheerfully*) You are, darling. (*Pats her knee.*) Just do
as I say. And tell him what I say in the way that I say it. It's
a doddle, darling. Just keep yer head, and *do what I say.*
Right? (*Pause. He looks – looks.*) Right?

LINDA: (*Subdued*) Right. (*She opens the car door, and then gives
him one quick glare back, of total hostility.*)

EXT. STREET/SQUARE. DAY

LINDA *click-clicking away from the car, shapely, but head down as
though in a wind.*

INT./EXT. RANGE ROVER. DAY

MAILION *watches her go. His expression hardens. Then – like a hiss
of hatred escaping from between his teeth –*

MAILION: *Unero Numo.*

CLOSE-UP – OLD CLOCK. RESTAURANT

Showing twenty-to-one, in a muffled tick.

INT. ITALIAN RESTAURANT. DAY

Finding in a room now with a few more lunchers a strung-up NICK,
*sick with the anxieties of the desire he thinks of as 'love'. His face
transforms. He half-rises, beaming, arm already extending in
welcome, as – fast along his eyeline –*

INT./EXT. STREET DOOR. RESTAURANT. DAY

LINDA *entering. And then she seems to stop dead on the threshold,
staring across at* NICK, *blank, before suddenly creating a model of a
smile and lilting her way forwards.*

EXT. WORKING-CLASS TERRACE. LONDON. DAY

*A surviving remnant of what was once an endless lattice of such
humdrum streets, tightly packed together – small houses with front
doors virtually opening straight on to the narrow pavement, and
small back yards behind them.*

And coming along the street, looking at the numbers, is DANIEL,
would-be sleuth, carrying a small briefcase.

INT. KITCHEN/LIVING ROOM. HAMMERSMITH HOUSE. DAY
A clock on the wall, battery, falsely 'Rosewood', shows twenty to one too. A woman of about forty, MRS HAYNES, obviously once shapely but who has 'let herself go' somewhat, rises from a chair by the half-net-curtained window looking out on to the yard and the backs of the next terrace of houses. She has been doing a jigsaw puzzle on the table up against the window, and she tuts annoyance at what must be by now a repeated knock, off, on the front door. But as she turns, and as she moves to –

INT. NARROW PASSAGE. THE HOUSE. DAY
Mrs Haynes's face, fully revealed, is one-third old scar tissue, an unsightly mess, and the eye on that side of her face is pulled down or askew, and is without doubt sightless. That side of her mouth, too, shows old damage. It is this figure who is about to open the street door on to –

EXT. HAMMERSMITH HOUSE. DAY
DANIEL *waits at the not-well-kept front door, his hand about to lift the knocker again, when –*

INT./EXT. DOOR AND PASSAGE BEYOND. DAY
DANIEL *cannot quite stop himself half-stepping back in surprise as Mrs Haynes's wrecked face looms out at him.*
MRS HAYNES: (*Not friendly*) Whatchawant?
DANIEL: (*Recovering*) I'm – uh – Excuse me. Are you, are you Mrs Sollars?
(MRS HAYNES *looks at him with her one good eye, and speaks with a slight distortion from the part-skewed mouth.*)
MRS HAYNES: No. Haynes me name. *Mrs* Haynes.
(*She goes to shut the door. There is already enough in her manner to suggest that she is not at all 'bright'. Her IQ is well below 'average'. And* DANIEL *is sharp enough on the uptake – he having the opposite problem with his own IQ – to realize that a sweetener of sorts will be needed.*)
DANIEL: (*Quickly – to closing door*) Money! I've got something for – !
(*But the door closes, nevertheless.*)

INT. PASSAGE. THE HOUSE. DAY
MRS HAYNES *turns away from the closed door, goes a foot or so down the drab passage, then stops dead. She turns to address the door, exactly as though it were open and* DANIEL *standing there.*
MRS HAYNES: Dosh? You say dosh, darling?

EXT. FRONT DOOR. HAMMERSMITH HOUSE. DAY
Some (correct) instinct has made DANIEL *wait at the door – but, even so, he is shifting from foot to foot in anxiety, in case he is wrong. Then – door opening –*

INT./EXT. DOOR AND PASSAGE BEYOND. DAY
MRS HAYNES: (*Instantly*) How much? And oo's it for, fella?
DANIEL: Um.
    (*The pitch of her slightly distorted voice rises alarmingly.*)
MRS HAYNES: How much? I said how much! And if you're on
    about insurance stuff and all that you can bugger bugger
    bugger off!
DANIEL: Where's Sandra?
    (*It looks for a moment as though she is going to slam the door again.*)
MRS HAYNES: Out!
DANIEL: (*Almost a gabble*) Money's for her and money's for
    you!
    (*Door widens. One good eye stares fiercely. And then looks down at Daniel's briefcase.*)
MRS HAYNES: How much? Is it in there? Eh? (*And she rubs the tips of two fingers together.*)
DANIEL: (*Severely*) I'm not going to tell you on the doorstep,
    now am I?
    (*She examines him again, just as fiercely as before, then – without closing the door – she turns abruptly away, going back down the passage.*
    DANIEL *understandably hesitates, and even looks swiftly up and down the terrace of houses, before following her on in, and shutting the door.*)

INT. CORRIDOR. THE HOUSE. DAY
DANIEL *hesitates again in the corridor. There is a stair climbing in*

front of him to his left, and a closed door off to his right (the 'front room') as well as the mottled-glass door directly ahead, at the end of the corridor, which is also closed. He clears his throat and remembers the name she had told him.

DANIEL: Mrs Haynes – ?

INT. KITCHEN/LIVING ROOM. THE HOUSE. DAY

MRS HAYNES *is back in the same seat as when the door knocked, and has already picked up a single piece of jigsaw. Momentarily, it seems she's already forgotten about* DANIEL, *intensely concentrating on the one-third-completed puzzle spread on the table before her. But then –*

MRS HAYNES: (*Calls*) In here! (*Muttering to self*) Muttonhead.
　　(DANIEL *comes in, comically over cautious. He looks at her. Her attention, however, is fixed on the jigsaw and the piece in her hand.*)

DANIEL: M – may I – sit down – ?

MRS HAYNES: (*Almost to self*) Where's this go, then? Where's this bit go? Looks like some of the girder, don't it?
　　(DANIEL, *who politely still has not sat, looks down at the incomplete jigsaw, trying to be friendly. Propped sideways against the half-net curtain of the window, the box lid shows a multicoloured picture of Hammersmith Bridge, gilded in sunlight.*)

DANIEL: Or the towpath – maybe?

MRS HAYNES: Towpath! Christ! (*Looks up at him at last.*) Listen, you. I know this bleed'n bridge like the back of me own hand. Don't you tell me! (*Then, in a sudden and disturbing fury, she throws the piece down, hard.*) They do it deliberate! Too soddin' hard!
　　(*And in the same inexplicable rage, she sweeps all the jigsaw pieces, the completed as well as the loose ones, on to the floor, in a wild scatter.*
　　A beat. They look at each other. Then – movingly, hopelessly – she puts her damaged face into her hands and starts to weep.)

CLOSE-UP – DANIEL. KITCHEN/LIVING ROOM
He doesn't know what to do. It is distressing. And his face shows that he is genuinely upset.

INT. KITCHEN/LIVING ROOM. DAY

Mrs Haynes's weeping, head in hands, elbows on the table, amidst bits of scattered jigsaw, has clearly moved on into much deeper terrain than her original anger and its apparently trivial reasons. Her crying is now sobbing: the awful, helpless, grief-laden kind of a broken life.

Full of pity and concern, DANIEL *tentatively touches the untidy mop of her hair as* MRS HAYNES *continues to sob, bent over the table. He becomes less tentative, a hint of wetness at his own eyes, and begins to stroke her head, speaking softly as he does so.*

DANIEL: There, there – anything as bad as that shouldn't be bottled up. Let it out. Oh, let it come! Oh, my dear – if there's anything – anything – there, there.

CLOSE-UP – MRS HAYNES AND DANIEL

The wretchedness of the sobs edges off and the shaking or juddering of her torso under their impact lessens and lessens. She becomes conscious of the stroking, stroking –

And then, suddenly, she turns her wet and mutilated face up to him, the weeping all but over, and her one good eye seems to express something new: half-way, so to speak, between bewilderment and gratitude. She holds the gaze for a moment.

INT. KITCHEN/LIVING ROOM. DAY

MRS HAYNES: (*Eventually*) It's not just – It's not just them pieces – I don't know. I – No, no, I don't know.

DANIEL: Do you want me to – ah – (*Looks around.*) Can I make you a cup of tea or something?

(*For a second, another spasm of crazed indignation threatens, but this time it is brought back under control.*)

MRS HAYNES: Tea? A cup of bloody tea? (*Controls.*) No. Ta. No. But – (*Attempts a wink.*) In there. See. A little drop of Mother's Ruin. That might do the trick. That cupboard. Up there!

INT. KITCHEN. THE HOUSE. DAY

DANIEL, *under instruction, moves into the small oblong of a kitchen, in which are squashed the basic units of DIY nature, including a pair of overhead cabinets.*

MRS HAYNES: (*Off screen*) No! The other one! For Christ's sake.

CLOSE-UP – THE CORRECT OVERHEAD CABINET
The knobbed door seems to stick and Daniel's hand tugs harder –
CRASH!

INT. KITCHEN. DAY
Worcestershire sauce, Bovril, mustard jar, Marmite, HP Sauce, a
folded-down half packet of sugar, a salt drum, some biscuits, a loose
box of teabags and about four packets of crisps come cascading down
from the top of the two shelves within the cabinet. The bottom one
has glasses – and the gin. They crack, bounce, bump and roll on to
the metal sink, and into it, and on to the floor, with some spillage,
and a lot of mess.
DANIEL: Oh, God! I'm – !

INT. LIVING ROOM/KITCHEN. DAY
A horrified half-second, then DANIEL *bobs down to try to gather up*
some of the fallen things. And unexpectedly, but with enormous
relish, MRS HAYNES *begins to laugh. Her laughter feeds on itself,*
until very soon – her hands on her hips – she is roaring helplessly.

CLOSE-UP – DANIEL. KITCHEN
Deeply embarrassed, DANIEL, *on his hands and knees in a crunchy*
mess of broken biscuits, spilled crisps and scattered teabags, tries to
scoop a splodge of ready-mixed mustard back into its jar – as though
he doesn't know what on earth he is doing. And MRS HAYNES *side-*
splits laughter, off screen.

INT. PASSAGE. THE HOUSE. DAY
SANDRA, *coming back from somewhere in what looks like a rush,*
stops dead in the drab passage, door keys still in her hand, astonished
or even suspicious about the yelps of helpless laughter she can hear her
mother making, off. Then, released, she rushes forward, snapping
open the mottled-glass door.

INT. LIVING ROOM/KITCHEN: FROM DOORWAY. DAY
Stunned SANDRA *sees her mother roaring with inordinate laughter,*
doubled up like a madwoman in the midst of scattered pieces of
jigsaw puzzle, and, beyond her, rising from all fours like a clown in a
circus, DANIEL, *who has somehow or other managed to get a blob of*

mustard and a smear of Bovril on his face, and particles of sugar or
salt in his hair and eyebrows.
SANDRA: What the f – ?! (*Then, at* DANIEL, *shrieking*)
Whatchewbleed'ndoin'ere!

CLOSE-UP – DANIEL
Flustered, and speaking out of a comically messy face, and very
relieved to see her.
DANIEL: Sandra. Thank God I've found you. It's important
that I – (*Tries to wipe at his mouth. Gets mustard on lip.*)
Don't be alarmed! Please!

INT. LIVING ROOM/KITCHEN
SANDRA: (*Angry, alarmed*) You're a bloody nutter! And you're
frightening the life out of me!
(*Her mother has stopped laughing, all at once, and looks from*
one to the other, her underlying mental confusion well and truly
showing.)
MRS HAYNES: (*Defensive*) He's not the insurance – ! Sanny?
What's up, love?
(DANIEL, *trying to wipe the mustard and the Bovril from his*
face with the back of his hand, has succeeded only in getting a
bit of both more generously spread across his lips. He can hardly
speak properly as a result of the sting and the taste.)
DANIEL: Sandra, I've brought your bag. It's – (*Half-spits out*)
Christ. Mustard. I – Oh, God. Excuse me –

INT. KITCHEN. DAY
DANIEL *quickly turns on the tap and puts his face or his mouth*
straight under it, half-gargles, half-gags, wipes at himself with a
rather grubby drying cloth.
DANIEL: I'll get this laundered, of course – I'm *so* sorry.

INT. LIVING ROOM/KITCHEN. DAY
As DANIEL *advances out of the small oblong, almost slipping on the*
mess or almost turning his ankle on a jar, bottle or salt drum.
SANDRA: (*Accusing*) You look inside it? Did you? My bag?
DANIEL: But I had to. I had to find out where you – Don't
worry. Everything's safe, Sandra.

(MRS HAYNES, *mental confusion more and more apparent, is beginning to flutter her hands and makes ties of bewilderment, indicating the strewn jigsaw pieces, but also a more general distress.*)

MRS HAYNES: (*Upset*) It was the girder. I know it was. 'E said towpath – towpath –

SANDRA: (*Calmly*) Sit down, Mum. Go on.

MRS HAYNES: Wha – ?

SANDRA: Sit down, there's a love. (*Pulls out the chair at table a little.*) Come on. You'll be all right in a minute, I promise. Sit down, my old love.

(SANDRA *seems calmly authoritative in a way which her mother accepts, and is calmed by.* MRS HAYNES *sits, stops twitching, and gradually begins to gather together the jigsaw pieces which are still on the table top.*)

DANIEL: (*Upset*) The last thing I wanted was to cause any disturbance or – or –

SANDRA: (*Fiercely to* DANIEL) You see her face? Do you?

DANIEL: I – yes.

SANDRA: Know who did that? Do you?

DANIEL: No –

SANDRA: (*Face twisting in hate*) Arthur Mailion! 'Pig' Mailion. The rotten ugly bastard!

EXT. ITALIAN RESTAURANT. SOHO. DAY
Still the lunch-hour rush surging all around. But a space is suddenly available almost directly opposite the restaurant, and a Range Rover backs into it, causing some aggro with other traffic, but succeeding by being as bullishly insistent as its driver, ignoring honks and a yell.

INT./EXT. RANGE ROVER. DAY
ARTHUR MAILION *buttons down a window to jeer back at a protesting driver.*

MAILION: (*Bellow*) Bloody stupid arsehole!

(*A mere daily routine, one feels. He settles, not at all disturbed, to look across at the Italian restaurant. He likes to check things out.*)

INT. NICK AND LINDA'S TABLE. THE RESTAURANT. DAY
Besotted NICK *is foolishly overlarding his comments while at the
same time making himself seem powerful, brave and all-knowing. He
does not appear to have noticed, so far, that* LINDA *is more playing
with than eating her main course, pushing it around her plate but
taking only the smallest nibbles.*

NICK: (*In mid-eulogy*) – and a perfect example of what I mean is
the way in that brasserie scene you tell the bat joke. You
know the one I mean?

LINDA: (*Too flat*) Yeah. The ones in the cave.
(*He doesn't notice the inadequate tone either.*)

NICK: Well, it was in the *timing*, wasn't it? The pacing of it. The
rhythm. Now, that's something you had instinctively, and
it's worth its weight in plutonium, Linda, believe you me.
And I know what I'm talking about.

LINDA: (*Small voice*) I just wish we –

NICK: Oh, you're going to be a star, my lovely! And I shall be
very, very proud that I had the foresight or insight or
whatever to have picked you out and lifted you up. Yes (*As
though a forced admission*) and the *guts* too. I had to stick to
my guns against all kind of – Believe me, Linda, most
people in this business grow *crusts* over their brain cells.
Habit. Custom. Usual practice. What worked before. God,
it – (*Belatedly*) What's the matter, my love?

LINDA: (*Quiver of near-tears in voice*) Oh. Everything. It's the
way – Us.

NICK: (*Blinking*) Us? You and me?

LINDA: I can't bear it no more. I can't bear what's happening –
(*She puts her knife and fork down, making no further pretence
to eat.*
    *Misunderstanding, though worried, he tries to reach across
and touch her hand – but at the same time he looks around to
see if he is being observed.*)

NICK: I don't like this hole-in-the-corner business any more
than you do. Linda? It breaks my heart. And I promise you
I'm doing all I can to – to –

LINDA: (*Breaking in*) It's my flat.
(*He looks at her, totally bemused.*)

NICK: Your flat. What about it? What are we talking about?

(*But she has lowered her head.*)

Linda? What is it?

(*A beat. She lifts her head, tears in her eyes, looks at him, then looks away from him as she speaks. If doubts have been expressed about the range of her skills in Daniel Feeld's* Karaoke, *there is no question now about her ability to put on an act in her real life.*)

LINDA: (*Eventually*) Me flat. Nick. Oh, Christ, Nick. It's been bugged.

(NICK *freezes. And then his voice tightens, as though squeezed out of a throat crawling with spiders.*)

NICK: How – how do you mean – ?

LINDA: I fought it was too cheap. (*Flash of anger.*) I should have bloody known, shouldn't I?

NICK: Known what? *What?* Linda! (*He is in panic.*)

LINDA: I told you, didden'I, that I got my place for just five hundred a monf – and feeding them fucking fish! Ought to have known. I mean, *you* said go for it too. *You* said it was a bargain. Some bargain!

NICK: (*Desperate – between his teeth*) Linda. Will you please stop *yattering* and tell me *precisely* what the hell is –

LINDA: Yattering? I like that!

NICK: Linda!

(*He has come close to shouting the name in his frightened exasperation, and now realizes that a few lunchers at nearby tables are beginning to cast looks in their direction.*)

LINDA: (*Normal tones*) Well, I've had the wool pulled over my eyes, enn'I? The flat's –

NICK: (*Near-whisper*) Sshh! Voice down.

(*They look at each other. Then – *)

LINDA: You'll have to come and see for yourself.

NICK: What? Go to the flat? Now? (*He looks up at the old clock on the wall.*) I've got to be in the cutting room in thirty-five minutes. Oh, shit. Yes. I don't know *what* you're talking about, but if it affects me then –

LINDA: (*Cutting in – oddly angry*) Course it affects you! Who else is on the bleed'n tape?

NICK: (*Gulp*) Tape?

LINDA: And I suppose you'd recognize your own bum,

wouldn't ya?
(NICK *shrinks into himself, eyes all a swivel, face crunching
with fear and humiliation. And then he sees* LUIGI *looking
straight at him, almost as though a participant. He straightens,
tries to right himself in every other detail, raises a hand, and in
a fair version of his normal voice and normal personal
assumption of authority –*)
NICK: Luigi. The clock is beating us. The bill, please.

INT./EXT. PARKED RANGE ROVER. SOHO STREET. DAY
MAILION *has been in and out of the car, it seems, for he is now
gorging down a cheeseburger. His full mouth stops chewing, grease on
his chin, as he sees –*

EXT. ITALIAN RESTAURANT. SOHO. DAY
NICK *and* LINDA *coming out, as seen from the Range Rover. And it
is clear from any distance that* NICK *is extremely agitated.*

CLOSE-UP – NICK AND LINDA. STREET. DAY
NICK *looks at his watch, and along the street, his words full of stress.*
NICK: You can never get a fucking taxi in Soho (*Jerks in
    anxiety.*) *Who's that?*
    (*Because hooot! A Range Rover is pulling alongside them, or as
    nearly as possible, making other traffic slow.*)
LINDA: Don't ask me – *Oh.* Hello, Arfur – !
    (*As, at the same time, window down –*)
MAILION: Linda! Linda Langer. I'll be blowed! Wanta lift, love?
NICK: (*Hisses*) No.
LINDA: Yeah! That'd be great if you can! (*To* NICK.) Don't be
    daft. Makes sense if you're in a hurry.
    (*She gets in the back without more ado. He has to follow. And
    the cars being temporarily held up honk! and parp!*)

INT./EXT. RANGE ROVER. STREETS. DAY
MAILION *throws a big-jawed grin over his shoulder.*
MAILION: Big 'earted Arfur, enn' I? Where to, Milady? And
    oo's yer boyfriend?
NICK: (*Quick, awkward laugh*) Not boyfriend. No.
LINDA: (*As though proudly*) He's me director, Arfur. George

Street, if you can. That'd be really nice. That's where I am now.

MAILION: George Street – ? Oh. Yeah. Know it. (*Then*) Blimey. Goin' up and up in the world, entcha? I heard you was in this film. Bit of luck, eh, Linda?

LINDA: I'll say! And it's all thanks to Nick, here. Me *director*.

MAILION: Pleased to meetcha, Nick. I'm Arfur.

NICK: (*Subdued*) Hello, Arthur.

LINDA: Nick saw me at this fashion show I was doing –

MAILION: (*Like one fascinated*) Yeah?

LINDA: (*Simper*) I don't know what he saw in me, but it must have been something.

MAILION: (*Half-turn, leer*) Hear that, Nick? She don't know what you saw in her? Don't take many guesses, do it!

CLOSE-UP – NICK. BACK OF CAR
He hates such contact with such a vulgar man, and hates the innuendo, all the more because of the truth in it. He controls his face, just.

NICK: No, no. It was her – it's my job to see what others cannot see . . .

INT./EXT. RANGE ROVER. DAY
LINDA *is looking at* NICK, *with a funny little smile, half-protective but also a little cruel.*

LINDA: Nick's done some good 'uns, Arfur. He's very well known.

MAILION: (*Interested*) Yeah?

LINDA: He done *Listen Who Dares* –

MAILION: Oh. Yes. I remember that one! Ooh – I'm honoured. Giving a bloke like you a lift, Nick. What's yer other name, then?

(NICK *doesn't answer.*)

LINDA: (*As though proudly*) He's Nicholas Balmer.

MAILION: Balmer? Balmer? Nicholas Balmer. (*Tiny pause, then – like revelation*) Oooh, yeah! Knew it, knew it. You was in the *Standard* the other night, wasn't you?

NICK: (*Fidgety*) Was I?

MAILION: Yes, you was! Picture and all. Your wife's that – cor,

I *am* going up in the world, enn'I? She's Lady Ruth
Balmer, entshe? Talks about cooking and that on the
wireless. That's her, ennit?
(*Tiny pause.* NICK *looks at* LINDA, *as though for help.*
Then –)
NICK: Yes.

CLOSE-UP – GETTING CLOSER – MAILION. CAR
Mailion's large, jowly face starting to glow-glow-glow as he positions
the punch, so to speak.
MAILION: Cor – ! You wouldn't think someone brought up like
her would bovver their heads about *cooking*, would ya? I
mean. I *mean.* Her dad was that funny old Lord
Collingwode, weren't he? No offence intended. But he had
more millions than he had brain cells, didnee? Left five
million flippin' quid for cats to have their balls cut off.
Christ. Didn't like cats much. (*Big big grin.*) Still, he left
her ten times as much, I'll give him that!

INT./EXT. RANGE ROVER. DAY
As the big, beaming, balding, bejowled face turns almost right
around to NICK *in the back of the car.*
MAILION: What a lucky boy you turned out to be, eh, Nick? No
offence meant. And none taken, I 'ope. (*Turning back.*)
Here we nearly are, Linda, me old love. Just tell me where
to stop, and you can give me a kiss on the cheek for me
trouble, eh?

EXT. THE HAMMERSMITH HOUSE. DAY
And curtains being closed at the top window of the little two-storey
terrace, even though it is the middle of the bright day.

INT. A BEDROOM. THE HOUSE. DAY
MRS HAYNES *is lying on the bed, the bad side of her face against the*
pillow. The pretty woman she had been can easily be seen at this
angle, and in this light.
SANDRA *turns from the closed curtains, whose blue, penetrated a little*
by the sunlight (no matter what the season), turns the little room into
a lagoon-like cool softness of muted colour.

SANDRA: Now you just try and get a little nap, lovie. I'll bring you a cup of tea and a nice biscuit 'bout four o'clock, right? You'll feel a lot be'er.

MRS HAYNES: (*Murmurs*) Good girl, Sanny.

(SANDRA *looks at her mother for a moment, then crosses to the bed.*)

SANDRA: I'll get you a new puzzle tomorrow. A real good 'un.

MRS HAYNES: Not too much sky. Eh?

(SANDRA *bends, and kisses her on the cheek. Her voice tries to hide a sudden emotion.*)

SANDRA: No, love. Them bloody blue bits can drive you mad.

INT. LIVING ROOM. DOWNSTAIRS. DAY

DANIEL *sits on the chair at the table where* MRS HAYNES *had sat doing the jigsaw puzzle. His briefcase is beside him. He has just pulled out of it an Olympus 'Pearlcorder' S912 microcassette recorder, which is battery-operated. Beyond it, on the table top, Sandra's bag glitters a little.*

SANDRA *can be heard, off, coming down the stairs. He lifts his head at the sound, and secretively smiles to himself, secretively tender. The door opens, but he deliberately does not turn his head.*

SANDRA *stands still for a small moment, looking at him, his seated back half to her. It is like a mini-examination. She moves on, towards the table.*

DANIEL: Before you say anything or before we try and sort any of this out, I want you to listen to this. Please.

SANDRA: What is it?

DANIEL: It's a message that was on my answer phone when I got home from the hospital this morning. Just listen, OK? (*He presses the button.*)

ANNA'S VOICE: (*On Pearlcorder*) Hello, Daniel. It's Anna here –

SANDRA: Who's she?

DANIEL: The producer.

ANNA'S VOICE: (*Continuous*) – I know you're out of St Christopher's this morning. I *do* hope you're feeling better, and I'm sorry to bother you at such a time –

CLOSE-UP – SANDRA. LIVING ROOM

Her eyes are fixed on DANIEL. *She still seems to be examining him.*

But there is a softening in her expression, as Anna's voice continues.

ANNA'S VOICE: (*Continuous*) – I'm calling early – well, actually it's five o'clock in the morning and to be honest I haven't had very much sleep, but I –

INT. LIVING ROOM. DAY

DANIEL *keeps his eyes on the Pearlcorder on the table in front of him, but he seems aware of her scrutiny, as Anna's voice continues.*

ANNA'S VOICE: (*Continuous*) – simply had to call you about this – um – little problem – (DANIEL *snorts*) which I know Nick will be – um –

DANIEL: (*At same time, not turning his head*) He's the director.

ANNA'S VOICE: (*Continuous*) – well, he'll want to talk to you about it, I'm afraid. The point is, Daniel, that by sheer bad luck, there is –
(*Now* DANIEL *looks straight at* SANDRA, *who is still gazing at him.*)
– there really is, somebody called Arthur Mailion, as in your script, and he is, really is, nicknamed 'Pig' Mailion, by –

EXTREME CLOSE-UP – SANDRA

Listening, her eyes flick away. The look of hatred transforms her face again as Anna's voice continues.

ANNA'S VOICE: (*Continuous*) – some of those who know him and he is apparently in what *could* be seen as the same line of business as *our* 'Pig' Mailion –

INT. LIVING ROOM. DAY

DANIEL *studies her, with concern. She realizes, and swings her eyes back to him, abandoning the so swift and so lethal look of sheer hatred, as Anna's voice continues.*

ANNA'S VOICE: (*Continuous*) – the fictional one, I mean. Now, I've gone through –

SANDRA: (*At same time*) What's 'fictional'?

DANIEL: Made up. Invented. By me.

ANNA'S VOICE: (*Continuous*) – the script and what we've shot – several times, believe you me – and I think –
(*Click!* DANIEL *shuts* ANNA *off.*)

A moment. They look at each other. SANDRA *is puzzled.*)

DANIEL: There's nothing more of any interest.

SANDRA: God. She sounds posh.

DANIEL: (*Amused*) Does she?

SANDRA: Not 'arf!

DANIEL: But do you see now what has happened?

SANDRA: (*With a frown*) Well – sort of – No. Not really. I mean –

DANIEL: When I was writing *Karaoke*, which was almost two
　　　years ago, Sandra, I used somebody's real name for one of
　　　my made-up names. Entirely by accident.

SANDRA: You'd never heard of him before? Is that right?

DANIEL: Dead right. Unless I'd heard about or read about a
　　　man with that name, then forgotten all about it. It *can*
　　　happen. It's called cryptomnesia.

SANDRA: Christ. That sounds nasty.

　　　(*He laughs. He finds her often unconscious comedy and
　　　directness enchanting.*)

DANIEL: Well, it *can* be nasty. On the pocket. That's why
　　　publishers and television and film companies have to check
　　　these things.

SANDRA: But somebody didn't?

DANIEL: (*Sighs*) Somebody didn't. (*Then, more positively*) So
　　　you see, I'm not what you called 'psychic' or anything like
　　　that. It's just *accidental*. When you ran away like that from
　　　the bench, I wondered *myself* whether my old bloody
　　　script, the karaoke thing, was sort of *reaching out* and
　　　tangling itself in *real* lives – God, that's what had been
　　　giving me the creeps! But it isn't, Sandra. It isn't! Do you
　　　see that? Do you *understand*? That script is just-a-story. Got
　　　it?

　　　(*A half-beat.*)

SANDRA: (*Half-reluctantly*) Yes.

　　　(*They look at each other. His voice softens, into a cajoling,
　　　earnest tone.*)

DANIEL: Sandra. Why do you have a gun? What sort of story
　　　does that come from?

　　　(SANDRA *looks at him, then very deliberately – as a child might
　　　– turns half her body away, giving no answer. He drums his
　　　fingers on the table, looks out of the window into the little back*

yard, then looks at her still half-turned figure again.)
Sandra. I want you to tell me. Please.
(She whirls back around, almost spitting.)
SANDRA: Go upstairs and take another look at me mum! Go on!
A really good look!
DANIEL: *(Wanting to flinch)* Hey. Steady.
SANDRA: Twenty-two years ago he did that. When she was
carrying me and I was due! Fink of it! And do you know
how he did it? Eh? *Eh?*
DANIEL: *(Shaken)* N – no –
SANDRA: Wiv a quart bot'le of milk! He went in and smashed
the bottom off of it and he chased her round and round the
room and he got her in the corner and he got her up
against the wall and he smashed it into her face and he
ground it in and ground it in and *dragged* it down her skin
and bone and then he kicked her in the hip and he walked
out to go to the bloody greyhound track. And he didn't do
a single day in the nick, not from that day to this.
*(SANDRA stares at him, eyes blazing, but she has finished. He is
badly shaken, and half-reaches out to try to touch her.)*
DANIEL: Sandra –
*(But she suddenly rushes into the kitchen like one trying to hold
down vomit.)*

INT. KITCHEN. THE HOUSE. DAY
SANDRA – *rather as* DANIEL *in more comic circumstance had done –
splashes running water from the tap over her face. But then her body
convulsively jerks forward, and she begins to retch.*

CLOSE-UP – DANIEL
*He winces and closes his eyes a moment at the sound, off, of desperate
retching. Then, opening his eyes, his expression heavy with pity, he
seems to catch sight of Sandra's bag – as though it insists on being
paid attention.*

SUDDEN CLOSE-UP – SANDRA'S BAG. TABLE
*Its sequins still sparkle in a tawdry manner, from the light slanting
through the window from the back yard.*

INT. AT THE TABLE. LIVING ROOM. DAY
As the retching sounds at last subside, off, DANIEL *makes a quick judgement and a swift movement, as though under compulsion. He reaches across to the bag, pulls out the 'silver' pistol and plunges it into his jacket pocket. He looks up, half-furtive, to see –*

INT. LIVING ROOM AND KITCHEN. DAY
SANDRA *stands in the undoored and uncurtained entrance to the oblong kitchen looking across at him, getting her breath back. It seems she has not seen him take the gun from her bag. He gets to his feet, awkward and flustered.*
DANIEL: Oh, Sandra. You poor girl. I'm so sorry.
SANDRA: All right now.
DANIEL: Please – sit down. Let me make you a drink or a, or a
    – Let me do *something* for you.
    (*Much more composed, she twists a smile, but doesn't move.*)
SANDRA: (*Quietly*) Nah.
DANIEL: But – but –
SANDRA: (*Interrupts*) Didn't track the bugger down till four
    months ago, did I? That's why I'm doing that job at this
    bleed'n club. I'll find him on his own-io there one of these
    days.
DANIEL: Sandra. Listen to me.
SANDRA: (*Taking no notice*) I'll get close to him, don't you
    worry. So bleed'n close I'd be able to squeeze aht one of
    his black'eads for him, wouldunt'I? (*Suddenly*)
    Wassamatter?
    (DANIEL, *standing, has suddenly clenched, clutching at his
    stomach or higher in obvious pain. He can only answer with a
    gasp.*)
DANIEL: (*Gasp*) It's – another smashed bottle.

INT. BRASSERIE. NIGHT
Oliver Morse's WAITER, *retreating from a wine-dampened* OLIVER, *looks back at him with a rather contemptuous or knowing glint – but Oliver's eyes (increasingly background as* WAITER *moves away) stay clamped on 'Sandra' (*LINDA*) and* PETER *on the other side of the brasserie.*

SUDDEN CLOSE-UP – OLIVER MORSE
The patrician old man's eyes absolutely still, staring, staring across.

INT. AT THE BAR. BRASSERIE. NIGHT
A section at the end where the long bar finally curves away to the swing doors of the kitchen, and where WAITERS/WAITRESSES *intermittently congregate for the occasional brief chat.*
OLIVER'S WAITER: (*Arriving*) God almighty.
WAITRESS: What's the matter?
OLIVER'S WAITER: He's found himself another one – our Big Tipper.
(*The* WAITRESS, *making out a bill on her pad for some other table, looks across at* OLIVER, *whose stance, and its degree of concentration, remain the same.*)
WAITRESS: Now that's what I call sick. (*A qualified smile.*) Poor old devil.

CLOSE-UP – OLIVER
Eyes fixed on the distant couple and voice 'in his head', with the similar sort of resonance in which an ill and near-drunken DANIEL *had 'heard' what he knew to be his own written dialogue.*
WOMAN'S VOICE: (*Over*) Don't fret, my darling. In the end, everything is all right. In the end, if your feelings are strong and true, you *will* know fulfilment, my love. You will.
(*As though along his eyeline, find –*)

CLOSE-UP – PETER (THE ACTOR)
PETER: – but Sandra, love, listen. I need a favour off him real bad, and he'd go for you in a big way. Do this for me! Please!

INT. PETER AND LINDA'S ('SANDRA') TABLE. BRASSERIE. NIGHT
LINDA, *virtually expressionless, takes no heed of the plea.*
LINDA: And the other bat says, 'Blimey, you're on the wrong track here, old mate –
PETER: (*Whining*) Sandra. Lis-ten –
LINDA: 'Christ, it's dawn out there, he says, bleed'n daybreak – So where you going to find fresh blood at this sort of time – ? Tell me that!

PETER: Oh. Shit.

LINDA: 'Dunno. But I'm effin hungry. You coming or what – ?'

PETER: I've heard this.

LINDA: The other bat – a downer, him – 'You won't find
nothing out there, not a fing!' (*Eyes hardening.*) Yeah. A
right downer. A real misery.

PETER: (*Reacting to her glare*) I'm telling you. I've heard this!
I've bloody well –

LINDA: (*Cutting in*) But off he goes anyway, the first one. Aht of
the cave – flap, flap – (*She seems to hesitate a fraction, and
half-covertly sneaks a look the length of the brasserie to –*)

INT. BRASSERIE. OLIVER'S TABLE. LINDA'S POINT OF VIEW
*The distantish figure staring across at her, fixedly, but so very
tenderly.*

PETER: (*Off, angry*) It's not even funny!

INT. PETER AND LINDA'S TABLE. NIGHT

LINDA: Flap. Flap. Back'e comes. Just a couple of minutes –
yeah? – Blood all round his beak –
(*Picture diminishing to –*)

INT. STEENBECK AND SCREEN. CUTTING ROOM. DAY
*Not yet wide enough to show who is in the room, except perhaps
Ian's hands near the control. But the little screen sharp and bright as
the brasserie scene continues.*

PETER: They don't even have beaks. You ignorant cow.

LINDA: (*Nasty little smile*) 'Je*sus*!' says the other bat. 'Where the
fuck do you find *that* at this time of day –'
(*Widening, during this, back fully into –*)

INT. BRASSERIE. NIGHT

PETER: (*Gritting teeth*) Sandra. If you don't stop –

LINDA: (*Takes no notice*) 'Where'd I get it? Where'd I get it?
Well, you see that tree over there? Do you see that fucking
tree – ?'

INT. CUTTING ROOM. SOHO. DAY
IAN *at the controls,* ANNA *sitting beside him, and 'back-to-front'*

BEN *half-on and half-off a higher chair further back from the Steenbeck, as the weak punch-line is played out.*

PETER: (*Sighs*) Go on, then.

LINDA: '*Do you see that tree?*' 'Yeah,' says the other bat, all irritated like. 'Yeah, I can see the bloody tree.' (*Tiny pause – other bat voice*) 'Well. *I* didn't.'

STEENBECK SCREEN

LINDA *delivers up the weak ending with as much panache as it allows, cackles a second, then stops dead, and once more looks across the fairly crowded brasserie. Her expression changes again, and picture widens back to –*

OLIVER'S TABLE. BRASSERIE. NIGHT

Linda's point of view of a now empty table, wine-stained napkin placed next to an as yet uncleared plate. OLIVER MORSE *has gone. The screen suddenly goes blank and scratchy.*

INT. CUTTING ROOM. DAY

IAN *stops the reel from spooling off altogether. The others are silent. Then, portentously –*

ANNA: You've gone out on a bit of a limb, Ian.

IAN: I've simply done what should be done, and recut it so that we're not on *that lassie* for every possible second of every possible minute. All I'm asking – all I ask – is that Nick at least sit down and look at it. I mean look at it properly. But where is he? What's happening?

(ANNA *looks at the clock on cutting-room wall. It shows twenty to three.*)

ANNA: (*Troubled*) Forty minutes. He's never usually late, is he?

IAN: Never.

ANNA: (*To* BEN) And where's Daniel? He *was* told two o'clock, wasn't he?

BEN: Of course he was. Told him myself. (*Irritated.*) This is all very – very –

ANNA: Yes. I know. I'm sorry.

BEN: (*Getting angry*) You told me that this was going to be the mig batch, the one that counts –

(IAN *is not used to Ben's little peculiarity.*)

IAN: The what? Sorry?

BEN: And here I am like a referee all kitted out with my shoots and borts and my whistle and neither team has even bothered to turn up!

ANNA: Well, Ben, I simply do not understand it at all. Unless – oh, God forbid!

IAN: Unless.

ANNA: They met up with each other in the street or something – bumped into each other –

IAN: (*Dour relish*) *Collided*, you mean?

(ANNA, *ever agitated* ANNA, *looks up at the clock, already perambulating.*)

ANNA: *Something's* going on, that's for sure. Something very fishy.

BEN: (*Muttering*) Bodes ill. Bodes ill.

INT. A SWINGING MIRROR. DAY

Unsettling visually for a moment, the entire screen tilts and slants as a very large mirror opens like a door. It is splitter-splatter decorated here and there with tiny ladybirds, all of which seem to be on the move – as do the faces and figures of NICK and LINDA, and, beyond, the bed and the soft, luxurious furnishings of –

INT. BEDROOM. LINDA'S APARTMENT. DAY

LINDA *has been 'opening' the mirror, which is normally flat on the wall, with no sign that it can be moved in such a way.* NICK *stares, aghast.*

A small automatic camera is buried in a mini-cavity within the wall behind where the immobile mirror would normally be. Its lens will fit one of the decorative ladybirds.

LINDA: Took me ages to find it – Running me fingers down the wall and the frames and everyfink – Couldn't find no button, no switch – then I just *pulled*, first on the wrong side, now this – and here the bloody thing is! See!

NICK: (*In a small croak*) Oh, my God –

EXTREME CLOSE-UP – SNOOP-CAMERA

As he reaches out the tip of a finger to touch it, with a slight tremble.

INT. LINDA'S BEDROOM. DAY

LINDA: I didn't even know they could make such fings as this. I mean, it's like some James Bond story, ennit?

NICK: (*Groans*) I wish to God it was. Just a – a *story* –

LINDA: Shall I shut it?

NICK: (*Near shout*) I don't care!

LINDA: Hey. Keep your 'air on, Nick.

(*She is closing the mirror, so that it is flat against the wall, as it obviously always 'normally' was.* NICK, *at a loss, brimming with dread, stares at his own reflection as it swings back across in front of him and settles.*)

CLOSE-UP – NICK AND HIS REFLECTION, STEADY MIRROR

Dread looks at dread. And then – jumping straight out of his head, so to speak – and preceded, just, by the appropriate sounds –

FLASH: LINDA AND NICK IN MIRROR

Rather as in Daniel Feeld's script: a sexual moment, where LINDA *with her palms flat against the big mirror, bending forward, provocatively half-underweared, appears to be being penetrated from behind by* NICK. *Very brief!*

CLOSE-UP – NICK

As the recollection of the sexual encounter hits him – and just how compromising it has now become. He lets out a slow hiss of breath.

INT. LINDA'S BEDROOM. DAY

NICK: (*In a whisper*) Absolutely done for.

(LINDA *has moved away from the mirror, towards the door.*)

LINDA: Sorry? What you say?

(*He turns, rage boiling up.*)

NICK: Are you in on this, you little bitch? Is this a set –

LINDA: (*Hotly cutting in*) Oy! Don't you fucking speak to me like that!

(*But a few quick paces and he has grabbed her by the arm, trying to shake her, physically shake her.*)

NICK: How do you know about it in the first place? What the hell's been going on? Who the hell've you been talking to – ?

(*She shakes herself free.*)

LINDA: Let go, you bugger! What sort of person do you fink I am?

(*He drops his hand. His face crumples, and his voice croaks again, part-plea, part-accusation.*)

NICK: That's what I want to know.

(*She looks at him. Her face softens. She takes hold of his hand, to lead him from the bedroom.*)

LINDA: Here. Come and see. Let me show you.

INT. LIVING ROOM. LINDA'S FLAT. DAY

Led by the hand, like a little boy, the now helplessly docile NICK *is brought into the living room.* LINDA *lets go of his hand, opens a drawer in an elegant, seemingly genuinely antique bureau, and takes out a long envelope.*

LINDA: Sit down, Nick.

NICK: (*Confused*) What?

LINDA: Sit down, there's a love. On the settee. Go on.

(*Childlike, he obeys, and stares up at her with a kind of dumb or deadening bewilderment, from a slumped position.*)

NICK: (*Croak*) I just can't take it all in – I –

LINDA: (*Giving him the envelope*) Read this. Go on.

(*He takes it, and opens what has already been opened, with slightly trembling hands. As he reads, he begins to stiffen, and to sit up straighter, the muscles on his face tightening. He takes a small photo from between the two pages of the letter.*)

CLOSE-UP – SMALL PHOTOGRAPH

A frozen moment, as it were, from a similar scene to the flash of compromised memory that had hit him a few moments ago. Nick's face is in clear view above Linda's naked shoulder, his hands cupping her breasts.

CLOSE-UP – NICK ON SOFA

Tears slowly well in his eyes. He wipes at them with his hand for a second, then makes himself read.

INT. LIVING ROOM. LINDA'S FLAT. DAY

LINDA, *standing, her arms folded, is watching him closely all the*

*time. There are moments when her look expresses cunning, but a few
more when they show sympathy and pity.*

EXTREME CLOSE-UP – PART OF THE LETTER
A line or so readable: the letter is written in not very gainly capitals.
BEEN FEEDING MORE THAN THE FISH AND I
KNOW THIS BLOKE ON THE SUN WHO WOULD BE
VERY

INT. LINDA'S FLAT. LIVING ROOM. DAY
As NICK *continues to read or maybe reread the two-page letter, the
little photograph once between the pages is on the sofa, beside him, its
face turned down.*
LINDA: (*Quietly*) You see? Nick?
NICK: (*More composed voice*) Everything. I see – everything.
LINDA: I mean, about *me* – Nick. Listen. *I* didn't set you up for
this – What's the matter – ?
(*This is because* NICK *is suddenly looking purposefully all
around the room.*)
NICK: Where *are* they, anyway?
LINDA: Where's the what?
NICK: The fish.
(*They look at each other. Unexpectedly, he starts to laugh –
really laugh.*)
LINDA: What's so funny?
NICK: (*Laughing*) I don't know – fish. I suppose the – *hoo! hoo!*
– fish!
(LINDA *starts to laugh too. He lets himself go for a while, in a
kind of aftershock.*)
LINDA: (*Laughing*) My plaice or your plaice. Place. You get it?
(*He nods, double nods, laughing – and then it suddenly stops,
and he is looking at her, his voice with an edge again.*)
NICK: But where are they? These fish in whose service you were
rewarded by so little rent?
LINDA: They're in that little room – the whatchacallit when you
– The study. You've seen them. Haven't you?
NICK: Yes. (*Glumly*) Of course. In the – yes. Sorry. (*Looks up at
her again.*) This Pete fellow. This bastard Beasley. Let me
get this straight, as I remember you telling me at the time.

LINDA: Yeah. Go ahead.

NICK: He was a – no, it wasn't an agent exactly, nor a booker, but nevertheless a kind of go-between between models and the advertising people and such like who sometimes used them –

LINDA: Right.

NICK: And that's how you knew him.

LINDA: That's how I knew him.

NICK: You weren't *lovers* at any time?

LINDA: Nah! Not my type. I just – well *knew* him, you know. Met at some office or other. Sometimes on location when you were away for a magazine, say – He was sort of – around. I liked him, and I thought he liked me – Christ!

NICK: And all this flat business came up just after you got the part?

LINDA: Yes. I thought wonders would never stop 'appening. The whole world seemed – well, felt like everybody wanted to give me everything I'd ever wanted. (*Twirls like a schoolgirl – with a flash of excitement.*) Oh, when I 'eard you on the phone! That part! My first job at real acting, and such a big, big part!
(*She stops the little twirl and rushes to him on the sofa, cradling his face in her hands, and kissing him enthusiastically.*)
You changed my life, Nick! I'll never forget it! Not never, Nick!
(*She kisses, kisses again; and, at first half-reluctant, he begins to respond.*)

CLOSE-UP – NICK (WITH LINDA) ON SOFA
He stops responding. He pulls his face away. There is a quick, hard look in his eyes for a micro-second.

INT. LIVING ROOM. LINDA'S FLAT. DAY
LINDA: What's the matter?

NICK: Then – bingo! – old friend Pete Beasley offers you a wonderful flat at a knock-down rent. Just like that.
(*She stiffens. They each pull apart.*)

LINDA: What you trying to say?

NICK: And you get this letter yesterday morning – but you wait to tell me. Then he rings you this morning as cool as a cucumber and says your rent is going up by a thousand pounds a week. Correct?

LINDA: (*Coldly*) Correct.

(*He looks at her and smiles nastily.*)

NICK: Then you'll have to move out, won't you?

LINDA: (*Evenly*) It's a thousand a week wherever I move, Nick.

NICK: (*Half-jeer*) Oooh. You poor thing. How on earth are you going to find it?

LINDA: How am *I* going to – You off your rocker or what? Read that bleed'n letter again, Nick –

(NICK *gets up, rips the letter into two pieces and lets it flutter to the thick-pile carpet.*)

NICK: I don't need to.

LINDA: (*Alarmed*) You what?

NICK: (*Calmly*) I said – I don't need to. It's not my problem.

(*And he is walking to the door, with every semblance of calm. She is agitated by this, then comes after him.*)

LINDA: Nick! What about the papers? That photograph!

(*He has gone on out to –*)

INT. HALL. LINDA'S FLAT. DAY

Tall, wide, smart, with door alarm and entry-phone, etc.

NICK: Have you ever read the script *Karaoke*, Linda? All the way through, I mean?

LINDA: What?

NICK: Or have you only read the pages that you're in?

LINDA: (*Confused, but indignant*) What the 'ell do I want them others for, if I ain't got to do nothing in them? – Nick? what you *talking* about? What you going to do about that letter?

(*Nick has his hand on the door, about to open it, but he pauses a little and looks back at her as she quivers near the door into her living room.*)

NICK: (*Not nice*) Well, my sweet, the script you have not read is not entirely irrelevant to the things that can happen in one's own life. I'll give Dan Feeld that. And *that* story of his shows that when a particular *obsession* cracks open – an obsession of any kind – there is a terrifying freedom poking

out, and in that freedom one might even see the faint
outlines of a funny little thing called dignity.

LINDA: (*Angry – near shout*) I don't know what the fuck you're
talking about.

(*He opens the door, with an ominous little smile.*)

NICK: No. I don't suppose you do. Goodbye, Linda. Good
luck. (*And he's gone.*)

CLOSE-UP – LINDA. HALL

*Eyes wide with shock, her fingers flutter up to her mouth, and then –
momentarily – it almost looks as though she is going to chew several
of her fingers all at once. Then she hurtles to the closed door.*

INT. LARGE HALL. SWEEPING CURVE OF STAIR. LINDA'S
BLOCK. DAY

'Luxury' all around. There is a discreet lift but NICK *is taking the
curve of a single flight of carpeted stair to the ground floor.* LINDA
appears, a little above him.

LINDA: (*Near-hysteria showing*) Why are you going, Nick? What
are you going to do? (*Little sob.*) Where are you going?
(*He looks up at her.*)

INT. STAIRS. DAY

NICK: (*Matter-of-fact*) Actually, I'm very late. Which is not very
professional. (*Ignores sound of her sob.*) As to what I'm
doing *precisely* – Well, I've got a lawyer, myself, and three
other people all waiting to eliminate someone called 'Pig'
Mailion – (*Moves on down – then – with real derision – half
over his shoulder.*) A joke which I've no doubt totally
escapes you.

CLOSE-UP – LINDA. BIG HALL

*Jump in close at her as though on a crash of music. It is funny. But
her shock is total, her fear palpable, and her fingers flutter up to her
mouth again. This time, one feels, she is actually going to chew all of
them, and swallow them too.*

KARAOKE SCREEN

Against montages of images with some relevance to the music, the

*words of a song come up on the lower half of the screen, in English,
sandwiched by Japanese.*

Your cheatin' heart
Will tell on you –

*At the same time, a male voice is singing, badly, the same words as
they march across the karaoke screens, darkening on cue.*

INT. KARAOKE CLUB. NIGHT
*The pan to find the singer shows what is obviously a different set to
the karaoke club seen at the start of Part 1 and visited later by*
DANIEL *in a poor state.*
*We are in Daniel Feeld's screenplay world, in other words. This is the
fictional karaoke bar.*
Finding the singer, 'PIG' MAILION, *a definite bull-necked heavy,
late forties, but definitely* not *the* ARTHUR MAILION *we have
hitherto seen and loathed.*
MAILION: (*Singing*)

– your cheatin' heart
Will make you weep –
(*Picture diminishing to – *)

STEENBECK AND SCREEN. CUTTING ROOM
On the sharp, bright little screen, the fictional MAILION *continues to
bellow so badly.*
MAILION:

But sleep won't come
The whole night through
Your cheatin' heart
Will tell on you –

INT. CUTTING ROOM. SOHO. DAY
DANIEL *has arrived. He is staring very intently at the Steenbeck
screen, clearly angry that his song ('Why Must I be a Teenager in
Love?') has been replaced by the Hank Williams original version of
'Your Cheatin' Heart'.*
BEN, ANNA *and, slightly awkwardly over his own shoulder at the
Steenbeck control lever,* IAN *are all watching* DANIEL *and not the
screen. And they are watching him with some anxiety.*
The song and picture have been continuing on the Steenbeck,

including the odd fade-out, fade-in exchange between MAILION *and*
Hank Williams.

STEENBECK AND SCREEN
As a front-on, tilted, head-masking big black umbrella lifts, like in a
theatrical cue, to reveal OLIVER MORSE, *the obsessive if patrician*
old man in Daniel's story.
OLIVER *'sings' the Hank Williams lines with a certain cruel, self-*
knowing relish.
OLIVER: (*Sings*)
> **But sleep won't come**
> **The whole night through**

EXTREME CLOSE-UP – DANIEL. CUTTING ROOM
The Steenbeck light from the bright screen on his face. And a
'Daniel' rage at his eyes.
OLIVER: (*Off, on Steenbeck*)
> **– your cheatin' heart**
> **Will tell on you**

INT. CUTTING ROOM. DAY
The other three still more concerned with Daniel's reaction than with
what is on the Steenbeck screen.

STEENBECK AND SCREEN
Now into the fictive *brasserie – everything has been continuous.*
> **– you'll toss around**
> **And call my name**
Widening for a moment, to lose the Steenbeck and plunge into this
fictive world.

CLOSE-UP – OLIVER MORSE AT TABLE. NIGHT
Alone, OLIVER *eats, the continuing music on brasserie speakers*
seeming not to trouble him at all.
> **– you'll walk the floor**
> **The way I do**
> **Your cheatin' heart**
> **Will tell on you!**
As the vocal gives way to a twangy musical interlude.

INT. CORRIDOR OUTSIDE SOHO CUTTING ROOM. DAY
NICK, *coming along, past several other cutting rooms where various shouts, shots, murmurs, backward-spooling dialogue and fragments of music are heard, from many different kinds of movie in the process of being edited.*
He is about to push open the door to his own cutting room when he hears the final twangs of the non-vocal music, from within the room.

CLOSE-UP – NICK
He smiles to himself briefly, and with a rueful twist. Then he seems to straighten his shoulders, set his jaw, and stride on in through the swing of the door into –

INT. CUTTING ROOM. SOHO. DAY
Just as IAN *stops the reel at the point where* OLIVER MORSE *is staring down into the wine glass with such a disturbing intensity, seeing the torpidly revolving flicker of the reflected ceiling fan on the surface of the wine.*
IAN: (*To* DANIEL – *cheerfully*) So? What ye think?
(*As though he doesn't know.*)
DANIEL: (*Splutter*) What do I think? What do I think? I'll tell you *this* and I'll say it *once* –
ANNA: (*Loudly, warningly*) Nick! Where've you *been*?
BEN: (*Agitated*) Lerry vate, old boy. And tad biming too, if you don't mind me saying so.
(DANIEL *turns and stares at* NICK.)
DANIEL: (*Severely*) Nick. Listen to me.
(*But* NICK *steps forward, with a warm smile, extending his hand. It looks like a real rapprochement – but it would also be entirely possible to interpret it as a suave sarcasm of the most arrogant and demeaning kind.*)
NICK: Daniel. Daniel, dear old chap.
DANIEL: (*Quivering*) What?
NICK: I've been thinking a hell of a lot about the different layers and resonances of your terrific screenplay – No! Really! And never more so, Daniel, than in the last hour.
(*Crack!* DANIEL, *fist swinging up out of nowhere, hits him smack in the eye, with enough force to make* NICK *stagger backwards.*

141

In staggering, a look of absolute shock on his face, NICK
*bumps backwards into a rack of film strips – and, clatter! Bang!
completes his fall on to the cutting-room floor, tangling in loops
of film.*)

ANNA: (*Screams*) Nick! Daniel!

(DANIEL *stands over fallen* NICK, *already ashamed, but also
not willing to yield.*)

DANIEL: Nick – that came across harder than I – Nick. Come
on. Get up. I'm sorry about that. But, look here, Nick –
listen, Nick – It's 'Why Must I be a Teenager in Love?'

CLOSE-UP – NICK

Head against the door, eye already beginning to puff, NICK *looks up
at* DANIEL *with utter goodwill and an almost beatific smile.*

NICK: You know, Daniel. I think that song 'Teenager in Love'
is *so* right in the wider context of the story –

INT. CUTTING ROOM. DAY

NICK *starts to get up. A startled and ashamed* DANIEL *gives him a
hand.*

DANIEL: Nick. My temper – it's – Nick. I apologize.

(*They look at each other.* NICK *smiles.*)

NICK: Me too, old bean.

(*The others are dumbstruck. Waa-waa music, almost – in self-
parodic comedy.*)

INT. THE REAL KARAOKE CLUB. DAY

*Empty. Waiting for the evening. All the complicated equipment off,
and all the many little karaoke screens blank.*

But, off, the sound of ringing telephone.

INT. OFFICE, OFF MAIN KARAOKE ROOM. WEST END KARAOKE/
HOSTESS CLUB. DAY

The real Arthur 'PIG' MAILION, *just coming in, his jacket draped
over his heavily muscular shoulders, grabs at the telephone.*

MAILION: (*Abrupt*) Yeah? Who? Wot you mean where I been?
That's – (*Sudden beam.*) Linda! Eh – went well, did it? Piece of
– (*Expression changing.*) What? (*Then*) What do you mean
they're on to me! (*Then, and looking around and about*) El-im-in-

ate me! You must be off your – Now you listen, girl – *listen!*
(*Snarl*) If you've dropped me in it, you're not going to like the
look of your face no more. Not one little bit. And that's a
promise.

INT. LIVING ROOM. LINDA'S FLAT. DAY
LINDA, *holding the phone, can see her own reflection in a mirror*
near at hand. She looks, sounds, frightened.
LINDA: (*Whining*) Don't say things like that, Arfur. Please.
P'raps we're dealing with the wrong class of people – ? I
only – (*She stares at –*)

CLOSE-UP – REFLECTION IN MIRROR
Her own face, scared, looking back at her. Going in closer, closer.
Pause.
LINDA'S REFLECTION: (*Near sob*) It's like – it's like – Oh, Arfur.
Don't. Don't, Arfur. It's like being in a – in some sort of
story. And it's gone all wrong.
(*Fade sound. A moment for her reflection, lips moving, but no*
words heard.
Fade picture.)

PART FOUR

EXT. POLICE CAR. LONDON STREETS. PRE-DAWN
Hurtling along largely empty streets, but its sirens screaming urban urgency.

EXT. DANIEL FEELD'S EDWARDIAN APARTMENT BLOCK. PRE-
DAWN/DAWN
The police car screaming past.

INT. DANIEL'S DESK. LIVING ROOM. PRE-DAWN/DAWN
Looking haggard, tired and stubble-chinned, as though he has been up all or most of the night, DANIEL *is hunched over his big but very littered desk, writing in long-hand on a fresh pad of paper in a small pool of light from his desk lamp. There is a stale third of a cup of undrunk coffee beside him.*
The police siren, receding, causes him to sit back a bit. A beat.
DANIEL: (*Derisive, to self*) 'Exterior stop police car comma pre hyphen dawn London streets stop.' (*Tiny pause.*) Screaming urban urgency.
   (*He gets up and goes to his windows, drawing open the heavy curtains, and looking down into the quiet side-street which is greying with dawn, and beyond – at his furthest horizon – the sky is streaking with reddish colour.*)

EXTREME CLOSE-UP – DANIEL
Looking as though he is seeing what must be familiar to him for the very first time. A moment. Then –
DANIEL: (*Very quietly, to self*) Good morning, Friday. (*Pause. He broods.*)

INT. DANIEL'S LIVING ROOM. DAWN
He turns from the window to go back to his desk. Half-way along he stops abruptly.
DANIEL: (*Loudly*) How many more Fridays?
   (*Then, as though the question has given new urgency, new life to everything, he returns at speed to his desk, instantly lighting a*

*cigarette as further fuel for the already crowded ashtray
squashed between piles of paper and the cup of stale coffee. He
writes –)*

CLOSE-UP – THE PAPER
Already to be seen –
I, DANIEL WALTER FEELD OF FLAT 26 STEDWOOD
HOUSE COLEDOWN STREET LONDON W1H 7DF,
HEREBY REVOKE ALL FORMER WILLS AND
TESTAMENTARY INSTRUMENTS MADE BY ME
AND DECLARE THIS TO BE MY LAST WILL.
And he is writing –
(1) I APPOINT MY LITERARY AGENT BENJAMIN
JOHN BAGLIN OF 40 SLOPEGATE STREET LONDON
W11 7DE TO BE EXECUTOR –

CLOSE-UP – DANIEL WRITING
With a little smile as he says aloud what he does not quite write –
DANIEL: (*At writing pad*) – and I declare that in this wy mill –
(*He stops, chuckles, drags on his cigarette, reaches unthinkingly
for his now rather scummy coffee and somehow manages to
knock the cup over, off screen.*)

INT. DANIEL'S DESK. DAWN
*The coffee cup on its side in its saucer, and spilt, cold black coffee
splattered across and into a loose, unevenly stacked pile of papers
(manuscripts, cuttings, folders, blank pages, jotted pages, etc. etc.).*
DANIEL: (*Roars*) Damn! Blast! And Bugger!
(*He pulls out his handkerchief, tries to dab and mop, but seems
only to make it worse. In the end, sighing and groaning
excessively, he has to lift up one whole pile, shaking off drops of
coffee, and then separate it out into its various constituents –
some stained, some not – on the floor beside the pile of virtual
reality and cryogenic books, etc., still where they were last seen.*)

CLOSE-UP – THE SCATTERED PAPERS ON FLOOR
And groaning DANIEL *stooped over them, putting dry ones to one
side, stained and/or dripping ones to the other. His hand stills. He
lifts up a particular sheet, which has a newspaper photograph and*

caption and some newsprint pasted on to it, with a scrawl of
handwriting alongside.
DANIEL: (*Slow hiss of escaping breath*) *Oh, my God –*

CLOSE-UP – THE PASTED SHEET
Showing a newspaper photograph of big, beaming ARTHUR 'PIG'
MAILION, *in evening dress, with or being presented to a member of*
the royal family, instantly recognizable – and preferably the Queen
Mother. The heading in newsprint says ' "PIG" MAILION SEES
THE JOKE!'
Alongside, beyond the couple of small columns of newsprint, a hand-
scrawled arrow and Daniel's handwriting, scrawled, saying HOW
ABOUT THIS 'GEEZER' FOR A CHARACTER! WORK ON
IT!

INT. DANIEL'S DESK. DAWN
DANIEL *puts the particular sheet back on to his desk, beside the*
telephone, with the air of a guilty man. He hesitates, looks at his
watch, starts to button a number, stops, hangs up, looks at his watch
again – Yes, it is too early to call people – and nevertheless dials
again.

CLOSE-UP – MATCHSTICK NOTRE-DAME
The great, wondrously intricate edifice looms, with the earnest, eager
and at these times childlike face of BENJAMIN JOHN BAGLIN
bobbing about behind and alongside it, three ready-shaved
matchsticks in his mouth, in the same kind of way a dressmaker on
the job might hold pins.
The telephone, of course, starts to ring, causing an instant flash of
anger at the bespectacled eyes. Ring – ring – ring.

INT. DANIEL'S DESK. DAWN/DAY
DANIEL *keeps the phone ringing, with determination, but jigging his*
foot and looking speculatively once more at –

CLOSE-UP – OLD PILE AT HIS FOOT
Virtual reality and cryogenics, from Daniel's point of view.

INT. BEN'S STUDY. DAWN/DAY

The primped and painted kimono-clad octogenarian, BEN'S
MOTHER, is opening the door in a very bad mood – the phone still
endlessly ringing.

BEN'S MOTHER: (*Shouting*) If you don't want to answer the
bloody phone, why don't you keep the bloody answer thing
bloody switched on!
(BEN, *who was already rising from his stooped position at his*
wondrous cathedral, takes the last of the three shaved
matchsticks from his mouth, in order to speak.)

BEN: (*Mildly*) Ma. Ma! Language.

BEN'S MOTHER: What do you think it does to my head! Eh!
Ring – ring – ring – bloody – ring!
(BEN *is crossing to his desk.*)

BEN: (*Mutters*) All right. All right. I was on a difficult bit of the
cross-lattice, Ma. (*Grabs phone, shouts ferociously*) Don't you
know the tucking fime!

INT. DANIEL'S LIVING ROOM. DAY

DANIEL *tries a soothing tone. At the same time, he reaches forward*
and buttons off the desk lamp.

DANIEL: (*Phone*) Now, now, Ben. It's Daniel. Ben! Stop it! No,
it's not *nearly* the dead of – I've just switched off my desk
lamp, Ben. And I had this feeling you'd be up and about
doing –

CLOSE-UP – BEN AT HIS DESK

BEN: (*Phone, instantly suspicious*) What you mean doing some
work? (*Relaxes.*) Scripts, yes. True, true. I *do* try to catch
up in these early hours. Awful lot of *words*, Daniel, and an
awful lot of those not particularly good, I'm afraid.
(*Mollified.*) Yes. I know. Still, have to earn a crust, dear boy
– (*Listens, stiffens.*) You *what?*
(*He frowns more as he listens again.*)

INT. DANIEL'S LIVING ROOM. DAY

DANIEL *swings a little in his revolving chair, confessing guilt.*

DANIEL: – and put it aside and thought no more about it. But,
yes, *mea culpa, mea culpa*, no doubt about it. It's in front of

me now, the clipping. This real bloke Mailion meeting the
Queen Mum at the Rothman Charity Gala. And, yes, even
the paper calls him 'Pig' Mailion – so, Jesus, I'm legally
speaking in a bit of a pickle – Yes?

INT. BEN'S STUDY. DAY
BEN, *on the phone, is flapping his arm and gesturing at his*
MOTHER, *who has stooped down about as far as she can get to
examine the matchstick edifice – far too close to the holy of holies for
Ben's comfort.*
BEN: (*Phone*) – signed the document, yes, so, yes, technically
     you are at fault, dear boy, but – (*Breaks off, covers phone
     with hand.*) Ma! Keep away from it! Do you hear me!
     Ma – !
BEN'S MOTHER: (*Airily*) Oh, cease. *Cease.*
     (*But she doesn't move, and* BEN *returns to the phone, but
     watching her all the time.*)
BEN: (*Phone*) Sorry about that. *Technically,* yes, I was saying,
     but I shouldn't worry about it moo tuch – (*Breaking off,
     agitated. He shouts*) Ma!

INT. 'CATHEDRAL' AREA. BEN'S STUDY. DAY
BEN'S MOTHER *is stooping as far forward as she can manage, a
wicked gleam in her eye, pretending to try out the pre-positioning for
the match she is holding. The genuinely shouted 'Ma!' makes her
hand jump and herself gasp.*

INT. DANIEL'S DESK. DAY
DANIEL *holds the phone away a little from his ear, at first puzzled
by the evident bellowing.*
DANIEL: (*Phone*) Ben – ?

INT. BEN'S STUDY. DAY
BEN'S MOTHER *is going back towards the door, wagging her finger
at him as he holds the lowered phone.*
BEN'S MOTHER: You'll get your just desserts for this, my lad,
     just you see if you don't. Frightening your poor old mother
     in such a barbarous, *barbarous* manner!
BEN: (*Soft tones*) Mother, I'm sorry – I didn't want to – but I

thought you might accidentally stumble into the – the –
(*But she has gone out of the door, with an imperious upturn of
the nose. He sighs, and lifts the phone again.*)
I don't often think it of you, Daniel, but you should
occasionally bless the last day you had any blood relatives.
Now – the important thing is to destroy and totally forget
the 'Pig' Mailion cutting or whatever it is. You never saw
it. You never heard his name. Never.

CLOSE-UP – DANIEL AT HIS DESK
DANIEL: (*Phone*) But I've obviously caused a lot of trouble, and
    if it leads to –

INT. BEN'S STUDY. DAY
BEN: (*Phone*) Anna's been useful for once. She went through
    the name mentions – (*Surprised*) Did I get that right? Mane
    nentions? Oh, thank goodness for that – And after all those
    truly amazing scenes yesterday evening, and the
    rapprochement – the *entente cordial* – well, she and I had a
    chittle lat, and *everything* can be sorted out, simply by –

INT. KITCHEN. BEN'S HOUSE. DAY
*The phone voice of her (in her opinion) errant son cannot be heard
from upstairs as* BEN'S MOTHER *poaches an egg, the toast in the
rack, and something half-way between a hummed tune and a cackle
plays about her vividly cherry-red lips.*

INT. DANIEL'S LIVING ROOM. DAY
DANIEL: (*Phone*) – your office before you so kindly take me to
    the hospital for the biopsies – well, they're the only two
    witnesses I can drum up at the moment. I haven't been to
    your office for donkey's –

CLOSE-UP – A TRAY. KITCHEN COUNTER. BEN'S HOUSE
*Next to the plate and the cup and the cutlery, the bright red-painted
false 'Glamour Girl' fingernails of a myriad-wrinkled, liver-spotted
old hand are placing a little pair of tweezers. In place, they receive an
extra little tap of blessing.*
Wider: BEN'S MOTHER *has a sweet smile, awaiting fulfilment.*

INT./EXT. NICK'S CAR. SOHO STREETS. DAY
Sporting a puffy black eye, the director NICK BALMER *is
approaching the small old heap of a block where the cutting rooms
are, making an early start. His eyes flick up to his interior mirror,
and he frowns slightly. He is not using the Rolls this morning: maybe
it's his wife's car!*

CLOSE-UP – NICK'S INTERIOR MIRROR
Showing a car close behind.

EXT. SOHO STREET. DAY
*Nick's car and a following car – with, at this time of the morning,
not much other traffic, so that when Nick's car makes a turn and the
other immediately does the same, it does look as though they are
sticking together.*

INT./EXT. FOLLOWING CAR. DAY
*There are two men in the car, one small and nasty, the other big and
nasty. The small one is called* SEAN *and the big one is called* DEAN,
the passenger. They are both in their mid-/late twenties.
DEAN: He's pulling in. Go past him a little bit, eh?
SEAN: (*Bored*) OK, Dean.
DEAN: I'll try and see what sort of place it is –

EXT. CUTTING ROOMS/VIEWING ROOMS BUILDING. SOHO. DAY
*An almost factory-like old building on the corner of the Soho street
and the wretched alley with the frequently raided bins. A newish sign
over the much older 'LICORICE WORKS' says Symonds Film
Facilities.*
NICK *is metering his car, and watches the other one go past, and
slow, with still only a mild interest or puzzlement.*

INT./EXT. INTERNAL MIRROR. FOLLOWING CAR. DAY
The reflection of NICK, *going into Symonds, without another look at
this car.*

INT. LINDA'S BEDROOM. DAY
*It is still early morning. This is the chintzy room with the compromised
mirror. The curtains are closed, the room in subdued lighting.*

Finding first LINDA, *in the bed, on her back, eyes wide open, staring up at the high ceiling. She is – if there is any greatly registerable expression – looking sadly thoughtful. She turns and lifts her head a little to look at –*

CLOSE-UP – ARTHUR MAILION IN BED
Fast asleep, with a soft wiffle of breathing, making the duvet rise and fall, rise and fall, covering the great half-buried hulk.

EXT. PAVEMENT. PARKED 'FOLLOWING CAR'. DAY
DEAN, *the big one, is ambling back from the direction of Symonds Film Facilities. He leans in to Sean's opened window, where the smaller man has been flicking cigarette ash and at least one cigarette-end on to the pavement. There are more people around now, more traffic, and much more sense of the day on the move.*

DEAN: There's a sort of Reception just inside the door, with a girl there, and so I –

SEAN: (*Interrupting*) What's she look like?

DEAN: (*Shrugs*) Nothing too much. Couldn't see her legs.

SEAN: (*Yawning*) That's the first place to look.

(DEAN *looks at his smaller colleague with some irritation.* DEAN *has a surprisingly high voice for a man of his size.*)

DEAN: Christ, Sean – you're always fucking tired. Yawning your head off.

SEAN: That's because I *do* know the first place to look.

DEAN: (*More irritated*) I said I wanted to know where Mr Mick Bamber was – And she said, No, there's no Bamber – She was looking down this list – Balmer – she says – Cutting Room 14 – Nick Balmer. No, no, I said, I got this thing to be signed and I can't afford no silly mistakes, can I? Lot she could care. Anyway, that's where he is. Cutting Room 14, whatever that is.

SEAN: It's where they make the sandwiches, Dean.

DEAN: What? Oh – shut up, willya! The point is –

SEAN: (*Looking at watch*) The point is Arthur'll fry our balls if we wake him before half-past eight. Let's just make sure that that's where the bugger is when we want to find him.

(DEAN *looks back down the street.*)

152

DEAN: Cutting Room 14. (*Half-beat.*) I bloody hate this sort of job. Don't you?

CLOSE-UP – PRETTY BEDSIDE CLOCK
Its hand about to tick quietly forward from eight twenty-nine, in the subdued lighting of a curtain-closed room.

INT. LINDA'S BEDROOM. DAY
LINDA, *still awake, now lies with her back to the whiffling* MAILION, *staring blankly at the pretty clock on the pretty bedside table.*
The telephone rings, making her start a little. It is on her side of the bed. As she lifts it, propping herself up a little, MAILION *makes dry-mouthed, lip-smacking sounds, and then a bullish groan.*
LINDA: (*Phone, slightly hesitant*) Yes? Who is it? (*Listens.*) How do you know 'e's 'ere? (*Listens.*) Oh. All right, then. 'Ang on.
(*She passes the phone across the bed to still grunting, very bleary and unappetizing* MAILION.)
'S for you, Arfur.
MAILION: Strewth – what's the bloody time? (*Into phone, snarling*) Whatchawant? Which one of you is – Dean? Yeah? Fuck me, I wish you two'd fucking sort your fucking selves out. I mean, you sound like fucking Minnie Mouse and you're as big as the side of bleed'n Buckingham Palace and wasname the fucking shrimp comes across like Paul Robeson wiv a bad cold!

INT./EXT. THE 'FOLLOWING' CAR. DAY
Still parked where it was, DEAN *on the carphone and little* SEAN, *staring ahead at a passing girl swaying alongside in front of the windscreen, still seems as though he wants to yawn and stretch.*
DEAN: (*Phone*) Sorry, guv. (*Comically tries to deepen his voice.*) Point is, guv, he's just up the road from us in this building and he's been there since ten to eight this morning – so it looks like he's going to stay there, don't it? And we –

INT. LINDA'S BEDROOM. DAY
LINDA, *in baby-doll-type nightie, has swung her long legs to the tuftily carpeted floor, and is shaking out multivitamins from a*

*labelled bottle into the palm of her hand. There is a glass of water on
the bedside table. She does not seem interested in the telephone
conversation, as heard from her end.*

MAILION: (*Phone*) But can you get in there? Can you get to
him? (*Listens.*) Well, then. That's what you do, right? Only
you don't say no names, no names at all, got it? And you
don't answer no questions, got it?

(*More awake, more vigorous,* MAILION *becomes aware of
shapely* LINDA *as, expressionless, she pads barefoot across the
tufty carpet towards the shower, passing the big mirror, into
which he is looking.*)

And I don't want nobody going too far. Hold off on the
last bit of bootin' and don't do it in the froat. Right?
(*Snarl.*) When? When you fink the coast is clear. When you
fink it's the right time, dickhead! (*Eyes gleam towards
direction* LINDA *has taken.*) Just make sure he gets the
fucking message!

(*Slams down phone, scratches the end of his nose, eyes still
where they were and how they were, then – loudly.*) Linda!
C'm here!

INT. CUTTING ROOM, ENTERING POINT OF VIEW. DAY
As seen through the opening door: NICK *diligent, if not altogether
with an editor's natural ease, at the Steenbeck, having clearly
reassembled a length of film.*

IAN: (*Entering, off screen*) Phew! Nick! Early, aren't we?

(NICK, *turning, reveals one hell of a shiner on his right eye.*)
Och, man! Your eye!

INT. CUTTING ROOM. DAY
NICK *gives a rueful grin, and almost goes to touch his eye, then
thinks better of it.* IAN *comes on into the cutting room, closing the
door.*

NICK: I must admit it's a bit sore – and I couldn't find my
damned sunglasses –

IAN: (*Sardonic*) Thought all film directors had them round their
neck on a silver chain.

NICK: But at least I can *see* out of it – My God, that mad bugger
really does pack a punch!

(IAN *already looking at the stilled picture on the Steenbeck screen.*)
IAN: (*Half-suspicious*) What have we here?

CLOSE-UP – STEENBECK SCREEN
The still frame shows the actor PETER *with* LINDA (*as 'Sandra'*) *in two-shot in a smart but vulgar living room. He is on a leather sofa, she standing.*

INT. CUTTING ROOM. DAY
NICK *half-spreads his hands. He always finds it difficult to make any kind of apology or admission of error. Yesterday evening, in this same room, had been an amazing exception, astounding everyone, including himself.*
NICK: I think I've been barking up the wrong skirt, Ian.
IAN: The lassie?
NICK: (*Drily*) Aye. The lassie.
IAN: You've been – reassembling?
NICK: (*Quickly*) Oh, only a rough go – that's for *you*, Ian. Of
    course. But only to show how it might be if I took the
    quote obsession unquote out of the lens, so to speak, and
    left it in Oliver's head – the old man's head – as Daniel no
    doubt meant.
    (IAN *is undoubtedly pleased – and very relieved. Momentarily –
    a rare sight too – he seems to shine with pleasure.*)
IAN: (*Beaming*) Well – let's have a gander, man.
NICK: Just take it back a bit – (*He works the lever.*)

STEENBECK AND SCREEN
Picture and speech move backwards for a few seconds.
PETER: nwod tis ?aylliw, ti tuoba esra elttil teews ruoy gniyrrow
    pots.

INT. CUTTING ROOM. DAY
NICK *gives way to* IAN *at the Steenbeck Controls, but both men lean in intently, watching the sharp little screen as the Reel restarts in the right direction.*
PETER: (*On screen*) Stop worrying your sweet little arse about –
    (*Picture widening to – *)

INT. 'SANDRA'S' (LINDA) FLAT. NIGHT

LINDA, *as 'Sandra', is standing in the middle of the room, troubled.*
PETER *is patting the leather beside him on the sofa, where he sits.*

PETER: (*Continuous*) – it, willya? Sit down. Come on! I know
we've had our differences, but I fought that was all sorted
out. Come on – give us a kiss, angel. I could do wiv some
affection, couldn't I?
(*But she doesn't move, twisting her hands anxiously. There is
more than a hint of an uncanny relationship between this,
Daniel Feeld's fictive world, and the real one that has been
going on around him. And also the suggestion that* LINDA *is not
above dipping into her own well-rehearsed lines when she needs
them outside the set.*)

LINDA: Peter. Listen – Pete, he's done a lot for me, enne? I
mean – I mean, I wouldn't be nuffink if he –

PETER: (*Cutting in*) That's a load of crap, and you know it.

LINDA: Yeah. But look what he give me. Look what he already
give me, that old bloke.

PETER: Number One. That's the first rule of life, pigeon.
Christ! Look after Number One and the rest'll look after
itself.

LINDA: (*Half-hostile*) Yeah.
(PETER *slaps the leather of the big white sofa, with macho
energy and enthusiasm.*)

PETER: Yes! Yes! Yes!

LINDA: But who is Number One, Peter?

PETER: (*Smiling*) You are, darling. *You*, Sandra.

LINDA: Not you – ?
(*Picture diminishes to –*)

STEENBECK AND SCREEN

Continuous with above. PETER *is staring up at her from the sofa.
His smile hardens and dies. She shifts, clearly now scared of him by
something that has happened in the* Karaoke *screenplay since we saw
her last with him (at the fictive brasserie).*

PETER: Sweetheart. Sweetheart. What are you trying to say?
Hey?

LINDA: (*Miserably*) I don't know.

INT. CUTTING ROOM. DAY

NICK *and* IAN *watching the little screen, each very still and concentrated, and – sounds off – the door to the cutting room opening. The Steenbeck screen is in view. Close-up of* PETER.

PETER: (*On Steenbeck*) What you mean, you don't fucking know?
>   (*Widening, on Steenbeck, to see* LINDA *half-turn away, wanting to cry.*)

LINDA: (*On Steenbeck*) All I know is – all I know, people keep trying to put words in my mouth.

NICK: (*To* IAN) Stop it there.

IAN: Right.
>   (*He looks up at* NICK, *approvingly. Both men are now so concentrated that they are completely unaware that someone has entered their domain.*)

NICK: It needs more subtlety than I can manage in the cutting, but –

IAN: Nick. It's a million times better, letting *him* so much more into –
>   (*Breaks off at the switch of* NICK*'s eyes, and* NICK*'s sudden frown.*)

NICK: Are you lost? Can I help you?
>   (*Wider: and big* DEAN, *little* SEAN *are standing there, staring at them.*)

SEAN: Which one of you is Nick Balmer?

NICK: Who are you? What's it to you?

SEAN: God. You've got a right shiner there.

DEAN: We have this thing to talk about with Mr Balmer.

NICK: What thing?

DEAN: Are *you* him – ?

NICK: And what if I am?

DEAN: Yeah. It *is* you. Wasn't sure from the car.

NICK: (*Twitching*) Car? What car?

SEAN: (*To* DEAN) Got a lot of questions, hasn't he? (*To* NICK) That how you got the black eye? Asking one too many?

NICK: Look – what's all this about?
>   (IAN *senses trouble beyond the normal irritations about intrusion into this self-contained little world. He wants to help.*)

IAN: We're very *busy*, y'know.

DEAN: (*To* NICK) It's about that unfinished business involving a young lady and her landlord, a Mr Beasley.
(NICK *stiffens. He looks from* DEAN *to* SEAN *to* DEAN, *and their faces look very set.*)
NICK: (*Slight croak*) Are you – um – is one of you Beasley?
SEAN: Oh, come on. Do we look like Beasleys?
NICK: (*Half-look at* IAN) This is not exactly the place to talk –
IAN: If it's private, I'll –
NICK: (*To* DEAN, *then to* SEAN) No, no. But – um – there isn't very much to talk about anyway, is there?
DEAN: Mr Beasley seems to think so.
SEAN: And *we* think so too.
NICK: There's a – Ian? Isn't there – A sort of empty office space or something at the end of –
IAN: Top end of corridor from the main door, yes. It's only got a wee table and a couple of chairs –
(DEAN *gives a big smile, for the first time. And then sounds suddenly amiable, even reassuring.*)
DEAN: That sounds just the right sort of place – and private too. (*To* NICK) You're quite right, sir. Being private is better. And there isn't all that much to say.
SEAN: (*Smirks*) Write it on a postcard, you could.
(NICK *starts to move out, addressing* IAN *as he does.*)
NICK: You can deconstruct the brasserie stuff as a start, Ian – in the way you always wanted, OK?
IAN: (*Pleased*) Sure, Nick.

INT. CUTTING ROOM. DOOR. CORRIDOR. DAY
As NICK *comes out, with* DEAN *and* SEAN, ANNA *is opening the doors at the other end of the corridor. They are walking away from her, to the 'spare office'.*
ANNA: (*Calls*) Nick!
(*All three men stop, and all three turn.*)
NICK: (*Calls to* ANNA) I'm just going to the spare office down here – Ian's there. We've made big decisions!
ANNA: Good! OK – thanks.
NICK: See you in a minute.
(*The three walk on,* SEAN *and* DEAN *looking at the mostly closed cutting room doors as they pass.*)

INT. CUTTING ROOM. DAY
IAN *already at work as* ANNA *comes in.*
ANNA: He was here early, wasn't he?
IAN: (*Chuckles*) I tell you – early and *bright* – The man has seen
the light! An overnight conversion. A *revelation.* There's no
other word for it.
ANNA: (*Pleased*) A smack in the eye can work wonders now and
again!
(*Abrupt cut.*)

CLOSE-UP – NICK. 'SPARE OFFICE'
Crack! as a big fist smashes into his open-jawed surprise.

INT. 'SPARE OFFICE'. DAY
As plain as IAN *had described, dustily capable of conversion to a
cutting room but without any of the heavy equipment. Without
warning, it seems, and without a word, and totally matter-of-fact
in expression and action,* DEAN *and* SEAN *instantly lay into* NICK,
*with punches to the head and body and kicks to the shins and
knee.*

INT. TREATMENT TABLE. RADIOLOGY ROOM. ST
CHRISTOPHER'S HOSPITAL. DAY
*A needle making its final, sudden biopsy-punch into Daniel's exposed
torso, in what seems to be slap in the middle of his stomach, above
the navel.* DANIEL *makes a single, half-gasp of a wince.*

INT. 'SPARE OFFICE'. DAY
NICK, *without a chance, gasps and yelps under the swift but utterly
relentless onslaught, then taking a final, crunching knee in groin.*

INT. TREATMENT TABLE. HOSPITAL. DAY
The CONSULTANT *is the same man we saw in the ward with*
DANIEL *in Part Two.*
CONSULTANT: (*With a smile*) Now for the liver.
DANIEL: Oo. Ta.
CONSULTANT: (*Broader smile*) Take in some breath. (*As* DANIEL
breathes in.) Not quite so much. (DANIEL *letting some out.*)
That's it. Hold it! One little –

(Punch! The biopsy needle makes its final plunge into Daniel's exposed right side, just below the ribs. Gasp!)

CLOSE-UP – NICK. 'SPARE OFFICE'
The final, sickening knee in the groin has brought NICK *hard down, doubling up on all fours, all but vomiting with the excruciating pain of it.*
SEAN, *the smaller and somehow more vicious one, grabs a hank of Nick's hair and lifts his face up, hissing venomously close into it –*
SEAN: That was the message, old son. The next one will be a
    fucking sight worse, if there is a next one. So *listen –*
NICK: *(Gurgle. Gasp.)*
    (SEAN *gives the hank of hair in his hand a nasty shake and jerk.)*
SEAN: *Listen!*
NICK: *(Choking)* I'm – listening –
SEAN: Call off your dogs. You leave a certain party out of it.
    Understand?
    (NICK *doesn't understand – but is in no condition to say so.*
    Another cruel tug –)
    Understand?
NICK: *(Gasps)* Yes.

INT. 'SPARE OFFICE'. DAY
DEAN *is already over by the door, listening for other sounds, alert for other possibilities, as* SEAN *lets go of Nick's hair.* NICK *collapses flat out on the bare floorboards as he is released. They look at him, then look at each other, and as though by a barely discernible nod to each other, leave.*

INT. CUTTING ROOM. CORRIDOR. DAY
DEAN *closes the door to the 'spare office' at the end of the corridor with an oddly quiet delicacy, rather as one might take leave of an elderly but ailing relative.*
As they walk back along the corridor, side by side, seemingly completely unruffled and at ease, they begin to react, at first startled and then with increasing interest, to the gunshot, the screaming car tyres, the woman's bloodcurdling scream, a madly barking or rabid dog, a gasp-asp! of sexual orgasm, and a growing police siren, at which, comically –

CLOSE-UP – SEAN AND DEAN. PASSAGE
The vicious pair look sidelong at each other in a micro-second of alarm.

INT. CUTTING ROOMS. CORRIDOR. DAY
Before proceeding safely on past a reassuring clip-clop of horses, a snatch of 'In the Good Old Summertime', a sudden laugh, and a backward-spooled male expletive delivered at full blast (and which unfit people may even try to decipher!), yelling rekcufrehtom! – all spilling out into the long, drab passage from this or that partly opened or opened door of the dozen or so busy cutting rooms.

INT./EXT. FRONT DOOR. HAMMERSMITH HOUSE. DAY
SANDRA – *the real one, of course – opening the door with a who-the-'ell-are-you? expression peculiar to her kind to see* BEN BAGLIN *standing there, a twinkle behind his glasses, a box under his arm, and a briefcase in the other hand.*
BEN: Miss Sollars? Is it?
SANDRA: (*Suspicious*) Ye-ah – ?
BEN: (*Ingratiating*) Ah, yes. As lovely as Daniel promised you'd be – I've –
SANDRA: (*Interrupting*) Daniel wasname? Well. He's a bleed'n fief, you tell him from me! He's pinched something of mine right from under my bloody nose!
BEN: The gun. Yes.
(*She stares at him. He keeps smiling.*)
SANDRA: What do *you* know about it? What's going on? Who are you, anyway? *I'm busy.*
BEN: I'm Ben, Ben Baglin. I'm Daniel's agent.
SANDRA: 'Is what?
BEN: Well – I sort of – look after his interests and I –
SANDRA: Deliver his messages.
(*Ben's smile cannot but falter a little.*)
BEN: No, it's not quite like – (*Beam.*) But in this case yes. I have various things for you and much good news as well as a present for your mear dother.
SANDRA: (*Blank*) Me what?
BEN: Your – (*Falters*) – A *gift*. From Daniel. Your – mother?
SANDRA: Oh! Me mum!

BEN: And good, good, *good* news!
>   (*She looks at him beaming and slightly twitching there, and her basic warmth floods out again.*)

SANDRA: (*Laughs*) What you doin' standing out here, then? Eh? Come on!
>   (*She leads the way in.*)

INT. PRIVATE ROOM. HOSPITAL. DAY
Long back from his double biopsies, DANIEL *is sitting up in bed, using the bed trolley as a bookstand, reading a fairly large, 'futuristically' designed, gaudily coloured and shiny paperback book called* Mondo 2000: A User's Guide to the New Edge. DANIEL *is reading with obvious interest and intention. A moment, then his 'reading' becomes available to us –*

DANIEL: (*Over, reads*) '– No one can know what will happen from one moment to the next in a cyberspace, not even the spacemaker. Every moment gives every participant an opportunity to create the next event.' (*Out loud*) Pooh. (*Mutter*) Do it all the time! *Sorry* – ?
>   (*The last word because a* NURSE *is suddenly beside him, to take his blood pressure.*)

NURSE: (*Smiling*) Blood pressure.

DANIEL: But you did it just a –

NURSE: Every quarter of an hour for the first few hours. Make sure you're not bleeding inside.

DANIEL: (*Looking around*) Well, I am bleeding inside.
>   (*She laughs, continuing with her task. He pulls his eyes back to the book.*)

DANIEL: (*Over, reads*) 'Whereas film is used to show a reality to an audience, cyberspace is – '
>   (*A thermometer goes into his mouth.*)

CLOSE-UP – PAGE 264, THE BOOK
Even the pages within have modernistic design.
>   CYBERSPACE IS USED TO GIVE A VIRTUAL BODY, AND
>   A ROLE, TO EVERYONE IN THE AUDIENCE.
Dissolving –

CLOSE-UP – COLOURED PICTURE ON JIGSAW BOX
DANIEL: (*Over, as in reading; it is continuous text*) 'Print and
radio tell. Stage and film show. Cyberspace embodies –'
(*The picture is of Notre-Dame in Paris.*)

INT. HAMMERSMITH HOUSE. LIVING ROOM. DAY
SANDRA'S MOTHER *has been holding the box, thoroughly scanning
the picture of what is to be made up, and is apparently pleased.*
MRS HAYNES: It's not got a lot of sky in it –
BEN: Oh, dear. I'm –
SANDRA: (*To* BEN) No, no. That's *good*.
(SANDRA *sits opposite her mother at the table, leaning forward
to watch her fondly, as a mother might a toddler examining a
nice gift.* BEN *hovers, standing, somewhere between them, still
holding his briefcase.*)
MRS HAYNES: And it's a very nice building whatever it is.
BEN: (*Pleased*) Yes. Isn't it! It's Notre-Dame in Paris. (*Proudly*)
I chose it when Daniel asked me to get a jigsaw to –
(*He trails off because* MRS HAYNES *has no interest in what he is
saying, and is clattering out all the jigsaw pieces from the box on
to the bare-topped table. He also realizes that* SANDRA *is now
studying him, and wondering what's afoot.*)
SANDRA: Made of *wood*. That's not one of yer cheap ones, then.
What's this Daniel up to? Eh?
BEN: I'm only here as his – his representative and I'm not sure
myself of –
SANDRA: (*Cutting in*) I mean that fing might be wood and all
that and Mum's pleased. (*To* MRS HAYNES) Entcha?
MRS HAYNES: (*Absorbed*) What?
SANDRA: *Pleased*. Entcha?
MRS HAYNES: Don't know yet, do I?
SANDRA: (*To* BEN) Only it ent worth what he took. You tell him
I want it back! *Or else!*
BEN: (*Agitated*) Do you mind if I dit sown?
SANDRA: If you want. (*Works it out.*) Oh, sit – yes – sorry. Sit
down. (*But she looks an 'old-fashioned look' at him, comically,
as puzzled that someone could speak in such a fashion as she
would be if his nose were made of gingerbread.*)
BEN: (*Sitting*) Thank you very much. Now – (*Takes up and opens*

briefcase.) I've been instructed by Daniel to show you this, and to read some particular part our loud to you. (*He is taking out a folded 'tube' of thick paper, a document about A4 size when flat.*)

SANDRA: What is it?

(*Ben peers over his glasses at her for a moment, adjusts his spectacles, holds open the document, and reads the opening paragraph in a deliberately inflated 'lawyer'-like voice.*)

BEN: (*Reads*) I, Daniel Walter Feeld of Flat 26 Stedwood House Coledown Street London WIH 7DF, hereby revoke all former wills and testamentary –

EXTREME CLOSE-UP – SANDRA

As incomprehension yields to a wide-eyed half-understanding, BEN *continuing, off.*

BEN: (*Continuous*) – instruments made by me and declare this to be my last will.

INT. SANDRA'S LIVING ROOM. DAY

Ben has stopped reading. He looks at her, quiet and still. She looks at him. MRS HAYNES *clacks wooden pieces. A moment. Then –*

MRS HAYNES: (*Triumphant*) There! I've got three of 'em joined up already! (*Looks at* BEN.) Oh, this is a good 'un! A real good 'un!

BEN: (*Looking at* SANDRA) I'm very glad.

(SANDRA *has not taken her gaze off him for a moment. Then, to another click and clack on the table, she is suddenly able to speak.*)

SANDRA: You're saying – you're saying that – what you got there is that bloke's will?

BEN: Correct.

SANDRA: Why? *What for?*

BEN: Because you are to be a beneficiary, on certain conditions.

(*She 'understands', but not quite, and doesn't want to get 'caught' or made to feel a fool – and so she half-laughs and half-frowns, if such a thing is possible.*)

SANDRA: What you talking about?

MRS HAYNES: Look, Sanny – they fit so nice. Better than that cardboard stuff, ennit?

SANDRA: (*Distracted*) Yes, Mum! Course it is. (*Eyes still on* BEN.) You mean, he's *leaving* me something? Is that what you're saying?
(BEN *seems, all at once, to be subdued and rather fidgety.*)

BEN: Yes.

SANDRA: (*Fierce*) *Why?*
(BEN *lightens, a little.*)

BEN: And I thought the first thing you'd ask would have been, 'Mow huch?'

SANDRA: (*Blank*) Wha – ?

BEN: (*Losing the lightness again*) Look, I have to say in all honesty that everything, *every single thing* about this whole situation, troubles me a great deal. In the first place, I find that what Dan is proposing to do is so odd that it would certainly be challenged in the courts if he had any family. And in the –

SANDRA: Has he? Got family?

BEN: (*Sighs*) No.

SANDRA: No wife, no kids, nothing?

BEN: No. His parents died fairly young. His brother – and it was his *twin* brother, by the way – well, he committed suicide five or six years ago –

SANDRA: Gawd.

BEN: And although he was once about to be married, something dreadful happened just a week or so wefore the bedding – I'm hardly sure what. He never lets one talk about it.

SANDRA: Christ.

BEN: He's left some – ah – legacies here and there, including to my – ah – my unworthy self – very very generous – but – ah – as for the bulk of his estate – and Dan's built up a considerable – um – high-earner over the years – well, as to that, two-thirds he proposes to throw away by donating the capital and its income to a cryogenic organization – (*Looks at her.*) Freep deeze. (*At her comic blankness, he picks up his hapless spoonerism, and smacks his own cheek rather harder than he intended.*) Deep freeze!
(*But the slap! sound has made* MRS HAYNES *look up from her wooden pieces in fascination, and* SANDRA *gapes, comically.*)

SANDRA: *Whatchewdothatfor?*

BEN: (*Twitch*) I have this little impediment that occasionally makes me reverse successive consonants.

SANDRA: (*Comically, no idea*) Oh dear. (*Then*) So he's going to leave a lot to some bleed'n deep-freeze outfit, is he?
(BEN, *recovering, laughs.*)

BEN: The sort that freezes human bodies and works on high technology at absolute zero temperatures. It was something his brother Christopher had been working on. That's the link, I suppose. (*Sudden switch.*) The point is that the other third he proposes to put into trust for the benefit of you and your mother. We're talking just short of one million pounds here.

SUDDEN CLOSE-UP – SANDRA

Her hand flies to her mouth, as though to catch hold of a gasp, and her eyes almost literally pop!

SUDDEN CLOSE-UP – MRS HAYNES

Comically – and with unexpected shrewdness –

MRS HAYNES: Ah, yes – but how bloomin' *old* is he? How long's he got, sir?

INT. SANDRA'S LIVING ROOM. DAY

BEN: (*Happily*) *That* none of us knows. And there *are* certain conditions.

SANDRA: (*Deflating*) You mean – there's a catch?
(BEN *nods, even more pleased.*)

BEN: (*Beams*) A bumbling stock.

INT. BRASSERIE. NIGHT

A segment that has been seen before, but overly favouring LINDA. *Now it is shown with more wide and many more two-shots, making it feel different. Cutting room capers. 'Peter' and 'Sandra' (*LINDA*) have not long arrived at their drinks-only table.*

LINDA: Don't want to do it with him at all, fanks very bleed'n much!

PETER: I mean, Christ – I mean it's not as though you haven't done it often enough before.

LINDA: (*Flashes*) Whatchewmean – ?
(*Picture diminishing to –*)

STEENBECK AND SCREEN
But this time more consistently close on PETER *and not, as before, a
big close-up on* LINDA *held while he was speaking.*
PETER: Oh, come on, angel. You've had more bonks wiv more
blokes than –

INT. CUTTING ROOM. DAY
Peter's face filling the Steenbeck screen as IAN *and* ANNA *watch –
but somehow not so intently as is normal in a cutting room.* ANNA, *in
particular, is darting glances at the door, and* IAN *seems troubled.*
PETER: (*On screen, continuous*) – I've had bleed'n Weetabix.
LINDA: (*In two-shot, screen*) Now look! I've hardly ever never
done it for the – No! Not for money!
(IAN *stops the spool. Looks up at* ANNA.)
IAN: I didn't like the look of them.
ANNA: Perhaps I'd better go and see?
IAN: I – well, it might be important business of some kind,
though I – (*Stops, rises.*) I'll come with you.

INT. 'SPARE OFFICE'. DAY
In the sparse, closed room, NICK *lies semi-conscious and well
bloodied. He seems, at some point, to have dragged himself half-
under the single, bare table in the room, before passing out again.
The door opens. With shock and incredulity,* IAN *and* ANNA *rush
towards him, each calling his name.*

CLOSE-UP – NICK
*As they gingerly prop him up a little, he spits out some blood from his
damaged mouth and broken teeth.*
NICK: (*Gasps*) Tidy.
ANNA: Nick! Oh, Nick! We've got to get you to hospital –
NICK: (*Louder*) Tidy.
IAN: What are you trying to say, Nick?
(NICK *makes a great effort, focuses on him.*)
NICK: Got to – tidy me up. Seeing *Ruth.*

EXT. HAMMERSMITH BROADWAY OR NEAR. DAY
*Ben's smart BMW, negotiating alternate streams of traffic, is cut up
in some potentially nasty situation by a car or van, so that* BEN *has
to brake fiercely.*

INT./EXT. BEN'S CAR. STREETS. DAY
BEN *gesticulates dangerously and shouts his rage.*

BEN: *Hoad rog!*

> (SANDRA *sitting beside him, gives him a comical, covert look.
> She can't work these speech distortions out at all, not one little
> bit.* BEN *quickly calms, however, and gives her a rueful little
> smile.*)

BEN: (*Again*) I'm afraid people – or, rather *men* – become
altogether a different kind of animal when on the Queen's
Highway. Mmm?
> (*Tiny pause.*)

SANDRA: (*Comically*) Yeah. (*Then, changing tone*) We didn't talk
for very long. I mean, I don't know the bloke, hardly at all.
This is *weird*. Ennit?

BEN: (*Heavily*) Yes. It is, rather.

SANDRA: Is this the visiting hours? I mean, they'll let me in to
where he is?

BEN: He has his own room.

SANDRA: Blimey.

BEN: So he can receive visitors at any time.

SANDRA: He's not *really* going to die. (*Anxiously*) Is he? Not
reeely.

BEN: I jolly well hope not!

SANDRA: (*Genuinely*) So do I! He seemed a real nice bloke. A
bit – well, sort of – (*Changes her mind, was going to say
'screwy'.*) No. A *nice* bloke. But what's he got then? What's
wrong with him?

BEN: That's what they're establishing. They're finding out. It –
oh dear, oh dear. I'm afraid it *does* seem rather serious.

EXTREME CLOSE-UP – SANDRA
*She gives a little nod and a little frown, dealing with suddenly
conflicting thoughts – and her continued bewilderment. She looks out
of the window at the bright day.*

168

INT. CUTTING ROOM. DAY

NICK, *very battered, is sitting on the mobile stool-like chair that is normally directly in front of the Steenbeck being tenderly powdered by* ANNA, *who has her full make-up kit and a box of tissues out on the flat deck of the editing machine. The Steenbeck is switched off.*

ANNA: (*To a wince*) I'm trying to be as gentle as I can, Nick.

NICK: (*Grimacing*) I know, I know –

ANNA: But you're still going to look pretty dreadful, you know.

NICK: I just – if it could be toned down a bit –

(IAN *comes through the door, with a paper bag full of chemist's things and toiletries.*)

IAN: You don't even know for sure that you haven't broken anything –

NICK: (*In a croak*) No. I haven't. No.

IAN: And if you *don't* see the doctor, and *won't* inform the police, then you're going to be ver-r-ry compromised when it comes to the film insurance people.

(*He is pulling out some sunglasses with different kinds of frames, lotion, sticking plasters, etc. from the bag.*)

ANNA: (*To* IAN) If you could put one of those small round plasters just here – see? –

IAN: Sure.

NICK: I'm very grateful to you. Both.

IAN: (*Mordant*) Ooch, you'll be needing more than face powder and sticking plasters, man. She'll think you've been hit by a lorry.

NICK: (*Brightening*) That's a good idea.

IAN: What?

NICK: That's what I'll tell her.

(IAN *and* ANNA *exchange glances as they tend to him.*)

INT. DANIEL'S ROOM. HOSPITAL. DAY

The same CONSULTANT *who had quipped with* DANIEL *in the public ward is carefully registering a reaction and carefully answering a question that has just been delivered.*

CONSULTANT: Time is always the most – any such prognosis, oddly enough, is based on – well, on *precedent*, on what usually happens.

DANIEL: (*Smiles*) We always need to look into the past to read the future. That's why I've got a crick in my neck.

(*The* CONSULTANT *is looking at him carefully, and sees that* DANIEL *is quite relaxed and, in what might almost be described as a perverse way, even serene.*)

CONSULTANT: Well, you should certainly think in terms of getting your affairs in order.

DANIEL: Yes. Thank you.

(*Small pause. The* CONSULTANT *examines his own hands.*)

CONSULTANT: And if there is anything of especial urgency that you've been wanting to do – ?

DANIEL: I am about to write a screenplay. About virtual reality and cryogenics. A frozen head, you know – (*Little dab of poison*) medical student type, I suppose one might say.

(*The* CONSULTANT *nods approval at the gibe, but –*)

CONSULTANT: And how long does it take you? This scribble-scribble-scribble?

(*Tiny pause.* DANIEL *looks at him carefully, then answers with deliberation.*)

DANIEL: About twelve weeks, and a bit. I always reckon to give myself eighty-eight days.

(*Tiny pause.*)

Any chance of putting the final full stop in place?

(*Tiny pause.*)

I mean, there's not all that much point in getting, say, two-thirds of the way through. I don't get paid per line or per page, more's the pity.

(*Tiny pause.*)

CONSULTANT: I couldn't guarantee that you would be able to finish.

DANIEL: I see. Perhaps something a bit shorter. With a nice and easy plot. There's an old favourite, for example, about who it is you would kill and help out humanity if you had, say, only, say – (*Looking closely at* CONSULTANT) eight weeks and a bit, more or less, to go –

CONSULTANT: Yes. I've often wondered who *I'd* execute if in such a circumstance. Apart from the Secretary of State for Health, of course.

DANIEL: (*Solemn agreement*) Of course.

CONSULTANT: Yes. I would say that such a plot was – *about right.*

DANIEL: (*As though still debating something else*) Mmm. Couple
of months. Yes?
(*They look at each other. The pause lengthens. Then –)*
CONSULTANT: I'm sorry.
(DANIEL *nods, digests, then starts to laugh: not in any way
hysterical or immoderate, but a genuine laugh, infectious enough
to make the* CONSULTANT *at first shift in his chair a little
uneasily, but then begin to smile.*)
CONSULTANT: (*Again*) Why are you laughing?

CLOSE-UP – DANIEL
DANIEL: I don't honestly know, to tell you the truth. I mean,
it's not *funny*. (*Laughs*) When all these dreadful pains
began – I mean, at the same time as they started to burn
me up – I was kind of, well, going a bit dippy. I thought
that a story I had written had somehow *got out* into the
world – like a contagious disease. My words, my script,
wandering about out there – right in front of me. But no.
They aren't, thank God. There's been another story going
on all the time. *This* one. The one I didn't know about.
(*Half laughs*) It's just that – well, the *ending* is sooner than I
thought. (*He falls silent, no longer with a smile.*)

INT. DANIEL'S ROOM. HOSPITAL. DAY
The CONSULTANT *leans forward, hands clasped, somehow knowing
that* DANIEL *is at this very moment steering himself around a
dangerous bend. He gives* DANIEL *a gentle prompt, so to speak.*
CONSULTANT: We're all in a kind of drama, perhaps. In which
each one of us is centre-stage – ?
DANIEL: (*Stirring, smiles again*) I always used to tell myself a
story when I was in pain or in fear as a child, and make
believe I was in the middle of a kind of book – the one
bright book! – in which there was a shape, a meaning, and
a good ending.
CONSULTANT: (*Half-rueful sigh*) Yes.
DANIEL: Yes. Where I can tidy up all the loose bits and bobs,
tie up all the loose ends, find the *shape* of it – Yes. That's
what I'll do. I can also do a damned good imitation of Bing
Crosby, by the way. (*Looks at him, steadily.*) I'm back in

charge of my own story. I can take control of it now. I've got it back into my own hands and my own words. I know what to do now.

(*The* CONSULTANT *nods briefly, smiles briefly, rises. They do not shake hands.*)

CONSULTANT: (*Quietly*) Good man.

(*The* CONSULTANT *leaves the room and carefully closes the door. Slowly settle on –*)

CLOSE-UP – DANIEL IN BED

His half-smile dies. His face goes momentarily blank. Then suddenly contorts –

INT. DANIEL'S ROOM. HOSPITAL. DAY

DANIEL *hurls the* Mondo 2000 *book he had been reading across the room – slap! – straight at the closed door.*

DANIEL: (*Yell*) Starting to throw things! (*And then he begins to laugh again.*)

INT. CORRIDOR. PRIVATE WING. ST CHRISTOPHER'S HOSPITAL. DAY

Shining glass double-doors swing open and closed as BEN *and* SANDRA *come through, and into a fairly long, wide, well-refurbished and smartly tiled corridor, with the doors of private rooms off it.*

BEN *slaps along flat-footed, whereas Sandra's high heels again make their insistent, strangely evocative tchick-tchack-tchick on the hard and shiny flooring. She is looking about, approvingly.*

SANDRA: Gawd. What money can do, eh?

BEN: (*Slightly shamefacedly*) Yes.

(*She laughs contentedly and makes a meaningless automatic remark, as though by rote.*)

SANDRA: The roo' of all evil.

(*At virtually the same time, the* CONSULTANT *passes them in the opposite direction, coming from Daniel's room. He cannot quite stop himself giving* SANDRA *a quick once-over of purely sexual appreciation, and, when past, even allows himself one swift look back over his shoulder.*)

INT. DANIEL'S DOOR. HOSPITAL CORRIDOR. DAY
BEN *and* SANDRA *come to his door, which has* DANIEL FEELD *in big letters on its slot.* BEN *seems suddenly nervous.*
BEN: In you go, then.
    (*And, oddly, so does she.*)
SANDRA: No, you first.
    (BEN *opens the door with a little frown, beginning to get one of his small flurries of agitation. He looks at* SANDRA *reprovingly.*)
BEN: Gadies before lentlemen.
DANIEL: (*Off screen*) I'd recognize that voice anywhere! Come in! Come!

EXT. THE ITALIAN RESTAURANT. SOHO. DAY
Lunchtime Soho swirl in the streets, and the sleek Rolls-Royce seen conveying NICK *in Part One – and almost flattening* DANIEL *– edges its way slowly to the kerbside through a sudden buzz of messenger motorbikes.*

INT. ITALIAN RESTAURANT. DAY
Height of lunch-hour business, and virtually every table occupied amidst the yammer-yammer of conviviality that always sounds too much in radio plays. Camera moving through, seeking, seeking, and then finding –

CLOSE-UP – NICK BALMER
So it's clearly not NICK *in the Rolls now edging to kerb outside. Nor is he at 'the usual' table he shared the day before with* LINDA. *He is in the extreme, odd-angled corner furthest from the entrance, next to the constantly swinging door to the busy kitchen – the least desirable or last allocated one, but on* this *occasion chosen deliberately. Because* NICK *still looks spectacularly damaged. He is wearing the largest of the dark glasses, and his face is matted with Anna's face powder, tempering the purplish hues of his beaten flesh. But even the cosmetic 'improvements' and the little circles and strips of plaster cannot in any really meaningful way hide the fact that he looks a beaten, battered man. He is sipping mineral water with a trembling hand.*

INT./EXT. RESTAURANT. DAY

RUTH, *Nick's aristocratic wife, entering from a gleam of Rolls-Royce outside, looks around the crowded restaurant, and hovers momentarily, unable to see* NICK. LUIGI, *the head waiter, ingratiatingly pounces – maybe he has glimpsed the grand vehicle outside.*

LUIGI: Signora. Please. I help you?

RUTH: Balmer table. Nicholas Balmer. (*She barely acknowledges* LUIGI, *not out of hauteur, but simply from the way she was brought up.*)

LUIGI: Ah, si, *si*! – Please. This way, Signora. I'm afraid – (*Stops himself.*) This way please.

(RUTH *registers him now, aware that he has checked something he had been about to say. But then she sees* NICK. *And stops dead. For the briefest moment it is as though she is not sure that it even is* NICK. *And then she rushes forward, immediately making* LUIGI *redundant. He goes towards the table, and then decides it is better to wait a while.*)

RUTH: Good Lord. Nick. What on earth –?

INT. NICK AND RUTH'S CORNER. RESTAURANT. DAY

NICK *tries a passable smile of rue. His speech is affected by his swollen mouth.*

NICK: Delivery van. Outside the cutting rooms. It backed so close up this little space as I very stupidly tried to cross the same space on foot – It was only a couple of inches – but – bam!

RUTH: Nick – oh, you look *dreadful*. Are you sure there's nothing broken?

NICK: Nothing.

RUTH: But, darling, you should at least be lying down, or – Really, you shouldn't have come!

NICK: I wanted you to come, Ruth. That's why I rang you so early from the flat –

RUTH: And you didn't sound quite *right*, then. Nick. What is it?

NICK: I so badly wanted you to come. And I especially wanted you to come *here*.

(*She half-looks around, mildly surprised.*)

RUTH: Why *here*? I've never been here before, or –

NICK: No. But *I* have.

(*Something in the way his swollen mouth says this makes her look at him with a different sort of attention.*)

RUTH: Nick?

NICK: I've been here – oh, fifteen, sixteen times – at least – with young Miss Langer.

(*The slightest quiver on Ruth's face.*)

RUTH: Linda?

NICK: (*Nods*) Linda Langer. My star. Or, at least, my leading lady.

(*He looks at her. She looks at him.*)

RUTH: Go on.

NICK: When you've ordered.

RUTH: Nick –

NICK: (*Firmly*) Order first. Please.

(*And like magic, as ever, the* WAITER *is there, little pad in hand. She doesn't even look at the menu.*)

RUTH: Oh, melon – No. No starter –

WAITER: (or LUIGI): No starter?

RUTH: No. I'll have Pollo Milanese and a green salad.

WAITER: Very good. Vegetables? Zucchini or –

RUTH: (*Still looking at* NICK) No. That's it. Thank you.

WAITER: Thank you, signora. Signor?

NICK: No starter.

WAITER: No starter?

NICK: (*Crisply*) No. I'll have Fegato alla Veneziana. Some zucchini fritte. That's it.

(*They are both looking straight at each other, and are unaware of the waiter's murmurings of withdrawal. There is wine already on the table: red Tignanello. Suddenly, he takes his dark glasses off and lays them beside his bread plate.*)

CLOSE-UP – RUTH
A gasp of reaction as two blue-black swellings protrude around his eyeballs.

EXTREME CLOSE-UP – NICK
Twisting his swollen mouth into a wry grin.

NICK: The van was delivering cans of my own film. I've been run over by my own story.

INT. NICK AND RUTH'S CORNER. RESTAURANT. DAY
RUTH: (*Suddenly*) I don't believe you.
NICK: No?
RUTH: No.
    (*Tiny pause. He nods. Then – *)
NICK: Some things, it doesn't matter. Lies. Fibs. Stories. It
    doesn't matter at all. But – that's why I asked you to come
    here, to *this* place, to where I had my discreet and cosy
    tête-à-têtes with Linda. When editing, that is. When in
    post-production around the corner. I am speaking in the
    past tense.

CLOSE-UP – RUTH
She visibly steels herself for something terrible to be said. A tiny
pause. Then it comes –
NICK: (*Off screen*) And then, if there was time, which there
    sometimes was, we used to take a taxi to her flat in George
    Street. (*Tiny pause.*) And make love.

INT. NICK AND RUTH'S CORNER. RESTAURANT. DAY
RUTH *shows no further deepening of reaction. She looks at him*
closely for a brief moment. She all but smiles. And then, as he stares
at her through puffed-up, blackened eyes, she gets up from the table,
without a word, and walks away.

INT. RESTAURANT. DAY
RUTH *strides rather than threads her way through the crowded*
tables.
Another WAITER, *holding two sets of dishes high, theatrical-waiter-*
style, is bumped into. Clatter! Crash! and scattered hot food all over
himself and an adjoining table. Such chaos seems to make no
difference to her, as she strides on to the entrance/exit door, without
any acknowledgement of responsibility, or any look back.

INT./EXT. THE PARKED ROLLS-ROYCE. DAY
The driver, TOM (*from Part One*), *is in a relaxed slump, picking at*
the edge of his nose, but straightens like a soldier caught at-ease by a
superior when he shouldn't be.
He has seen RUTH *coming out of the restaurant door. Before he has*

time to get out, she has opened the back door and got in.
TOM: (*Unsure*) Lady Ruth? Is there – ?
RUTH: (*Bleakly*) Please. Sit still. And say nothing until I say so.
Please, Thomas. Not a word.

INT. NICK'S CORNER. RESTAURANT. DAY
LUIGI, *coming into shot from the depths of the crowded and now extra-humming restaurant (at all the chatter and consternation caused), cannot quite control the glare of twitchy fury he arrows at* NICK. *Approaching closer, however, he hesitates, partly at the physical state of the man, but mostly at the evident emotional distress.*
LUIGI: (*Unsure*) Mr Bamber. What shall we – ?
(*He trails off. Stands still.*)

CLOSE-UP – NICK
Mindlessly breaking breadsticks into fragments with trembling fingers, his swollen jaw seeming to speak and yet not speak, and very slow, almost viscous tears dribbling slowly down his powdered but pulpy cheeks from between his blackened and puffed-up eyelids. He senses LUIGI's *nearby hover, rather than looks up at him. And squeezes out a croak of a voice, would-be sardonic.*
NICK: Throw of the dice, Luigi. And I lost.

EXT. ROAD. ITALIAN RESTAURANT. DAY
The gleaming Rolls-Royce has not moved off, strangely. It remains in front of the restaurant, not quite perfectly opposite the door.
TOM, *the driver, has his cap back on.* RUTH *can be seen, sitting still, in the back.*

INT. NICK'S CORNER. RESTAURANT. DAY
NICK, *not crying now, shakily tries to sip some of his Tignanello, but spills it down his shirt. He groans quietly to himself. And then, decisive all at once, he pulls out his wallet, counts out several twenty-pound notes, gives up and puts the whole wad of folded twenties on to the table, and gets up, passing through –*

INT. ITALIAN RESTAURANT. DAY
Ironic 'Colonel Bogey' music – as in the bedraggled march of the

wounded Brit prisoners in The Bridge on the River Kwai –
momentarily swells as the badly injured NICK *limps and threads his
way through the restaurant towards the street door.*
*Every table stops its chatter, its scrape of knife and fork, its clink of
plate and glass. Every eye is fixed on him. He doesn't notice.*

EXT. RESTAURANT. DAY
NICK *turns to his left as soon as he comes out, limping along the
pavement, past the bonnet of the Rolls, and attracting many a look
from passers-by. It is a moot point whether he has observed that
Ruth's car is still there or not. Certainly, he gives no visible sign of
acknowledging its presence.*

CLOSE-UP – TOM
*In his peaked cap, his face showing anxiety and bewilderment as he
sees, through his windscreen,* NICK *limping slowly away from the
car, through throngs of pedestrians, his back to the car.*

INT./EXT. THE PARKED ROLLS. DAY
RUTH, *too, has obviously seen Nick's exit and passage from the
restaurant. But she stays quite still, virtually expressionless, turning
things over in her mind. In front,* TOM *makes too marked a throat-
clearing, then half turns his head.*
TOM: (*Nervous*) Lady Ruth – I –
RUTH: (*Half-shutting eyes*) Please!
    (*Meaning, Please be Quiet.*)

EXT. SOHO STREET. DAY
Limp, shuffle, limp, NICK *makes his way back towards the old
cutting rooms building, without once looking back, his face set with
pain and other kinds of distress. And still people look at him.
Then, wider, the Rolls-Royce is crawling forward, just behind him,
keeping pace, as close to the kerb as it can get – and heedless of the
irritations of other vehicles.* RUTH *must have given* TOM *some
instruction after all.*

INT./EXT. ROLLS. STREET. DAY
*A strange sight, now. The Rolls is inching along no longer behind but
exactly parallel with limping* NICK. *But he doesn't look sidelong at*

it. And in the car, RUTH *does not look sidelong at him.*

EXT. SOHO STREET. DAY
Strangeness upon strangeness. The slow procession continues. And then, suddenly, as though something were imploding within him, NICK *half-crouches, then springs at the rear passenger door of the creeping Rolls and all but falls into the inside of the car.*

INT./EXT. ROLLS. DAY
NICK *and* RUTH *are suddenly kissing and kissing, with enough force to suggest momentarily that they might even be attacking each other.*

CLOSE-UP — TOM AND HIS INTERIOR MIRROR
A sort of relief and a deal of bewilderment upon his face as he checks out the back seats in his mirror. He clears his throat again.
TOM: (*Eventually*) Pardon me, but – Where to? I mean –

INT./EXT. ROLLS. DAY
NICK/RUTH: (*Together*) *Home, James!*
NICK: (*Twisted grin*) And don't spare the horses.
TOM: Sir!

EXT. STREET. DAY
The gleaming Rolls-Royce pulls out and smoothly accelerates. Whatever problems it contains will have to be dealt with by the two in the back; but, it would seem, at least on the basis of truth, or forms of truth.

EXT. ST CHRISTOPHER'S HOSPITAL. DAY
And for the sake of a story-teller's symmetry, to be permitted on this one occasion, the Rolls – ten minutes or so later – sweeps past the old hospital.

INT. DANIEL'S ROOM. ST CHRISTOPHER'S HOSPITAL. DAY
BEN *is hovering at the half-opened door, like one reluctant to make a final exit.* DANIEL *is sitting on the bed in his dressing gown and* SANDRA *is sitting on one of the bedside chairs.*
BEN: (*Severely, but very agitated*) – and, Daniel, it mehoves be to say one tinal fime – for God's sake think this thing through for just one tast lime!

179

DANIEL: (*Amused*) Ben. Whenever you're upset your speech goes out of the window. I *have* thought it through. From every angle. Just *you* make sure the will is safe and that you do your level best to carry out my wishes.

BEN: The will is already in my solicitor's safe, Daniel. All done up with rue blibbon. (*Smacks his own face.*) Blue ribbon!

DANIEL: I'll see you tomorrow, Ben.

BEN: Tomorrow, Daniel. And – ah – and take care!

DANIEL: (*Warmly*) Thanks, Ben. I'll even go so far as to cake tare. (BEN *shrugs an indifferent guilt – about spoonerisms – waves, and closes the door behind him.*)

CLOSE-UP – SANDRA
Intercut with above as she tries to work things out, and comically bewildered by Ben's speech, always even more spoonerish in emotion, and ending on her, as she looks at DANIEL *and nervously smiles.*

INT. CORRIDOR BEYOND DANIEL'S ROOM. DAY
Walking away from Daniel's room, his back to us, BEN *suddenly stops and puts his hands up to his face. His body suddenly shakes with the first stab of grief. Seen from behind, and briefly, giving it more emotional power.*

INT. DANIEL'S HOSPITAL ROOM. DAY
DANIEL *and* SANDRA. *Her smile to him has faltered a little in the time it has taken* BEN *to give his brief sob outside. She nods at the closed door.*

SANDRA: (*Tentative*) Funny sort of b – But you can see 'e likes you, can'tcha?

DANIEL: Can you?

SANDRA: Not 'arf. That twinkle behind them thick glasses! But I can't seem to fiddle-faddle out what he was on about.

DANIEL: He was trying to make me change my mind.

SANDRA: Oh, I could see *that*. And it makes sense, too!

DANIEL: Oh?

SANDRA: Christ, you don't know me from Adam.

DANIEL: Or Eve.

SANDRA: Who? (*Laughs*) Oh. Yeah. Ought to say Eve, being a woman, enn'I?

DANIEL: No doubt about it. (*Looks at her, changes tone.*) I want to say something about you and to you.
(*Tiny pause. She fidgets a little, puzzled.*)

SANDRA: What?

DANIEL: Don't get worried or upset. I'm not going to jump on you or anything like that. I don't want to offend you – but I must say something.

SANDRA: Blimey. You'd better say it then.
(*Tiny pause. Basically timid with women, he half-looks away, then looks back at her.*)

DANIEL: I'll tell you now what I didn't exactly or *precisely* lay on poor old Ben. I have about eight weeks to live.

SANDRA: (*Gasps*) Oh-h!

CLOSE-UP – DANIEL

DANIEL: (*Smiles, nervously*) So I have time enough and the world to tell you that you, Sandra Sollars, *you* are utterly enchanting. You are fresh air to me. I feel

INT. DANIEL'S ROOM. DAY

DANIEL: (*Continuous*) lifted up in your presence. (*Holds up his hand to stop her attempted interjection.*) I once knew a young woman whom all the songs were about. A green-eyed dazzler I met in a Forest of Nead dance hall. I've always carried her inside

CLOSE-UP – DANIEL

DANIEL: (*Continuous*) me, through thick and thin, though she was killed before you were born, Sandra. (*Half-stops, lights cigarette, but holds up hand again to stop her speaking.*)

INT. DANIEL'S ROOM. DAY

DANIEL: Ever since – (*Drags in smoke.*) Ever since, I've been sort of pulled to this girl or that girl, but the song was always in the wrong key, or –
(SANDRA, *bewildered, is affected by the way he is speaking as much as by what he is saying. The simple warmth and the glow on him when he looks at her are palpable. Her eyes threaten to moisten.*)

181

SANDRA: (*Not aggressive*) Leave it out, willya?
(*He smiles his delight at her manner.*)

DANIEL: When I was staring and staring at you in that brasserie
on – God, it was only Tuesday night and this is Friday. It
seems *years* ago –

SANDRA: Tuesday, that's right. I was wiv that bugger Peter. Last
time an' all!

DANIEL: (*Pleased*) I stared and stared. I know I was more than
half-way nuts at the time, what with the drink and the pain
and the way I'd been feeling – and even though I was
putting my words-on-the-page into your mouth I could
still *feel something else* going on inside me – things were
stirring again. Feelings that had been dormant for years!

SANDRA: Been what?

DANIEL: Asleep.

SANDRA: Oh.

DANIEL: And you woke me up. I – was – awakened.

SANDRA: But I hardly spoke a –

DANIEL: (*Insistent, cuts in*) You woke a part of me that knew the
words but didn't know the song.

CLOSE-UP – SANDRA

*Concentrating earnestly, as one might for rapid speech in a foreign
language one knows but has not used for a long time.*

DANIEL: (*Off screen*) Of course I know as a *sometimes* rational
man, of course, of *course* it's physical, it's sexual, erotic –
(*Her face changing, comically. This she wholly gets.*)

INT. DANIEL'S HOSPITAL ROOM. DAY

SANDRA: (*Pleased*) 'Ang about a minute –

DANIEL: (*Sweeping on*) And of course I'd like to lie beside you
and stroke you and hold you and kiss you and – *rhapsodize*
you –

SANDRA: What me?

DANIEL: (*Laughs*) Exactly.
(*Tiny pause. She considers the matter.*)

SANDRA: Well. I could – um – I mean – (*Looks at closed door.*)
Do you want a hand job or something – ?
(DANIEL *bursts out laughing. She frowns, half-rises, sits again,*

not sure whether to be offended, or whether she has given offence.)

DANIEL: (*Gasping back laughter*) Oh, you dear girl – You funny, funny little –

SANDRA: But that's only because I want to help you out. I mean, what's happening to you and all – Christ, must be awful! (*He has stopped laughing, and is considering her again.*)

DANIEL: (*Quietly*) You don't really want to work in that place, that karaoke club or whatever it is. Do you?

SANDRA: (*Contempt*) Nah!
(*She gets up, walks about, as he follows her every movement, every gesture.*)
You're sposed to offer yourself, you know. Get 'em going. Champagne at three hundred pounds a bo'le and anyfink else on top. But I usually get out of it.

DANIEL: Usually.

SANDRA: I get caught sometimes. (*Little shudder.*) But by then they're usually too pissed to – (*Looks at him, a sudden spurt of rage.*) I hate it! I hate the whole fucking world sometimes!
(*Silence. She is chewing her mouth in pent-up disgust.*)

DANIEL: (*Gently*) Sandra. Listen to me –
(*But her rage has not abated.*)

SANDRA: And where's my bleed'n gun! I paid a lot for that! You nicked it – Where is it?
(*He simply looks at her until she calms a little. She plonks herself down on the chair again, face set, arms folded, legs crossed, and the freer one jiggling.*)

DANIEL: What would you like to do? What sort of work?

SANDRA: (*Instantly*) Manicure 'n' hairdressin'.

DANIEL: Then can't you?

SANDRA: I was! On this whatchacallit – like apprentice. Nice place 'n' all. They paid nothing, or nearly, but I *loved* it. But me mum – she has these turns, you know, and had to go to this place – he did more than smash up her face, that cruel bugger, he banged up her mind as well. (*Deflated.*) Anyway, it all fell frew. And I – oh, I dunno – (*Sudden tears.*) I've got meself stuck, enn'I? Like I'm – like it's all – I dunno – *useless.*

183

(DANIEL *gets off the bed, with a surge of energy it seems, perhaps because he is suddenly more sure than before that – however odd it may be – he is doing the right thing.*)

DANIEL: Two conditions. One, you don't go back to that karaoke place, or anything else like it, again – not ever. Never! Two, you take a proper course, apprenticeship or whatever it is, in this hairdressing, nail thing you like doing – No. *Three* conditions. Forget about the gun, and everything that means.

SANDRA: Oh, yeah? And if pigs 'ad wings –

DANIEL: (*Interrupts*) In return – you will get two thousand five hundred pounds a month for the rest of your life –

SANDRA: *What?*

(*He holds her shoulders, stopping her rising.*)

DANIEL: And your mother will get a thousand pounds a month for as long as *she* needs it.

SANDRA: (*Spluttering*) But – but –

CLOSE-UP – DANIEL AND SANDRA

His hands move from her shoulders, tenderly, to rest on the bare flesh at the sides of her neck. She is immobile, and dumb with shock.

DANIEL: All of this will be set up just as soon as possible. Ben Baglin, dear Ben, the man who brought you here, will make all the arrangements, him and his solicitor, Andrew Adam. It'll all be safe. It'll all be guaranteed. But here and now, Sandra, once and for all, promise, solemnly *promise* to do and not to do the things I said.

(*She stares up at him, blank. She tries to move her lips, but her tongue won't make the words.*

He leans in a little more, and kisses her. Then, urgently –)

Promise!

SANDRA: (*Released*) I promise. I promise. I really bloody do!

(*And then she cups her face with her hands and bursts into tears. He holds off, and his own new smile trembles on the edge of tears too.*)

DANIEL: And now you must go.

SANDRA: Go? Oh, but –

DANIEL: Everything is all right. Everything will be as I said it will be. Come on. Stand up.

(SANDRA *rises, like a small child being told what to do*.)

SANDRA: (*Barely audible*) I – I – oh, my God – I don't know
what to say. (*She looks at him, woman now, not child, and
flings her arms around him.*) Thank you! Thank you! Thank
you! (*And then realizes the squeeze is actually, physically
hurting him.*)

INT. DANIEL'S HOSPITAL ROOM. DAY

DANIEL: (*Quickly*) No, no – it's OK – just a twinge, and and a –
(*But he sucks in his breath, holding back agony.*) Look –
somebody's coming along in about five minutes to shove
something up my bum.

SANDRA: (*Almost indignant*) To *what*?

DANIEL: (*Smiles*) To help me, Sandra. (*Turns to his table, picks
up notebook, gives it to her.*) Everything is written down in
here in clear language in a way that you are sure to
understand. Ben's address, numbers, the amounts, how
it'll be paid, oh, the whole lot. Take it.

SANDRA: (*Numbed*) Ta. Yes – I mean, thank you.

DANIEL: And Ben will talk to you on Monday. Go to his office
– it's all written down in there, how to get there and so on
– go there at twelve o'clock. He'll take you somewhere nice
to lunch –

SANDRA: (*Beaming*) Will he?

CLOSE-UP – DANIEL AND SANDRA

DANIEL: And answer all your questions, or any you think of in
the future. Now – not tightly, *please* – (*Laughs*) give us a kiss.

SANDRA: Oh, you darling!

(*And they kiss. He breaks first, moisture at his eyes.*)

INT. DANIEL'S ROOM. DAY

*He takes her by the arm towards his door. She is in a dream, unable
to take her eyes off him.*

DANIEL: (*Matter-of-fact*) Goodbye, Sandra.

SANDRA: (*Protests*) But ent I going to see you again nor nuffink – !

DANIEL: We'll see. (*Then*) Goodbye, Sandra.

(*He stands still, leaving her to complete the few feet to the door.*)

SANDRA: (*Shakily*) G-goodbye, Daniel. (*Shaking, she opens the*

*door, looks back at him, bewildered, almost goes through to the
corridor, but then − suddenly, in harsh tones, totally
unexpected −)* I'm still going to get that bugger though.
You see if I don't!
(*And the door shuts.*)

EXTREME CLOSE-UP − DANIEL
*Astounded, he holds his breath. And then slowly expels the air in a
hiss of anxiety and disappointment.*

EXT. ST CHRISTOPHER'S HOSPITAL. DUSK/NIGHT
Lights splash out into the thickening dusk.

CLOSE-UP − DANIEL. HIS BED
The roll is taken from his arm after the blood-pressure readings.
NURSE: There. That was fine. We shan't bother you now for
      eight hours. A holiday!
DANIEL: (*Dully*) Ta.
NURSE: Your tablets are in the little pot. Here. Take them now,
      or in the next few minutes. Yes?
DANIEL: (*Dully*) Yes. Thank you. I will.
NURSE: (*Falsely bright*) See you!
      (*He doesn't answer. The door closes, off.*)

INT. DANIEL'S ROOM. DUSK/NIGHT
DANIEL *lies still a moment, like a dead man.*
SANDRA: (*Over*) I'm still going to get that bugger though.
      (*He turns his head, as though she were in the room. And then,
      suddenly, he is on the move. Fast out of bed, pad-pad to the
      door, opens it −)*

INT. CORRIDOR. DANIEL'S POINT OF VIEW. DUSK/NIGHT
Nothing on the move, in either direction.

INT. DANIEL'S ROOM. DUSK/NIGHT
Moving fast, DANIEL *rushes to and opens the narrow cupboard,
which is wide enough to hold the clothes one comes in, with a shoe
rack, and spaces for a bag the size of a brief case. He picks up the case.*

CLOSE-UP — INSIDE BRIEFCASE
Hands grope, unwrap tissue paper, reveal the 'silver' pistol, lift it out.

INT. DANIEL'S ROOM. DUSK/NIGHT
DANIEL clicks open the pistol, making sure (yet again, one feels) that it is loaded. He shoves the gun under the top bedclothes, and takes his clothes on their hanger over to the bed, holding or half-holding his breath with tension all the time.

INT. CORRIDOR OUTSIDE ROOM. DUSKY/NIGHT
A rubber-wheeled drugs cart clinks its contents a little as it returns from the last room on the other side to DANIEL, pushed by the same nurse and her companion nurse.

INT. DANIEL'S ROOM. DUSK/NIGHT
Shirt on, pyjamas off. DANIEL, about to step into his trousers, freezes at the faint sound, off, of jiggling or tinkling medicines, and a rodentine squeak-squeak of rubber wheels.

INT. CORRIDOR. DUSK/NIGHT
The cart goes on through the glass doors at the far end. Daniel's cautious head, peeping around his door, pops back in again, relieved. The corridor is once again empty, almost eerily so, as in a story.

EXT. HOSPITAL. NIGHT
An hour, maybe, has passed. A figure is descending normally unused iron steps, threading down the original part of the old ramshackle building via neglected balconies. The figure, discernible only in movement, is alternately swift and cautious depending upon the splashes of light from the windows on each floor, at angles to the balconies.

EXT. 'HALF-SECRET' CENTRAL GARDEN. HOSPITAL. NIGHT
DANIEL, more discernible now, moving through scruffy bushes, off the path, passes the damaged Eros that was once the pride of a fountain. Near it, he is suddenly wrenched with pain, and has to stop and clench his body. He is fully clothed – and, indeed, rather smart: the clothes of this morning.

CLOSE-UP – DANIEL
He has to suck in his breath hard and wait a moment for the spasm of hot agony to pass. He contorts a sort of smile, and whispers to himself –
DANIEL: Happy ending. Happy ending! Must write a happy –
    (*He swallows, winces, looks up at Eros –*)

EXTREME CLOSE-UP – EROS
With every appearance of looking directly back at him, its soiled, chipped and damaged face, half-mobile in the fleeting scuds of moon and cloud, cloud and moon, seems to leer.

EXT. CENTRE OF 'HIDDEN' GARDEN. NIGHT
DANIEL, *wincing less, but half-stooping with pain, makes himself address the almost-alive stone figure, in his old 'chapel language'.*
DANIEL: (*Softly*)
    Will there be any stars, any stars in my crown,
    When at evening the sun goes down?
    When I wake with the blest,
    In the Mansion of Rest,
    Will there be any stars in my –
    (*He stops abruptly. He straightens. He moves off, towards an old wooden gate that probably issues on to the side-street beyond, where traffic can be heard.*)

KARAOKE SCREEN
Against crude montages of 'appropriate' images with some relevance to the music ('Life is Just a Bowl of Cherries') the words come up in English, sandwiched by Japanese – almost at the end of the song.
    The sweet things in life
    To you were just loaned
    (*At same time, a Japanese voice is singing the same bit in Japanese. Pull out and pan across other karaoke screens to singer, and widen –*)

INT. KARAOKE CLUB. NIGHT
At the karaoke stand, a small Japanese businessman ends the familiar, bouncy tune in his unfamiliar tongue.
SINGER:
    So how can you lose

What you've never owned?
Life is just a bowl of cherries
So live and laugh at it all!
During which, find the hostesses (not Sandra), a few new Japanese
(obviously a favourite haunt), the bar, barmaid, etc., and – at the
scatter of applause, mainly from the singer's compatriots – a figure,
back to us, hunched over his champagne at the end of the bar –
vaguely thriller-like.

INT. BAR. KARAOKE CLUB. NIGHT
It is, of course, DANIEL. *He sips, puts his glass down, amused, then*
goes into the body of the club where a HOSTESS *is trying to inveigle a*
group of English males – with three half-clad hostesses – into
'performing', holding a big, decorative book of available karaoke
numbers.

INT. KARAOKE CLUB. NIGHT
TOUTING HOSTESS: (*To group*) – and it's fun! Come on, one of
    you gents! Let's have a bit of English up there, eh?
DANIEL: (*Cutting in*) I'm game.
TOUTING HOSTESS: (*Pleased*) You are? Here. Pick a good 'un.
    (DANIEL *riffles through the book, jabs his thumb on the*
    number, smiles, and turns towards the karaoke stand.)
DANIEL: (*Leaving*) I've always wanted to do this.
TOUTING HOSTESS: (*Calls across*) Number twenty-seven!
    (*This to the karaoke operator in a little oblong cubicle near the*
    top end of the bar. He inserts a CD-like disc into a winking,
    twinkling, flashing slab of high-tech equipment.)

INT. KARAOKE STAND. NIGHT
Music starts. Pictures start on all the little screens. Then up come the
words in English and Japanese. But instead of his own voice, DANIEL
actually perfectly lip-syncs to a singer he has already claimed (to the
CONSULTANT *in the hospital) that he can perfectly imitate –*
DANIEL: (*'Sings' Bing Crosby*)
    A long time ago a million years BC
    The best things in life were absolutely free
    But no one appreciated
    A sky that was always blue

And no one congratulated
A moon that was always new –

INT. MAILION'S OFFICE. OFF MAIN CLUB ROOM. NIGHT
MAILION, *counting out a stack of fifty pound notes with a moistening
thumb-pad – dib, dab, dib, dab – is suddenly caught by the music, off,
and naturally impressed by the remarkable quality of the singer.*
CROSBY: (*Off*)
So it was planned that they would vanish now and
then
And you must pay
Before you get them back again.

INT. KARAOKE CLUB. NIGHT
*The whole place goes uncannily quiet, every single person astounded
by the quality of the singing. They stop in mid-sip, mid-word, mid-
hand-on-thigh fumble, open-mouthed.*
CROSBY: (*Off*)
– that's what storms were made for
And you shouldn't be afraid for –
(*And find* MAILION, *coming out of his office and leaning
against the door to stare admiringly at –*)

INT. KARAOKE STAND. NIGHT
DANIEL: (*'Sings' Crosby*)
Every time it rains it rains
Pennies from heaven.
Don't you know each cloud contains
Pennies from heaven –
(*As he slightly turns, theatrically gesturing as a crooner might,
enjoying it all hugely, a new glint flashes in his eye. He sees*
MAILION.)
You'll find your future falling
All over town
Be sure that your umbrella –

EXTREME CLOSE-UP – 'SINGING' DANIEL
*The glint and the grin becoming wickedly enthusiastic as Bing sings
in his mouth.*

    – is upside down
    Trade them for a package of
    Sunshine and flowers –

INT. KARAOKE CLUB. NIGHT
*'PIG' MAILION moves on into the body of the club from his office
door, apparently fascinated, as, slightly off, the music continues.*
    If you want the things you love

EXTREME CLOSE-UP – MAILION
*The admiration and fascination changing to a look of calculation
and speculation. One can almost track the thought into 'I could do
something with this bloke'.*
    You must have showers –

INT. KARAOKE STAND. NIGHT
DANIEL (*and Bing*) *give it their all in a final, splendidly Vaudeville-
style excess of open-armed gesture.*
DANIEL: (*'Sings'*)
    So when you hear it thunder
    Don't run under
    A tree,
    There'll be pennies from heaven
    For you and me!

INT. KARAOKE CLUB. NIGHT
*The whole place erupts into roars, claps, cheers as, now in fairly long
shot,* DANIEL *bows, grins, bows, and* MAILION *comes up to him and
half-whispers in his ear.*
As everything subsides back to normal in the club, MAILION *can be
seen leading* DANIEL *towards and into his office.*

INT. MAILION'S OFFICE. CLUB. NIGHT
Coming in, DANIEL *pretends to be impressed by the pile of fifty-
pound notes.*
DANIEL: My goodness – ! Now *that's* what I call cash.
    ('PIG' MAILION, *pleased, claps* DANIEL *on the shoulder with
    his meaty, beringed hand.*)
MAILION: That's nothing. Nothing! Pocket money. Know why

they call me 'Pig'? 'Pig' Mailion?

DANIEL: Um. It doesn't sound very nice.

MAILION: (*Cackle*) It's cos I like me dosh by the *trough*-load, fella!
(*He slaps Daniel's shoulder again. Daniel winces pain, then
manages to hide it.*)

DANIEL: (*Suppressed pain*) Well, that's the – (*Half-turns away.*)
Sorry. Frog in my throat.

MAILION: Nah. Not a frog. You got *gold* in them tonsils, I'll tell
you. Now, listen, what you need is a good manager,
somebody who'll – *Hey. What is this?*
(*Because, fully turning back,* DANIEL *is pointing the pistol
straight at him.*)

DANIEL: (*Mildly*) You need a few stars in your crown, Arthur.
(*And he fires, at point-blank range.*)

CLOSE-UP – MATCHSTICK NOTRE-DAME. NIGHT
*Lit by Ben's work lamps, the wondrous edifice seems alive with light
and shadow, as* BEN *hums happily above or alongside it.*

BEN:

Mm – ma maa
Funshine and plowers
If you mm – ma –mmm –
(*Ring! Ring! Ring! on telephone. The usual Tut! Tcha!, but at
least he answers.*)
Who is – ? Daniel! Dan – it's lucking fate, old boy! Do what?

INT. MAILION'S OFFICE. CLUB. NIGHT
MAILION *sprawled backwards across his desk, dead, alongside the
phone a calm* DANIEL *is using.*

DANIEL: (*Phone*) I said *note the time*. You called *me*, right? No,
just do as I say. And then in – a – in – (*Looks at his watch.*)
In thirty-five minutes telephone my room in the hospital.
No – forty minutes. I'll be there. (*Puts phone down, gives
dead Mailion's cheek a little friendly pat.*) It's called an alibi,
old chum. (*Tiny pause.*) It's called a capital A alibi comma
old chum full stop capital initials. The End full stop. And
underline.

COLD LAZARUS

Cold Lazarus was first broadcast by Channel Four in April 1996.
The cast was as follows:

EMMA PORLOCK	Frances de la Tour
TONY WATSON	Grant Masters
DANIEL FEELD	Albert Finney
FYODOR GLAZUNOV	Ciaran Hinds
LUANDA PARTINGTON	Ganiat Kasumu
BLINDA	Carmen Ejogo
KAYA	Claudia Malkovich
MARTINA MASDON	Diane Ladd
DAVID SILTZ	Henry Goodman
ANDREW MILTON	David Foxxe
NAT	Jonathan Cake
NIGEL	Richard Karlsson
BILL	Ian Kelly
MANOLO	Antonio Elliott
CELESTINE	Lisa Shingler
BETH CARTER	Tara Woodward
YOUNG CHRIS (TWIN OF DANIEL)	Joe Roberts
YOUNG DANIEL	Joe Roberts
TRAMP	John Forgeham
DANIEL'S FATHER	Adam Bareham
STUDENT DANIEL	John Light
JIM	John Higgins
TED	Edward Woodall
JOHN	Miles Harvey
BETH'S MOTHER	Susan Porrett
PREACHER	Malcolm Rogers
LOCAL SINGER	Tim Whitnall
HARRY SCHUMPET	Harry Ditson
POLICE CHIEF	Guy Masterson
DR RAWL	Donald Sumpter
POLICE COMMANDER	Paul McNeilly
INSPECTOR GENERAL CHALLENDER	Michael Culkin

VALERIE	Sophie McConnell
GEORGE	Philip Dupuy
1ST MSC GUARD (HOPKINS)	Terrence Maynard
2ND MSC GUARD/1ST SENTRY	Silas Carson
3RD MSC GUARD/2ND SENTRY	Jason Salkey
MARTINA'S WATCH TOWER GUARD	Peter Warnock
APARTMENT GUARD (FYODOR'S)	James Peck
POLICEMAN	Todd Boyce
1ST SEARCHER	Nick Sampson
2ND SEARCHER	Aron Paramor
3RD SEARCHER	David Royle
APARTMENT GUARD (BLINDA'S)	Steve Speirs
DOOR COP	Victor Power
HARRY THE DOORMAN	Leon Greene
KARL	Rob Brydon
POLICEMAN (RESTAURANT)	John Altman
PRISON GUARD	Darren Bancroft
SILTZ EMPLOYEE	Geoffrey Lardor
YOUTH ONE	Craster Pringle
YOUTH TWO	Simon Meacock
MILITIAMAN ONE	Adam James
MILITIAMAN TWO	Rod Woodruff

Written by	Dennis Potter
Production company	Whistling Gypsy
Producers	Kenith Trodd
	Rosemarie Whitman
Executive Producers	Michael Wearing
	Peter Ansorge
Director	Renny Rye
Editor	Clare Douglas
Production Designer	Christopher Hobbs
Director of Photography	Remi Adefarasin
Costume Designer	Charlotte Holdich

PART ONE

SCREEN
*A screen which in fact occupies a whole wall, but we do not yet know
this. It is alive with myriad floating, cell-like dots, of every hue, but
utterly incomprehensible.*
*But then, very gradually, many of the dots seem to float together and
coalesce into larger blobs.*
MALE VOICE: (*Off*) Hey – wey . . . ! What is this – ?

CLOSE-UP – SECTION OF SCREEN
*A group of blobs reaches out glutinously to another group of blobs
and, in a micro-second or so, the shape of something near human
oozes itself into existence.*
MALE VOICE: (*Very excited*) My God! It's coming – !
    (*The oozing blob settles into a real figure of a man, though still
    enveloped in multicoloured swirls and flows of dots and other
    blobs.*)

INT. CRYOGENIC LABORATORY. YEAR 2368. DAY
*One whole wall is the screen. In front of the screen is a thirtyish
scientist* TONY WATSON, *skilled assistant to and disciple of the
renowned cryobiologist* EMMA PORLOCK, *acknowledged world
authority on biotechnology at absolute zero temperatures.*
Behind and beyond WATSON, *who is alone in this section of the lab,
various black machines wink, twinkle, murmur with light and
subdued resonances.*
TONY: (*Almost screaming with excitement*) Everybody! Quick!
    Quickly!
    (*So excited that he is rising from the autocube in which he sits:
    basically, a motorized cube of a chair, with electronic buttons
    and control pads, the cube yielding where and when necessary to
    the shape of a body.*)

INT. OUTER LABORATORIES. DAY
*As in an open-plan office separated into varying spaces of near-
privacy or illusory-privacy by folding dividers, the cryogenic*

laboratory extends and extends into sections – and from several of these, autocubes come racing, towards the excited shouts, off.
TONY: (*Off, yelling*) It's happening! It's happening!

INT. CRYOGENIC LAB. DAY
TONY WATSON *sinks slowly back into the soft folds of his autocube, eyes riveted to the 'live' wall in front of him, his mouth all but sagging open with the overwhelming sense of wonder which has so manifestly invaded him. At the same time, the first of the other autocubes racing towards this part of the lab bursts in, bearing the fairly elderly* EMMA PORLOCK, *whose hands fly to her mouth as though she were once again an enchanted little girl, as she sees –*
More and more of the bigger blobs are metamorphosing into recognizable shapes within the mesh and lattice of surrounding, still swirling dots –

WALL SCREEN
Now fast shaping itself into a location of some 374 years ago, way back in 1994 – and then, all at once, the surrounding swirl settles, and the juddery picture steadies with a strange plop-p! of over-sound, like air being suddenly released.

INT. A ROOM. A HOSPITAL. 1994. DAY
But all as seen from the point of view of someone in the bed. Gathered around are a paunchy, bespectacled, middle-aged literary agent, BEN BAGLIN, *a thirtyish and always somewhat harrassed-looking film/television producer,* ANNA GRIFFITHS, *an approaching-middle-age film director,* NICK BALMER, *and a very attractive young woman,* SANDRA SOLLARS.
They seem to be speaking to each other, but there is no sound.

INT. CRYOGENIC LAB. DAY
TONY *and his boss,* EMMA, *have by now been joined by a middle-aged Slav,* FYODOR GLAZUNOV, *a black 'brain specialist',* LUANDA PARTINGTON, *and two young women laboratory technicians – one black, one Asian –* BLINDA *and* KAYA.
All six are leaning forward eagerly in their autocubes, as though willing the 'live' wall to emit sounds that have been lost for nearly 400 years.

FYODOR: (*Between teeth*) C'mon c'mon c'mon! Speak!
(*The wall picture wobbles. There is a collective gasp.*)

WALL SCREEN
The hospital room, silent, is gradually being swamped by blobs again as each figure, each object, starts to lose definition and ooze at the edges. And then, suddenly, with another strange plop-p! the entire wall is once again full of floating, cell-like, multi-coloured dots, as at the beginning.

INT. CRYOGENIC LAB. DAY
A collective groan. Then silence, apart from faint bleeps and murmurs from nearby equipment. Each face turns to look at the formidable EMMA PORLOCK, *clearly the person in charge, and the one who 'knows most'. She stares straight ahead, but at nothing, interlacing her bony fingers, as though unaware (but she isn't) of the collective gaze upon her. Then –*

EMMA: (*Quietly, in even tones*) I have never been quite so delighted in the entire span of my professional life. Or, indeed, my life in general. To be able to reach into the actual memory, the actual mind, of a human being who died (*Awed, shifts*) three hundred and seventy-four years ago . . . (*Pause*) And then to lose it. Lose it.

FYODOR: For the time being.

TONY: We will surely be able to –
(EMMA *holds up her hand, imperiously, as one uninterested in optimistic burble, and turns to address* LUANDA PARTINGTON, *the black scientist who specializes in cryogenic biotechnology.*)

EMMA: Luanda.

LUANDA: Professor?

EMMA: Our circuits have involved – what – four and a half billion neurones in this man's cerebral cortex.

LUANDA: Out of more than ten billion, yes. Say, about 43 per cent of the neurones. The highest we have ever attempted.

FYODOR: So it's – overload?

LUANDA: I have concentrated on those areas of the brain where it is easiest to stimulate emotions or the . . . or the *memories* or – yes, *desires* – like the front part of the hypothalamus and the septal area.

FYODOR: Which of course is near by.

LUANDA: Of course.

(*Something about the way she says this, and the tiny subsequent look between the two, indicates that they have a controlled hostility towards each other.*)

EMMA: Fyodor. Do we need a running commentary?

(*Fyodor stiffens, in a stonily Slav manner, and becomes more formal.*)

FYODOR: I am sorry if that is what you think it is, Professor Porlock.

EMMA: (*Ignoring him, to* LUANDA) Can we bear a wider spread? Same percentage of neurones, but more span?

LUANDA: I – well, Emma, we're in zonko new territory here – and – (*Little twinkle of a laugh, which she often does.*) I just don't know.

(*Silence. They stare at the live wall, full of floating dots, the disappointment palpable.*)

CLOSE-UP – TONY

Eyes on the screen wall, he fiddles anxiously with what has succeeded and is still rather like the cuff of his jacket. His finger brushes, accidentally, briefly, against one of the small buttons on the bracelet he wears. Then he sits bolt upright, startled, as –

THE LIVE WALL

Again, the dots start to float together and coalesce into blobs, seeming to seek each other out.

INT. CRYOGENIC LAB. DAY

The autocubed watchers are suddenly transfixed, as – on the wall before them –

EXT. FOOTBALL GAME. LATE 1970S. DAY

It is at Craven Cottage – home of Fulham FC – and the white-shirted Fulham captain, Alan Mullery, smashes in a volley from about thirty yards out, which is so powerfully struck that the Leicester City goalkeeper, Peter Shilton, brilliantly diving, is nevertheless in mid-air only as the ball bulges the back of the net. Huge roar from the crowd is heard.

Plop-p! the brilliant scene very quickly degenerates.

INT. CRYOGENIC LAB. DAY
*The four women and two men watching, having immediately
whooped! in the irritating American style of instant enthusiasm
which has, by now,* AD *2368, become utterly universal, subside again
as the living wall collapses back into eddying dots.*

TONY: But there was *sound*! This time there was –

EMMA: (*Cutting in*) We're obviously on the rim of it, there's
some process we're missing out on or –
(KAYA, *the Asian young woman, and much a junior in status
to the others, except her colleague* BLINDA, *has been looking at*
TONY, *with especial interest.*)

KAYA: Dr Watson – what were you doing with your biobrace?
(*Puts hand to mouth, charmingly.*) I'm sorry. That sounds
rude.

TONY: (*Puzzled*) Doing? Why – nothing that I know of.
(*He looks at what we, back here in the dark ages, would call his
bracelet.* BLINDA, *the black young technician, laughs, not
entirely without a dig at* KAYA.)

BLINDA: Kaya notices *everything* you do, sir. If she says –

KAYA: (*Embarrassed*) Blinda! That's – !
(*She half-turns away in confusion.* FYODOR *is amused. But
elderly, formidable* PROFESSOR PORLOCK *is not interested in
these trivial emotions – as she sees them – and intervenes in the
parlance of the day, her eyes as keen as a bird of prey as she
looks at* KAYA.)

EMMA: If you want to take ten for a fuck, go ahead, dear. But
what *did* you see?

KAYA: (*Still embarrassed*) Um – well, I –

EMMA: (*Snaps*) Come on! Out with it!

KAYA: Tony was – Dr Watson was kind of – (*Switches from
Emma's too sharp laser gaze, to* TONY.) You were fiddling
about a little with your cuff. And I – happened to notice
that your fingers brushed against the biobrace.
(TONY *looks at his bracelet, dubious.*)

TONY: Well, if you say so, but –

CLOSE-UP – TONY AND FYODOR

As the heavy Slav unexpectedly pounces, gripping TONY *quite hard half-way between elbow and wrist, making him extend his right arm.*

FYODOR: (*Angrily*) *Why you wearing this one!*

TONY: Hey. Loosen your – What do you mean?

EXTREME CLOSE-UP – EMMA PORLOCK

The predatory eyes take on an even sharper gleam of avid interest. Her mouth seems to go dry, for she moistens her lips with the tip of her tongue.

FYODOR: (*Off screen, angrily*) This is the hibernation-peptide biobrace! Totally, *totally* out of order!

INT. CRYOGENIC LAB. DAY

TONY *is discomforted, but greatly dislikes Fyodor's tone and implicit suggestion of 'authority', which he does not have.*

TONY: OK. OK. So I left on yesterday's tooling, but I don't see –

EMMA: (*Cuts in*) Fyodor. What were you using on those cells?

FYODOR: Alpha-neuropeptide 1042.

TONY: (*Defensive*) But it's all been discharged by now and – (*He is taking off his biobrace, a little shamefacedly.*)

FYODOR: That's not the point! If you haven't put it through the chemostere there could still be a trace of –

EMMA: (*Cuts in again, fiercely*) 1042. 1042. That was hitting the synaptic cleft, right?

(FYODOR *is the pure chemist among these experts and their assistants.*)

FYODOR: Yes, but only on the outer membrane of that area where the cortex of a hibernating animal – (*Stops, looks at her.*) My God.

EMMA: (*Snaps*) Precisely!

TONY: (*Puzzled*) Emma? What have I – ?

(*But she is already punching a button on her autocube. She speaks as though to someone in the room, but it is obviously a command going elsewhere.*)

CLOSE-UP – EMMA

Excitement is rekindled in her hawk-like eyes or face.

EMMA: Porlock, Cryolab A. Fuel – (*Looks around.*) Three, no
   four, biobraces with alpha-neuropeptide 1042. That's mine,
   Dr Watson, Dr Glazunov, Dr Partington. Priority A plus.
VOICE FROM HER AUTOCUBE: (*Laconic*) Cost a lot.
EMMA: Keep your accountant's snout *out* of it, Karl.
VOICE: (*Same tones*) You're on the rim of your budget, you
   nasty old bitch.
EMMA: Just do it! And *now*.
   (*Behind her, just in shot, with a tiny bleep-bleep-bleep, letters
   are forming in a strip on the nearest piece of the other wall – not
   screen wall.*)

INT. CRYOGENIC LAB. DAY
*The words streaming out on an upper part of the wall or divider
behind* EMMA, *are not at first picked up by the others because of the
sheer power of Professor Porlock's authority and enthusiasm.*
EMMA: Budgets! Budgets! They'll strangle us yet! But accident,
   sheer accident, bee-oo-ti-ful serendipity has played a
   bigger part in all science than any – What?
   (*Seeing the switch in the direction of their eyes, she swivels her
   autocube a few degrees to see -*)

CLOSE-UP – BLEEPED WORDS ON SECONDARY WALL
   FILE 1 REF 1 DANIEL FEELD MEMORY:
   ASSOCIATION FOOTBALL GAME AT CRAVEN
   COTTAGE, ONCE FOOTBALL STADIUM IN
   LONDON. GOAL BY ALAN MULLERY OF FULHAM
   AGAINST LEICESTER CITY, FOOTBALL
   ASSOCIATION CUP (ROUND 4, SATURDAY, 26
   JANUARY 1974).

INT. CRYOGENIC LAB. DAY
As the six variously digest the, to them, utterly arcane information.
TONY: What amazes me – *stupefies* me – is the sound of the
   crowd, I mean, that must be *hundreds* upon *hundreds* of
   people all gathered together at the same place –
FYODOR: (*Sniffs*) Thousands, actually. If you know your history.
LUANDA: Oh, we know all that in *theory*, of course – but to
   experience it, wow – mind-slant slot!

BLINDA: (*To* LUANDA) That they could feel *safe*.

KAYA: (*Awed*) They must have been almost touching each other –

EMMA: Oh, but that is just the tiniest fragment, the merest gleam of a hint, of what we have in store for us if if *if*! we can break into this man's synapses. (*She is so excited, so obsessed, that she is unknowingly making her autocube all but. spin in circles or thread in parabolas in and around them.*) Imagine the wonder of it all. And if we wear our VR helmets we will live for hours at a time in the *real* past, the *authentic* past – and and – (*Her voice, her expression change; a small shadow falls.*) And perhaps escape.

(*Fyodor, in particular, is watching her keenly. He is about to say something, but – and this is clear – at the very last second changes it into a simple question.*)

FYODOR: (*Quietly*) Escape from what, Emma?

EXT. CRYOGENIC LAB. DAY

This particular lab and its divided offlabs are housed in what at first sight – model shot – looks like a giant but smooth golfball on its tee – that is, it globularly bulges upward and outward from a comparatively narrow entrance stalk, which seems difficult to enter. This is the Masdon Science Center Inc.

Beyond it, similar constructs swell on similar stalks, with rail-like lattice interconnecting them all. And in the background, a huge, thick iron fence, intermittently sparking little flashes. The sign MASDON SCIENCE CENTER INC. *glows, high above all.*

EXT. ENTRANCE, CRYOGENIC LAB. DAY

Tight, narrowed almost right down to a trio of armed guards at the lab entrance doors, which are seamless with the beginning of the bulge of the outer wall and electronically operated.

CLOSE-UP – FIRST GUARD

He stands at the apex of the triangle the three make, so to speak. His futuristic, laser-like weapon held ready cradled, his eyes narrowing as he seems to pick up and attend to something well beyond us, in his middle-distance view. Eyes seen through an enclosing, plated, 'buttoned' helmet.

He looks, and is, instantly menacing. *The* MASDON SCIENCE
CENTER *in metal on his leathery, electronic-button-studded quasi-
uniform is very like a police badge. (In fact, in this world of 2368 all
public services are 'privatized', and for at least a century past.)
Zoom his eyeline.*

EXT. SMALL 'TRUCK'. RAIL. DAY
*Armour-plated, not fast, slit front 'window', a Masdon delivery
container quietly hums on the narrow gleam of rail, approaching the
Cryogenic lab. It has a number, 787, flashing on-off on-off.*

EXT. ENTRANCE. CRYOGENIC LAB. DAY
*The 'triangle' of guards evidently do not need to turn their heads to
speak to each other. Their voices sound amplified and a little
distorted.*
FIRST GUARD: 787. Coming at angle 6.25.
SECOND GUARD: Angle correct for Lazarus.
THIRD GUARD: Number correct for Lazarus.
FIRST GUARD: (*To someone 'beyond'*) Please say 'gain. How
    many phials?

CLOSE-UP – FIRST GUARD
*He seems to listen inside his helmet, with a slight tilt of the head. One
of the little buttons on the helmet lights up green.*
FIRST GUARD: Seven phials alpha-neuropeptide 1042. Gotcha!
    Cleared! (*Then, in different tone.*) Hey? Cosby – ? Me gonna
    see you Clubside after hour? Yeah? We'll play
    Schmuckdies [pronounced 'Schmuck Dies'], OK? – U-uh,
    all right, misery. But remember, I'm one up with only two
    smacks to go. Cave your chest, pal!
    (*The 'truck' approaching, its number flashing.*)

INT. CRYOGENIC LAB. DAY
*On another of the walls, a type of hatch raises itself open with a buzz
and a twice-repeated automatic voice saying 'Attention!', and a
shelf protrudes, bearing a small rack of sealed phials.
Even as the autocube-scuttling EMMA reaches out with eager hands –
as for the Holy Grail – a voice from somewhere above, God-like,
with a deep resonance for added power, speaks in a way which seems*

to know what she is doing at the moment she does it.

It is not the same autocube-borne voice ('Karl') as before, and does not sound like one which would permit any casual badinage. Indeed it is a female voice. It is that of MARTINA MATILDA MASDON, *an American, a tycoon, owner, power-broker, would-be autocrat, carefully preserved sixty-five-year-old witch.*

MASDON'S VOICE: Professor Emma Porlock. This is Martina Matilda Masdon at eight-twenty-two a.m. Los Angeles time, five-twenty-two p.m. your west Europe time. Register what I have to say!

> (EMMA, *about to catch the phials, stiffens in mid-grasp, and the other five look at each other in covert foreboding. They are all scared of her.*)

EMMA: (*Quietly*) I am registering, Ms Masdon.

MASDON'S VOICE: Ordering up seven phials of alpha-neuropeptide 1042 without so much as even a token reference to the –

INT./EXT. POOLSIDE BREAKFAST, CALIFORNIA. DAY
MARTINA MATILDA MASDON *is not alone.*

MASDON: (*Continuous*)– biochemical tranche of your very specifically allotted budget is – (*Uses her beringed fingers, with an excess relish*) A, an impertinence, pure and simple – (*Smirks*) if not impure and complex. B, a plain ignorance when you have no knowledge of, nor any apparent desire to find out, the *market price* of that particular neuropeptide. And C, an almost certain –

CLOSE-UP – EMMA. CRYOGENIC LAB
Back in what is still in sentiment called 'England', the PROFESSOR *sits in her autocube as one frozen, but then she moves her lips slightly as though to protest.*

MASDON'S VOICE: (*Continuous*) – guarantee you foolish woman, that your whole two-ounce frogshit operation will end up splattered on your own face. And why? Because –

INT./EXT. POOLSIDE. CALIFORNIA. DAY
MASDON: (*Wet-mouthed relish, continuous*) – you've tilted tit-up into overspend – overspend! – o-ver spend! On next

Thursday's intercontinent agenda, your Lazarus Operation
will be listed for discussion as either A, suspension or B,
aband-on-ment. Got it?
(MASDON *smacks her liver-spotted hand down unnecessarily
hard on a large rubbery pad inset into the table at which she
sits, under a vivid awning, with an apparently speechless
Adonis, a young man called* NAT, *and a rotund, somehow
twinkly, seemingly amiable middle-aged 'showbiz' type,* DAVE
SILTZ.

    *The table is meloned, fruited, juiced and coffeed under its
awning, on bright tiles edging to a Hockney-like dream of big,
sunsplashed pool. Everything could be late twentieth-century
Beverly Hills except for some near-at-hand autocubes and a
wheeled partition containing scores of little monitor screens. And
in the background a few armed guards, cousins to the ones at
the 'Science Center'.*

    DAVE SILTZ *has been looking at Masdon's female bitch-act
with sardonic amusement, occasionally flashing glances at* NAT
*as though wanting to share it, but finding only beautiful
blankness in response as the young Adonis spoons down an ice-
cream dish.*)

SILTZ: (*To* MASDON) Which side of the bed did you get out of
    this morning, Martina?

MASDON: (*Grins*) Hey now, Dave. That was me being a
    reasonable lady. (*Looks at* NAT.) Correct, my boy?

NAT: (*Toneless*) Correct –
    (*She squeezes a bit of his long, bare thigh. He is in swimming
    costume and loose robe only.*)

MASDON: (*To* SILTZ) Fear and/or greed or both, boy. You tell
    me a better stick, a better carrot.

SILTZ: But how do you do it?

MASDON: Do what?

SILTZ: Voice-call this little nothing of a place about a little bit of
    damn-all while you're still chewing your berries?
    (*Which is exactly what* MARTINA *is doing, chomp-chomp, from
    one of a scatter of dishes around her, taking a tiny bit here, a
    tiny bit there, messily.*)

MASDON: (*Chewing*) What's a God s'posed to be, Mis-ter Siltz?
    Christ, you know this in your own glitzy biz even better

than I do, Dave. Come on! A God ain't a God unless He slash She is omnipotent, right?

SILTZ: Sure. Give or take the odd cardiac or earthquake.

MASDON: Well, then – see those monitors over there – (*Indicates the wheeled 'divider' near pool.*) I got, what, thirty-two of my lab complexes dotted here, there, everyfuckingwhere – (*So excited by this measurement of her own power,* MARTINA MASDON *cannot avoid getting up and pacing near to the edge of the glistening blue pool, on ludicrously teetering heels.*)

CLOSE-UP – MASDON. POOLSIDE

MASDON: (*Pacing*) Yeah – all over, *all* over – And most of them, twenty-eight of them, in fact, give me no more trouble than a kink in my tube of toothpaste – you know, just a little squish . . .

CLOSE-UP – NAT. TABLE

Paying absolutely no attention, now licking the end of the long spoon he has been using to eat his ice-cream, he seems unaware that MASDON, *spouting away, but widening her self-obsessed walk, is passing just behind him.*

MASDON: (*Half off screen*) And I mean if money is shit – and it is, it is! –
(*Comically, Nat's tongue pauses on the spoon, and the first flicker of expression – amazement, incredulity – enters the dead perfection of his features.*)

CLOSE-UP – SILTZ. TABLE

SILTZ *is paying attention, and the harder glint of scorn or even dislike can just be glimpsed behind the seemingly constant twinkle of amiable amusement.*

MASDON: (*Half off screen*) Then most of my Centers are as fat as a full colon. I mean –

INT./EXT. POOLSIDE. DAY

MASDON: (*Continuous*) – they can't *avoid* making profit. They fill the pan as regular as a boy on prunes!
(NAT *puts his spoon down at last.*)
But even so – look at those monitors! (*Gestures at screen*

again.) I make it a habit to check in now and then. Voice only. Make them think every move is under scrutiny. And as for the others, the more problematic ones – (*Sits back at table.*) I kinda *hover.* In each finance department I have my own personal agent, working direct to *me* outside any other form or discipline. And as soon as any one section of any one Center makes any one expenditure decision for any one tranche of any one internal subsectioned budget, I get a coded *bleep* – at once.

SILTZ: Ah. So *that* was what I heard when I spilt the coffee.

MASDON: (*Proudly*) Yup. Sorry, Dave. Then I look up at those monitors – (*Gestures at them again.*) And I punch in my own close-shot of any one work room in the whole damned place. *Look.* (MARTINA *presses the rubbery pad on the table again, and – it being voice-activated – says –*) *Twenty-nine* – (*Aside, to* SILTZ) That's the place in England. A shithouse. *Sixteen* – (*Aside, to* SILTZ) The lab ordering an overspend – *See!*

CLOSE-UP – RUBBER PAD. TABLE

It flickers into a (silent) animated picture. The picture is that of the English cryogenic laboratory that had ordered up extra and too-expensive biochemicals. Just discernible: the six lab people positioned at the living wall, where blobs are again forming into recognizable shapes.

CLOSE-UP – SILTZ. TABLE

Putting on his horn-rimmed glasses, he peers down at and into the rubber-pad picture, very interested. His interest seems to grow.

MASDON: (*Off screen*) And if you want to wear a helmet, Dave – Why, you can of course get –

INT./EXT. POOLSIDE TABLE. DAY

MASDON: (*Continuous*) – right there and smell, taste what's a-cooking, eh?

(SILTZ, *peering, suddenly looks like one trying to control or hide a very, very keen interest. But* MASDON *has stopped looking at the picture, her bullying-for-the-day done so far as she is concerned. Her hand now rests on Nat's shoulder.*)

SILTZ: (*Acting half-indignant*) Well, I've no meeting due for –
Sure, Martina. Why not?
(MASDON *gives* NAT *a proprietorial tap, and the Adonis rises
instantly, with a more than obedient smile.*)
MASDON: (*Calls to house beyond*) Manolo! VR helmet for my
guest! Pronto. And some data gloves, eh? (*Leans in to*
SILTZ.) Got another little matter first, Dave. Best exercise I
know of, Dave. You should try it more often.
SILTZ: (*Scarcely listening*) Right.
MASDON: (*Nasty snigger*) But not with *me*, babe.
(*Still sniggering,* MARTINA MASDON *leads* NAT *away with a
little smack of his behind, going towards the – model or false
façade – weird-looking, turret-and-guard-watch-towered house
teetering on her silly shoes in ungainly fashion.*)

CLOSE-UP – SILTZ. TABLE
*Hardly able to contain his excitement, he pushes his face even closer
to the rubber-pad picture.*

CLOSE-UP – RUBBER PAD
*As – discernible even on this flat-bed, miniature, soundless pad –
more and more of the largest blobs on the living wall in front of the
six viewers in the lab settle into the recognizable location of 374 years
ago: a room in a hospital, with four figures gathered around a bed
and someone in the bed who cannot be seen.*

INT./EXT. POOLSIDE. CALIFORNIA. DAY
A servant, MANOLO, *uniformed with* MASDON SC INC. *insignia,
puts or helps put a computerized virtual reality helmet and
computerized virtual reality data gloves on a now desperately
impatient* SILTZ.
SILTZ: OK, OK. Thanks, Manolo. Got it –
MANOLO: (*Hispanic*) Meesis Masdon say *stop* when you bored,
sir. She say that be *soon*.
(*But* SILTZ *is already settling back into his autocube or chair as
the lead from both helmet and data gloves plugs in to a tiny
socket alongside the rubber pad.*)

EXTREME CLOSE-UP – SILTZ. VR HELMET

A very strange sight to our eyes. The upper two-thirds of Siltz's head is completely encased by a seamless black shell, dome-shaped, almost ominous, with the lead coming out of it at the back to lace once around him and join with the lead of the mitten-like shell of the gloves before reaching the table socket. Siltz's eyes are within the encasement, and he can – in this mode – see nothing *of the real world unless he releases the just visible eyeslit hatch.*

Going closer, closer into the black dome – and dissolving slowly at the same ratio as the movement into –

INT. CRYOGENIC LAB. DAY

The same six transformed by what they are seeing on the living wall, into which we begin to plunge – losing all laboratory surroundings.

INT. PRIVATE ROOM. ST CHRISTOPHER'S HOSPITAL, LONDON. 1994. DAY

BEN BAGLIN, *agent, is at the immediate right, top end of the bed of the patient,* DANIEL FEELD. SANDRA SOLLARS, *young beneficiary of part of Feeld's will and his (idealized, platonic) last love, is at Feeld's immediate left, top of the bed, holding his hand.* ANNA GRIFFITHS, *producer, is next to* BEN, *nearer the bottom of the bed, and* NICK BALMER, *director, uneasily not sitting and uneasily not quite standing, is at the foot of the bed. All seems to be from the point of view of the man in the bed,* DANIEL.

BEN: (*Leaning in*) Say again, old chap. We didn't quite catch –

SANDRA: He said No sumfink. Definitely No. (*Squeezes his hand, sudden tears.*) Oh, the poor bugger.

DANIEL: (*Off screen, faint croak*) Ben – ?

CLOSE-UP – BEN BAGLIN

His bespectacled, chubby-ish face, slightly agleam with sweat, looking in with the hint of the slight distortion of a morphined point of view, full of love and concern.

BEN: (*Hoarse*) Yes, dear old friend. It's 'back to front' Ben.

INT. DANIEL'S HOSPITAL ROOM. DAY

ANNA, *seemingly a perpetually flustered woman, is anxious to be recognized, or something similar.*

ANNA: You were deeply asleep, Daniel.

DANIEL: (*Off screen, croak*) No – not asle – No. I wanted –
(*But he stops.* NICK *shifts about at the foot of the bed, not knowing what to do with his hands.*)

NICK: If only you could see the assembly of *Karaoke* we now have, Dan. It's beautifully written. You'd be rightly proud of it, I assure you.

ANNA: Yes! It's marvellous
(*Wet-eyed* SANDRA, *who has more common sense than most, flashes them a lethal look, close, even, to hatred. Her strong London accent in full flight.*)

SANDRA: Christ. 'E don't want to 'ear about none of that *now* – do he?
(NICK *gives a roll of his eyes in condescension, and as if to say 'What's* she *doing here, anyway?' But* –)

BEN: No. Quite right. He's desperately trying to sell us tomething.

INT. CRYOGENIC LAB. DAY/DUSK
Pulling back, DR TONY WATSON *looks puzzled.*

TONY: Curious speech pattern.

EMMA: (*Snaps*) Query it. And *shut up!* (*Her eyes never leaving the wall.*)

ANNA: (*Wall, meanwhile*) Perhaps as the sleep clears – morphine dries out the –
(TONY *presses a small button with question mark on it, on his tunic-or-jacket, and mumbles, inaudibly, his query.*)
mouth terribly. Perhaps he wants –

INT. DANIEL'S HOSPITAL ROOM. DAY
ANNA: (*Continuous*) a drink, or just his lips moistened.

CLOSE-UP. SANDRA – (DANIEL'S POINT OF VIEW)
Without ado, SANDRA *dips her free hand into the water jug and leans forward, evidently to moisten Daniel's lips. Her face, streaked with tears, momentarily fills the screen.*

SANDRA: There, y'are, love.

DANIEL: (*Off screen, croak*) Ta.

INT. DANIEL'S HOSPITAL ROOM. DAY
BEN: (*As to a child, to* DANIEL) Better? Eh?
DANIEL: (*Off screen, urgent croak*) Ben. Ben, I – listen.
  (*But he stops. They are desperately attentive. They wait.
  Then –*)
BEN: (*Quietly*) Daniel. Say it. Say it, old lad.
  (*Sound of noise in Daniel's throat. Then, after an evident
  struggle, almost incomprehensibe words are gasped out.*)
DANIEL: (*Off screen*) No biog-g-gah –

EXTREME CLOSE-UP – BEN
*Looming in, filling the screen, face puckering with the strain of
listening to what is only on the brink of comprehensibility.*
BEN: What? No what?
  (*Sounds, off screen, from* DANIEL, *of final struggle, and
  eventually a released near-shout.*)
DANIEL: Ben!

INT. DANIEL'S HOSPITAL ROOM. DAY
*All around the bed frozen as though in the still-life of terror in the
face of actual death. A gurgle off screen, and then the very last heave
of the last two words the mortal* DANIEL *will ever speak.*
DANIEL: (*Off screen, near-scream*) No biography!
  (*Suddenly, and as a shock –*)

INT. CEILING VIEW. BED AND ROOM. DAY
DANIEL *can now be seen in the bed, from on high, the death rattle in
or at his throat. It is a sudden and weird change of angle, on the cut,
and not made a gradual upward rise in any way.*
Sharp cut.

CLOSE-UP – SILTZ. CALIFORNIA
*The helmet-encased, hand-encased, plugged-in figure jerks forward,
showing surprise only by body-language.*
Sharp cut.

INT. CRYOGENIC LAB. DAY/DUSK
LUANDA: What the – ! Oh-h-h. *Yes.*
  (*On the living wall,* BEN, SANDRA, ANNA *reacting in their*

different ways to Daniel's obvious moment of death – and NICK, *panic in his eyes, runs towards the door, as though for help. And all of it, all of the time, is seen from above, as though from something or someone stuck on the ceiling.*)

EMMA: (*To* LUANDA) What mean, *Yes,* like that?

LUANDA: It's the out-of-body experience. It's been recorded many times by those who have been brought back from the brink.

TONY: (*Keenly interested*) So – he's not actually *dead* at this precise moment?

FYODOR: (*Abruptly dismissive*) How can he be?

(TONY *flashes the Slav a look of genuine personal dislike.* KAYA, *sentimental, has her hands half up to her face, tensely watching the wall, where, beyond the half-silhouettes of the watchers, an emergency doctor is running in, followed by* NICK.)

BEN: (*Standing*) I'm afraid –

INT. DANIEL'S HOSPITAL ROOM. HIGH POINT OF VIEW STILL. DAY

BEN: (*Continuous*) he is no more. (*And bursts into tears.*)

SANDRA: (*Screams*) Daniel – Dan! Don't go!

(*But suddenly –*)

BLACKNESS. SILENCE
Both total.

INT. CRYOGENIC LAB. DAY/DUSK
The living wall is totally black. It does not last long, but seems an eternity of tension. Now, instead of semi-silhouettes against the brightness of the living wall, the figures of EMMA PORLOCK, TONY WATSON, FYODOR GLAZUNOV, LUANDA PARTINGTON *and their lab assistants* BLINDA *and* KAYA *now stand out sharply in the glow of their autocubes.*

FYODOR: (*To* TONY) Well. You may take it that he is dead *now.*

TONY: (*With edge*) Quote dead unquote.

KAYA: Oh-h –

(*She says it like someone watching a sentimental story.* EMMA *snorts.*)

EMMA: Don't be silly, girl.

KAYA: S-sorry.
> (*But* EMMA *almost* softens – unaware, as yet, of the way LUANDA *is leaning forward so eagerly in her autocube.*)

CLOSE-UP – LUANDA. LAB
Eyes glowing in anticipation, lips parted in held-in hope or excitement.
EMMA: (*Off screen*) But, yes, it is *rather* like a little tale already. Imagine what we –
> (*Her voice breaks off as* LUANDA, *all but jumping up, claps her hands together in a single loud noise and calls out –)*
LUANDA: Here it comes! Coming!

INT. CRYOGENIC LAB. DAY/DUSK
All suddenly rigid as the blackness of the living wall begins to swirl in a centrifugal motion, streaked with faint light, coming from the centre.
Swirl – swirl – swirl, gradually making what looks or feels like a deepening tunnel.
EMMA: (*Hissing to* LUANDA) *What is going on?*
LUANDA: (*Excitedly near-breathless*) The second most often recorded experience by those brought back from the brink, Emma – a *tunnel* with – There's supposed to be a bright light at the end of it. *Let's see.*

THE LIVING WALL
Losing all surrounding people and paraphernalia from the laboratory, the faint light (at the very centre of the now fast-moving, faster-moving centrifugal waves of variegated black and half-black, grey and half-grey) is growing brighter, brighter in a swift series of pulses.
LUANDA: (*Off screen, yell of excitement*) You see! It's happening!
> (*And then odd or slightly echo-like sounds begin to come out of the living wall –)*
YOUNG WOMAN'S VOICE: (*Receding cry*) Dani-e-el!

WITHIN SWIRLING TUNNEL
The light, small but pulsing yet brighter at the far end of the centrifugal 'tunnel', suddenly yields up a tinkle of syncopated music,

*as though heard in a soft breeze or from the 'other' side of distant
walls or doors, magically evocative, tantalizingly elusive –
The brief snatch of music is a little of the intro or intervocal of 'Hush,
Hush, Hush, Here comes the Bogeyman', performed by Henry Hall
and His Orchestra. Then, suddenly, on the first soft 'Hush' of the
vocal –*

INT. SMALL BEDROOM. NIGHT (WITHIN SWIRLING TUNNEL).
1940s
A six- or seven-year-old DANIEL FEELD *in a little room with a
sloping ceiling and a curtain opening directly on to the narrow stairs
pulls the bedsheet up over his nose and mouth, his eyes – candlelit by
a guttering stump on small chest of drawers – as wireless music drifts
up the stairs –*
SINGER: (*Minus* one *'Hush'*)
  – Hush, Hush,
  Here comes the bogeyman,
  Don't let him come too close to you,
  He'll catch you if he can!
YOUNG DAN: (*During, in terrified whisper*) Chris!
  (*The six- or seven-year-old twin next to him in the narrow bed
  is fast asleep.*)

SWIRLING TUNNEL
*The image, flickering so briefly, is lost within the grey-black-white
swirl, the light at the end swelling a little more and steadying out of
its pulse.
A great crowd roar suddenly bursts out –*

EXT. TWICKENHAM. 1990s. DAY (WITHIN SWIRLING TUNNEL)
*Flash: Rory Underwood or any white-jerseyed England Rugby player
crashes over the try line in an international with an exhilarating,
skidding dive.*

SWIRLING TUNNEL
Image lost, but light expanding at the central depth, then, flash –

X-RAY MONITOR SCREEN (WITHIN SWIRLING TUNNEL). 1994
An internal digestive system at work, as seen in a quick sidelong

glance by off-screen DANIEL *on X-ray table. Succeeded immediately by –*

EXT. TREE TOP. FOREST OF NEAD. 1940S. DAY (WITHIN
SWIRLING TUNNEL)
SMALL DANIEL, *top of an oak, clings for dear life, as though he has climbed too far. 'Instantly' succeeded by –*

INT. THEATRE STAGE. NIGHT
MAX WALL *doing his funny walk in a comic routine, becoming –*

INT. CHAPEL. FOREST OF NEAD. 1940S. DAY (WITHIN
SWIRLING TUNNEL)
Bright faces of CHILDREN *singing – to an accompanying harmonium.*
CHILDREN:
> **Will there be any stars any stars in my crown –**
> *(Yielding, as the exuberant voices seem to take on richer and richer resonance, to –)*

INT. BEDROOM. LONDON FLAT. 1980S. NIGHT (WITHIN
SWIRLING TUNNEL)
An attractive young woman later identified as BETH, *her bare back turned from the bed point of view, undoes her bra strap from the back, then turns shyly towards the bed, saying something, but her words overwhelmed by the chapel singing* CHILDREN.
CHILDREN: (*Continuous*)
> **When at evening the sun goes down?**
> **When I wake –**

EXT. NEW COLLEGE LANE. OXFORD. LATE 1950S. DAY
(WITHIN SWIRLING TUNNEL)
Seen from back, a young man on a bicycle, gown flapping, at speed, obviously delighted by something, suddenly spreads his arms wide – the bike wobbles – he begins to fall with a 'Whoopeee!' that can be heard even over –
CHILDREN: (*Continuous*)
> **– with the blest**
> **In the mansion of rest**
> **Will there –**

CLOSE-UP – DANIEL. A WINE BAR. 1990S. NIGHT (WITHIN
SWIRLING TUNNEL)
*Draining a glass of red wine with a deliberately vulgar little burp of
enormous satisfaction,* DANIEL *cackles a glee of a challenge to
someone mostly off screen.*
CHILDREN: (*Continuous*)
   – **be any stars in my crown?**

SWIRLING TUNNEL. BRIGHT LIGHT
*Suddenly, a tropical bird flutters briefly, all colour, and the beat of its
gaudy wings is, so to speak, the last remnant of the swirl as we seem
to plunge headlong into the very bright light.*
*And briefly, comically, yet movingly, a fragment (amplified, double-
or treble-tracked) of Ronnie Ronalde whistling 'Birdsong at
Eventide' with Robert Farnon and his orchestra completing the
passage or plunge into –*

BRILLIANT WHITE SCREEN
*With the barest, scarcely discernible hint of something like a child's
image of angel wings, white on white, and cherubs, white on white.*

INT. CRYOGENIC LAB. DAY/DUSK
*The six watchers enthralled in front of the vivid white, 'angel-
brushed' living wall, but then they visibly jerk or recoil as the entire
lab of winking, twinkling high-tech plus 374 years more high-tech
equipment is filled with an almost subhuman scream, not really
recognizable as Daniel Feeld's – but that's whose scream it is.*
DANIEL: (*Over*) No-o-o-o-o-o-o-o-o – !
LUANDA: (*Agitated*) He's in mortal pain because of being
   dragged back from the light. This was when he was so-say
   'cured' while in absolute zero temperature.
   (*And the living wall in front of them collapses into black dots,
   which eddy and swirl.* KAYA's *hands fly to her face; and this
   time, so do* BLINDA's.)

CLOSE-UP – SILTZ'S VR HELMET
*His data gloves flutter up to try to touch the sides of his domed black
shell, as one unable to bear the sights or sounds coming from within
it. The reverberating horror of the scream carries over, momentarily.*

INT. A BEDROOM. THE MARTINA MASDON HOUSE.
CALIFORNIA. DAY
A circular room. Indeed, it would be like being in a globe were it not for the flat floor, which is laid with a very springy, thick white carpet, with soft tufts that are almost grass-high in length, all but reaching one's ankles. Various small, tiny, light-glowing pads and consoles are dotted here and there amongst what can be easily recognized as centuries-on variants of present-day bedroom furniture.
MARTINA MASDON, *half-dressed now but still showing a lot of scraggy old flesh, is lying propped-up on the gadget-buttoned bed, looking across the room to* NAT *and an opened 'wardrobe' door.*

INT. AT WARDROBE. THE ROUND BEDROOM. DAY
NAT, *an Adonis clad only in the briefest of briefs now, has opened only the section of the multi-divided wardrobe he has been commanded to, and he makes a loud whoop! or gasp! of sheer pleasure.*
The only thing hanging there in this subsection is a cowboy suit, exactly in the very, very old Wild West style, complete with Gene Autry or Roy Rogers hat and cowboy boots with silver spurs, as well as all the Range Rider rest of it.
NAT: (*Gushing*) Oh-h-h! *This* is nice – ! Martina! Oh, Martina. It's lovely! It's something I've always wanted. Thank you, my darling. Thank you. (*He is pulling out the big cowboy hat, almost as though too awed to touch it.*)

INT. MASDON BEDROOM. DAY
MARTINA, *pleased, is swinging her scraggy legs down to the carpet, sitting on the bed, searching with her toenail-painted sixty-five-year-old feet for her ridiculous platform-style shoes.*
MARTINA: Well, that's for being a good boy. (*Sudden, crude cackle.*) Let's hope we can continue to come together, eh?
NAT: (*Turning*) This hat – isn't it just wondroso!
MARTINA: Try it on.
NAT: (*Swallowing*) Dare I?
MARTINA: That's what it's for, Nat. Go on. Put it on.
(*Almost nervously,* NAT *puts on the tall, wide-brimmed cowboy hat.*)

NAT: (*Enthused*) He-e-ey. (*He turns back to the long inset mirror in the wardrobe.*)

CLOSE-UP – NAT AND MIRROR
Naked except for his briefs, NAT *preens, with the huge cowboy hat tilting on his head, very proud.*
NAT: Heckorose! It's like – what – way way back when you hunted sheep and Indians – twenty-second-century stuff. Marvelloso!

INT. THE MASDON BEDROOM. DAY
MARTINA MASDON *has her shoes on now and ankle-glides through the soft, tufty white carpet to put her scrawny arms around Nat's bare waist.*
MASDON: You can put it all on in a sec, pally. But Natty, dear, Natty, dearest, another little pressieroso ['nice little present'] – !
NAT: (*Beaming, hugging her hands round his waist*) More? You mean, *more*, Martina Matilda?
(*She turns, letting go of him, to a small console/table near the window, which, metal-slatted like a Venetian blind, looks out on to the pool, its horizontals at present quite narrow, not letting much be seen outside, and nothing in from outside. She sits in a prettily decorated autocube.*)
MASDON: Press the button four down on the left side inside the robehold ['wardrobe'] where the cowboy rides. (*Sniffs*) Incidentally, don't show your ignorance. Cowboys were mid-twentieth century.
NAT: Oops. Sorry.
MASDON: (*Baby talk*) Shall smack oo, lickle one.
NAT: (*Simper*) Yes, please. (*Presses button.*) What is it?

CLOSE-UP – TINY PROTRUSION OF LEDGE RELEASED BY
BUTTON IN WARDROBE
A small metal object, peculiarly shaped. Nat's hand picking it up, gingerly.

INT. THE MASDON BEDROOM. DAY
MASDON: A key.

NAT: Key? I thought key meant an answer or an analogical representation of other qualities.

MASDON: (*Amused*) Oh, there's an older meaning. You still find it used occasionally, other than as a metaphor . . .

(NAT *is bringing the key across to her.*)

NAT: A what? Metaphor? What's that?

MASDON: (*Mildly*) You dumb shit.

NAT: (*Grins*) Sure am, ma'am.

(*She takes the key, inserts it into a small keyhole in the table/ console.*)

MASDON: This was the original meaning – now we use pads or numbers or bioprints to get at something secure – but no cop is bright enough to work out what the fuck you do with *this* little fella –

(*She opens the little 'door' in the console and takes out a filter-tipped cigarette and a little lighter.* NAT *audibly gasps and even takes half a step back.*)

NAT: Great Godolo!

MASDON: (*Smirks*) Surprised?

NAT: (*Stuttering*) But – but – Martina – you're – Martina! What are you doing! That's a – whatyoucallit! – a –

MASDON: It's a – (*Unconsciously lowers voice*) cigarette.

(NAT *watches wide-eyed as she puts it in her mouth and lights it. Again, he takes the quaver of a quarter-step back as she suddenly blows smoke out of her mouth. Clearly, something he has never, ever seen.*)

NAT: (*Awed*) Does it *burn* your mouth – ?

MASDON: No. But you'll see, I'll give you a try.

NAT: (*Excited*) Will you? Will you really? (*But then, a shadow.*) But if anyone ever finds out –

MASDON: (*Snaps*) They won't! And which force would *dare* raid *my* personal – Oh, come on – (*Blows smoke.*) Don't be such a dickhead. Here. Taste the joys of the illicit, my boy.

(*She hands the cigarette across. He takes it fearfully, cannot avoid a quick look around, drags in too much, blows out smoke through his mouth and his nose in a helpless, spluttering, tears-to-the-eyes cough.*)

NAT: Hoo – hoo – ! Christ – !

MASDON: (*Cackles*) Take a smaller pull. Go on. Then you'll see the effect.

NAT: (*Gasps*) I'm – ah – I've gone all – I'm *giddy*, Martina.

MASDON: (*Peremptory*) Go on!

CLOSE-UP – NAT. CIGARETTE
A comical little cameo as, all but trembling, NAT, *virtually naked except for his enormous cowboy hat, takes the most tentative of puffs, holds the quarter-mouthful of smoke for an eye-popping second of pure music hall, then lets it out as though it were vomit.*

INT. THE MASDON BEDROOM. DAY
MARTINA *is laughing. She takes the cigarette back.*

MASDON: There! All of life's pleasures, Nat. Plus the luxury of the purely criminal.

NAT: (*Coughs*) Thirty years' prison!

MASDON: And the good old needle death if you sell it. See, I trust you, boy. Mind you, you'd be wiped out within a minute of opening your chops.

CLOSE-UP – MARTINA AND CONSOLE TOP
She takes another drag, then drops the only quarter-smoked cigarette into a small orifice on the table console top, where, with a faint whirr, it is macerated to nothing.

INT. THE MASDON BEDROOM. DAY
NAT, *considerably shaken by the whole exotic experience, is leaning with one hand against the wall, as though for support. He wipes his brow with the back of his hand.*

NAT: I feel – I feel sort of – giddyish and – (*Slow, he has to think about it. But then he takes his hand away from the wall, thinks a little bit more, and, with a sudden beatific smile –*) Yes. I can feel the *power*. The what is it? Nico-nicotine – Yeah. My *mind*. It's working faster. Holy Moseoso! I could do an *equation* now – just like that! (*Breaks off.*) What's the matter, Martina Matilda?

INT. AT WINDOW. THE MASDON BEDROOM. DAY
The metal slats widening slowly as she presses on the sill, there is that sudden suspicious tension, or similar, in Martina's body to provoke

*the question. She stays staring out and does not turn around to speak
to him.*

MASDON: (*Abrupt*) Get yourself dressed. I'll see you at eight
    o'clock this evening. Go on!

CLOSE-UP – NAT
*He hesitates, frightened that he has done something to offend, but
then, with the faintest shrug, turns away.*

NAT: All right, my sweet darling.

INT. AT WINDOW. THE MASDON BEDROOM. DAY
MARTINA *makes no reply, but leans forward, sharp-eyed, looking
out at –*

INT./EXT. POOLSIDE. THE CALIFORNIA HOUSE. DAY
Latticed by the horizontals of the window blind, DAVE SILTZ, *in his
VR helmet and data gloves, is in a posture so totally still that it
suggests* absolute *concentration.*

EXTREME CLOSE-UP – MASDON
Her eyes distinctly narrow under their false lashes.
MASDON: (*To self, in a mutter*) What am I missing?

INT./EXT. POOLSIDE. DAY
SILTZ, *cut off from any sight or sound of the world immediately
around him, is – especially this much closer – quite obviously
absorbed, utterly immobile with what must be the highest degree of
fascination.*

EXTREME CLOSE-UP – SILTZ'S VR HELMET
*Going right into the shining, shell-like, enclosing black dome, and at
the same ratio as the approach to it, so to speak, slowly dissolve
into –*

INT. CRYOGENIC LAB. DUSK
*The living wall is much as it was at the very beginning, alive with
myriad floating, cell-like 'dots', of every colour, incomprehensible.*
EMMA *is holding forth to* FYODOR, TONY *and* LUANDA. *The two
assistants (*BLINDA *and* KAYA*) seem to have left.*

EMMA: Now we are in a really serious pickle if that – (*Raises her eyes to ceiling, adjusts her words, in case: she was going to say 'bitch'*) if our limited funds mean we cannot get enough of what I know to be, what I admit, is *the* most expensive by far of *any* of the very latest neuropeptides – I mean, we're talking megabucks here . . .

EXT. POOLSIDE. CALIFORNIA. DAY
MASDON *comes up behind* SILTZ, *by the glistening pool. She is carrying her own data gloves.* MANOLO, *her manservant, bears the big VR helmet contraption.*
She puts on the gloves. MANOLO *helps fit the enclosing helmet around her.* SILTZ, *of course, is so cut off within his own similar devices that he cannot see any of this.* MANOLO *takes the joint lead and plugs it into another small socket at the side of the 'rubber pad' on the table. Click!*

INT. CRYOGENIC LAB. DUSK
At exactly the same moment, a small flash of light, like a white bar, crosses the picture, for a micro-second. But it is enough of a clue for the always-very-alert (sometimes deceptively so) SILTZ.
SILTZ: (*Voice-over, resonant voice-in-head*) She's plugged in!
   Watch it!
   (*At the same time – and, fortunately, rather boringly or overacademic –*)
EMMA: I mean, it's been known for centuries that some of the neuropeptides of the order then available could or *did* act as neurotransmitters at cerebral synaptic junctions in at least a few neuronal areas, some of which, as I'm sure you know . . .

INT./EXT. POOLSIDE. CALIFORNIA. DAY
MASDON, *her hands already slipped out of the data gloves, gestures, and* MANOLO, *dutifully standing sufficiently far back, comes to help her take off the helmet.*
He goes to pull the lead out, but, sharply –
MASDON: *Wait!*
MANOLO: Meesis – ?
MASDON: *I'll* do it. You can go back to the house.

MANOLO: Yes. Thank you. Yes.

CLOSE-UP – MARTINA MASDON. POOLSIDE. DAY
*An absolutely intense, absolutely total scrutiny of every nuance of
Siltz's position. Her hand is on the jack, ready to pull out the lead.*

CLOSE-UP – SILTZ
*Intercut with the above: the object of the scrutiny, who has not moved
a millimetre, suggesting either total, mind-fixed absorption – or
something else.*

INT./EXT. POOLSIDE. DAY
MASDON *knows that when she pulls the plug, so to speak, Siltz's
head-world will cease to exist. And he is bound to make some sort of
jerk or any other kind of reaction.*
*Still studying him closely, she yanks out the lead with an almost
brutal precision. And looks at him all the time.*

CLOSE-UP – SILTZ. POOLSIDE. DAY
Not the slightest quiver of change.

INT./EXT. POOLSIDE. DAY
*Martina's glint leaves her eye. She bursts out in a single roar of
laughter, like a man. And then she begins, gently, to ease off the big
shell-like dome of an enclosure from Siltz's head.*

CLOSE-UP – SILTZ/MASDON. DAY
*As the helmet raises, the sound of deep, nasal snoring rises and she
laughs, more extendedly.*
*Released, he gives it the full works. First, the pitch of his snore
changes, then he grunts, then his cheeks quiver, then his mouth
makes dry, smacking noises and then, at last, his eyes open, with a
look of comic incredulity. A beat.*
SILTZ: (*Slurred*) Yes. Yes. Very interest – (*Looks around, as
though confused*) No. I mean. That was *absolutely*
fascinating, Martina. Wonderful. I wouldn't have missed it
for . . .
(*His voice trails off in the face of her cackle. Then she addresses
him severely.*)

MASDON: David Siltz.

SILTZ: Y-yes . . . ?

MASDON: You are a complete and utter fraud.

SILTZ: Now look here, Martina –

> (*But she slaps him hard on the back – hard enough to dislodge a fishbone.*)

MASDON: Oh, don't worry. I don't blame you. These biochemists and what have you would make a camel piss its hump away just for something more interesting to do. (*Slaps him on back again, irritatingly.*) Come on, boy. You need a livener.

> (*Siltz swallows down irritation, rises, sliding his hands out of the data gloves.*)

SILTZ: I guess I do.

INT. CRYOGENIC LAB. THE LIVING WALL. DUSK

As we left it, myriad floating multicoloured 'dots'.

TONY: (*Off*) But will he have had any sense of being – well, *alive* again?

INT. CRYOGENIC LAB. DUSK/NIGHT

EMMA, TONY, FYODOR *and* LUANDA *still chewing the cud, with an edge of unease.* FYODOR *seems an exception: he looks sidelong at* TONY, *with a hint of derision.*

FYODOR: Does that trouble you, Dr Watson?

> (TONY *returns like for like.*)

TONY: Does it *not* trouble you, Dr Glazunov?

> (LUANDA, *the black brain-biochemist, is out of her autocube and walking up and down a little.* EMMA *watches her from her own autocube.*)

EMMA: Whenever one is at any sort of new edge, a new question will always pose itself. I don't know, *yet*, whether we are going to face one of those *absolute* dilemmas or not. It's not yet Yea or Nay and nothing in between. (*Slight pause.*) Luanda.

> (LUANDA *stands still.*)

LUANDA: (*Eventually*) Now – we know from our own experience, and I know very well as a cortex-biochemist who has been working at the deepest levels of nanotechnology applied to injured brain cells that *much* memory *most* of the time is involuntary. *We* don't summon it up, so to speak. *It*, the memory, beckons to *us*.

TONY: (*Frown*) True. But –

EMMA: (*With a frown at* TONY) Go on, Luanda.

LUANDA: But you can see this more especially in sleep. If you think about it.

(FYODOR *yawns and tries a joke.*)

FYODOR: I'm thinking about it.

EMMA: (*Snaps*) You can leave any time you wish, Fyodor.

FYODOR: Hey. *Hey.*

EMMA: (*Turning away*) Luanda.

LUANDA: A host of past memories, past inventions, whole distortions, odd fragments out of place in our past – like we're suddenly back at school again, say. But the sleeper, the *dreamer*, is not usually aware that he or she is asleep.

TONY: (*Relaxing a little*) True.

EMMA: There is no *volition* in it, is there? And so, in a sense, no *identity*. I mean –

LUANDA: (*Cutting in*) Yes. Daniel Feeld, this man from all those centuries ago, is not any more aware that he has a partly functioning brain than a dreamer is that he is asleep.

FYODOR: And another thing – (*Looks at* EMMA, *with a satiric gleam.*) *If* I may dare to intrude, Professor Porlock.

EMMA: (*With a snort*) Oh, don't be so silly!

(FYODOR *spreads his hands. Then –*)

FYODOR: When we saw Daniel Feeld in that tunnel-like whirl, as opposed to his pre-death bed scene with all those people around him, the man saw *himself* in the scene. As when he was a small child scared of that silly little song.

EMMA: (*Thoughtful*) Mmm. Do we see ourselves as objects, as *actors* in our own memory? No. I don't think we do.

TONY: (*Eager*) So he doesn't know he's quote alive unquote.

INT. SECTION OF LAB. DUSK/NIGHT
Words begin softly bleeping across the same strip of wall as before, when identifying the Fulham goal.

FILE 1 QUERY 1 DANIEL FEELD MEMORY: THE SPEECH PATTERN OF BESPECTACLED MAN

DANIEL FEELD'S RIGHT USED TO BE CALLED 'SPOONERISM'.

INT. CRYOGENIC LAB. DUSK/NIGHT
The four watch the words spill out –
TONY: My God. They took long enough!
   (*As the words continue to bleep out –*)
   THAT IS, INITIAL SOUNDS OF SPOKEN WORDS
   ARE REVERSED TO MAKE A TYPE OF NEW SENSE
   AS IN –

CLOSE-UP – BLEEPING LETTERS
   'QUEER DEAN' INSTEAD OF 'DEAR QUEEN'.
   CALLED AFTER REV. W. A. SPOONER, 1844–1930.
   QUERY COST 385 UNIDOLLARS.

INT. CRYOGENIC LAB. DUSK/NIGHT
TONY *claps his hands across his mouth.*
TONY: Oops. I'm sorry, Emma. I'll try not to ask too many
   questions. The tight-arsed sods.
EMMA: Oh, it's this precious internal market of the Masdon
   Group. They'll charge a fee for *anything* that could be
   argued as outside our remit.
FYODOR: Well, in this case, all one can say in 'reversed initial
   sound' is – muck fee!
   (*For once, they all laugh at one of his interjections. The heavy-
   faced Slav seems pleased, like one who is sure he is not loved.*)
LUANDA: (*To* EMMA) But, Professor, if we're on so tight a rein –
   I mean, this is a tragedy across every arts and science
   discipline I can think of. History. Memory enhancement.
   Brain surgery. Grammar. A perspective on ourselves –
EMMA: (*Between teeth*) I know. I know.
TONY: Can't we appeal direct to Martina Masdon? Can't we
   make her see!
   (*But he looks ceilingwards, half-cautiously.*)
EMMA: (*Angry and heedless*) No. She is walled in by prejudice as
   fat as her profits and as thick as her armed guards. You'd
   need thermonuclear back-up to get even a quarter of a
   millimetre into her skull!

EXT. MASDON HOUSE. CALIFORNIA. DAY
Looking as though you'd certainly need nuclear weapons to crack open this *house. Basically ovoid, bristling with defence devices, with armed watch-towers. Model shot.*

CLOSE-UP – INSIDE WATCH-TOWER. DAY
A Masdon-insigniaed guard, laser-gun cradled, peering out, chewing gum. He stops chewing suddenly and raises tiny binoculars, searching the sky.

INT. A LIVING ROOM. THE MASDON HOUSE. DAY
MANOLO *pours a vividly coloured liquid into Siltz's glass and withdraws.* MARTINA *already has hers. She raises her glass.*
MASDON: To boredom.
    (*Then cackles.*)
SILTZ: (*Mock rueful*) Well – I suppose I'd better drink to that, when all's said and done.
MASDON: You went into showbiz, Dave, because you always did have ants crawling up your orifice. Excitement – excitement – all that glitz, eh?
SILTZ: I have eight hundred million subscribers, Martina. And a link-in to three times that with my Memory Lane programmes. From a baseline like that, I can't lose.
MASDON: (*Drinks*) Sure. Sure.
SILTZ: Plus all the offshoot and secondary activities – actor management, pre-packaging other entertainment products. Food and drink via interactive media, video, virtual reality games and – biggest spinner of the lot, needless to say – interactive sex with whomever you like, however you like it, with your virtual reality body-suit.
MASDON: (*With a faint snigger*) I prefer the real thing.
SILTZ: (*Chuckles*) Yeah – but you gotta think of the cripples and misfits, darling.
    (*He drinks for the first time and pulls a slight face, which she doesn't notice.*)
MASDON: (*Drinks*) OK. Here's to the biz there's no biz like. *We're* not in competition. In fact, I want to discuss a particular deal with you, Dave boy.

EXT. SKY ABOVE MASDON HOUSE. DAY
What looks like (and actually is, for our purposes) a small, box-shaped, guided 'kite' is descending from a small dot in the deep Californian blue into something with discernible shape. It can be as 'futuristic' in design as anyone chooses: bristling with various antennae, etc.

CLOSE-UP – THE PARTICULAR WATCH-TOWER GUARD
Training his weapon on the descending, then hovering, then descending object in the sky, he speaks –
WATCH-TOWER GUARD: Snoop Kestrel! Snoop Kestrel!
    Angle 2.40 from Tower 3. Snoop Kestrel approach!

INT. MASDON LIVING ROOM. DAY
A small speaker somewhere unseen conveys the alert, just as MARTINA *leans in to* DAVE *to begin her pitch.*
VOICE: Snoop Kestrel approaching! Snoop Kestrel
    approaching!
MASDON: Shit!
    (*Slamming her drink down so that it slip-slops and spills, she rushes to the wall by the door and –*)

CLOSE-UP – CIRCULAR PLATE INSET BY DOOR IN WALL
The flat of Masdon's hand smacks hard against the plate, twice.

INT. MASDON LIVING ROOM. DAY
All the many bits and pieces of electronic equipment scattered among, and sometimes masquerading as, the furniture stops winking, twinkling or faintly humming.
SILTZ: (*Startled*) What is – ?
    (*She holds up her hand, urgently, and whispers.*)
MASDON: *Say nothing. Nothing.*

CLOSE-UP – SNOOP KESTREL. SKY
A weird-looking thing, dipping then steadying, then dipping downwards again, antennae revolving. It emits a small pee-ep pee-eep peeee-eeep. Going ever closer, closer until it occupies the entire screen, then dissolving into what purports to be its interior – Dissolve.

INT. SNOOP KESTREL
In the small space, miniaturized detecting devices, with minitape spooling, etc, etc. There is, of course, no operator.
MASDON: (*Whisper, over*) *They can pick up a plop of shit in a pan at twenty-five yards' distance.*
    (*Dissolving back to –*)

CLOSE-UP – SNOOP KESTREL
As it steadies, goes to dip again, then Whoomph! The whole weird 'kite' explodes into tiny fragments.

CLOSE-UP – WATCH-TOWER GUARD
Lowering his laser gun with a glint of pleasure.
GUARD (*Macho enthusiasm*) Problem e-lim-in-at-ed. (*And he resumes chewing, jaws like grinders.*)

INT. MASDON LIVING ROOM. DAY
MARTINA *and* SILTZ *are in frozen position, like children in a game of 'Simon says . . .'*
VOICE: Snoop Kestrel destroyed. All clear. All clear.
MASDON: (*Snarls*) Bastards!
SILTZ: Martina – what the hell is – ?
MASDON: (*Cuts in*) Those bastards from Chemocure! They'll bribe and backhand and steal and snoop their way into any damn thing of ours they get a sniff of! It's war, Dave, nothing short of all-fucking-out wam-bam *war*. (*Smacks fist into her open palm.*) Womph!
SILTZ: *I* don't have these problems, for Chrissakes.
MASDON: Why should you? Oh, you'll get poaching of stars or directors or storylines, but, hell, Dave – and no disrespect here – your formulae are pretty much standard, yes? You *know* how to maximize your audience, or at least how you might be able to!

CLOSE-UP – SILTZ
SILTZ: (*Proudly*) Too damned right, gal. Our seat sensors tell us exactly how the viewer or interactivator is reacting. Every four seconds we get this info, from everywhere. We know when a killing or a fuck or a droplet from the tear duct is

231

needed – you betcha. But it's a constant fight, I can tell you.

INT. MASDON LIVING ROOM. DAY

MASDON: Ah, but it keeps us on our tootsie-wootsies, Dave. I
love a good scrap!

SILTZ: If I lose nought point two of an audience in any of my
shows, we calculate we lose nought point *three* of
advertising revenue – so, believe you me, anybody on my
team on any of my shows who slips under that line gets a
kick-arse applied on more than just the right orifice!

MASDON: Our formulae, you see, are radically different each
time. (*Ticks off on her fingers, a habit of hers.*) You got A,
anti-depressants. B, sleeping pills. C, fuck stimulants. D,
wake-up-and-enjoy-pills, and E, flavour enhancers. All the
rest is just crumbs off the table. Now, we jiggle-jaggle the
right biochemicals, or find new ones, or – (*Breaks off, looks
at him: a different tone.*) The sleepers are on a bit of a slide
with us at the moment. This is confidential information,
understood?

(SILTZ *is suddenly very alert, sensing 'deal' in the offing.*)

SILTZ: (*Vigorously*) Understood.

MASDON: I want to sponsor a half-hour, Western world, any
half between nine-fifteen and eleven-fifteen p.m.

(*Tiny pause.*)

SILTZ: Cost you.

MASDON: Don't I fucking know it!

(*They look at each other.*)

SILTZ: (*Cautiously*) What kinda show?

MASDON: Horror.

(SILTZ *nods, not unrelieved.*)

SILTZ: What kinda horror?

MASDON: Psychological.

SILTZ: (*With a faint twinkle*) No axes, chisels, chainsaws,
gouged eyeballs, blood-sucking, asphyxiation – that
whatchewmean?

CLOSE-UP – MARTINA MASDON

MASDON: No. The shadow at the top of the stair. The half-voice
that half-whispers in the head. (*A nasty, peculiarly sadistic*

gleam enters her eyes.) The hollow nothing at the back of the
eye. The sound of the wind in the chimney and the
footstep that wasn't there. The darkness outside the door.
Dark. Da-a-ark. Da-a-a-ark!

INT. MASDON LIVING ROOM. DAY
At the odd climax, SILTZ *steps back, almost in defence. In speaking,
she has advanced upon him, and on the last two words her hands
have made something of a claw-like gesture.*
SILTZ: OK. OK. I got the category, Martina.
MASDON: Unease.
SILTZ: You're not kidding.
MASDON: Angst.
SILTZ: Gotcha.
    (*They look at each other. She becomes more matter-of-fact.*)
MASDON: Anyway, an unsettling half-hour for those with that
    kind of disposition. But people *like* being scared, don't
    they?
SILTZ: Oh, sure. *If* they're safe. That's a good market.
MASDON: Well, it's the one I'm after. Masdon Science Centers
    will stand the heat on this, cost-wise. I want the kind of
    show where the hey-feel-good pills have long since worn
    off, and the sleepers have a kinda *scary* feeling about them
    – know what I mean?
SILTZ: (*Comically, uneasily*) I'm beginning to, dear.

CLOSE-UP – MARTINA MASDON
The predatory, witch-like glint bounces back into her expression.
MASDON: Dave. We've been working on encaphalins – that's a
    group of peptides in the brain, OK? – and we *think* we've
    found one little cluster that blocks the messages being
    transmitted from one segment of the brain to another –
    you with me?
SILTZ: (*Off, unsure*) Y-yes.
MASDON: And the message that *this* group of peptides stops is –
    wait for it! – *anxiety*. We put up a road-block. Angst – No
    entry! Got me?
SILTZ: (*Off, unsure*) Sort of.

INT. MASDON LIVING ROOM. DAY

MASDON: But first – well, shit – it's as plain as a boil on a fat man's arse, Dave – *first* you gotta make a whole damn zillion of folks feel mighty *anxious*. And that's where your TV and VR and whatthehellelse comes in.

SILTZ: You want a half-hour of terror so that you can –

MASDON: (*Cuts in*) Not terror! No! *Unease.* The shadow at the top of the stair. Wake *up*, willya!
(*She gives* SILTZ *what is more than a playful little push and shove; and he doesn't like it.*)

SILTZ: Maybe you should take some kind of pill yourself, Martina.
(*But she just cackles.*)

INT./EXT. 2368 'CAR'. STREETS. DUSK/NIGHT

EMMA, TONY, LUANDA, FYODOR *squashed inside a bubble of moving glass with just one or two wheels, electric, and with no driver – just voice-recognition controls. This is passing, not very fast, through what is in effect a* dressed *building site or similar, as at abandoned warehouses in dockland. Through the hazy glass, the 'street' looks unutterably dangerous and vandalized. The powerful lights of the 'car' cut a swathe through it all.*

FYODOR *is looking morosely out, somehow cut off from the others by his own temperament.*

EMMA: (*Too warmly*) – but you're *very* welcome, Fyodor. It's ages since we ventured beyond the company diner. I'm looking forward to it! It's been quite a day. *Please* come.

FYODOR: (*Still looking out*) No. Thank you. I want to watch the big movie. (*Then*) RON. RON. Look – it's getting to be everywhere – !

EXT. SIDE OF RAT-WARREN BUILDING. DUSK/NIGHT

In fluorescent paint the initials RON in crude capitals, as seen from the moving glass bubble.

CLOSE-UP – LUANDA

LUANDA: (*Laughing*) You know, for *ages* I thought it was just a name – Ron. Who is this Ron? I thought. And too stupid to ask.

INT./EXT. 'CAR'. STREET. DUSK/NIGHT

TONY: Ask the wrong person and you get the cuffs biting into your wrists, honey.

FYODOR: (*Suddenly*) OK. This is FG 170535. Stop here on left, twenty yards up.
(*The 'car' slowing, at once. In the distance, wailing police sirens.*)

EMMA: You're sure – ?

FYODOR: (*Almost a snap*) *Quite* sure. Thank you (*Presses a button, a section opens.*) Some other time, though.

EXT. FYODOR'S APARTMENT BLOCK. DUSK/NIGHT

Less vandalized, more obviously 'city-normal' type, another ovoid building, with private armed guard – but by no means a warm or welcoming sight. FYODOR, *getting out of the car, leans back in –sardonic.*

FYODOR: 'Reality or Nothing'. RON. What a piss-arse nomenclature for those killers, eh? There must be an acronym for what they want which would spell out ess aitch eye tee.
(*Inside the 'car', they laugh, a little uneasy, and chorus 'Good night.'*)

EXT. ENTRANCE AND PAVEMENT, FYODOR'S BLOCK. DUSK/NIGHT

He looks at the departing glass bubble as it moves slowly away, then turns to the door and the –

APARTMENT GUARD: Evening, Mr Glazunov.

FYODOR: Evening. (*He inserts a 'smart card' into a sidelong slot by or in the door.*)

DOOR VOICE: (*Automatic resonance*) *Checking.*

APARTMENT GUARD: There was a shoot-out down the street just twenty minutes ago, sir –
(*As* FYODOR *stiffens, the* GUARD *points with his laser gun.* FYODOR *looks.*)

EXT. SIDE-STREET. DUSK/NIGHT

The ovoid block is on a corner. Beyond it, off the road the electric 'car' had travelled, arc lamps illuminate a row of covered and half-

*covered bodies with a bloodied arm or leg protruding here and there.
A morgue globule-like cart is being backed up to them, with police
gestures.*

EXTREME CLOSE-UP – FYODOR
*A sick look, momentarily hooding his eyes, with the first hint that he
might be something else as well as what he is professionally.*
APARTMENT GUARD: Seems they caught a bunch of those –

EXT. ENTRANCE FYODOR'S BLOCK. DUSK/NIGHT
APARTMENT GUARD: (*Continuous*) RON people on their way to
    a meeting or some –
FYODOR: (*Abruptly*) Good.
    (*At same time –*)
DOOR VOICE: *Entrance cleared. Welcome.*
    (*The door clicks open on a brief buzz-zz, and* FYODOR *goes
    through without further acknowledgement to the* GUARD.)
APARTMENT GUARD: Pity we can't get all the bastards – !

INT. COMMUNAL HALLWAY. FYODOR'S BLOCK. NIGHT
*The guard's possible further expletives cut off by the closing door. The
hall is smart, clean, even luxurious – unexpectedly so, from the
outside. Its walls have monitors showing street outside and a variety
of TV programmes. More and more evidently in this future world,
the 'private' is high-tech luxury and wealth, the 'public' shabby,
soulless and dangerous.*

CLOSE-UP – FYODOR
*He leans back against the closed door for the briefest moment. And
there are tears in his eyes.*

INT. MASDON LIVING ROOM. DAY
SILTZ *drains his glass of prettily coloured liquid, but not as though he
likes it, and rises.*
SILTZ: Well, Martina, good to meet with you, as always. I'll get
    a team of scripters on to it as soon as you come up with
    some development money.
MASDON: How much?
    (*They look at each other. Then –*)

SILTZ: (*Laughs*) Hey. We got agents for that.
(*They look at each other. And laugh.*)

MASDON: OK, Dave. But it's not bug-eyed monsters, right? It's spiders crawling up the lining of your throat.

SILTZ: (*As though casually*) Is that what your troublesome lot in London are working on – those encaphalins or whatever it was – ?

MASDON: Nah! We extract those from cerebrospinal fluid. Those bums over there are working on memory enhancers – it's such a tiny sector of the market, they're just *asking* for trouble if they go into overspend. (*Suddenly.*) Why? Why you ask?

SILTZ: That woman you were balling out – I got a feeling I was at cybercollege with her.

MASDON: (*Relaxing*) Yeah? That so?

SILTZ: So many years ago, but there was something about her – Christ. To look back so far gives me the shudders. But, yes, I'm off to England tomorrow –

MASDON: You are?

SILTZ: (*Laughs*) Troublesome little dump!

MASDON: Why the laugh?

SILTZ: Oh, I dunno – it's the way we say 'England' when no such place even exists as a political entity. Not for – what? – two hundred years.

MASDON: But they still call it that themselves. My God, they're almost more trouble than they're worth. That's where the RONs have their *real* power base, if you ask me! Anyway – safe trip, Dave.
(*They are going through to – *)

INT. LARGE VESTIBULE. DAY

Vaulting to the very top of the dome, almost cathedral-like, luxuriant with high-tech trimmings and many monitor screens showing many programmes, soundlessly, waiting to be chosen.

SILTZ: (*Disingenuous, with a laugh*) Maybe I should look this old broad up – and frighten her with a description of your present mood.

MASDON: Emma Porlock? Nah! She's –

SILTZ: (*Gleaming*) Yes. That was her name!

MASDON: (*Continuing*) – a brilliant cryobiologist, but otherwise *the* pain in the rectum of all time. (*Opens door.*) Anyway. She'll be frightened enough already, Dave. The bitch has barked and shown her fangs. (*Taps bosom.*) *This* bitch, I mean. Bye.

SILTZ: (*Laughs*) Good-bye, Martina. Don't bite *me*, gal.

INT./EXT. COURTYARD BEYOND VESTIBULE. DAY
The door shuts behind him. The witch disappears. Coming in closer and closer to SILTZ, *and settle on:*

SILTZ: (*Quiet, speculative*) Emma Porlock. Professor Emma Porlock.

EXT. LONDON RESTAURANT. NIGHT
An old building, recognizably London still, though again an armed guard patrols the narrow perimeters of the entrance. Once more, far beyond, sirens wail.

INT. RESTAURANT. NIGHT
EMMA, TONY, LUANDA *in the middle of their meal – a good one, by the looks of it.*

TONY: No – he's strange that way. There are times when you persuade yourself that he positively *wants* to be liked, and then he deliberately says and does the wrong thing. To me – (*Shrugs*) Fyodor's a total enigma.

EMMA: (*Who doesn't like* FYODOR, *but is fair*) Yes. (*Sighs*) But – he's a very great scientist in his own area: the central question of how *memory* is held by differing groups of cells in a way that suggests 'memory' itself cannot be *located* as such, at all –

LUANDA: That's right. It's our real problem. I mean, if you stimulate any one part of the brain, electrically or pharmacologically, you can see that *that* part is definitely related to certain functions, like sex, say, or fear. But 'memory', in quotes, escapes this labelling.

EMMA: Whereas if you excite the front end of the hypothalamus as well as its septal area, you *will* get sexual excitation.

TONY: (*With a half-laugh*) I'm stiff with excitement.

LUANDA: (*Laughs*) You would be if I tickled your hypothalamus!

(*This rather high-scale conversation is broken up a lot by the eating and the drinking, and by loud guffaws from a table beyond them, equally preoccupied with itself.*)

TONY: Ah. (*Chews*) Then we might make our Daniel Feeld have a purely *sexual* memory if we use the –

EMMA: (*Interrupts, gloomily*) If we can do anything at all with Daniel.

(*They look at her and stop eating.*)

LUANDA: Emma – ?

EMMA: She'll cut us off. I sense it. I know it in my bones. That witch (*jeer*) Martina Matilda Masdon. We simply won't be able to *afford* any submicroscopic modifications of *any* of Daniel's surviving brain circuits. We might as well throw him in the bin!

TONY: Surely if we show what can be done – what we've *already* done –

LUANDA: The first time ever anyone has broken into a head with any memory from near-antiquity. Surely, surely, she can't stand in the way of –

EMMA: She's not, the company's not, in the slightest degree interested in science for its own sake. We stand about as much chance of –

(*She breaks off, startled, at the sound of laser gunfire outside. An invented sound: high-pitched, long whine, then deadly whomp! of explosion or implosion. People in restaurant start to stand. Some begin to scream.*)

TONY: (*Urgently*) Get under the table! Quickly!

EXT. RESTAURANT. NIGHT

Wheeeeeeeee! Whompa!, repeated, repeated, as the restaurant guard, lying flat on the rutted pavement, attempts to return fire on a trio of hooded men: members of the extremist wing of RON (Reality or Nothing).

Beyond and too far away, but definitely approaching, police sirens wail.

EXT. LONDON STREETS. NIGHT

Two armour-plated 'bubbles', fast, with gun turrets, slit windows, rocket through what looks like a half-derelict no man's land which seems to be all that is left of Whitehall or Trafalgar Square (Nelson's Column and/or Houses of Parliament modelled or matted in, with appropriate additional decay in background.)

INT. RESTAURANT. NIGHT
Diners, in panic, hurry, scurry, back up against the far wall, hurtle towards the kitchens, anywhere, everywhere, but –

INT. UNDER TABLE. RESTAURANT. NIGHT
The overhang of the table-cloth is just about long enough to provide a little sheltered cave under the table top, where EMMA, TONY *and* LUANDA *crouch, holding on to each other and to the edge of the cloth to make sure that the visual protection is at its maximum.*

EXT. STREET AND RESTAURANT. NIGHT
Outnumbered, outgunned, the restaurant guard sprawls dead in the gutter and the three (seemingly uninjured) RON *rebels are trying to smash their way into the restaurant. The door, heavily plated, will not yield. They crab sideways, aware of ever-nearer-approaching police sirens, crab, scuttle, crab, until they reach a less well-protected, small side window.*

INT./EXT. KITCHEN. RESTAURANT
The meshed side window is at the back, waste-disposal end of the very well-equipped kitchens of the restaurant.
Those diners who had rushed for safety towards the kitchen, screaming and shouting now as they scurry back again. The mesh of the window is buckling, buckling, breaking –
And then the first of the three rebels is half-torso in, half-torso out, firing all the time from what must be a virtually endlessly automatic 'self-generating-bullet gun'.

EXT. RESTAURANT. NIGHT
The two armoured police 'bubbles' arriving. They align themselves to smash their way into the restaurant, regardless of any 'civilian' casualties, as, at the same time –

INT. RESTAURANT. NIGHT
All three rebels are crashing in from the kitchens, into the main

*body of the restaurant, firing at random as the petrified diners are
cut down, screaming, diving, crashing, trying to hide, trying
anything.*

INT. UNDER TABLE. RESTAURANT. NIGHT
EMMA, LUANDA and TONY, *all trembling, cling to each other for
dear life in the table-cloth-made shelter under the table, hearing the
mayhem all around them.*
*A slaughtered diner's head and part of his shoulder, crashing to the
floor, flops partly into their perilous little space and* LUANDA *puts her
fist in her mouth to stop screaming as the bloodied head lolls and
spurts into and over her lap or her thigh.*
*The laser gun noises increasing, above, around and beyond them,
as –*

INT. RESTAURANT. NIGHT
*Half a dozen 'police' – more like the militia – cascade from the
armoured bubbles that have smashed their way in, firing, as do the
mounted gun turrets on the bubbles themselves. They seem almost as
indiscriminate as the rebels, with little or no regard for 'civilian'
safety.*
*In a few seconds of blood and thunder, splattered flesh and bone,
broken crockery and mangled food amongst the fallen, it is all over.
Two dead policemen, three dead rebels, a dozen or so dead diners,
and most of the rest injured.*

INT. UNDER TABLE. RESTAURANT. NIGHT
*Cautiously – and carefully pushing or lifting aside the fallen, blood-
oozing body –* TONY, EMMA *and* LUANDA *emerge from their
makeshift but (in the event) effective shelter.*

INT. RESTAURANT. NIGHT
As the three emerge to the carnage around them, a POLICEMAN
*coldly trains his weapon upon them. Two pairs of hands go up in fear
and incredulity. Then – fierce and unyielding, not raising her
hands –*
EMMA: I am Professor Porlock of Masdon Science Centers Inc.,
and these are my colleagues, Drs Watson and Partington.
(*The* POLICEMAN *touches a button on the shaft of his weapon.*

Three MSC ID badges light up on their clothing, but EMMA
does not stop talking.)
Why were you so appallingly late? And why do you pay so
little regard for ordinary civilian life?
(*The* POLICEMAN *lowers his weapon, but under his mostly
enclosing helmet, his eyes flash scorn, even hatred.*)
POLICEMAN: Shut your food-hole, you dried-up old bag. Try
doing what *we* do for a week, and then yap-yap about it!
(*In the background another policeman is radioing for the
morgue carts and the paramedics. The unpleasant cop talking to*
EMMA *motions at the three dead rebels, sprawled together in a
multi-lacerated huddle.*)
Those bastards there – those RONs – rot the beasts! – but
they've got more spunk juice in them than all you sit-on-
your-arse scientists and button-pushers put together!
(*Feisty* EMMA *snorts, then she looks at the bodies all around, a
real shambles of death and destruction. One dead diner, for
example, has a scooped-out, berry-filled pineapple cradled in his
arms, upon which blood from his head has dripped. Then she
looks at the* POLICEMAN.)
EMMA: (*To* POLICEMAN) You know something. You might even
be right. For once. (*Turns to others.*) Let's get out of here,
for God's sake.
POLICEMAN: Hey. Wait a moment. You can't just –
(*But she ignores him.* TONY *looks at the* POLICEMAN,
uneasily, but turns and follows EMMA *and the more instantly
obedient* LUANDA. *They pick their way past the rubble of the
entrance, leaving behind sounds of moans, sobs and radiophonic
voices from the police.*)

EXT. STREET OUTSIDE AND BEYOND RESTAURANT. NIGHT
EMMA, TONY *and* LUANDA *walk a few yards in subdued and
depressed silence. It is amazing how few people are out and about ,
even after all the noise and spectacle of the rebel raid.* EMMA *is
touching, or has touched, a module on the outer rim of her biobrace
(bracelet).* LUANDA *is very quietly crying to herself.* TONY *sniff-sniffs
the air.*
TONY: Godolo – the *air.* You know. It sort of, sort of – it –
LUANDA: (*Suppressing quick half-sob*) Stinks.

TONY: And to think in days gone by, people used to go for long walks – half a mile sometimes – breathing all this in.

EMMA: Don't worry. I've ordered up my bubble on the biobrace – I'll drop both of you off at your places. (*To* TONY) It wasn't like this, then. The air. (*Then, vigorously but with anguish/regret.*) Oh, we have so much to learn or relearn from the past. Daniel Feeld! In a way, he could have been our – our – yes! Our teacher!

EXT. CAR AND FURTHER ALONG STREET. NIGHT
A small 'bubble' auto is coming slowly up alongside them, driverless. It will just about seat the three of them. For a little while, it dutifully keeps pace with them at the edge of the pitted and broken pavement, its beam bright, splashing light ahead of them.

CLOSE-UP – LUANDA. STREET
Her tears have dried. She is back in emotional control of herself.

LUANDA: I *think* I've satisfied myself on the ethical side of Daniel Feeld's half-life. Odd, isn't it, what goes on in your head when you're scared out of your wits. But it came to me when I was cowering under that table.

EXT. STREET. 'BUBBLE'. NIGHT
The little auto gives a small beep! as though for attention.

EMMA: (*Fiercely, to 'car'*) Shut up! And wait!

CAR VOICE: Identify. Please ident.

EMMA: EP 110761. Shut up and wait.
(*The 'car', satisfied, is silent, and crawls along beside them.*)
Go on, Luanda. Explain.

TONY: Yes, please!

LUANDA: We have the answer in front of us every time we look at the living wall in the laboratory. As long as that screen stays blank – or free of real images – then it means Daniel only quote remembers, only quote thinks, when under biochemic stimulation, right?

EMMA: (*Stops*) No volition, you mean. He has no independent will.

TONY: (*Stops*) Of course! So when it's blank he himself, or the bits of himself we have left, *cannot* be aware.

243

LUANDA: (*Stops*) And if you're not aware, you're not alive. You're in no mental and no spiritual and no physical torment.

(EMMA *unexpectedly, gives* LUANDA *a dry little peck on the cheek, as they stop walking.*)

EMMA: Clever girl!

(TONY, *looking up ahead by the dazzling splash of light from the auto 'bubble', sees what looks like a gang of young layabouts tormenting a down-and-out, with hoots of laughter.*)

TONY: Come on. Let's get into the car.

EXT. STREET UP AHEAD. NIGHT

An equivalent of today's wino, cradling a bottle of some oddly coloured liquid as though for protection, is being rolled over and over on the broken paving stones by five or six youths.

FIRST YOUTH: C'mon, pop. Give it to us!

SECOND YOUTH: It'll kill you in the end!

(*They cackle with their own wit.*)

THIRD YOUTH: We'll kill you if you don't stop drinking that stuff!

(*They kick him and break the bottle. The wino weeps as the liquid pours all over him.*)

FIRST YOUTH: Let's make the bugolo lick it up!

CHORUS: Lick it up! Lick it up!

(*They dance all around him, cavorting with glee.*)

INT. CRYOGENIC LAB. NIGHT

Nobody about. Dim night lights bathe everything in soft silvery grey, not unlike moonlight. The autocubes are unoccupied, mere silhouettes. The living wall is blank. And then, in a slow, slow movement towards it – virtually a creep – a few black dots begin to float on the screen wall.

THE LIVING WALL

Soon, it is made up of myriad dots, which take first one, then a few, then many colours. The dots start to blob and coalesce. The blobs gradually take shapes.

INT. CRYOGENIC LAB. NIGHT
The living wall, alive again, throwing out light across the empty lab,
and its unmanned equipment.
Pulling back, back, wider and wider, as, on the wall –

INT. DANIEL'S HOSPITAL ROOM. 1994. DAY
Daniel's lips have just been moistened by SANDRA, *and* BEN *is*
speaking to DANIEL *as one might to an injured or fretful child.*
BEN: Better? Eh?
DANIEL: (*Off screen, urgent croak*) Ben. Ben I – listen.
BEN: Daniel. Say it. Say it, old lad.
DANIEL: (*Off screen*) No biog-g-gah –
    (*Not really comprehensible.*)
BEN: (*Looming in*) What? No what?

INT. CORNER OF CRYOGENIC LAB. NIGHT
Now the width of the lab away from the living wall, where the
above, repeated scene from Daniel's last on-earth moments is still
clearly visible and audible – dominating the empty lab. The angle is
reversed, so that we are now looking straight at the lab wall exactly
opposite the living wall.
DANIEL: (*Off, shouts*) Ben!
    (*Narrowing down in the terrorized pause that followed Daniel's*
    *cry in the hospital room to find - *)

CLOSE-UP – A BLACK BOX
More and more discernible, and hideously upsetting, a head seems to
float in liquid nitrogen, all wired-up with antennae,
neurotransmitters and hair-thin coils of tubes. But the eyes are open,
full of terror, and the mouth seems to be trying to make word-shapes,
and the flesh is a ghastly, slightly fluorescent, silver grey. The cry
from the unseen living wall opposite, off-screen, might as well come
from the box.
DANIEL: (*Off, near scream*) No biography!
    (*For the severed, part-thawed, electronically transmitting head*
    is DANIEL's *head. And, clearly, it has transmitted the pictures*
    of its own volition. Clearly, it knows that it is 'alive'.
       Slowly fade the grotesque and unbearably cruel image of the
    wired-up, discoloured yet recognizable head of DANIEL FEELD,

245

trying to scream the ultimate terror of a mortal soul made immortal. Separated from God.)

PART TWO

EXT. SMALL STONE CHAPEL. 'FOREST OF NEAD'. DAY
*On the edge of a hilly line of trees, among village houses, old, grey,
proletarian – but a bright day and the sense of 'another land'. We
are way, way back, somewhere in the twentieth century.*
*The steady approach to the chapel (simple Protestant) is matched by
the steady rise of children's voices singing – and, since this must be a
special occasion, by the sound of brass band instruments playing
'Amazing Grace'.*
CHILDREN: (*Singing, off*)
   Amazing Grace! How sweet the sound,
   That saved a wretch like me.
   (*Dissolving –*)

INT. CHAPEL. DAY
*A full congregation of children, only children, except for the village
brass band to the left of the pulpit and a preacher who remains
sternly silent. There is an embroidered banner behind the pulpit,
hanging tasselled on the stone wall, showing a version of Holman-
Hunt's* Light of the World.
CHILDREN: (*Singing, continuous*)
   I once was lost, But now am found,
   Was blind, but now I see.
   (*They are seven–ten-year-olds, singing their hearts out. It
   moves.*)

INT. WINDOW. SIDE OF CHAPEL. DAY
*Seeking and finding a chapel-shaped window half-way along the
rows of singing benches, as the hymn continues.*
CHILDREN: (*Continuous*)
   'Twas grace that taught my heart to fear
   And grace my fears relieved –
   (*There is a bowl or vase of fresh cut flowers on the sill. And
   then, suddenly, peering around the flowers – a face.*)

EXTREME CLOSE-UP – FACE AT CHAPEL WINDOW
It is the face of DANIEL FEELD *as he was in* Karaoke: *that is, 1994.*
So we presume this is not a 'childhood' memory. The singing
continues.
CHILDREN (*Continuous*)
   How precious did that grace appear –

EXT. SIDE OF CHAPEL. DAY
DANIEL, *hands flat against the stone wall on either side of the*
window, is standing on an empty upturned grocer's wholesale tin of
Oxo Cubes to give him the extra few inches needed to peer right in to
the singing children.
CHILDREN: (*Singing, off, continuous*)
   – the hour I first believed!
   Through many dangers, toils and snares –
(*Behind him, a tufty grass hillock reaches towards outlying trees,*
part of a real forest. Alongside him, patiently sitting, ears cocked is
the very double of the old 'His Master's Voice' advertising dog. But
then DANIEL, *on the upturned tin, stiffens.*)

INT./EXT. THROUGH CHAPEL WINDOW. DAY
DANIEL *sees a knitted-jerseyed, short-trousered, tousle-haired seven-*
or eight-year-old boy point at him, accusingly, from the end of a
crowded bench, and other faces soon start to turn. He quickly bobs
down and, in doing so, falls, making the Oxo tin clatter under him,
and the dog bark.
CHILDREN: (*Off, continuous*)
   I have already come
   'Tis grace that brought me safe thus far
   And grace will lead me home.

EXT. GRASSY HILLOCK. DAY
DANIEL *rights himself and, with an odd desperation, begins to run*
up the hill towards the outlying fringe of trees, the dog following,
excitedly. As he runs, the band and the children's voices recede, but
in these spaces they can be heard, distantly, for quite a time, like
Sunday bells, so to speak (or clang).
CHILDREN: (*Off, receding, continuous*)
   Yes, when this heart and flesh shall fail,

And mortal life shall cease –

EXT. THE WOODS. DAY
*Getting into and under the canopy of trees – oak and beech, mostly –
the chapel sounds are just on the veriest edge of earshot, heartachingly
evocative even if not properly heard.*

CHILDREN: (*Far off*)
**I shall possess within the veil
A life of joy and peace!**
(*Running deeper into the woods,* DANIEL *becomes less anxious.
But by now, there is something about the whole situation, and
in particular his body-language, which suggests something is
wrong, out of order, out of what is possible.
He picks up a stick or loose, fallen piece of branch, and hurls it
as far as he can. Thwack! it goes against another tree, and birds
fly up in noisy alarm.* DANIEL*'s movements and gestures are
those of a small child.*)

DANIEL: Fetch! Good boy!
(*The dog, whose ears have been pricked, head cocked,
delightedly bolts away after the thrown stick.*)

INT. CRYOGENIC LAB. DAY
*It is, of course, the year 2368 – 374 years on from Daniel's death.
The living wall – one whole length and depth of the big laboratory –
has been (and continues) showing the above.*

EMMA, LUANDA, TONY, BLINDA *and* KAYA *are watching.*
FYODOR *is missing. But now, as the forest scene continues (see
below), they are beginning to shuffle their autocubes uneasily and to
look at each other as much as at the screen or living wall.*

EXT. THE WOODS. DAY
*The dog, tail wagging, bringing back the stick and laying it proudly
at* DANIEL*'s feet.*

DANIEL: (*Heavy accent*) Aw, good old Mick! Thou bist a good
'un, Mickey, o'butt. Best dog as ever there was – only
doosn't thee go and tell on I, mind.
(*At which he falls to the soft under-tree ground and wrestles with
the happy animal.*)

CLOSE-UP – TONY. CRYOGENIC LAB
He shifts discontentedly and mutters, more to himself than to the others.
TONY: This doesn't make sensolo. It's ridiculous.

INT. CRYOGENIC LAB. DAY
His mumbled unease is obviously being shared by the others, as, on the living wall, 'boy' and dog stop wrestling, yelping and barking, and head off at a lick further and further into the seemingly endless trees.
DANIEL *wallops his own backside as he runs, as though he himself were his own horse.*
DANIEL: Giddy-up! Giddy-up! Up! Up!
EMMA: (*Suddenly*) Luanda! *Stop the drip!* The alpha-
    neuropeptide 1042!
    (*As running, horse-riding 'boy' and barking dog recede into the deeper and deeper bowers of greenery,* LUANDA *fast autocubes to the opposite wall to the living screen, to a –*)

INT. RACK OF 'FEED' CHANNELS. THE LAB. DAY
Above and to the right of a strange black box – the one holding Daniel's severed head, seen at the end of Part One – virtually hair-thin loops of viscous liquid lead to the box from a rack of small neuropeptide containers, differently numbered.
LUANDA *buttons off one of the containers from a simple two-position button above the rack – a button for each peptide.* KAYA *has gone across with her and checks that the flow has stopped, stooping in front of the black box.*

CLOSE-UP – THE DEADLY BLACK BOX
Floating in its liquid nitrogen, with a sort of cold steam blurring the image a little, the electrode-plugged, tube-fed, hole-drilled, ghastly silvery face of DANIEL FEELD *seems to fall into a kind of repose.*
KAYA: (*With pity*) Overt activity has ceased, Professor.

INT. CRYOGENIC LAB. DAY
On the opposite wall the images of DANIEL, *dog, over-arching trees slide almost stickily into blobs, the blobs suck apart from each other and with a distinct plop-p! the living wall becomes once again a*

myriad multicoloured dots. Silent KAYA *turns to watch, a sparkle of wet in her eyes.*

And silence from the other four present, too, for a beat. Then –

EMMA: We have so damnably *little* of the 1042 that we must always, always make absolutely sure that we gain the maximum use or value out of it. Now – what is going on up there at the moment – (*Gestures at screen*) is to me so – so – *distorted* and out of any sort of norm *I* can accept – ! We're either feeding in too much 1042 or too little.

TONY: It began real enough –

LUANDA: (*Brooding, trying to speak*) But perhaps, perhaps this is only a –

(EMMA *is not really listening to the others. Out of her autocube in her agitation and disappointment, she gives Fyodor's empty autocube a thwack! of temper with the flat of her hand.*)

EMMA: And, of course, *of course*, just when we need Glazunov's biochemistry the most, he chooses to take the morning off! We're underfunded, understaffed, underdisciplined, and undereveryfuckolo else! I'm sick of it!

LUANDA: (*Quietly*) Emma.

EMMA: (*Who happens to be looking in Kaya's direction*) Sick of it! Sick of it, d'you hear!

KAYA: (*Confused*) I – I – I'm sorry. I –

LUANDA: Emma!

EMMA: (*As though* LUANDA *has only now spoken*) *What?*

LUANDA: I've been thinking –

EMMA: Well, I'm glad someone around here has been doing *something*! (*Looks at* LUANDA, *tone changes.*) Oh, bugolo! I'm sorry. I'm sorry! It's just – well, everything's getting me down this morning. And it's not simply the delayed shock from last night.

TONY: We actually made the *Breakfast News* this morning – well, at least on the *Orange Juice Hour* – which shows the RONs must have been after somebody really –

(*His voice trails off as he realizes* EMMA *is staring at him indignantly for interrupting her plaint.*)

SUDDEN CLOSE-UP – EMMA. LAB

EMMA: *Orange Juice Hour. Orange Juice Hour!* And what vidfax was I getting? Eh? Any fucking idea? Juice-head!

INT. CRYOGENIC LAB. DAY

TONY: (*Subdued*) Sorry, Professor.

(*He sneaks a quick look at* KAYA, *the lovely Asian, and gets a quick answering warmth.*)

EMMA: There's that dear, sweet old *shag-hag* Martina Matilda. Masdon popping up behind my toaster, all her teeth grinning at me, saying that our contracts are being reduced from eighteen months to *eight* and our budget per month is cut by 15 per cent with an absolute ceiling!

(TONY, LUANDA, BLINDA *and* KAYA *gulp down suppressed gasps of disappointment and anxiety.* EMMA *looks at them, her expression softens – she spreads her arms in an I'm-so-sorry gesture.* LUANDA, *recovering, tries to make a joke.*)

LUANDA: Maybe sly old Fyodor is already out looking for a job.

(BLINDA *covers her mouth with her hand, amused.*)

EMMA: Hah! The job we need is right here, right now. I thought if we could assemble enough material from our resurrected Lazarus – (*Gestures towards the black box*) we *might*, just might, be able to pitch a case for continuation, or at least to hold the budget at its present level. But if all we're going to get is unreliable distortion, and comic maladjustment, then even –

LUANDA: (*Interrupts*) But it may not *be* that!

(EMMA *stops dead.*)

EMMA: What?

TONY: (*Hopeful*) Luanda?

LUANDA: We-e-ll – we can't expect perfectly formed memory when so many of the brain cells are not 'tuned in' to our peptides and so many more have still to be thawed out –

EMMA: No, but –

LUANDA: (*Keeps going*) But even then, even if we could, we would surely expect to see some sort of duplication of what we get in our *own* memories. Aren't we sometimes – I mean, rather, don't we sometimes place ourselves as we are now back into the unravelling of an old recollection – ? Don't we?

EMMA: (*Half-dubious, but interested*) Mmmm. Not sure.

LUANDA: I can be as I am now when I dream of my childhood, for instance. Do you, Blinda?

BLINDA: (*Laughs*) Oh, yes. Doctor. It's the only way I can thump the other kids!

EMMA: (*Irritated*) Very funny. Oh, yes – but that's not the same thing, is it? Dream, memory. Memory, dream.

LUANDA: It's first cousin to it!

(EMMA *gives her a sharply questioning look, then nods half-assent, half-reluctantly. Going in – in – on* LUANDA *as her eyes brighten with thought.*)

CLOSE-UP – LUANDA

LUANDA: First cousin. And of the same blood. My dreams are built from the things that happen to me in the waking world. And my memories can also adapt and shape the past. I can put myself in a better light than I actually was, for instance. I can work up an accidental slight from a former friend into a deliberate act of villainy from a now sworn enemy. I can disown this or that piece of behaviour. My memory, Emma, is also a tool, an editor, a judge, a jury!

INT. CRYOGENIC LAB. DAY

TONY: (*To* EMMA) That's true. It's true! And there's something else – now we've done enough work on *amnesia*, haven't we? We *know* that we can block out entirely things that are too painful to remember. Right?

EMMA: (*Rather chilly at being addressed didactically*) Right.

TONY: Well – that's what we might be seeing here – (*Gestures at living wall*) Daniel Feeld half letting in a *real* memory. A bad one, maybe. A shameful one, perhaps. We don't yet know. These distortions we're seeing – OK, they could be just that, a failure in our alpha-neuropeptide 1042, or wrong mix of it – OK, yes – But it could, just could be that we are seeing the infinitely cunning operations of an infinitely complex mind actually at work!

(*They all look at the living wall and its myriad floating, multicoloured dots. Then, suddenly, decisively – *)

EMMA: All right. We'll risk more of our precious fluid. Switch him on again!

LUANDA: Kaya. On the point zero two two mark.

(KAYA, *pleased by the responsibility, goes quickly across to the 'feed' rack.*)

KAYA: Thank you, Doctor.

BLINDA (*Mock indignant*) When do *I* get to do that?

EMMA: (*Matter-of-fact*) Oh, shut up, girl.

(*Her eyes, like those of the others, are fixed on the living wall, where, faster now, dots slide to blobs, which slide to bigger blobs, greening all the time and becoming –*)

EXT. THE FOREST. TWENTIETH CENTURY. DAY

The great old trees, arching towards each other at the tops, like the nave of an enormous cathedral, seem to go on and on for ever, letting in dapples and pools of sunlight here and there, and softening all other colours in their greenish hues. Move through it like a slow memory forming.

Finding – as though looking and looking for him – DANIEL, *sitting behind a big bush just off a path of sorts through the trees towards a distant stile.*

EXT. THE BUSH. FOREST. DAY

It is, indeed, the physical simulacrum of DANIEL *as he was in 1994 (in Karaoke) but now he is dressed as a working-class schoolboy of 1944 or so (this can be adjusted if necessary, decade-wise). He is carefully taking out the one single three-quarters-unsmoked, untipped 'Woodbine' cigarette from its otherwise empty green-paper packet of five. The dog squats beside him, head cocked with interest.*

CLOSE-UP – LUANDA. LAB

A glow of triumph on her – and the greeny-glow from the living wall.

LUANDA: (*Half-whisper*) You see! Look at the clothes! The memory is adjusting back to childhood. At base, it's real. It's true!

EXT. THE BUSH. FOREST. DAY

DANIEL *now takes out a box of England's Glory matches, but there is only one match in the box. He addresses the dog solemnly, and the dog solemnly listens.*

DANIEL: (*To dog*) One match, mind. 'Sall I got, Mick, o'butty.

Im'll have to work fust time. There yunt no second chance. (*He has the unburnt end of the three-quarter cigarette in his mouth. Scrape-scrape, the match flares. He lights the cigarette, successfully, draws in smoke, coughs, leans back on the ground, cradling his head with the back of his free arm, comically contemplative.*) Oy. There yunt nothing like a fag when tha bist in a bad mood, our Mick. (*Puffs, thinks.*) Make I giddy, mind. (*One more illicit puff, then he carefully pinches out the cigarette with a little 'ow!', blows on it to make sure it is quite extinguished and puts it back in the packet. He doesn't get up, but sits up a little, patting the dog and ruffling its hair.*) Doost thou think Chris'll tell on I not going to chapel? Bet him ool! And I shall be in dead *bloody buggering bloody* bloody trouble. (*Sniff.*) I cont half *cuss*, eh, Mick? (*Giggles, strokes.*) But look – tuppence collection money! (*He shows the dog two big old pennies. The dog sniffs at them, interested, and then not interested.*) Another ha'penny and I can buy me a *Sunny Stories* at the post office, cont I? Tuppence-yuppeny. That's a *lot*, yunnit? Nowadays. But I'da like them little stories – *Wassamatter?* (*This last marginally anxious question because the dog is suddenly extra-alert.*)

CLOSE-UP – DOG
Ears cocked, a faint growl, then his hair ruffles at the neck.

EXT. BUSH. DAY
DANIEL *gets up, brushing the seat of his short trousers, a bit concerned.*
DANIEL: Who is it, Mick? I hope it chunt Mr Harris or one of thoy –
(*But the dog is suddenly running, fast, deeper into the dense trees, further and further away from the rough forest path, with that excited, persistent, vaguely threatening yelp-yelp-yelp common to terriers.*

   DANIEL *follows the dog, at less speed, and with less certainty of purpose.*)
(*Gasping*) Here, boy. Come, here! Wos wrong with thee – !
Mick! Here, Mick!

EXT. FOREST THICKET. DAY

The undergrowth seems to meet the lower branches, and the trees are tightly packed together, reducing the normal dapples and pools of invading sunlight into narrow shafts, and the ambient pale greeny glow into something rather darker, and somehow more foreboding. The predominantly white flash (with darker spots) of the dog – yelp! yelp! yelp! yelp! – is seen for a moment, plunging in a streak deeper and deeper into the thicket.

DANIEL: *(Off, further back)* Mick! Come th'on here, boy! Mick! Mickey!

INT. CRYOGENIC LAB. DAY

The five watchers, staring at the huge, vivid living wall, would be hard put to explain the tension in their bodies, but it is evident even as they sit in their autocubes. In front of them, the forest scenes above and below are being played out.

CLOSE-UP – KAYA

She has so far consistently been shown as the one real 'romantic' amongst them. The laboratory assistant, caught as though accidentally in the sudden plunge of the big close-up, has her hand going towards her face again, her eyes stilling in an incipient fear, and she seems to be holding her breath, as –

EXT. FOREST. DAY

DANIEL, *standing off a little from the very densest part of one of the thickets that regularly knot themselves into a real forest (as opposed to small, 'managed' woods), keeps calling the dog's name, and, out of his view but near, the dog keeps yelping. But now, oddly, his voice is octaves higher!*

DANIEL: Mickey! Mick! C'mhere! Bad boy! Bad, bad boy!

INT. CRYOGENIC LAB. DAY

Reverse angle. The five watchers are seen front-on, as from the living wall, which momentarily cannot be seen. And, with shock, with consternation, with excitement, with incredulity, their faces react to something on the living wall that is clearly knocking their minds sideways. Reverse to –

INT. CRYOGENIC LAB AND ITS LIVING WALL. DAY
*There, now, before them, calling out the same words from the same
(locked-off) camera position to the same yelp-yelp-yelp! from the
same (as yet unseen) dog is a genuine seven- or eight-year-old boy in
(cut-down, obviously) identical 1940s working-class schoolboy
clothing.*
DANIEL: Mickey! Mick! Bad boy! You come here, you bugger!
  Come here!
  (*And it seems to be the same knitted-jerseyed, short-trousered,
  tousle-haired seven- or eight-year-old boy who pointed at
  Daniel's face at the chapel window, accusingly, from the end of
  a crowded bench – except that that boy, safely in chapel, safely
  singing 'Amazing Grace', is Daniel's twin brother*
  CHRISTOPHER.)

EXT. FOREST. DAY
*The yelping of the dog, off, near, suddenly ends in one long yelp of an
utterly different kind and then is silent.*

CLOSE-UP – DANIEL. FOREST
*The boy stands still a moment, suddenly very frightened. He whispers
to himself out of a dry throat.*
DANIEL: (*To self*) Mick? What's wrong? Mick? – Wassamatter,
  old butty?

FLASH: EXTREME CLOSE-UP – KAYA
Eyes dead still, lips slightly parted, anxiety in every facial muscle.

EXT. FOREST AND THICKET. DAY
*The boy, swallowing a bit, cautiously edges forward (his back to
camera) into the outer fringes of the thicket, the ground beginning to
slope downward, as is often the case. This type of thicket will
sometimes surround a small grassy hollow or dell.*
DANIEL: (*Quietly*) Mick? Where bist? Mickey – ?

EXT. THICKET AND DELL. DAY
*Reverse, now, so that the boy's cautious or stealthy approach into the
heart of the thorny, woody, frond-like entanglement is seen head-on,
and not from the back.*

Boy DANIEL *'s hands part fronds of fern, branch or briar, and then his face emerges, and then he cries out in a sob.*
DANIEL: *Mi-i-i-i-ick!*

EXT. THE DELL. DAY
A scooped-out grassy steep-sided little dell entirely surrounded, as though in dense protection, by the thicket. But in the middle of the dell, the dog lies still.
Approach the dog as though on tiptoe, even though boy DANIEL – *momentarily paralysed – does not move and hence goes off screen.*

EXTREME CLOSE-UP – THE DOG
It is *dead. The sharper, bloodied end of a stone lies beside it, though there is little or no sign of the (cosmetic!) wound to the poor old dog.*

EXT. THE DELL. DAY
Released, the boy charges forward, a sob in his throat, clearly realizing that MICK *is dead. He half-lifts or half-cradles the motionless animal.*
DANIEL: (*Weeping*) Oh, Mick – Mick, Mick – What happened o'butty? What – (*He stops dead, looking up, as though straight at the camera looking down on him into the hollow – Reverse –*)

EXT. RIM OF DELL OR HOLLOW. DAY
A rustle of undergrowth and suddenly, menacingly, a huge pair of working boots, steel-tipped, scuffed and studded, and above them sturdy male legs, in dirty, patched, scuffed corduroy, tied with cord just below the knees, top of frame.

INT. CRYOGENIC LAB. DAY
Close against the giant living wall, the comparatively small figures of EMMA, TONY, LUANDA, BLINDA *and* KAYA *stare at the image with a palpable sense of tension filling the laboratory.* KAYA *is already out of her autocube, standing stock still.*

EXT. BOTTOM OF DELL. DAY
Reversed again, so that we see from the point of view of the booted figure looking down upon the boy and his slaughtered pet.
MAN'S VOICE:(*Off screen, strong London accent*) 'E come at me

like a bleed'n *animal*, didn't he? What sort of bloody critter
would do that, then? I didn't have no chance, sonny Jim.
Christ, I fought it was a fucking tiger. Ooops! Watch me
langwidge, eh? (*And he jumps down into* –)

EXT. DELL AND THICKET. DAY
The boy DANIEL *backs away, scared, horrified, as the great hulk-
like frame of the* TRAMP *momentarily fills the screen.*
Wider – and the TRAMP *can be seen as a real, half-mad ruffian, his
upper clothing stained and tattered, and one of his trunk-thick arms
bare to the elbow, with a Sacred Heart tattoo on it.*
TRAMP: Hey, now. No call to be scared, sonny Jim. You're a
lad after me own heart. But dogs is dogs is dogs. If I told
you 'alf the bleed'n trouble they've caused me – well, you'd
soon see. Hoy! *Stand still!*
(*This last peremptory bark of a command because the boy, who
has all the time been slowly backing off, suddenly makes a bolt
for it – scrambling up the slope of the dell.*)
DANIEL: (*Yelling*) Leave I alone!
(*But already big hands are lunging towards him.*)

FLASH: CLOSE-UP – KAYA. LAB
*A micro-second of sheer horror on her watching face, so vivid and
immediate is her identification with the contents of Daniel's
neuropeptided memory.*

EXT. RIM OF DELL AND THICKET. FOREST. DAY
Scrabble as he might, desperately trying to get away, boy DANIEL
cannot quite elude the big man's clutches. First, the TRAMP *grabs a
retreating ankle, then both ankles, and then – as boy* DANIEL
screams a hopeless scream, the TRAMP *drags him back, back.*

CLOSE-UP – BOY'S HANDS. EARTH
Boy DANIEL's *hands try to gain purchase on the soft underwood
earth, clawing, clawing, but being pulled down, down – the scream
continuing –*

EXT. DELL. FOREST. DAY
DANIEL *has stopped screaming as the big* TRAMP *towers in a*

lurching stoop above him, twisting the boy around.

DANIEL: (*Whimpers*) Please, Mister – Please, Mister – I be very sorry about the dog! Please, Mister, don't hurt I, oot?

TRAMP: (*Cackles*) Cheeky little bugger, entcha? Whatchewdoin' aht here in all these bleed'n trees? Eh?

DANIEL: (*Terrified whisper*) I be s'posed to be in chapel, mister, and thoy'll –

TRAMP: (*Cutting in, derisive*) Chapel!

DANIEL: (*Continuous*) – come a-lookin' for me, that's for sure. You watch out! They'll *catch* tha!
(*Whap! The* TRAMP *smacks the boy around the mouth, hard, making him cry out in pain.*)

TRAMP: (*Psychotic glee*) Catch me? Catch me? They'll have a bloody job, won't they?
(*The little face looking up at him with such absolute terror is already smeared with blood from his mouth.*)

DANIEL: (*Barely audible*) Please, Mister –

TRAMP: Please what? Please. Please. Please. Christ, is that all you can bloody say?

DANIEL: (*Weeping*) S-sorry – (*His arms are now pinioned in a spread-eagled position.*)

TRAMP: (*Jeering mimicry*) Pleeeese. Pleeeeeese. Sowwy. Sowwy. What sort of bleed'n talk is that, then? How was *you* dragged up?
(*As he speaks, softly rising through the surrounding thicket, the unaccompanied singing voices of children are heard again.*)

CHILDREN: (*Singing, over*)
Amazing grace, How sweet the sound,
That saved a wretch like me.

TRAMP: I'll give you something real nice to say please for, my boy. Real nice. I promise. (*Snarl*) Keep your arms where they was!
(*This because he has released his pinioning grip. Meanwhile, continuous, rising –)*

CHILDREN:
I once was lost, but now am found,
Was blind, but now I see.
(*The* TRAMP *starts to pull the boy's knitted jersey, so that it eventually covers* DANIEL'*s face.*)

INT. CRYOGENIC LAB. DAY
The above, slow process continuing on the living wall for the now visibly horrified and sickened watchers. EMMA *stands up from her autocube, her fists clenching and unclenching as they hang loose.*

CLOSE-UP – KAYA. LAB
Reverse angle from the living wall so that we cannot see *what she is seeing, only hear the muffled cries of the boy, the hard-breathing mutter of the* TRAMP, *and the now full swell of the children's voices.*
DANIEL: *(Off, muffled)* Please, mister – Mister – No, mister . . . No . . .
TRAMP: *(Off, muttering)* Keep still, you little bugger –
CHILDREN: *(Same time, singing)*
   'Twas grace that taught my heart to fear
   And grace my fears relieved –
   (The sick horror on KAYA'*s face cannot hold out a second longer. She turns. She* runs.*)*

INT. EXT. CRYOGENIC LAB. DAY
Hands to her mouth, KAYA *hurtles blindly through the exit door, out into –*

INT. OUTER LAB. CRYOGENIC LABS. DAY
Some startled technicians at work on a whole human brain, removed from a head, look up as the weeping KAYA *plunges past them, and on out into –*

INT. LONG CORRIDOR. THE COMPLEX. DAY
As the outer, golf-ball shape seen in Part One would suggest, a very long connecting corridor would be circular, and anyone running its length would end up where they started. But mostly people autocube. And long before a near-hysterically distressed KAYA *can do the complete circle, she crashes almost headlong into a man coming out of the office rather than a laboratory door (the distinction being made visually evident during her run). It is* FYODOR.
KAYA: Oof!
FYODOR: Oof! Why the fuckolo –
   (He stops. He grips her shoulders.) Kaya! *(He sees the tears. His*

261

voice changes.) Kaya. What is it? Oh, my dear. Whatever has happened?

KAYA: (*Passionately*) It's cruel! It's so *cruel!*

FYODOR: (*Blinking*) What is?

KAYA: (*Passionately*) What we do! Day after day after day! What it is we do. I can't stand it. I can't take it any more!
(*Deeply upset, she puts her hands to her face again and cries – only this time in a subdued grief rather than in near-screaming hysteria. He looks at her, his Slav slab of features softening. Then* FYODOR *– rather oddly – looks up and down the corridor quickly, and draws her closer to the door he has just left.*)

CLOSE-UP – DOOR. FYODOR AND KAYA
The wide door is plated impressively with the name ANDREW Q. MILTON, DIRECTOR OF PUBLIC AFFAIRS.

FYODOR: (*To* KAYA) Look – you need to calm down a minute, and you don't want people to think you're – Come in here. I've just had some good old-fashioned coffee with an old friend of mine – The real stuff, I mean. Not a trace of Anjola or whitener in it!
(*He taps once and takes her in, pulling at her wrist as she half-wants to hang back.*)

KAYA: I don't think I –
(*But the door is closing. Fast-track back to find – *)

INT. CIRCULAR CORRIDOR. THE COMPLEX. DAY
BLINDA *is standing just at the other side of the clear glass double-doors which space out the corridor with the letters MSC in vivid red.*

EXTREME CLOSE-UP – BLINDA
She has obviously been sent after KAYA, *to bring her back, and she must have seen her equally young colleague being spoken to and half-pulled into the office. Her face looks thoughtful. Her eyes narrow. She moves.*

INT. CIRCULAR CORRIDOR. DAY
BLINDA *opens the glass doors and goes on the few yards to stop outside the office door* KAYA *had entered. She lifts a tiny note*

recorder from her electronic-button-studded belt and speaks softly into it even as she moves back in the direction whence she came. The recorder is no bigger than an aspirin tablet attached to the belt on a hair-thin thread or wire.

BLINDA: Kaya. Eleven oh five. Met by Fyodor at door of Andrew Q. Milton, Director of Public Affairs. Looks as though Fyodor had been in that office. He took her in.

INT. MILTON'S OFFICE. DAY

A very spacious, elegant and it could even be said luxurious room, except 'taste' would form itself first rather than the more gross adjective. There are a few good paintings and some objets d'art, even shelves of well-bound books, a rarity in this number-orientated, picture-dominated world, where literacy is not of particularly high standing.

KAYA *is in the process of sitting in a proper old-fashioned chair rather than an autocube, sinking down on to it under the gentle pressure of Fyodor's hand on her shoulder.*

FYODOR: That's it, my girl. Andrew, I'm afraid I have another customer and potential devotee of your extraordinary coffee.

ANDREW: (*Mock rueful*) Well, I *suppose* so – so long as it is one person at a time, Fyodor.
(*Over her head, so to speak, they are exchanging silently questioning looks, optimistic from* ANDREW, *wary or half-warning from* FYODOR.)

FYODOR: Andrew, this is Kaya. She works in the Lazarus laboratory with me. A biochemical research assistant.

ANDREW: (*To* KAYA) And would-be lackey, I presume, if dear old Emma has not changed overnight. (*Then, belatedly, notices the tear streaks.*) Oh. Is – um – I'm sorry. You must have your coffee straight away.
(*He goes to the old-style pot on a warming plate near to the expanse of his vast desk.* FYODOR *offers up what is both an explanation* and *a probe at Kaya's position in general.*)

FYODOR: Kaya thinks that what we do is cruel! It's beginning to scrape at her feelings and thoughts.

ANDREW: (*Pouring coffee*) Oh, dear. What – in general?
(*He brings the coffee across to her. She takes it with a brave*

attempt at a smile, but the cup tinkles against its saucer as her hand shakes.)

KAYA: No. I . . . this is very kind –

ANDREW: (*Soft purr*) No, no . . .

KAYA: It's just that – this man's head. It's been frozen for nearly four hundred years – and now we're slowly regenerating whole clusters of brain cells and billions of the neurones in the cerebral part of the – (*Looks at* FYODOR.) Sorry, Doctor. You know far better than I do what we're doing. I'm not trying to criticize anyone personally, not at all, but – but – (*Starts gently to weep a little again.*) These memories are starting to tumble out, and – and – Excuse me.

(*Her hand is shaking so much she has to put the cup down on Andrew's desk.* FYODOR *and* ANDREW *are looking at each other.* FYODOR *seems a little disappointed, edgily so.*)

FYODOR: Oh. You mean you're upset by the nature of the memories you are seeing, rather than by the process itself.

KAYA: Pardon?

FYODOR: (*Brutally*) You don't mind the frozen head in itself so much as you care about the stories it is telling.

(*She hears the 'wrong note' in this observation and turns to look at him, her composure restored, her voice suddenly steady and full of dignity.*)

KAYA: I care about both, sir. And I care very much. (*Tiny pause. She holds her gaze.*)

FYODOR: I beg your pardon.

(ANDREW *blazes a brief look of 'you fucked that up!' over* KAYA, *to* FYODOR, *and intervenes himself. It should be obvious to some, by now, that they are in some sense subversives, whether or not connected to the RONs, who are seeking a possible recruit, but sounding out the dangers.*)

ANDREW: Well, my dear, I can see you are both a sensitive and a dignified young woman, and I would be very sorry indeed if any aspect of our work here at this particular Masdon Science Center were to disturb you to such a – to such obvious distress. Please. Drink your coffee. (*Gives her the cup again.*) It's the real thing, you know. But don't ask me how I manage to get hold of it.

(KAYA *half-shares his smoothly amiable smile and takes the coffee again. She sips.*)

KAYA: Mmmm.

ANDREW: Nice?

KAYA: Very – um – Yes. But it's rather – strange. A sort of pure – um – Yes, it gives you an elevation.

ANDREW: Ah. A woman of taste! Thank you. (*Then he looks 'meaningfully' at* FYODOR. *A 'leave her to me' look.*)

KAYA: I – (*Starts again*) Perhaps things in general have been preying on my nerves. I should have talked to someone about it, but –

ANDREW: But it never seems possible. *I* know. Fyodor. They'll be screaming for *your* head to be in the box if you don't return to your duties.

KAYA: And I'll get dismissed for sure!

ANDREW: No, no. We'll invent some concoction of a tale that *explains all.*

FYODOR: (*Leaving*) You're in good hands, Kaya. I won't say I saw you. You won't say you saw me. Just relax here a while. And listen to Andrew. He has even better things than *real* coffee on offer! (*With a would-be smile –* FYODOR *doesn't find it easy to crack his face in that way – he leaves the room.*)

INT. CHAPEL. FOREST VILLAGE. DAY
The brass band plays softly while the children finish their hymn – the end of the fairly tuneful 'There is a Green Hill Far Away . . .'

CHILDREN: (*Singing*)
Oh, dearly, dearly has he loved
And we must love him too.
(*Finding.*)

CLOSE-UP – CHRIS, DANIEL'S TWIN
CHRIS AND CHILDREN: (*Singing*)
And trust in his redeeming blood
And try his work to do.
(CHRIS *seems to be seeking the eyes of one particular uniformed* BANDSMAN, *playing the heavy euphonium.*)

INT. CHAPEL. BAND SECTION. DAY
And the euphonium player seems to be doing the same, seeking out
CHRIS *among the sea of young, bright, upturned faces as the band*
alone now thunder the last chorus. The euphonium player is Daniel
and Christopher's FATHER.

INT. CRYOGENIC LAB. DAY
The band oompahs hymnally on the living wall as a quiet, almost
furtive FYODOR *returns, hovering in the doorway. For a moment, no*
one notices that he is back – except BLINDA. *He stands to the rear of*
the watchers, arms folded.

CLOSE-UP – BLINDA. LAB
A sharply covert look across at an apparently unaware FYODOR, *as*
the band plays on.

INT. CHAPEL. FOREST. DAY
The band finishes the final 'Green Hill' chorus, and the children all
sit back on their benches with a clatter of boots and shoes. When
chapel silence is restored, the PREACHER *– standing in the pulpit*
throughout – rustles a few sheets of lined paper and, looking over the
top of his glasses, begins.
PREACHER: Brothers and sisters, children in Jesus, today has
    been a special day in our chapel because the band has
    marched through the street carrying our banner, and come
    right into this plain little house of God to give musical
    thanks to –
    (*He breaks off in consternation. He is facing the chapel door,*
    whereas the children have their backs to it.)

INT./EXT. PORCH ENTRANCE. CHAPEL. DAY
The door swings slowly open, weirdly. No one is to be seen, but there
is the sound of a child's sob.

INT. CHAPEL. DAY
All the children swivel their heads around to see what has stopped
their PREACHER *in mid-sentence. And some of the bandsmen put*
down their heavier instruments to stand – in particular, DANIEL'S
FATHER.

INT. ENTRANCE. CHAPEL
Suddenly – almost as in a thriller, or with the deliberately perverse timing of a 'horror' film – a body in disarray thumps heavily to the floor, like one who has been thrown through the door. Consternation.

CLOSE-UP – THE BODY. CHAPEL DOORWAY
Shockingly, it is the 1994 DANIEL FEELD, *as seen in* Karaoke. *The close shot must come with the sudden jab or swoop of a coup de théâtre.*
DANIEL, *mouth and face bloodied, wearing the larger versions of the boy Daniel's clothing, unrolls himself from the bundle he has made of himself to crash so dramatically into the chapel, and with just one single howl of misery, begins to crawl.*

INT. CHAPEL. BAND AND PREACHER SECTION. DAY
Led by DANIEL'S FATHER, *several of the quicker bandsmen rush from their slightly raised platform at the side of the pulpit. The* PREACHER *stays frozen, hands oddly clawing at the air.*
DANIEL'S FATHER: Daniel! Oh, Danny! Danny! My Dan!

CLOSE-UP – CHRIS
On the end of a bench, rising with the other children, open-mouthed, eyes wide with concern and fear, the twin is of course the boy who played young DANIEL *in the woods.*

INT. CHAPEL. DAY
A whole throng of bandsmen and children around DANIEL, *who has stopped crawling on his hands and knees up the aisle towards the rearing pulpit.*
DANIEL'S FATHER: Give him some air, oot! Dan. Dan o'butty!
    Oh, Dan – What's happened – ?

INT. CRYOGENIC LAB. DAY
The scene is playing on the gigantic living wall, but as they watch – EMMA, LUANDA, TONY, BLINDA *and now* FYODOR *– the images of the crowding around* DANIEL *start to slip and slide and overlap in a way that we have not seen before.*
EMMA: (*Hissing*) What's the –
    (*But* FYODOR *is quick off the mark, rushing to – *)

CLOSE-UP – 'FEED' RACK. ABOVE BLACK BOX
FYODOR *turns off the particular hair-fine loop that coils into the black box marked* ALPHA-NEUROPEPTIDE 1042.

LIVING WALL
The slipping, sliding, overlapping, double and triple overlapping chapel pictures collapse into each other and become, via a swift intermediate phase of near-recognizable blobs, a mesh of myriad floating, multicoloured dots once more.

INT. CRYOGENIC LAB. DAY
Everyone turns to look at FYODOR, *who seems to deliberately ignore them and half-stoop down to the black box.*
EMMA: Fyodor –
FYODOR: (*Peremptorily*) A minute.

CLOSE-UP – FYODOR: AS FROM BLACK BOX
He is looking straight into camera, taking up the whole screen, as though the camera were Daniel's severed head.
Fyodor's expression – hidden from the others – is heavy with grief. Then he speaks very quietly, as though making a wish or even a prayer for DANIEL.
FYODOR: (*Softly*) Repose.
EMMA: (*Off*) What are you saying . . .?

INT. CRYOGENIC LAB. DAY
FYODOR *straightens and turns, sounding angry in a controlled manner.*
FYODOR: You were perilously close to aborting the whole programme, Emma. You are already a whole percentage point above the limits of this peptide, Luanda.
LUANDA: No!
FYODOR: Yes! And if it had gone on much longer – (*Gestures at the living wall*) all of that, *all* of it, wouldn't even be the floating corpuscle-dots of minimum consciousness. *Our man would be no more.*
(*His words have a strong effect upon them. There is a small silence. Then, feisty* EMMA *attempts to turn the table.*)
EMMA: Of course *you* are the specialist biochemist in cerebral

circuits and Luanda is more on the surgical and regenerative side – (*Quick aside to* LUANDA) No, Luanda, you're not at fault. (*Back to* FYODOR) But there would have been no danger and no problem in the first place if you had been where you should have been. *Here.* Doing your job! Where the hell have you been, Dr Glazunov?

FLASH: CLOSE-UP – BLINDA
A sudden sharpness in her eyes as she waits for his response.

INT. CRYOGENIC LAB. DAY
FYODOR: When you were out dining last night (*Little edge*) and I hope enjoying yourselves – I made a few important vis-calls and videofaxes –
TONY: What do you mean, 'enjoying ourselves'? (TONY *can never resist picking up on what he takes to be* FYODOR'*s perpetual sarcasm.*)
FYODOR: (*Blinks*) Well – You did, didn't you?
TONY: Being shot at and bombed? You've got a weird sense of humour, Fyodor –
(FYODOR *goes absolutely still. His voice comes out as through a strainer.*)
FYODOR: You mean – you mean –
EMMA: Yes. We went to the Holly Tree. Didn't you know? You chose wisely, my man.

CLOSE-UP – FYODOR
He looks in shock. He grips the back of the nearest empty autocube.
A moment –
FYODOR: I had no idea until this moment you had gone to *that* restaurant. Holy Moseolo! You could so easily have – Jesus. You could have been *slaughtered* – !

INT. CRYOGENIC LAB. DAY
They are rather surprised, even moved, by the extent of his shock about their endangerment.
EMMA: (*Softer tones*) I thought you knew where we were going. The food's good there.
FYODOR: If I'd known you were going there, I'd – (*But he stops*

himself, too suddenly for it not to be noticeable, especially,
again, by –)

FLASH: CLOSE-UP – BLINDA
With the look of one filing away another minuscule scrap in her
mental dossier.

INT. CRYOGENIC LAB. DAY
TONY *doesn't notice most things, however, and remains surprised by*
Fyodor's concern. He speaks to him rather more warmly.

TONY: Well, Fyodor, the bloody RONs didn't attack during the
first course – *and* we didn't have to pay the bill! (*Stops*) U-
oh. (*He is looking at the message wall, at right angles to the*
living wall, where previous information – e.g. about Fulham
and Spoonerisms – has been bleep-bleep-bleeped out.)

MESSAGE WALL
Softly bleeping –

> PRIORITY. PRESIDENT OF UNIPLANET TOTAL
> ENTERTAINMENT DAVID SILTZ SEEKS MEET
> HERE LONDON ENGLAND WITH PROFESSOR
> EMMA PORLOCK OF MSC CRYOGENIC
> LABORATORY AT UNIPLANET HOTEL HYDE PARK
> SOONEST SOONEST SOONEST PLEASE VIDCALL
> A1011.

INT. CRYOGENIC LAB. DAY
Incredulity. And then laughter.

EMMA: Me? With Siltz? With UTE?

TONY: (*Snorting laughter*) Maybe a new children's programme,
Emma.

LUANDA: (*Laughing*) UTE? Universal Total Entertainment!
God almighty, what have you *done*, Emma!
(*Only* FYODOR *is not laughing.*)

FYODOR: (*Savagely*) Universal Total Debasement. Universal
Total Pollution.
(*They stop laughing.*)

EMMA: But – but what on earth can such a creature want with
(*Deliberate irony*) poor insignificant withered-up little old

me? Am I to be the booby prize in some horrible new game show?

LUANDA: (*Half-excited*) Won't hurt to call.

TONY: And milk him for a grand meal at the very least.
(*Despite their amusement and contempt, the name excites or intrigues, giving some sense of his power.*)

LUANDA: He's like the old whatsit, Tsar of All the Russias.

FYODOR: Genghis Khan's a better analogy.

TONY: (*To* EMMA, *half-giggles*) Go on, then.

EMMA: Shall I? Shall I reply? (*And there is a little touch of the impressed schoolgirl in the normally feisty and quite elderly lady.*)

LUANDA: (*Giggles*) Oooo – yes please! Hell-o, big-bad-wolf!
(*They all crowd around the videophone unit as* EMMA *punches in the number – except* FYODOR, *who stands off, arms folded, eyes blazing hatred.*)

CLOSE-UP – EMMA. VIDEOPHONE
She finishes the last 'I' of the digits. On the little screen, sharply defined, a soaring skylark sings in blue sky and the letters UTE form themselves. They all roar with laughter. Then a cultured female voice says –

VIDEOPHONE: (*Over*) Please say who you are and wait for a few moments. We would be very grateful for your patience.
(*They stop laughing, so that – *)

EMMA: (*Suddenly nervous*) This is Professor Emma Porlock of MSC Cryonic Laboratory A in Kensington, London.

INT. MASSAGE ROOM. DAY
A large marbled room off the large marble bathroom and off the enormous bedroom of Dave Siltz's wantonly spacious hotel suite.
DAVE SILTZ, *naked but for a strategic towel, is being pounded and manipulated by two attractive masseuses, genuine article. One of them is sploshing a palmful of butter-like grease all over his paunch and the other kneads it in, fiercely. But another noise makes her jump: Brrrrrrrrr! Then –*

VOICE: Professor Porlock on Six, Mr President.

SILTZ: Tell her one and a half seconds and apologize. (*To* GIRLS, *instantly*) Out!

FIRST GIRL: Mr Siltz – ?

SILTZ: Out, I said. Out! Now!

> (SILTZ *sits up, all slippery and gleaming, adjusting the towel. He leans across to the edge of the massage table and, rather slithery in his movements, and an 'Oops!' at his mouth as he almost slides off the edge, presses one of a recessed row of buttons.*
>
> *A little red light blinks on at the top corner of the marbled massage room. He does not speak into any instrument, as* EMMA *had to do. He is immediately ingratiating.*)

SILTZ: Hi! I'm sorry to keep you, Professor. And I'm so very grateful that you called me back as soon as you did!

INT. CRYOGENIC LAB. DAY

As they all (except FYODOR*) crowd around* EMMA*, her sharp videophone screen shows a man gleaming with grease sitting on the edge of a table, naked except for the towel.*

TONY: Jee-ee-sus!

> (*He explodes with laughter, followed by the others. It is too loud.*)

EMMA: (*Flustered*) I – I'm sorry about the –

INT. MASSAGE ROOM. DAY

Below the little red light and to its left, on the wall, a large screen has slid down. The screen shows flustered EMMA *and her sniggering colleagues.*

SILTZ *puts down a frown and now, holding the small control pad which he has picked up from the recess with the buttons below the lip of the massage table, and looking to his right at a smaller but still large second screen which shows* his *image as transmitted, control-pads his image into a narrower, head-and-shoulders-only band.*

SILTZ: As you can see, and as your companions so *amusingly* appreciate, I happened to be having my mid-morning massage, Professor. I'm endeavouring to make myself a little less unseemly.

INT. CRYOGENIC LAB. DAY

EMMA *dislikes bad manners from her subordinates and glares them into silence.*

EMMA: It's all right now, Mr Siltz – it was more due to the – the

– unexpectedness of me calling you in the first place, Mr
  Siltz.
SILTZ: (*Video, simpering*) Please. It's Dave. Call me Dave. And
  may I address you as Emma – ?

INT. MASSAGE ROOM. DAY
*If the floor-to-ceiling wall-to-wall marble has not given the room a
coldish-looking edge, the big screen certainly does, as* EMMA'S *frosty
image glitters down on* SILTZ.
EMMA: No. You certainly may not, Mr Siltz. We have never
  met each other, and I do not intend to break the habits of –

CLOSE-UP – EMMA. VIDEOPHONE
EMMA: (*Continuous*) a lifetime merely because you are such a
  powerful man, sir.

INT. CRYOGENIC LAB. DAY
TONY *holds his breath,* LUANDA *grins from ear to ear,* BLINDA *claps
her hand over her mouth and* FYODOR, *still a little apart, nods with
deep satisfaction.*
SILTZ: (*Video*) Well, that's – well, that's just fine by me, Professor.
  (*Slightly forced laugh.*) There may not be an England any
  more, but, by God, there are still the English, eh?
EMMA: (*Imperious*) There'll *always* be an England, Mr Siltz.
  (TONY *has to turn away, wanting to split his sides.*)

CLOSE-UP – SILTZ. MASSAGE ROOM
*He has difficulty in controlling what is in fact anger, but manages (to
a degree) to pass if off as something more sardonic.*
SILTZ: Well, maybe there will, Professor. I'm not blessed with
  your sort of – what shall we call it? – *foresight.* Right now,
  I'm more concerned with what is happening right now and
  in particular what happened at breakfast time yesterday in
  California. (*Tiny pause, then lobs the news like a little bomb.*)
  A breakfast I shared with Martina Matilda Masdon. In
  point of fact, Professor, I was helping myself to some of her
  juice when she grabbed hold of your short hairs and
  threatened to close down the whole neat little caboodle
  you got going for you over here. You listening?

INT. CRYOGENIC LAB. DAY

Everyone has gone still and tense – and there are no lingering traces of condescending smiles or English uppittyness.

EMMA: (*Suddenly quieter*) I'm listening, Mr Siltz.

SILTZ: (*Video*) Now, I *know* for sure that she means it. That's the sort of cow she is, Professor. And it's just possible – I calculate the clock and the odds at 9,854 to 1 that she is peeking in at you all right now – in which case it'll be bye-bye any chance of helping you. And I want to help you. (*Tiny pause.* EMMA *looks for* FYODOR, *finds him, because he has now moved forward, and her worried expression seems to be asking a question of him.*)

FYODOR: (*Urgent whisper*) Ask him why?

EMMA: But – why would someone like you want to help *me*, Mr Siltz?

SILTZ: (*Video*) Because 'someone like me' –

INT. MASSAGE ROOM. DAY

SILTZ, *all slippery and shiny, dangling his legs over the side of the table, is now into territory he enjoys. He swing-swing-swings his greased legs in sheer pleasure.*

SILTZ: (*Continuous*) and incidentally I do so hope there is *no one* else like me, which would suggest a slight adjustment in your English grammar, Prof – because someone *such as* I might have a certain pecuniary interest of his own to pursue.

EMMA: (*On big screen*) I can't imagine what interests we could possibly –

EXTREME CLOSE-UP – SILTZ

With an almost manic shine on his face.

SILTZ: (*Cuts in, chuckling*) No. I bet you can't. But here's a simple Yes/No situation. Tick one box. We can't chat on *these* devices without risk to you and your colleagues. We *can* chat over lunch, one o'clock today, the David Siltz Room at this hotel of mine in Hyde Park. At that lunch I'll *guarantee* you all the fucking alpha-neuropeptide one zero whatfuckever that you need. *Guarantee!* So, you come? Today? Tick one box, lady. Now.

INT. CRYOGENIC LAB. DAY

EMMA *hesitates. The Devil has shown her all the kingdoms of earth. She looks at her colleagues, one by one, but they are frozen into immobility. Even* FYODOR – *who had seemed about to nod.*

INT. MASSAGE ROOM. DAY

SILTZ, *suddenly tensing, stops swinging his legs. But he will say no more.*

INT. CRYOGENIC LAB. DAY

After what has seemed an eternity, and with a strange, half-subdued croak in her voice –

EMMA: Yes. I'll – Yes. I will be there at one o'clock.
   (*Click! The sharp little screen picture of* SILTZ *is gone, without smile, without acknowledgement.* EMMA *looks at the hovering others.*)
   What am I *doing* – ?

INT. MASSAGE ROOM. DAY

DAVE SILTZ *flops back on the massage table and smacks his own hairy, greasy chest in a momentary Tarzan gesture. Then –*

SILTZ: (*Mimic 'English'*) 'Certainly not, Mr Siltz.' (*Chuckles, then bellows*) Girls! Girls! C'm here!
   (*As though waiting a bare few inches away, the two attractive* MASSEUSES *coming running, speaking virtually together.*)
TWO MASSEUSES: Yes, Mr President.
SILTZ: (*Immensely self-satisfied*) *This* time I want you to grease around an area I'm very fond of – but it tends to get rather dryolo and overused in Califuckinoria. Know what I mean?

INT. CRYOGENIC LAB. DAY

They are all in a bemused state, half-way between fantastic hope and pious disapproval. TONY *ventures to put an arm around* EMMA'S *shoulder, then adjusts, thinking better of it.*

TONY: Doesn't matter, does it? I mean, *meeting* a monster doesn't turn you into one, does it?
LUANDA: Or what would have happened to Saint George?
   (*They laugh, easing the tension. Behind and beyond them, the huge, utterly dominating living wall is meaninglessly vibrant*

with its ever-swirling, multicoloured dots. It seems, again, to compel *their collective attention.*)

FYODOR: I was about to say, before all this, that I'd made some calls last night, and this morning I've been trawling with my inadequate nets through every so-called independent foundation or academic centre for whatever scraps they might sort of accidentally drop from their tables. But – (*Shrugs, spreads hands.*) How can people of such high IQ be so absolutely blind?

EMMA: No luck then?

FYODOR: A few thousand unidollars. Enough for five minutes of Daniel Feeld's brain at full capacity. I'm sorry I didn't tell you. I wanted to be the unannounced hero.

EMMA: (*Morose*) Forget it. I feel a bit – Any moment now, I'm going to upchuck.

TONY: No, no. You're not.

LUANDA: (*To* FYODOR) We got some very vivid stuff. Puzzling at first. But – you must catch up on tape.

FYODOR: I will.

TONY: But it drove poor little Kaya away – it was so – Jesus, it was very graphic.

LUANDA: I'm terrified to think how near we came to a blow-out. My God – there must be a treasure house waiting for us in Daniel's head.

FYODOR: (*Bitterly*) That's what that malignant oaf Siltz thinks too.

BLINDA: (*Out of nowhere, to* FYODOR) Have *you* seen her, Doctor? Kaya, I mean?

FYODOR: Me?

BLINDA: I mean – oh, excuse me – I'm getting worried about her.

FYODOR: (*Blink of mock surprise*) *I* haven't seen her. No. Why should I?

BLINDA: Sorry.

EMMA: She's a silly, overemotional little – still, I felt upset myself.

TONY: We all did.

LUANDA: (*To* FYODOR) The question is – can we reactivate again? Soon, I mean?

(FYODOR *paces, hand on chin, brooding. He goes over to –*)

CLOSE-UP – 'FEED' RACK AND ADJOINING BOX
FYODOR *half-stoops to examine the levels of the various differently numbered neuropeptides.*
FYODOR: The biochemical problem with quote memory unquote is that there is no one particular cluster of cells in which you can say – OK, *there* it is, *there* we can tap it. Now we've overloaded – or come close to overloading – exactly those parts of the temporal lobes which in living psychiatric or psychopathic patients under treatment cause fear.

INT. CRYOGENIC LAB. DAY
FYODOR *turns, looks at them. The repeated word tolls ominously, like a bell.*
FYODOR: *Fear.*
    (*The others look at each other.*)
EMMA: (*Drily*) Yes. It is an appropriate word for what his head threw out at us. The vomit of an abused soul.
    (*Tiny pause, as the graphic words sink in.*)
FYODOR: I think it is relatively safe to try again, straight away, but not in the same temporal lobe. Luanda –
LUANDA: Yes?
FYODOR: *I'm* sure about the particular neuropeptide. Are *you* sure you can get it to the septal area and the front end of the hypothalamus?
    (LUANDA *considers.*)
LUANDA: Yes.
EMMA: (*Sharply*) Are you sure?
LUANDA: Yes. But I wish I had Kaya here. She is very deft and exceptionally useful when I try to switch the neurotransmitters.
EMMA: Damn the girl!
TONY: (*To* LUANDA) I'm not *so* rusty on that, Luanda. I can put myself under your control. And Blinda can help *me.*
LUANDA: Well. Yes. Then – (*Decisive*) OK. We'll start transpositioning.
EMMA: How long?
LUANDA: (*Swiftly*) Seventy-five minutes.
    (EMMA *looks at the clock. It is now almost ten-thirty a.m. Then she looks at* FYODOR.)

EMMA: Then I'll be able to see some before breaking bread with
the Devil.

TONY: Caviare, more like.

LUANDA: Just take a long spoon.

EMMA: (*To* FYODOR) So, while they get on with it – and *please*
be careful – let you and I take a little walk.

FYODOR: *Walk?*
(*He sounds so astonished or incredulous that they have to
laugh.*)

BLINDA: (*Cheekily*) You know, it's where you put one leg in front
of the other, and then do the same thing all over again.

EMMA: Don't be impertinent, girl. (*But she is smiling.*)

INT. CIRCULAR CORRIDOR 5. THE COMPLEX. DAY
*The glass doors opening just before Andrew Q. Milton's office and,
front on,* EMMA *and* FYODOR *come through, scarcely talking.*
As they pass the door marked ANDREW Q. MILTON, DIRECTOR OF
PUBLIC AFFAIRS, FYODOR *cannot quite help a little sideways flick
of his eyes.*

EMMA: (*Alert*) I'm told Milton has access to a private supply of
real coffee. (*She is slowing.*)

FYODOR: Mmm.

EMMA: Shall we importune? (*She is about to raise her knuckles to
tap on the door.*)

FYODOR: (*Too loud*) No!

CLOSE-UP – AT MILTON'S DOOR
EMMA, *hand still raised, looks at him in surprise.*

FYODOR: (*Again, quickly*) Emma. I can't stand the man. I'd
rather have unfiltered ditchwater.
(*She lowers her hand, to his relief, and they walk on.*)

INT. CIRCULAR CORRIDOR 5. THE COMPLEX. DAY
Going through another set of glass doors. EMMA, *half-amused in a
dry way, has been looking sidelong at* FYODOR.

EMMA: (*Slyly*) You don't like too many people, do you, Fyodor?

FYODOR: (*Surly*) I wouldn't say that.

EMMA: Is that because you imagine that too many of them
don't like *you?*

(*He stops walking and faces her, stung.*)

FYODOR: I have my friends, Professor. But as for the social life in general – in this world, in *this* hell we are making of it – I say no. No, thank you! I'd rather lock myself in my own room and howl on all fours.

(*He strides on, almost too fast for her. She has a grim little smile, trying to keep up with him. But then he suddenly stops again and faces her, accusingly.*)

Is *that* what you want to walk and talk about? My demeanour in the lab or my private life or something? *Is it?*

EMMA: Fyodor –

FYODOR: (*Angrily*) Because if it is, I propose to proceed not one step further. Do you understand?

CLOSE-UP – EMMA. CORRIDOR

She studies him. There are stirrings of a new respect in her expression.

EMMA: Understood. (*A beat.*) I want, actually, I want to talk to you about this lunch with Siltz – for I have a good idea that you know what is likely to be involved as much as I do. I feel I need to get some bearings. The whole idea of any kind of dealing with his mass entertainment business disorientates me. And yet – well, there's all that money, all those possible doors to open with it. I'm at a total loss, Fyodor. Am I to be *willingly* seduced? Or what?

LIVING WALL

At the point where the blobs are seeking each other, it seems to become bigger still and ooze into recognizable shapes.

INT. CRYOGENIC LAB. DAY

LUANDA, TONY *and* BLINDA *high-palm each other in triumph.*

LUANDA: Success!

TONY: Smack in the hypothalamus and septal.

BLINDA: (*Pertly*) And *I* was brilliant, you two!

(*They laugh. On the living wall, dominating the lab, two figures are now almost formed, in a corridor, opening a door, still a bit blobby or smeary.*

LUANDA *rushes across the lab.*)

CLOSE-UP – 'FEED' RACK
LUANDA *turns off the particular numbered alpha-neuropeptide, then turns.*
LUANDA: We'd better wait for the big guns.

INT. CRYOGENIC LAB. DAY
The dominating living wall quickly turning back to its swirl of multicoloured, floating dots.
TONY: (*A touch jealous*) Wonder what they found to talk about, those two? I mean, they're not exactly – (*He stops, abruptly.*)
EMMA: (*Amused*) Not exactly what, Tony?
(*For* EMMA *and* FYODOR *are suddenly in the lab's main doorway.*)
TONY: (*Embarrassed*) I beg your pardon.
FYODOR: (*Gratingly*) Oh, we're buddy-buddies, Dr Watson.
EMMA: (*To* FYODOR) Now, now, you miserable Slav.
(FYODOR *actually grins.*)
FYODOR: Well – so you're ready! You've done it!
LUANDA: We've done it!
(EMMA *dry-pecks her on the cheek.*)
EMMA: Then let the show begin.
FYODOR: (*Frowning*) Show?
(*But* LUANDA *has already released the correct peptide into the new area of Daniel Feeld's cortex. On the huge living wall, the blobs suck together, swirl, swell, take shape, then – as they take their positions in their autocubes –*)

INT. END OF CORRIDOR AND BALCONY DOORS. HOSPITAL.
1994. DUSK/NIGHT
DANIEL: (*Opening balcony doors*) Twenty-two. (*Wistful*) Oh, my God.
SANDRA: (*Misunderstanding*) Yeah. Getting on a bit, ennit?
(*They walk on to and along –*)

EXT. HOSPITAL BALCONY. DUSK/NIGHT
Untouched Victoriana from the original building, and the thickening twilight adds to its fading or neglected charms. DANIEL *looks around, appreciatively, but then –*

DANIEL: Places like this – bits left over from other times, other people – (*Wry laugh.*) You see, my life's been given over to *writing* words. Words. Fucking words.

SANDRA: (*Comic reproof*) Oooh.

DANIEL: Words. That's all I've ever been any good at, if I'm any good at all. And I've an idea that I'm soon going to find out about that, one way or the other.

SANDRA: Whatchewmean?

(DANIEL *deflects the question by pointing out something ahead of them.*)

DANIEL: Look – if we go to the end of this balcony, and if that funny little gate thing opens, we can go all the way down past the other balconies –

SANDRA: To the garden, yeah. You like gardens?

DANIEL: (*Smiles*) I like the *word* 'garden'. It has a – well, the ring of primal innocence.

SANDRA: The what?

DANIEL: Adam and Eve.

(*Suddenly, abruptly, breaking into the 'original'.*)

EXT. SCHOOL PLAYGROUND. FOREST. 1940S. DAY
The boy who played CHRIS – *Daniel's identical twin – is surrounded by a ring of other eight-year-old* BOYS, *who are chanting, in a jeery sort of way* –

BOYS:

Adam and Eve and Pinch-me
Went down to the river to bathe.
Adam and Eve got drowned,
who dost thou think was saved?
(*They jab and push in a tighter and tighter circle around boy* DANIEL, *demanding response.*)

BOYS: Who? *Who?* Come th'on! Say *who!*

DANIEL: No-o-o!

(*They hugger-mugger more tightly around him, punching and pushing as they chant all over again.*)

BOYS:

AdamandEveandPinch-me
Wentdowntotherivertobathe.
AdamandEvegotdrownded,

281

Whodostthouthinkwassaved!
WHO! WHO! WHO!

(*Boy* DANIEL *is now at the bottom of a whole heap of them,
virtually out of sight.*)

DANIEL: (*Muffled despair*) Pinch-me!

BOYS: (*Cackling*) Pinch him! Pinch him! Him have asked for it!
Pinch! Pinch!

(*But suddenly* CHRIS, *the twin – i.e. the same boy, as* DANIEL
*cannot now be seen under the tormenting heap – is wading in at
the edge of the gang, throwing punches.*)

CHRIS: Let'n alone! Dost hear I! Let him alone!

(CHRIS's *punches have power. They soon take effect, with
many an ow! and ooch!, thump and yelp! Then, suddenly,
abruptly, seemingly without apparent reason –*)

EXT. DESERT. KUWAIT. 1991. DAY

*A sequence – without commentary, which in this case is especially
redundant – from Pathé News BBC archives* A Year to
Remember: 1991.

*First, a line of drab-looking Iraqi soldiers, hands on heads, come
marching, under white flags. Then there is a shot of a line of bunkers
in the sand. Four Iraqis come out, hands on heads, gibbering in real
fear, weeping, begging for their lives. They are made to sit down by a
US soldier. They clearly think this is a prelude to their execution.
They moan and gibber, and one tries to make a kissing gesture – a
really abject surrender.*

US SOLDIER: (*Soothingly, as to disturbed dogs*) All right. It's all
right.

(*But still they tremble and still they weep. Then – jolt – sound of
feet on iron steps, and –*)

EXT. BALCONIES AND IRON STAIRS. HOSPITAL. 1994. DUSK/
NIGHT

*The balconies are threaded by iron steps between them, each with a
creaky, unused little gate.*

DANIEL: What a lovely sound your heels make on this old iron.

SANDRA: (*Pleased*) Do they? Ta.

DANIEL: I have that sound in –

INT. CRYOGENIC LAB. DAY
Dominated by the living wall, the five watchers exchange glances at this confirmation of DANIEL*'s profession 374 years ago –*
DANIEL: (*On wall, continuous*) one of my stage directions in the last script I finished.

EXT. BALCONIES, STEPS. HOSPITAL. 1994. DUSK/NIGHT
DANIEL *makes a small, half-uneasy laugh.*
DANIEL: (*Continuous*) Just one of the little things that's been bothering me.
SANDRA: What's it called, your story?
(He looks sidelong at her, then pushes open the last little iron 'gate', which is an awkward one. There is a significant change in his answer.)
DANIEL: (*Puffing*) Cold Lazarus.

FLASH: CLOSE-UP – EMMA. LAB
Her eyes practically pop! and her jaw sags a little, in real shock.

EXT. GRAVEL PATH. HOSPITAL GARDEN. 1994. DUSK/NIGHT
They crunch in silence along a narrow gravel path between dusty and malnourished bushes towards a small, chipped Eros, a garden statue of stone that was once the centrepiece of a fountain. Some dialogue here seems to have fled from his memory, but then –
DANIEL: (*Pleased*) Oh, look! A real old garden bench!
SANDRA: Bit dirty an' all.

EXT. BENCH. HOSPITAL GARDEN. DUSK/NIGHT
He makes a pantomime show of dusting off the seat for Milady, and she laughs, agreeing to sit.
DANIEL: There. Perfectly clean, my dear.
SANDRA: (*Laughs*) Ta! You're a gent.
(As he sits, he suddenly winces. She notices, but says nothing – and waits.)
DANIEL: (*Eventually*) As you can see, I haven't been feeling too great lately.
SANDRA: What's wrong then?

INT. CRYOGENIC LAB. DAY

The dominating living wall and the avid watchers, and what he says – which had a double resonance at the time – seem to have yet one more layer of meaning, one more sense of plea.

DANIEL: (*With a half-laugh*) I've been on the wrong diet. Eating and drinking my own thoughts. And I kept hearing what I thought were my lines coming back at me.

(Then, looming so hugely in front of them, something strange and dream-like happens on the living wall, completely different to the in any case differently shot scene in Karaoke *Part Two.*

DANIEL gets up from the bench, abruptly. Then stands still, appearing to stare at camera, or right at his 374-years-later watchers.)

CLOSE-UP – DANIEL

He walks all around the bench, but as he does so it becomes evident that SANDRA *is no longer sitting on the bench. She is, in fact, nowhere to be seen at all.*

DANIEL *runs his hand along the top of the bench, at the back, then comes to the front of the bench and sits down, and stares straight at camera, repeating himself, but in the present and not past tense. It chills.*

DANIEL: I am on the wrong diet.

INT. CRYOGENIC LAB. DAY

EMMA, FYODOR, LUANDA, TONY, BLINDA *seem to stiffen, as though under direct accusation, as the huge face looms in front and above them on the living wall.*

DANIEL: (*Continuous*) I am being made to eat and to drink my own thoughts. And I keep hearing what I think are my own lines and my own life coming back at me. (*A beat, infinitely sad.*) My own life.

(And then his face, as though made of rubber, begins to buckle and squash and widen and stretch all at the same time, into something monstrous. LUANDA *is already racing towards –)*

INT. 'FEED' RACK. LAB. DAY

LUANDA *stems the tiny flow of the alpha-neuropeptide through its capillaries into the black box, then half-stoops to look into –*

CLOSE-UP – BLACK BOX
*The ghastly, slightly luminous, silvery-grey face registering an agony
of mouth movement – for a micro-second – before 'repose' of a kind
from the cessation of the neuropeptide.*

INT. CRYOGENIC LAB. DAY
Disturbed, LUANDA *turns back to the others. In front of them the
living wall is returning via the floating blobs into its multi-coloured
myriad of dots.*
LUANDA: It's almost as though – almost as if – (*Tiny shudder.*)
No. That doesn't bear thinking about. It cannot be.
EMMA: (*Troubled*) Or are we saying it *must* not be?
TONY: He certainly – (*Swallows*) I mean, it was as near as you
can get to a – a – The word I would normally use is a 'plea'.
FYODOR: Technically, Luanda knows that it is not possible, not
within the scope of the percentage of his brain in activity.
Biochemically, I would be forced to the same conclusion.
(*Between his teeth*) It-cannot-be-that-*that*-damaged –
remnant – knows its own condition.
(*Silence. Then, out of nowhere, so to speak,* LUANDA *turns her
elegant frame away, puts her hand up to her face and quietly
weeps.*
BLINDA *hesitates, then goes over to her, and puts an arm
around her shoulders.* EMMA, *briskly, tries to pull the issue
away.*)
EMMA: So – to sum up – we know he had an identical twin. We
know he was a writer, and it seems a successful one. And
there is something else we ought to bear in mind about
writers.
TONY: And that's – ?
EMMA: The fact that they tell stories.
FYODOR: Sorry?
EMMA: They tell *tales*. They make things up.
(FYODOR *blinks, then throws back his head with a dry single
bark of a laugh.*)
FYODOR: You mean – they are *liars*.
EMMA: (*A little shamefaced*) Well – it's something to bear in
mind. (*Looks at them.*) Isn't it?
(*But before anyone can say anything more, a shatteringly loud*

voice breaks through, on a big, 'old-style' – almost –
loudspeaker above entrance door – and presumably all entrance
doors in the golf-ball complex.)

CLOSE-UP – LOUDSPEAKER
ATTENTION! ATTENTION! BODY FOUND ON
GROUND IMMEDIATELY BELOW COMPLEX.

INT. CRYOGENIC LAB. DAY
They all look at each other, startled, as the voice booms on.
THIS IS A MASDON SCIENCE CENTER POLICE
COMMAND. STAY EXACTLY WHERE YOU ARE
UNLESS IN A SCIENTIFICALLY ENDANGERED
POSITION. ATTENTION! ATTENTION! A BODY HAS
BEEN FOUND BENEATH THE WINDOWS OF THE
COMPLEX.
(*Dissolving during this –*)

INT. ANDREW Q. MILTON'S OFFICE. DAY
The latter part of the loudspeaker voice is also heard in this elegant
office, so obviously the working abode of a cultivated man. But
MILTON, *the man in question, has his elbows on his virtually*
gadget-free desk, his head in his hands. He is crying, softly – but in
total despair.

EXT. CRYOGENIC COMPLEX A. MSC. DAY
At the rear of the golf-ball-on-tee-shaped edifice, a huddle of
helmeted armed guards have gathered in the universally useless way
of their kind around a small figure spread-eagled on the ground.
Beyond them, alien and peculiarly desolate in feel, other golf-ball
buildings and the intermittently flashing electrified perimeter fence.
An unnecessarily howling paramedic bubble with a green cross on its
sides is hubble-bubbling at speed towards them.
The guards pull back a little, looking in the direction of the
approaching vehicle, revealing a broken figure on the ground.

CLOSE-UP – KAYA
Sprawled, head on one side, in a way that suggests her back has been
broken.

INT. ANDREW Q. MILTON'S OFFICE. DAY
MILTON stops weeping. He blows his nose. He makes himself stand up, and makes himself go and stand in front of one of his 'beautiful' paintings, which he makes himself examine. Pause. Then he looks at his fingernails.
ANDREW: (*Whispers, to self*) Ars longa. Vita brevis.

INT. CRYOGENIC LAB. DAY
They have not, of course, stayed exactly where they are, but have gone to the one window in this part of the lab, opposite the door and the 'message' wall. From the way they crane to look down, one has a sense of great height. But from here, it seems, they can see nothing.

CLOSE-UP – THE WINDOW
Looking straight out, there seems to be a strange-looking crow in the sky, sweeping close to and then past the window, as though it is injured or unable to fly quite properly. It makes an authentic 'Aak' of a noise – and it is not odd enough for anyone to make a comment. But odd *it definitely is!*

INT. CRYOGENIC LAB. DAY
They come back from the window, a little tense or excitable.
TONY: Think somebody jumped?
LUANDA: (*With apparent conviction*) Christ, *I* would if I worked here.
(*They laugh at the way she says it, then stop laughing, in case it's not appropriate.*)
EMMA: Well, if it *is* someone who did the honourable thing, let's hope it is Martina Matilda Masdon, over on a quick visit.
(*They seem to look up at the ceiling in half-alarm.*)
TONY: (*Grinning*) Careful. Ceilings have ears.
EMMA: And eyes. And arseholes.
(FYODOR, *restless, fidgety, looks at the clock.*)
FYODOR: Emma. Your lunch.
EMMA: God, I'm dreading the –
(*With sudden boom, loudspeaker – *)
PLEASE RESUME ACTIVITIES. THE BODY IS NOT THAT OF AN OUTSIDER AND IT IS NOT BOOBY-

TRAPPED. WE REGRET TO INFORM YOU OF THE
DEATH OF MSC PERSONNEL NUMBER 124549 KAYA
CHANG OF LABORATORY A.

INT. MILTON'S OFFICE. DAY
Loudspeaker, continuous –
UNLESS UNDER APPOINTMENTS ALREADY SET
AND GATE-APPROVED, ALL PERSONNEL WILL
RENDER THEMSELVES FOR QUESTIONING BY THE
MSC POLICE, BEGINNING ON FLOOR THREE.
(MILTON *is still staring at the painting, which is rural but only
semi-idyllic* Larchant, 1939, *by Balthus, for example, though it
could be any painting so long as it has* some *sense of the idyllic,
rural past. The door behind him swings open. He turns,
stiffening. In reverse –*)

CLOSE-UP – FYODOR. MILTON'S OFFICE
Mouth a tight line of rage, eyes burning hatred, FYODOR *stalks
across the wide room towards* MILTON, *virtually hissing with rage.*
FYODOR: You. It was you. You!

INT. MILTON'S OFFICE. DAY
MILTON, *by now back in the suave composure which is his
predominant style, gives a neat little sidestep and a calm reply.*
ANDREW: I'm very much afraid to say that it is the other way
around, Fyodor.
FYODOR: (*Rage-tremble*) What?
(ANDREW *sighs, spreads his arms a little.*)
ANDREW: (*Evenly toned*) You should not have brought her in to
see me. You had had no conversation with her at all, as I
was soon to discover. (*Same tones, no breath.*) And it is not
possible to discuss your funding issue in terms of the
public domain in any sense of the word that comes into *my*
territory, Doctor.
(FYODOR *realizes that someone has come to the door he had left
open in the plunge of his rage. His back is to the door and he
closes his eyes, clamps his teeth, in an effort to regain control.*)

INT. DOORWAY. OFFICE AND CORRIDOR BEYOND. DAY

EMMA: I'm surprised you should even *try* to begin to coax a farthing piece out of *this* smooth fellow, Fyodor.

ANDREW: Emma. Emma. Your assumptions are out of order, dear lady. I help when I can help.

EMMA: (*Departing*) You need to be a speleologist to enter the unfathomable depths of your mind, Mr Milton.

ANDREW: (*Blinking*) Speleologist? The word temporarily eludes me.

FYODOR: (*Almost spits the words*) One who studies *caves*, and usually finds nothing more than *bat shit*. Emma! Wait – !
(*He whirls away, after her, still leaving the door open.*
MILTON *grips the edge of his desk, half-closes his eyes, shivers, then slowly levers himself down into his desk chair.*)

INT. CIRCULAR CORRIDOR A. DAY

FYODOR *lopes up alongside* EMMA. *She gives a quick look.*

EMMA: She was unhappy, Fyodor.

FYODOR: Oh, the poor, poor –
(*He suppresses a half-sob. She is a little surprised. They come to – *)

INT. ELEVATORS. DAY

Long row of lifts, at least one stopping each five seconds, plus a 'Straight Through'-labelled lift. EMMA *is showing how bleak a woman she can be. Strong emotions are often atrophied in this future world.*

EMMA: (*Uncompromising*) Fyodor. There is nothing we can do about it. What are you – ? Are you trying to accompany me, or what? I'll be quite safe, you know. Siltz will not rape me. Alas.
(*She steps into elevator. As the doors slide shut, he calls after her.*)

FYODOR: *No one is safe!*
(*The doors have closed. Alone, he looks down at his boots, speaking quietly.*)
No one.

EXT. SILTZ'S HOTEL. DAY

Model shot. Extravaganza-built, towered, crenellated, bristling with all types of self-protective devices.

EXT. SKY AROUND, ABOVE HOTEL. DAY

Again, among maybe other city birds, especially pigeons, a weird, slightly ominous black crow awkwardly flip-flap-flaps like something with an injured wing. All vaguely disturbing, like a sickness in the air.
It approaches a very high-up window of the hotel, as though ready to crash into it, but then veers to one side at the last moment, wings spreading.

CLOSE-UP – HUGE WINDOW

With glimmerings of spacious room – near football-field size – beyond the shining glass.

INT. SILTZ'S DINING ROOM. THE HOTEL. DAY

Big windows look out into a polluted sky, about sixty floors up.
Finding EMMA walking the length of the long, long room to meet her host, who uses an old dictator's trick of forcing a lengthy approach upon his visitors and supplicants. Reverse –

INT. DINING TABLE. DAY

The room could take scores of such tables, and even so this table could seat thirty. But it is the only table, at the very top end of the room – nearest the biggest of the big windows – and SILTZ sits at its top, expressionless as he watches her long walk. When EMMA has completed it, she will have to sit on Siltz's right, where the only other table-place is laid.
Eventually, SILTZ slowly rises, taking his time to lift and extend his hand.

SILTZ: Professor Porlock. It is an honour indeed for a Barnum and Bailey such as I to meet so distinguished an expert in the cryogenic sciences.
  (*All but out of breath, EMMA tokenly takes the proffered hand, drops it and sinks with relief into her dining chair.*)
EMMA: Goodness. I thought one was supposed to take exercise *after* one's meal and not before it.

(SILTZ *laughs, and pours her some red wine.*)

SILTZ: Never mind. *Mental* gymnastics will shortly be in order.
Taste that. Tell me what you think.
(*He looks at her, expectant, proud, as she lifts the glass.*)

CLOSE-UP – EMMA
*She takes a careful sip, as a connoisseur might, holding the wine
momentarily in her mouth before swallowing. She knows what is
expected from her, but she is not presently disposed to oblige.*
EMMA: Mmmm. (*A beat.*) Not bad. Not bad at all.

INT. DINING TABLE. DAY
SILTZ *is incredulous.*
SILTZ: Not bad? Not *bad?* Do you have any idea what you're
drinking – a Margaux before that region was torched –
know how difficult it is to get that? How much it cost!
EMMA: Oh, dear. I wasn't aware that price was a *taste*, Mr Siltz.
Forgive my ignorance.
(*He looks at her. She returns the gaze. He smiles.*)
SILTZ: Know something? I *like* you. And that astonishes me.
Truly!
EMMA: Not half as much as it astonishes me.
SILTZ: OK. Let's eat. You wanna eat?
EMMA: If it tastes – *expensive.*
(*He roars approval and slaps her too hard on the back. If she
wore false teeth, they would have flown out.*)
SILTZ: Attagirl!

CLOSE-UP – EMMA
A frown, a cough and then a threat –
EMMA: If you do that again, or anything like it –

INT. DINING TABLE. DAY
But realizing his mistake SILTZ *has already put his hands up, in
exaggerated surrender.*
SILTZ: OK. OK. Promise. Promise! (*Looks at her.*) I thought
maybe cold cherry soup. A Hungarian dish with lotsa nice,
nice other things – ?
EMMA: Fine.

SILTZ: Then, keeping the light theme, an all-around-the-world salad with some fruits on a whole Dover sole. That do?

EMMA: (*Secretly pleased*) That will do.

SILTZ: Good. Got that, kitchen?

VOICE: (*Over, off*) Got it, Mr Siltz.

CLOSE-UP – UNDER TABLE. SILTZ'S PLACE-SETTING
He presses a button under the table, his side. She can't see this.

CLOSE-UP – EMMA. TABLE
EMMA: (*Surprised*) The kitchen can hear all this?

INT. DINING TABLE. DAY
SILTZ: Well, they're all too thick to understand a word we're saying. I only employ *Irish* people there, you see. (*Looks at her.*) Laugh. Try it. Won't hurt.

EMMA: It's not much of a joke.

SILTZ: (*Sighs*) S'pose not – but, no, I've buttoned them out of earshot – here, under the table, see – ?
(SILTZ *lifts the edge of the cloth, shows her an array of electronic buttons.*)
Try one. Press the blue one.
(*She looks at him and senses this is no idle chat.*)

EMMA: Blue?

SILTZ: Blue.

CLOSE-UP – EMMA AND 'BUTTONS'
Her old face bends and looms under the table a little, then finds and presses the blue button of the many differently coloured ones.

INT. DINING ROOM. DAY
Two figures at the far end of the vast room, and a familiar voice from Part One filling the great spaces –
MARTINA MASDON: (*Over, off*) I kinda *hover*. In each finance department I have my own personal agent, working direct to *me* outside any other form or discipline.

CLOSE-UP – EMMA
Dislike, even hatred, etching into her already well-etched features as

she listens. The dreaded voice is continuous.

MARTINA MASDON: (*Over, off*) And as soon as any one section of any one Center makes any one expenditure decision for any one tranche of any one internal –

INT. DINING TABLE. DAY

SILTZ *closely studies* EMMA, *who is rock still. The voice continuous.* subsectioned budget, I get a coded *bleep* – at once.

CLOSE-UP – SILTZ

Making a little bow or nod as his own voice comes up on the tape. The soup arrives.

SILTZ: (*Over*) Ah. So *that* was what I heard when I spilt the coffee.

INT. DINING TABLE. DAY

As the Masdon voice continues ('Yup . . . whole damned place').

EMMA: So you recorded it when you were a guest at her house?
(*She looks down at her cherry-coloured soup, a bit unsure.*)

SILTZ: Go on. It won't bite. Eat.

MASDON VOICE: *Look. Twenty-nine.* That's the place in England. A shit-house. *Sixteen* –
(EMMA PICKS UP HER SPOON, GRIMLY.)
The Lab ordering an overspend – *See!*
(*Click! Off goes the voice.*)

SILTZ: And then I saw right into your lab.
(*Pause. They each have some soup, with a slight slurping noise from each.*)
And then she told me she was going to cut you out. Completely. So –

EMMA: So?

SILTZ: You might as well give that man's head to the zoo. Soup nice?

EMMA: I'll go elsewhere for funds. Yes, very nice.

SILTZ: Wild cherries.

EMMA: (*Putting spoon down*) Get to it.
(*He slurps some more soup, deliberately taking his time. Then –*)

SILTZ: Well, *I* like it. The soup. *And* what you're doing. Some of that stuff today for example. Great!

EMMA: (*Startled*) Today? What do you mean? How the hell do
   you know what –
   (SILTZ *laughs, pushes his soup bowl away, and shouts – sing-shouts –*)

SILTZ:
   Bye-bye-blackbird!
   (*From 'Pack up all your cares and woe', etc.*)

INT./EXT. BIG WINDOW. DINING ROOM. DAY
*With a shock, and a distinct smack! against the glass, the weird crow
suddenly flitter-flutters straight at the window. And, even more
strangely, as it smacks belly-up into the glass, it sticks there.*

INT. DINING TABLE. DAY
EMMA *half-rises in dismay and consternation, whereas* SILTZ *calmly
gets up, goes to the window, slides a lever on the narrow metal sill,
and the glass does a complete turn in its own orbit.*

INT./EXT. BIG WINDOW. DAY
The 'crow' is now room-side of the glass. Using both hands, SILTZ
*pulls it off the glass with a sucking sound, then a plop! He carries
what now looks less and less like a creature across to the table.*

INT. DINING TABLE. DAY
SILTZ: You've heard of or maybe even seen Snoop Kestrels –
   God! Primitive! My people just take things that little bit
   further, that little bit better, in every communications field
   you can think of.

CLOSE-UP – 'CROW' AND SILTZ'S HANDS
As SILTZ *speaks, he lays the powered 'crow' flat and unzips its entire
middle, pulling out an oblong box, soft-sided, full of the most
miniature recording devices imaginable: the nanotechnology of
communications.*

INT. DINING TABLE. DAY
EMMA *is watching all this open-mouthed, still half-way up out of her
chair. Eventually, gripping the edge of the table, she sits, and
swallows, and stares, and swallows.*

SILTZ: We send out a dozen of these and they almost always get back. The navigational system is – well, just out of this world . . . Now, if I fit this in – here –

CLOSE-UP – TABLE TOP

He lays the oblong box into a marginally indented slot the same size on the table top. With a faint whirrr! followed by a click! from somewhere below, the oblong is pulled down into the table, ready to transmit.

INT. DINING TABLE. DAY

SILTZ: (*Pleased with himself*) Are you ready for your sole, Professor?
    (*Tiniest pause.*)
EMMA: Soul.
SILTZ: I beg your pardon?

CLOSE-UP – EMMA

She has an inner quiver, her nerves stretching.

EMMA: (*Voice thickening*) Soul. I said soul. Ess oh you ell. (*Then she pulls her hands to her face, to try to stop the sudden rush of tears.*)

INT. DINING TABLE. DAY

SILTZ: Oh, come, my dear. Just wait until you see this – and pray to God that Martina Masdon doesn't clap her sharp, piggy little mascaras on it first! Just wait until you hear my offer, Professor! I'll knock you out! (*Then – stupidly, but just in case.*) I meant, are you ready for your fish, lady?
    (*Tiniest pause. She controls tears. Just.*)
EMMA: Fish?
    (*Music starts, and she swivels her head, sharply, to see, on a screen rising slowly from the bottom end of the table, a sea of bright young faces from nearly 400 years before.*)

RISING SCREEN, END OF TABLE

Still slowly rising as the children sing.

CHILDREN:
    Amazing grace! How sweet the sound

That saved a wretch like me.
I once was lost –
(*Dissolving.*)

CLOSE-UP – BLACK BOX. LAB. DAY
DANIEL FEELD, *the alpha-neuropeptide 1042 staunched, seems in
some kind of silvery, capillary-wired and tubed repose. Music
continuing through dissolve.*
CHILDREN: (*Over*)
But now am found,
Was blind, but now I see.
(*Fade picture.*)

BLACK OR BLANK SCREEN
CHILDREN: (*Over*)
'Twas grace that taught my heart to fear
And grace my fears relieved –
(*Fade sound.*)

PART THREE

EXT. THE SILTZ HOTEL. NIGHT
*Model shot. The grandiloquent, looming, gigantic tower, winking
and twinkling with what looks like millions of fairy lights now that
darkness has fallen.*

EXT. AT ORNATE ENTRANCE. THE HOTEL. NIGHT
*A standardly posh hotel doorman, top-hatted, is chatting idly with
three distinctly non-standard heavily armed guards, as a few guests
pass to and fro, showing 'smart cards' or similar as they reach the
quietly swinging glass doors.*
*Suddenly, looking into the depths of the lobby after the long legs of a
pretty woman –*

INT./EXT. LOBBY. ENTRANCE. HOTEL. NIGHT
*– the doorman stiffens and hisses some sort of warning to the guards,
who immediately take a more alert, more hostile-looking stance.
This is because the doorman can see, coming towards the doors,*
DAVID SILTZ *and* PROFESSOR EMMA PORLOCK. *She is
(uncharacteristically) holding on to his arm. In fact, she is on the
verge of being drunk. The meeting must have lasted hours and hours.*

EXT. ENTRANCE. HOTEL
It is all salutes, all attention, all eyes on SILTZ, *the president of the
great entertainment corporation which owns the hotel, as well as as
much as it can of 'the hearts and minds' of never less than half of the
world's population,* AD 2368.
SILTZ: (*Coming into earshot*) – send you back in one of my
    specials. You just speak your instructions –
EMMA: (*Slightly slurred*) We have those. *Our* corp-corporation
    has those too.
SILTZ: (*Mischievous glint*) With a bar in back?
EMMA: A bar? Well – no – but in any cashe – I – (*Giggle*) Oh.
    All right. Why not? You naughty man.
SILTZ: Just ID yourself with SAIG – ess ay one gee – that, in
    case you should wonder, stands for Siltz AI guest.

(*She looks sidelong at him and a flash of the sober* EMMA
appears, making her take her hand off his arm.)

EMMA: Siltz high-interest trade would have done. And it makes
a better acronym.

SILTZ: What?

EMMA: Capital initials. Ess aitch eye tee.

(SILTZ *twists a smile, beckons obsequious doorman.*)

SILTZ: Call up the guest car, Harry.

HARRY: Yes, *sir*, Mr Siltz!

(*And he gets a roll of notes for his pains.*)

Thank *you*, Mr President, sir!

(*He blows a two-note whistle, and from a gleaming row of
bubble-like vehicles a very polished one emerges.*)

SILTZ: (*To* EMMA, *as he turns away*) Ess ay one gee will have to
do. And remember. Answer by noon tomorrow. Tick one
box.

EMMA: (*Slight giggle*) Tick one box.

SILTZ: (*His back to her*) Good night, Professor.

EMMA: Good night.

CLOSE-UP – SILTZ

Reverse. And his face shows what he really thinks of her.

SILTZ: (*Mutters to self*) I'll squeeze that milk from your withered
udders, you hoity old cow. Just you see!

(*Unaware, it seems, that all eyes are upon him. Clearly, an
extraordinarily famous and feared man.*)

INT./EXT. GRAND 'BUBBLE'. STREETS. NIGHT

*The non-driver autobubble soon leaves the vivid lights of the hotel
environs. It passes through alternate patches of desolation,
vandalized buildings,* RON *graffiti, occasional pools of light and
luxury – a strange new world.*

EMMA, *alone, tipsy, rather endearing and becoming more and more
so as we get to know her, is half talking to herself.*

EMMA: Mmm-um – tried to – wants me pissed – (*Pause.*) Nasty
man. (*Pause, very clearly*) I – just – don't – know.

(*Looking out, she sees a pattern of buildings like that on the
way to the attacked restaurant. She pours herself a drink from a
little rack of bottles and glasses, then – *)

Stop here!

CAR VOICE: Identify, please.

EMMA: Oh, um – oh, shit!

CAR VOICE: Not recognized. Identify, please.

> (*Befuddled, she has to think hard. It comes. She tosses back her drink, smacks her lips.*)

EMMA: Ess ay one gee. Stop.

CAR VOICE: Am stopping.

EMMA: Ess ay one gee. Reverse. Slowly.

CAR VOICE: Am reversing slowly.

EXT. NEAR ENTRANCE FYODOR'S APARTMENT BLOCK. NIGHT
The 'bubble'-like car slowly crawling backwards, virtually clinging to the pavement edge.

INT./EXT. 'CAR'. NIGHT

EMMA: Stop!

CAR VOICE: Am stopping.

EMMA: (*Giggles, replacing drinks glass*) And shut your mouth!

> (*She starts to get out, but falls back a little, with a tipsy giggle.*)
> Oopsy-doopsy Prof! (*Then*) Wait here.

CAR VOICE: Will wait.

EMMA: Shut up.

INT. KITCHEN. FYODOR'S APARTMENT. NIGHT
Stooped over a sink, making odd juddery breathing noises, FYODOR *seems to be washing something, the water running.*

CLOSE-UP – SINK
An art-deco-type piece of table sculpture is being sluiced heavily with fast running water – but even so, some blood is still coming off it, and FYODOR, *off screen, is making suppressed, dry half-sobbing sounds deep at the back of his throat.*

INT. FYODOR'S KITCHEN. NIGHT
Then he starts to retch. But, almost at the same time, bzzzzzzzz!

EXT. ENTRANCE. FYODOR'S BLOCK. NIGHT
The armed apartment guard stands warily near as EMMA *presses an*

*entry button, and a small videocam swivels to her. She has to press
again.*

EMMA: (*To self, fidgety*) Come on. Come on. I want to go to
     wee-wees.

INT. HALL. FYODOR'S APARTMENT. NIGHT
Breathing heavily, wiping his hands, FYODOR *looks at the
videoviewer, to see* EMMA *waiting there. He sucks in his breath in
dismay.*

FYODOR: (*To self*) Oh, dear sweet Jesus. (*To microphone, harshly*)
     What do you want?

EMMA: (*On video, scratchy*) Fyodor. Let me in. It's important!

FYODOR: (*Growls*) I'm asleep! Go away!

EXT. ENTRANCE. FYODOR'S BLOCK. NIGHT
*The guard's attention has switched to a group of youths at the edge of
the frame, so to speak, while* EMMA *stamps in fury.*

EMMA: Fyodor! Let me in! At once! How dare you keep me out
     here in the –

GUARD: Get down, lady.

INT. HALL. FYODOR'S APARTMENT. NIGHT
FYODOR *cannot see but he can hear the* GUARD, *as Emma's angry
face looms in his video entry oblong.*

GUARD: (*Off, scratchy*) I think it's just robbers and not – Jee-sus!
     Get down!
     (*As a shot is heard.*)

EXT. FYODOR'S ENTRANCE. STREET. NIGHT
The GUARD *goes down on one knee and opens fire, warningly, over
the heads of four teenagers, one of whom has fired at the building,
apparently for no reason.*

EMMA: Fyodor! There's trouble down here!
     (*She has not stooped or taken cover.*
     Bzzzz! The door clicks open for her, as – beyond – the YOUTHS
     laugh and jeer.)

YOUTHS: Nervy cop! Nervy cop!
     (*And she is in.*)

INT. FYODOR'S LIVING ROOM. NIGHT
Sweating and panting, FYODOR *is dragging a body by the legs, across the living-room carpet. He is in a panic, holding on to the ankles. Looking around and about, he drags the body behind a long, soft leather sofa, near a wall of books. It just about fits.*

CLOSE-UP – BODY
As, panting, FYODOR *bends to adjust its position, the body is seen to be that of* ANDREW MILTON.

INT. UPPER HALL. BEYOND ELEVATOR. NIGHT
EMMA *comes out of the lift, faintly humming 'Amazing Grace', still a bit tipsy but getting less and less so by the minute. She stops at Fyodor's door.*

INT. HALL. FYODOR'S. NIGHT
Still out of breath, with a stone in his chest, FYODOR *pointlessly dabs a fluttery hand at his awry hair in the mirror by the door and opens it to* EMMA's *irritatingly persistent buzz.*

INT. HALL TO LIVING ROOM. FYODOR'S. NIGHT
EMMA, *self-preoccupied, at first notices nothing wrong with the manner of his appearance.*
EMMA: You certainly took your time, young man. And what do you mean, you were *asleep?*

INT. LIVING ROOM. FYODOR'S. NIGHT
She plumps herself straight down on a sofa – directly opposite the one behind which Milton's body lies.
EMMA: How can you go to sleep so early – What time is it, anyway?
(FYODOR *brushes his hand through his hair, utterl;y distracted.*)
FYODOR: I – eleven o'clock. Nearly.
EMMA: (*Exclaims*) My God!
FYODOR: (*Nervous*) W–what – ?
EMMA: That means I've been with *that man* for close on ten hours! (*Looks at him.*) Fyodor?
FYODOR: What?

EMMA: Have I come at – (*Hiccups slightly.*) Oops. Oh, dear. He's given me too much to – Fyodor. You look *terrible*. What is the matter? Oh, please, will you sit down! You're hovering over me like a – like a – (*Frowns at him.*) Fyodor. Are you ill? (*He sits on the dangerous sofa, jumps up immediately, sits on another chair, pulls his hand haplessly to his throat, lowers it again.*)

FYODOR: (*Nods*) I – yes. A – some sort of fever or – or – (*Babbles*) Fell asleep at my desk, and – I –

EMMA: And had a nightmare, by the looks of you. (*He tries to smooth his hair down, to no purpose. His forehead gleams with sweat. She is really looking at him now.*)

FYODOR: Excuse me. I'm – not myself. (*Hollow, to self*) Oh, God. (*She goes to get up, to cross to him, concerned.*)

EMMA: Fyodor, my dear - (*But he gets up himself, and goes – oddly jerkily – to a trolley-like side-table.*)

INT. DRINKS TABLE. LIVING ROOM. NIGHT
Hands shaking badly, so that cut-glass decanter and glasses chink and ring, FYODOR *pours himself a brandy, then remembers to do one for* EMMA *too.*

FYODOR: Maybe it's some bug, or – And poor Kaya. That really got to me.

EMMA: I know. She keeps flashing in and out of my mind, too. Such a sweet and – What could possibly have happened? (*He crosses to her, a little more composed.*)

INT. LIVING ROOM. NIGHT
FYODOR: I don't think I can let you stay long, Emma. I'm just about all in.

EMMA: I'm sorry. I've intruded, I can see. (*Takes drink from him.*) I shouldn't have any more but suddenly I feel stone cold sober and badly in need of a talk. I doubt very much whether *I* shall get any rest this night.

FYODOR: (*Sitting*) Siltz?

EMMA: Siltz. (FYODOR *gulps down a long drink and half-shudders. She misunderstands.*)

302

I know, All such people make me feel contaminated.

FYODOR: (*Flat*) Contaminated.

EMMA: But then again, I don't suppose he's all that much worse
than the Martina Masdons of this world. We're entirely
run by giant corporations, and they in turn are entirely run
by people who have no regard for any other structure, any
other systems, any other values, any other feelings than
what shows in the number-cruncher.

(FYODOR *does not seem to have been listening. He repeats a
word, making it sound like something disgusting lodged in his
throat.*)

FYODOR: Contaminated.

EMMA: (*Slightly irritated*) What?

(*He looks at her, then stands up.*)

FYODOR: Emma. I – I – (*He sways, alarmingly.*)

EMMA: Fyodor!

(*He seems to steady himself, and even to smile at her, but then,
all at once, glass still in hand, he keels over and slumps to the
floor.* EMMA *claps her own drink down on a table and rushes to
him, shocked.*)

EMMA: Fyodor – ! What's the – ! Fyodor – ! (*She lifts his head,
sees he's out cold, and rushes for the nearest source of water – the
kitchen.*)

INT. KITCHEN. FYODOR'S. NIGHT
*She wets a kitchen cloth that seems clean, and notices, as an oddity,
the little table statue or figurine art-deco style on the drainer.*

INT. LIVING ROOM. NIGHT
*Rushing back in, she stops dead. From her slightly new angle she can
now see --*

CLOSE-UP – FEET BEHIND SOFA
A pair of shoes, soles up, and a stretch of legs – the body of ANDREW
MILTON.

INT. LIVING ROOM. NIGHT
At almost the same time that EMMA *gasps,* FYODOR *makes a low
rumbling moan, coming to, trying to sit up.*

She stops beside him and inexpertly, indeed rather comically, splosh-splashes the soaking cloth across his face, making him twist his head and splutter.

FYODOR: Aah – No – enough – (*He succeeds in sitting up, and then puts his hands to the sides of his head.*)

INT. LIVING ROOM. NIGHT
Still holding the sodden, dripping cloth, EMMA *edges and edges sideways, then, suddenly abrupt in movement, thrusts her head over the back of the sofa and sees the face of* MILTON.
EMMA: (*Matter-of-fact*) Andrew Q. Milton.

CLOSE-UP – FYODOR
Sitting on the floor, his hands go still at the sides of his head. A beat.
FYODOR: (*Croaks*) Director of Public Affairs.

INT. LIVING ROOM. NIGHT
EMMA *returns to her chair and picks up her drink again. A remarkable woman. She sips, looking at* FYODOR *all the time, virtually expressionless. Then –*
EMMA: Ex-Director of Public Affairs. (*She takes another sip.*)
　　Come on. Get up. Drink your drink. And explain.
　　(FYODOR, *steadier now, and almost with a smile, hauls himself to his feet, looks over the back of the particular sofa, and resumes his place at the chair in which he previously sat, taking a sip of brandy, too.*)
FYODOR: We had a row.
EMMA: What about?
FYODOR: Leave that a minute. I might be able to tell you.
　　(*She tilts her head, considers, then nods.*)
EMMA: You had a row.
FYODOR: I totally lost my temper. I mean totally. I picked up my delicate-looking little art-deco figurine – and it turned out to be far less delicate than it seems. (*Sips.*) I hit him on the head with it. (*Sips.*) And as he fell, I hit him again. As hard as I could.
EMMA: You're quite sure he's dead?
FYODOR: (*Gloomily*) Absolutely.
　　(*Pause.*)

EMMA: What are you going to do?
(*Smaller pause.*)
FYODOR: I haven't the faintest idea.
(*They look at each other – indeed, seem to examine each other.*
It is suddenly tense.)
EMMA: Are you going to kill me, too?
(*He makes a small, ambivalent gesture, a sort of I-don't-know,*
with his hand.)

CLOSE-UP – EMMA
She considers the matter, apparently calm, and decides to take
another small sip. Then she puts her glass down, and rises.

INT. LIVING-ROOM. NIGHT
EMMA *makes her way to the door, seemingly unimpeded. But*
suddenly, very fast, he lurches out of his chair, gets in front of her,
and stands with his back to the living room door.
EMMA: No?
FYODOR: No, Emma.
(*She sighs, and goes back to where she was sitting. He does not*
move.)

CLOSE-UP – FYODOR. AT DOOR
He stares across the comfortable room at her, absolutely bewildered.
FYODOR: I am so terribly sorry. He k – (*Stops himself: was going*
to say 'killed Kaya'.) I'm sorry. I have to think. And in
order to think, really think, you have to talk about and
think about something else, haven't you? It's like referred
pain.

INT. LIVING ROOM. NIGHT
EMMA *thinks about this 'lateral-thinking' approach, and decides to*
accept it for the time being.
EMMA: Siltz. He's offered me – us – the kingdoms of the world.
He can guarantee all our funding, double all our salaries,
move us into our *own* laboratories, and provide us with all
the alpha-neuropeptide 1042 and all the cerebrospinal
fluids we'll ever need –
FYODOR: (*Gasping throughout*) What – ? What? *What?*

EMMA: And to cap it all, he'll enable us to make submicroscopic modifications in many, many more cerebral circuits by pushing us from 40 per cent to 80 per cent of those ten billion neurones in the cerebral cortex.
(FYODOR, *astounded, is moving away from the door, open-mouthed.*)

FYODOR: But – but – but that would cost *zillions* – I mean billions and billions – it would be one of the costliest –

EMMA: Plus the law suits –

FYODOR: The what?

EMMA: Well, it's *theft*, isn't it? Siltz's corporation purloining the Masdon material. We'd have to get that boxed-up head out of there, for a start. (*Excited.*) But think of it! Our *own* lab! Those resources! That percentage of the cortex! My God in blue heaven!
(*They look at each other, each suddenly a little dry-mouthed.*)

FYODOR: And in return?

EMMA: (*Blunt*) We prostitute ourselves.

FYODOR: Exactly.

INT. BY THE 'MILTON SOFA'. NIGHT
Emma's eyes start to move to the particular body-hiding sofa again.
FYODOR *hovers in front of it, comically, as though (ludicrously) trying to prevent her from even thinking about the corpse behind the sofa.*

FYODOR: And what, *what* does he get for all those zillions? *What?*

EMMA: (*Off screen*) Ah now. This is the thing.

INT. LIVING ROOM. NIGHT
EMMA: He gets the right to take the memories of Daniel Feeld, edit them, and transmit them all over the world on his TV, his cable, his VRs, his videos, his whole crock of shit. *He's* convinced that he'll sweep all the ratings when people out there see what it was *really* like to walk and talk and play and screw and eat and drink nearly four hundred years ago. *He* says the marrow in what we must presume to be his bones tells him so – and that he's only – (*Snorts*) once been wrong in thirty years in the business, as he calls it.
(FYODOR *sits down, reeling with contending thoughts.*)

CLOSE-UP – FYODOR

FYODOR: And maybe, just maybe, he's *too* smart for his own
good. (*Thinks, all but chuckles*) Maybe. *Maybe!*

CLOSE-UP – EMMA

*Taken by his sudden change of expression – and needing it. She peers
at him with a glint.*

INT. LIVING ROOM. NIGHT

FYODOR: (*Getting up*) You see, he's *right* in a way – how
stupendous to see the real past through the eyes and the
feelings of someone who lived in it. God! What an escape!
Can't you just imagine how *avidly* people would lap it up!
And then – *and then!* – oh, if only! – and then they might
look at the world around them, the world as it is *now*, and
start to ask questions! *Why* do we have to live like this?
Why cannot *we* walk the streets? Why can't we mingle and
touch and hope in the way our forefathers and mothers
used to do? Why? Why? Why?

EMMA: You're getting to sound like a RON.
(*Silence. He makes a decision.*)

FYODOR: (*Quietly*) I am. Reality or Nothing. I believe it.

EMMA: (*Shocked*) You – !

FYODOR: I joined like hundreds, no thousands, of others for
political reasons. Not to terrorize. Not to shed blood. But
to sabotage. To throw up the right questions in the right
places, to *rescue* – (*Stops.*) And now – (*Stops.*) And now I
can't get out. You can't resign from the party. It's for life.
It's for life or death.
(EMMA, *trembling a little, nods at the sofa.*)

EMMA: And Milton there – he found out about you. Is that it?

FYODOR: (*Bitter laugh*) He's my section leader! He recruited me
in the first place.

EMMA: Andrew Milton!

FYODOR: Oh, we're here, there, everywhere.

EMMA: Then – what were you . . . ?

FYODOR: That poor little girl Kaya. I met her in the corridor
when she ran out of the lab. Her *disgust* with the work was
promising. I left her with Andrew.

(*Pause.*)

EMMA: (*Shakily*) You mean – Andrew killed her.

FYODOR: (*Nods*) My fault. She was horrified by the very thought of the RONs. And he'd gone so far that he'd compromised himself. That's what he came to me for, tonight, to explain, to justify – But how can you explain, how can you justify? I just felt this – this hot mist, this rage – I picked up whatever it was I could pick up, and – and – (*He covers his face again, momentarily. When he speaks again, it sounds like stone, so bleak.*) Oh, dear God. Oh, dear Christ in Heaven. (*Silence.*)

EMMA: So – now you'll have to kill me.

FYODOR: (*Gulps*) Will I?
(*Silence.*)

EMMA: Do you intend to try to sabotage my project?

FYODOR: I *did* intend to, yes. It is an obscenity.

EMMA: But now?
(*Silence.*)

FYODOR: (*Heavily*) No.
(*Silence.*)

EMMA: (*Tense*) Are you sure?

FYODOR: Yes. I'm sure. No – I will not sabotage this. Not now. I still have a few shreds and tatters of hope in us as citizens rather than simply consumers – (*Then the rage suddenly goes out of him, like wind leaving a billowing sail.*) OK. OK. This is how I see it. You should take the tainted silver, scrape out our poor creature's memories, and show *billions* of people out there that, yes, there were other ways to live. The past can stand in front of us for once, challengingly, and not be safely anaesthetized in the long, long ago. Let the past speak! Let it *accuse*!

EMMA: (*Pleased*) So it backfires on Siltz?

FYODOR: Explodes in his face! And the ugly mugs of all the other little Siltz's, all the little Masdon's and their related turds. (*Looks at her.*) Do it, Emma. Go for it.
(*Silence. Then, looking at him all the time, almost but not quite scared, she walks again towards the living-room door.*

He simply watches her go. He makes no attempt to stop her. She opens the door, looks back at him.)

EMMA: Don't be late for work.

EXT. MASDON SCIENCE CENTER. DAY
The alien, desolate golf-ball buildings, fences, etc., slanted with morning sunshine.

INT. CRYOGENIC LAB. DAY
EMMA, TONY, LUANDA and BLINDA *watching the living wall, towering in front of them, with a sort of half-amused stupefaction.* KAYA, *of course, is no more, and* FYODOR *is not there. On the living wall is Daniel's memory of a karaoke bar, and he is 'singing': not in his real voice, but in that of Bing Crosby. They don't know this.*
DANIEL:
> **– don't you know each cloud contains**
> **Pennies from Heaven –**
> (*Going straight into the living wall -*)

INT. KARAOKE STAND. KARAOKE CLUB. 1994. NIGHT
As DANIEL *slightly turns, theatrically gesturing, enjoying it all hugely, a new glint flashes in his eyes. He sees a brutish, balding, middle-aged man,* MAILION, *standing at the open doorway of what looks like his office, off the fifth floor.*
DANIEL: (*Singing*)
> **You'll find your fortune falling**
> **All over town,**
> **Be sure that your umbrella –**

EXTREME CLOSE-UP – 'SINGING' DANIEL
The glint and the grin becoming wickedly enthusiastic as 'Bing Crosby' sings in his mouth.
> **– is upside down,**
> **Trade them for a package of**
> **Sunshine and flowers.**
> (*Suddenly, like a jump in memory, music abruptly stops, and we are in –*)

INT. MAILION'S OFFICE. DAY
MAILION *claps* DANIEL *on the shoulder with a meaty, beringed hand.*

MAILION: Know why they call me 'Pig'? 'Pig' Mailion?

DANIEL: Um. It doesn't sound very nice.

MAILION: (*Cackling*) It's cos I like me dosh by the *trough* load, fella.

(*He slaps* DANIEL'*s shoulder again.* DANIEL *winces in pain, then manages to hide it.*)

INT. CRYOGENIC LAB. DAY

The four watchers, dominated by the huge, glittering living wall, on which, continuous –

DANIEL: (*Suppressed pain*) Well, that's the – (*Half-turns away.*) Sorry. Frog in my throat.

MAILION: Nah. Not a frog. You got *gold* in them tonsils, I'll tell you. Now, listen, what you need is a good manager, somebody who'll – *Hey, what is this?*

(*The four watchers audibly gasp, too, as, with* MAILION *up on the living wall, they see* DANIEL, *fully turning back, pointing a pistol straight at him.*)

CLOSE-UP – MAILION. DANIEL'S POINT OF VIEW

Terror widening on his face, as –

DANIEL: (*Off screen*) You need a few stars in your crown, Arthur.

(*And the shot explodes at point blank range:* MAILION *splatters, sinks below frame.*
    The picture goes black.)

INT. CRYOGENIC LAB. DAY

The living wall is black. It is as though unconsciousness had invaded Daniel's plugged-in brain cells. This has never happened before; at previous failures or overloads, the blobs have appeared, then the collapse into the myriad dots.

EMMA: It's not overload. It can't be.

LUANDA: No. Not overload.

TONY: If it were not impossible, technically impossible, I would say it was a pure black-out, I mean total loss of consciousness in trauma. The most extreme form of amnesia you can get.

LUANDA: Well – why do you say 'technically impossible'?

(*He looks at her hard, then –*)

TONY: My God. You're right. Those cells, the stimulated ones, could behave in any normal brain pattern within the parameters we've set. Yes.

EMMA: That means – that would mean we have to distinguish what type of amnesia we've got here – anterograde, retrograde or post-traumatic. And that gunshot – the killing, my God – our man was a murderer!

(*At which precise moment,* FYODOR *appears in the doorway. He looks across at* EMMA. *She looks back at him. The others – and especially* BLINDA – *are aware of 'something' but know not what.* FYODOR *seems as stiff as a pole.*)

Fyodor. We've just discovered that our Daniel Feeld as was shot a man at virtually point-blank.

(FYODOR *visibly relaxes.*)

FYODOR: I'm sorry I'm late. Again.

EMMA: (*Snaps.*) Yes. So am I.

FYODOR: I had a bad night – and then an intolerably real, authentic-seeming *nightmare* in which I was about to be executed for being a RON terrorist.

TONY: Jesus.

BLINDA: But why *that*, Doctor?

FYODOR: (*Shrugs*) There are no whys in nightmares. Only whats.

EMMA: Which is more or less the problem we now have – (*Gestures at wall.*) I'd say post-traumatic amnesia, but arrested, and we can't move him back, can't move him on. (*Looks at* FYODOR, *who knows what she means.*) Today of all days.

TONY: Today? What do you mean?

(*She ignores the question.*)

EMMA: Fyodor? Help.

(*He stares at the black living wall.*)

FYODOR: Mmmm. It's possible – oh, there's so much leakage, so much after-freeze damage between the – Maybe the amygdala has been overstimulated – by accident, so to speak. You know, that whole fight or flight syndrome. And here the motor and autonomic responses have simply *ceased.* We need to use switching mechanisms – serotoein, noradrenalin and so on –

LUANDA: Noradrenalin, yes. Arouse that state of attentiveness.

TONY: Can't we reverse the whole process – and feed *him* a memory?

LUANDA: What? Not one of his own.

TONY: Well, if it was some public event that he might have seen or have heard talked about –

LUANDA: (*Excited*) With you. With you!

(*But* EMMA, *shrewd, is already off the mark. They turn and look as they hear her speak, pressing a button on her autocube.*)

CLOSE-UP – EMMA. LAB

EMMA: Archive 2611. Pick random twenty to thirty seconds' public event – say – um – say – yes, 1983. Zip it through the capillaries into our Feedbox, Cryonic Lab A.

VOICE: Cost you.

(*This seems a standard MSC response for ordered material.*)

EMMA: (*Hisses*) Oh, and some STFU.

VOICE: Some what?

EMMA: Shut the fuck up!

INT. CRYOGENIC LAB. DAY

Some laughter - BLINDA, *characteristically, covering her mouth with her hand.* FYODOR *quietly puts his hand on Emma's shoulder. She understands it as a gesture of thanks and briefly touches his hand – almost unnoticed. Meanwhile –*

INT. AT 'FEED' RACK. LAB. DAY

LUANDA *is jacking into a small available socket a new but very small ganglion of capillary-like 'tubes', differently coloured.*

LUANDA: The beta grade neo-noradrenalin will be ready when the archive stuff flows –

INT. CRYOGENIC LAB. DAY

The totally black living wall still dominates as TONY *and* BLINDA *take a mini-cassette out of the delivering slat in the 'message wall' and start transferring it on small spools into a machine like a cotton reel spinning out hair-thin thread towards the various phials of the 'feed' rack.*

TONY: (*Gloomily*) If I know archive, this'll be utterly useless –

CLOSE-UP – EMMA AND FYODOR. LAB
They aren't interested in the others for a moment. A quick, quiet exchange.
EMMA: Disposed of?
FYODOR: Yes. Gone.

INT. CRYOGENIC LAB. DAY
LUANDA *straightens from the 'feed' rack, and* TONY *and* BLINDA *complete spooling 'fine hair'.*
LUANDA: (*To* TONY) Have the police questioned you yet about poor Kaya?
TONY: (*Rolls eyes*) Only for an hour. By the time they finished, I was beginning to think *I'd* done it.
    (BLINDA *and* LUANDA *say the same thing at almost the same time.*)
BLINDA: Me, too.
LUANDA: Me, too.
EMMA: (*Smiling*) Well – you *sound* like conspirators. (*Stops smiling.*) Oh, the poor girl.
BLINDA: (*To* FYODOR) Have they questioned you, Dr Glazunov?
    (FYODOR *is gradually becoming aware of her perpetual interest in him. He is a bit cold in response.*)
FYODOR: Of course.
EMMA: (*Impatient*) Are we ready?
LUANDA: (*To* FYODOR) What mark? The noradrenalin?
FYODOR: As soon as the spool light comes on – 3 – no, 2.9!
TONY: Spool light on!
    (*They turn to look at the living wall as* LUANDA *bends to the 'feed' rack.*
    The wall bursts into colour: hordes of children at an Australian Flying Doctor school broadcast in the open air, during the 1983 tour of Australia by Prince Charles and Princess Diana, the happily married couple.)

INT./EXT. AUSTRALIA FD SCHOOL
Under a canvas awning sit, from left to right, Prince Charles, Princess Di and a very Australian DJ/BROADCASTER. *There is an unnecessary Pathé News interpolation which is easily removed. This piece is about twenty-five seconds long.*

BROADCASTER: Now for all our students, on air today, good morning, girls and boys!

CHILDREN: (*Roar*) Good morning!

(*So much noise that Charles sort of guffaws and Di sort of shrinks. It starts getting immediately funny/embarrassing, like an English music-hall double act.*)

BROADCASTER: Jamie wants to know, Does Prince William have a favourite *toy*?

(*Whisper-whisper in a neighing sort of mumble from Charles to Diana.*)

DIANA: Um, Jamie. He loves his koala bear he's got.

(*And for no apparent reason, makes an exaggerated 'Ha Ha' gesture, hand curling to mouth.*)

But he hasn't got anything particular. He just likes to make a bit of noise.

(*Whisper-whisper, including 'Plahstic whale' from Charles. She nod-nod-nods.*)

He's got a plastic whale that throws things out at the top. Little balls.

(*She starts to giggle at 'balls'. Charles's hand goes up to his face. Then – black screen.*)

INT. CRYOGENIC LAB. DAY

The living wall is black again, as –

TONY: (*Incredulous*) What on earth was *that*?

EMMA: Whatever it was, it doesn't w –

(*She stops dead as, suddenly, the living wall comes alive again. SANDRA is sitting in a hospital room, with DANIEL.*)

SANDRA: (*On living wall*) Christ, you don't know me from Adam.

DANIEL: (*On living wall*) Or Eve.

INT. DANIEL'S HOSPITAL ROOM. 1994. DAY

Although the scene is substantially as it is in all positional and many verbal respects to the would-be 'identical' scene in Part Four of Karaoke, *the 'trigger' they have used to unblock the Mailion-murder trauma has got comically tangled in Daniel's maltreated remnants of a brain.*

SANDRA: Who? (*Laughs.*) Oh. Yeah. Ought to say Eve, being a

woman, enni? And I love my Koala bear a lot.
(*And for no apparent reason, she makes an exaggerated 'Ha Ha' gesture, hand curling to mouth.*)

DANIEL: No doubt about it. (*Looks at her, changes tone.*) I want to say something about you and to you.
(*Tiny pause. She fidgets a little, puzzled.*)

SANDRA: What?

DANIEL: Mumble, umble plahstic whale mumm.

SANDRA: (*Exactly as before.*) What?

DANIEL: Don't get worried or upset. I'm not going to jump on you or anything like that. I don't want to offend you – but I must say something.

SANDRA: But he hasn't got anyfink in particular. He just likes to make a bit of noise.
(*Tiny pause. Basically timid with women, he half-looks away, then looks back at her.*)

DANIEL: You are utterly enchanting. You are fresh air to me. I feel lifted up in your presence. (*Holds up his hand to stop her attempted interjection.*) I once knew a young woman whom all the songs were about.

SANDRA: She throws things out at the top. Little balls.
(SANDRA *starts to giggle, in a Diana-ish sort of way.*)

DANIEL: All the songs. All of them. A green-eyed dazzler I met in a Forest of Nead dance hall.
(*Dissolving.*)

EXT. SMALL TOWN DANCE HALL. 1950S. NIGHT
The sob of a saxophone taking blue ribbons out of 'Smoke Gets in Your Eyes', on a starry night, with some young people hanging around the entrance. Way beyond, under the moon, the fringe of the tree-line as the forest climbs and spreads all around the drab little township.

INT. STAGE. DANCE HALL. NIGHT
More a slightly raised platform than an authentic 'stage', easy to step up on to. Half a dozen amateur or, as they would prefer, semi-pro musicians are stepping rather heavily on the delicate smoke of 'Smoke Gets in Your Eyes'. They wear snazzy 'uniforms', but not all of them quite match.

INT. DANCE HALL. NIGHT
*Thirty to forty couples in the 1950s swirl of clothing, with proper
ballroom etiquette and strictly strict tempo, dominated by the not-bad
sax. All very evocative. Finding –*

INT. BAR. DANCE HALL. NIGHT
*Two-thirds of one side of the largely wooden, or stone and wood hall,
is taken up by a bar which is not quite makeshift, but hardly the real
thing. Groups of lads drink beer loudly, and groups of girls allow
themselves to be eyed. Homing in on –*

INT. BOTTOM END OF BAR. NIGHT
*Nearest to the amateur musicians a group of three young men, one of
whom (youngish* DANIEL*) has his back to us. He is one of the two
listeners to* JIM*, a card, a jokesmith of about twenty-two, with a
rubbery face and a small, unwise moustache, doomed to talk about
sex a lot and practise it a little.*
*The music continues, loud enough to make raised voices necessary,
gliding eventually from 'Smoke Gets in Your Eyes' to a more upbeat
'Did You Ever See a Dream Walking?' The young men's forest
accents are fairly strong, but not as dialect-thick as the very young or
the much older.*

JIM: And thoy be sitting on these here beach at Porthcawl all
    bloody morning. Her with next to nothing on, mind. Bikini
    – thou's know!

TED: Two cups full, eh, Dan?
    (DANIEL *just laughs. They drink. We don't see Daniel's face.*)

JIM: 'I got to touch her, just got to, bloody *got* to,' him said to I.
    Cos her kept looking sort of sideways at'n. I mean, with a
    bit of encouragement and that –

TED: Jim. Is this true? Or just one of your stories?

JIM: True as I be standing here. *Anyway*, him thought the best
    approach'd be by a bit of horseplay.

DANIEL: (*Off screen*) Well, that'd be fine if she were a mare.
    (TED *sniggers.* JIM *is a bit irritated.*)

JIM: 'Old on, 'old on, Daniel. Tha bist always trying to go one
    better on I, ent you? (*There is just a faint edge of other
    resentments here.*)

DANIEL: (*Off screen*) Oops.

JIM: *So* – (*Grins*) They go for a walk in the afternoon, see –
along the sand – and suddenly him jumps on her – 'I'd like
to duck you!' he says, pushing her towards the water.
'Duck me?' she says. 'Christ, you con even bloody spell it!'
(*Mild groans and laughs, and the weak ending is in any case
further spoiled by the intrusion of a fourth young man,* JOHN.)

JOHN: Daniel –

DANIEL: (*Laughing, over-compensating for his interruption, still off-
screen*) Oh hi, John. How is it?
(*He seems to pull by the hand a pretty young woman of about
twenty, as if from nowhere, in the thicker crush at this end of the
bar.*)

JOHN: I'd like you to meet *my girlfriend*, Dan. Beth. Beth
Carter. Beth, this is an old pal of mine from the grammar
school, Daniel Feeld. 'Double E' Feeld, eh, Dan?

DANIEL: That's right. Pleased to meet you, Beth.
(*Something about the way* JOHN *has said 'my girlfriend'
indicates that excess of pride which in turn indicates doubt about
security of tenure.*)

EXTREME CLOSE-UP – BETH

The suddenness of the close shot is like a swift arrow of desire.

BETH: And nice to meet you, too, Daniel. John says you're at
Oxford – is that right?

JIM: (*Edge, off screen*) Yeah. Clever bugger, ent he?

DANIEL: (*Off screen*) Well. It beats work, that's for sure! (*Then*)
Um. (*Then*) How long have you been, um, going out with
old John here?
(*She looks sidelong, towards off-screen* JOHN. *This close shot is
relentlessly held. Music switching to 'Did You Ever See a
Dream Walking?' smack on the nose.*)

BETH: Well, I wouldn't really say that we –

JOHN: (*Butts in, off screen*) Two months.

INT. CRYOGENIC LAB. DAY

As the relentless close shot of BETH *flicks off, like a turn of Dan's
head to look at the dancers swirling slowly past, just beyond the bar,
while a not-bad* LOCAL SINGER *fronts the band, bow-tie slightly
askew.*

LOCAL SINGER:

Did you ever see a dream walking?
Well I did.
Did you ever hear a dream talking?
Well I did!

(*All this on the dominating living wall, where the five watchers are made into near-silhouettes by the strength of the glow from the vast, glittering wall. The image changing –*)

EXT. BUS STOP. BUS QUEUE. FOREST TOWN. DAY

A line of ten, eleven people by a rail with a bus-stop sign saying 'Monmouth. Staunton. Berry Hill'.

Moving along them at walking pace until find, penultimately, BETH *alone. All from point of view of walker.*

DANIEL: (*Off screen*) Well, well – it's – um – it's Beth, isn't it? Beth Carter. We met on Saturday at –

(*Her response is swift, and the smile both sweet and immediate.*)

BETH: At the dance. Daniel Feeld.

BETH/DANIEL: (*Same time*) With two Es.

(*They laugh. She stops laughing and seems to study him for a micro-second.*)

INT. CRYOGENIC LAB. DAY

Reverse from the previous lab angle, so that the faces of EMMA, FYODOR, TONY, LUANDA *and* BLINDA *are seen watching, the glow of the gigantic but now off-screen living wall on their slightly uptilted faces.*

And it is the glow of watching someone fall in love, as, continuous –

DANIEL: (*Off*) Where are you going? If I may dare to ask?

BETH: (*Off*) Monmouth. To get my hair done.

DANIEL: (*Off, too quickly*) Oh, not *cut*. Not cut, I hope – !

EXTREME CLOSE-UP – BETH

A shy little fluster, full of uncalculated charm.

BETH: But it's a bit raggedy at the ends – and –

DANIEL: (*Off screen*) It's *perfect*, Beth.

(*Too emphatic. Too glowing. She looks at him, faintly puzzled.*)

INT. CRYOGENIC LAB. DAY
Two-shot, screen-free, of LUANDA *and* BLINDA.
LUANDA: (*Side of hand*) Not too great with the women, is he?
BLINDA: (*Giggles*) I'd run a mile.
LUANDA: (*Smiles*) Towards?
BLINDA: Away from!

EXT. COUNCIL HOUSE. FOREST VILLAGE. DAY
*A young man, his back to us, knocking half-nervously on the glass
panel inset into the front door of a typical 1930s-built council house.
Obviously,* DANIEL.

INT./EXT. DOOR AND 'HALL'. COUNCIL HOUSE. DAY
*Opening door, and a woman of about forty-five. Going close in on
her.*
BETH'S MOTHER: Yes? Can I – ?
DANIEL: (*Off screen*) I – ah – Is Beth at home by any chance?
BETH'S MOTHER: At three o'clock on a weekday?
DANIEL: (*Off screen*) I meant – um – If I –
BETH'S MOTHER: Hers at work, o'butty. At Mallard's.
DANIEL: (*Off screen*) Oh. Yes. Of course. The grocery place – ?

INT. CRYOGENIC LAB. DAY (REVERSE)
*Luanda's eyes, watching the living wall we cannot see at this angle,
are beginning to shine with the slightly ludicrous enjoyment readers
are alleged to get from a Mills and Boon romance.*
BETH'S MOTHER: (*Off, on screen*) Her's cashier there. Good wi'
    figures, mind, our Beth. Always was.

EXT. PAVEMENT. SHOP WINDOWS. FOREST TOWN. DAY
The camera is again DANIEL *as it 'walks' past a butcher's, with
hanging slabs of meat, and a chemist's, with big glass jars in the
window and Brylcreem ads featuring Denis Compton, then hesitates
at the brink of another window.
Then moves again –*

EXT. MALLARD'S GROCERY SHOP WINDOW. DAY
*Through the slightly curved, highly polished glass, a traditional non-
self-service shop with a pair of long counters, at least four assistants,*

*and, towards the back, a cashier's kiosk, fed by pneumatic tubes for
delivery and send-back of notes and coins. Stand and watch.* BETH
*is the figure in the glass 'kiosk', like someone on a little stage of her
own.*

INT. CASHIER'S KIOSK. DAY

*Taking Daniel's eyeline on a kind of zoom, as though there is
nothing else in the way – a purely mental act, so to speak, a
'metaphor' of sorts for extreme concentration of feeling, made more
vividly so when –*

CLOSE-UP – CASHIER'S KIOSK

Everything *literally has disappeared. The kiosk occupies whiteness.
And the figure of* BETH *within it, in a red dress, seems almost
incandescent.*

CLOSE-UP – EMMA. LAB

Unexpectedly sentimental.

EMMA: (*Quietly*) We *do* that, you know. At certain times in our
   – (*But her voice trails off in embarrassment.*)

INT. CRYOGENIC LAB. DAY

*The living wall in front of them – a great slab of picture – is suddenly
changing, almost as though in a self-defensive gesture against the
intensity of the 'concentration' and the means used to show it. We are
looking at a more-than-a-little tipsy* DANIEL *and* ANNA, *at table in
the brasserie, as in Part One of* Karaoke.

DANIEL: (*To* ANNA) The way we hear – see – *think* that what is
   so – say *out there* – (*Gestures around*) in front of us – the way
   we feel it's somehow or other been *arranged* in advance by
   – by – Oh, I don't know what to call it.

ANNA: Paranoia?
   (*He half-glares, then nods, and* drinks *– and laughs.*)

DANIEL: (*Half-hiccup*) I've always longed to be an artsy-fartsy
   arsehole, Anna, which is why I want to work for the Arts
   Council or that magazine, what's it? *Sight and Sound?* I'd
   make a – (*He stops in mid-word. His face changes. He stares
   across the brasserie.*)

INT. BAR/'DRINKS' TABLES. BRASSERIE. 1994. NIGHT
*Just about to sit, and again it comes with the shock of a coup de
théâtre, is* BETH, *the Forest of Nead girl, with a much older,
distinctly Essex man,* PETER (*not the actor, the 'real' Peter), who is
thumping down an opened bottle of wine by its neck, rather as
though it were a chicken being strangled.*
*This (if explanation really is needed) reaches far back into the source
of Daniel's original* Karaoke *script, in which an otherwise sane old
man, Oliver Morse, gives the face and voice of a girl he had loved
and lost many years ago to other young women in the present day,
when particularly struck by them. It is also a clue to the immediacy
of Daniel's feelings for* SANDRA – *and their similarity to what he had
felt long ago for* BETH.

INT. DANIEL'S TABLE. BRASSERIE. NIGHT
ANNA – *puzzled by the dramatic change in Daniel's expression –
turns to see what he can see.*
DANIEL: (*Hisses*) It's straight out of – it's the second page of my
    – (*Almost a shudder*) *What's happening here?* (*Small beads of
    sweat are suddenly glistening on his forehead. It seems he is in a
    metaphysical terror.*)
ANNA: Daniel? What on earth are you on about?
    (*He looks at her, haunted. A beat.*)
DANIEL: (*Awed*) *They are speaking my lines.*

INT. CRYOGENIC LAB. DAY
*The pictures on the living wall suddenly collapse into smeary blobs,
disassembling themselves, slipping and slithering away from each
other before further disintegrating into myriad multi-coloured dots.*
FYODOR: (*Reassuring and pleased*) To the second. That's all
    right. That's perfect! We're well clear of the trauma
    syndrome.
TONY: But did you notice the way the 'memory' we fed him
    bumped into his real ones?
EMMA: And his real ones bumped into his own real ones, if you
    follow me.
LUANDA: But we all do that, don't we?
    (BLINDA *is looking at* FYODOR.)
BLINDA: All the time.

(FYODOR *again picks up on this attention. She tries to flick her eyes away, but is a fraction too late.*)

EXTREME CLOSE-UP – FYODOR
A warning sounds in his head: at least, that is what his face looks like.

EXT. SILTZ'S GRAND HOTEL. DAY
Ornate vulgarity, luxury, and the bristle of menace protecting it all around.

INT. SILTZ'S SUITE. 'LIVING AREA'. DAY
Judge this by the dining room and massage room already seen in this suite: acres of marbled, fluffed, puffed, neo-antiquity and twinkling, winkling high-high-tech, the sky at all the windows, so far up is it. He is with a senior, middle-aged member of his staff, HARRY SCHUMPET.

HARRY: Just so I get it on the record, Dave, just so as you don't get up there, four months from now and yell for Harry Schumpet to be dewhatsipated, I want to be adamant –

SILTZ: (*Glinting*) To be what?

HARRY: Adamant.

SILTZ: With *me*?

HARRY: I want to be as near to adamant as your bullying cruelty will allow.

SILTZ: Your what?

HARRY: I want to cringe, Dave.

SILTZ: OK. Go ahead.

HARRY: And whine and crawl and wring my hands.

SILTZ: Consider it done. About what, though?

HARRY: This *head*.

SILTZ: I'm right. I'm right even when I'm wrong, Harry.

HARRY: It-ain't-gonna-work.

SILTZ: How much you bet?

HARRY: Not my job, that's for sure.

SILTZ: OK. I promise: Not your job. You've gone on record. The record is noted, right *here* – (*Smacks forehead with butt of his palm.*) That head, Harry, is going to outrate every damned show we got.

322

HARRY: But it's so fucking *old*, Dave. It's like – like – God, like one of those cheeses –

SILTZ: (*Puzzled*) One of those what?

HARRY: Crawling with maggots. Gives me the shudders. Eating stuff like that. C'mon!

(SILTZ, *excited by his own genius, is starting to move about the room, picking up objets d'art and putting them down again after cursory non-examination.*)

SILTZ: It'll be the most exciting, most unexpected, most storiest of all the j – You know, our biz, showbiz, call it what you will biz, is all about taking a trip. A journey. That's all. Looking over the next guy's fence. Right?

HARRY: (*Glum*) Right.

SILTZ: Five minutes to zero.

HARRY: Yeah. Noon. I know. (*Brightens.*) Maybe she'll say No, no, no!

(SILTZ *stops and looks at him as though at a crass idiot.*)

CLOSE-UP – SILTZ
A credo.

SILTZ: Listen, fella. Those with high principles stuffed like a pole up their arse are no trouble at all. You just reach out and take them. They're always ready to fall outa the tree, the right and proper and the good and true ones. It's the people with *no* principles you gotta worry about!

EXT. MASDON SCIENCE CENTER. DAY
The soulless golf-ball-on-tee buildings, the patchwork of narrow paths, the flash-flash-flashing perimeter fence.

EXT. A PATH BETWEEN BUILDINGS. DAY (BINOCULAR VIEW)
As seen by a GUARD at the entrance to Emma's building. An old woman walking alone, seemingly talking to herself, hands seemingly clasped together.

CLOSE-UP – EMMA
EMMA *is actually using a voice-only phone, holding down one button on her biobrace (bracelet) as she speaks.*

EMMA: I have no means of ensuring this will not be recorded.

323

I'll be brief. I tick the yes box. Now what do I do? I'll wait instructions at home at seven.

EXT. ENTRANCE TO CRYOGENIC LAB BLOCK
The GUARD *recesses his tiny binoculars back into the helmet. Behind the glass shield, his eyes are narrowing with suspicion. But* EMMA *is returning. As she approaches, he moves a little towards her.*
GUARD: Professor Porlock.
EMMA: Correct.
GUARD: What are you doing?
EMMA: Minding my own business.
    (*The* GUARD *sighs a world-weary sigh.*)
GUARD: Come on, Professor. I shall have to report that at eleven fifty-nine hours you made what appeared to be an audio call in circumstances that suggest – Well, you tell me.
EMMA: Good. And add that at eleven fifty-eight hours I finished a wee-wee, and at twelve oh one hours I talked to an impertinent oaf. (*With which she sweeps past, using her 'smart card' to enter the building.*)
GUARD: Hey! You!
    (*But she ignores him and disappears into the lobby.*)
    (*Fade.*)
    (*Fade in.*)

INT./EXT. POOLSIDE. MASDON HOUSE. CALIFORNIA. DAY
Witch-like MARTINA MATILDA MASDON, *stretched on a lounger in an inappropriate bathing costume, is having her toenails buffed and painted by a young maid,* CELESTINE. *Seated beside her is a different Adonis from the last one. This beautiful fellow is called* NIGEL. *But he would appear to have the same IQ as his immediate predecessor.*
MARTINA *looks at him, crooks a twist of a smile to herself and, with a long sweep of her skinny, bare, wrinkled but bracelet-adorned arm, indicates all that surrounds her.*
MASDON: You see all this, Nigel?
NIGEL: Yes'm.
MASDON: Well, one day it won't be all yours.
NIGEL: No'm.

MASDON: But you can have some very nice sweet and juicy slices of it, boy.

NIGEL: Yes'm.

(CELESTINE *hides a smile, not too well.*)

MASDON: Celestine!

CELESTINE: Ms Masdon?

MASDON: Split your face later. Not now.

CELESTINE: Sorry, Ms Masdon.

(MARTINA MATILDA *spreads a wider smile, turns her attention back to the muscular Einstein.*)

MASDON: Be a good boy, Nigel. Fix us a drinkolo. And give me a kiss.

NIGEL: (*Rising*) Yes'm. (*Pause.*) Which first?

MASDON: (*Sighs*) Go get the drinks.

NIGEL: Yes'm.

MASDON: Bonehead.

NIGEL: Yes'm.

(*He swaggers off towards the house, somehow or other pleased with himself.* CELESTINE, *finishing the last little toe in a vivid purple, tries not to lift her head. But* MARTINA *is looking at her, with a wicked gleam.*)

MASDON: Well – whatchathink?

(*Tiniest pause.*)

CELESTINE: Don't let him finish your crossword puzzle, ma'am.

MASDON: (*Cackles*) Ah, no. But what about his pectorals?

CELESTINE: (*Rising*) I wouldn't even be *starting* the puzzle, Ms Masdon!

MASDON: (*Another dirty cackle*) Good girl, Celestine. (*Wiggles her toes.*) Nice colour, yes?

CELESTINE: Deep purple. *Definitely* nice.

(*But* MASDON *is already looking across at the bank of monitors beside the blue glitter of Californian pool. Her whole face seems to focus, in the way a setter dog's does. She ignores* CELESTINE *altogether, as the girl packs away her cosmetics and eventually leaves.*)

CLOSE-UP – MARTINA MASDON. POOLSIDE

MASDON *presses the rubbery pad (voice activated) on the table beside her.*

MASDON: Twenty-nine.

CLOSE-UP – RUBBER PAD. TABLE
It flickers into a (silent) animated picture: the golf-ball-on-tee-shaped cryogenic laboratories. No sound.

CLOSE-UP – MARTINA MASDON. POOLSIDE
MASDON: (*Off screen*) Sixteen.

CLOSE-UP – RUBBER PAD. TABLE
*Flickering into view, the cryogenic laboratory, late afternoon 'English' time, with all five present (*EMMA, LUANDA, BLINDA, TONY, FYODOR*). No sound. But they are watching the living wall, where blobs are once again forming themselves into recognizable shapes.*
The shapes are those of a woman with a disfigured face and DANIEL, *in the living room of a dingy little house, speaking to each other – but no sound.*

INT./EXT. POOLSIDE. MASDON HOUSE. DAY
Something about the configuration on the rubber pad has obviously caught Martina's attention. As she turns to yell for NIGEL, *he is already bending, behind her, to lick her earlobe or something similarly unappetizing, holding two glasses of luridly coloured 'drinks'.*
NIGEL: (*Dumb grin*) You like this, huh?
MASDON: (*Brisk*) Yes. Later! Quick! Get my VR helmet and data gloves. They're on the side table by the poolside window.
NIGEL: Yes'm. (*But he doesn't move, unsure what to do with the glasses.*)
MASDON: (*Screeching*) Then do it! Now!
NIGEL: Yes'm.
(*Awkwardly, he puts the glasses down and lopes off, muscularly.* MASDON *stares at the rubber pad, thinking suspicious thoughts.*)
MASDON: (*To self*) I wonder. I wonder if –
(*She sits bolt upright, suddenly, and presses another button on table. Some taped sounds whizz by, incomprehensible. She*

presses the button again. The sound emerges.)

WOMAN'S VOICE: At eleven forty-seven in Laboratory F there
was a double ordering of the same –
(*She tuts, buttons again, whizz again, buttons, and –*)
Guard Hopkins observed Professor Porlock making what
he considers to be an outside audiocall while walking to no
other purpose to and from Laboratory A –
(MARTINA *buttons off the sound, face setting harder and
harder.*)

MASDON: (*Again, to self*) I *wonder.*
(*But* NIGEL *is at her back again. He begins to put on the
weird, enclosing, black-domed virtual reality helmet. She is
putting on the data gloves.*)

CLOSE-UP – RUBBER PAD
Showing the same two figures (the woman and DANIEL) *as the jack
goes into its socket and –*

INT. KITCHEN/LIVING ROOM. HAMMERSMITH HOUSE. DAY
*Propped sideways against the half-net curtain of a window looking
on to a drab backyard, the box lid of a jigsaw puzzle shows a
multicoloured picture of Hammersmith Bridge, gilded in sunlight.
The woman with the damaged face, a* MRS HAYNES (*Sandra's
mother*) *is muttering discontentedly, a piece of wooden jigsaw in her
hand.*

DANIEL: Or the towpath – maybe?

MRS HAYNES: Towpath! Christ! (*Looks up at him.*) Listen, you. I
know this bleed'n bridge like the back of me own hand.
Don't you tell me! (*Then, in a sudden and disturbing fury, she
throws the piece down, hard.*) They do it deliberate! Too
soddin' hard!
(*And in the same inexplicable rage, she sweeps all the jigsaw
pieces, the completed as well as the loose ones, on to the floor, in
a wild scatter. A beat. They look at each other. Then –
movingly, helplessly – she puts her damaged face into her hands
and starts to weep.*)

INT./EXT. POOLSIDE. MASDON'S. DAY
In her VR helmet and gloves, MARTINA *looks strange, and cut-off*

from the world around her, like something that has landed from another galaxy.
Swimming-trunked NIGEL *sits beside her, sipping his Technicolor drink, looking and looking at her, comically unsure what to do. He goes to touch her leg, then withdraws his hand, then half-shrugs, then sips again.*

EXTREME CLOSE-UP – MARTINA MASDON
All her body-language indicates absolutely close attention to whatever it is that is going on inside her strange, enclosing helmet.
Fast dissolve.

CLOSE-UP – MRS HAYNES AND DANIEL
She turns her wet and mutilated face up to him, the weeping all but over, and her one good eye seeming to express both bewilderment and gratitude. She holds the gaze.

INT. KITCHEN/LIVING ROOM. HAMMERSMITH HOUSE. DAY
MRS HAYNES: (*Eventually*) It's not just – it's not just them pieces – I don't know. I – No, no, I don't know.
DANIEL: Do you want me to – ah – (*Looks around.*) Can I make you a cup of tea or something?
(*For a second, another spasm of crazed indignation threatens, but this time it is brought back under control.*)
MRS HAYNES: Tea. A cup of bloody *tea*? No. Ta. No. But – (*Attempt at a wink.*) In there. See. A little drop of mother's ruin. That might do the trick. That cupboard. Up there!

INT. KITCHEN. THE HOUSE. DAY
DANIEL, *under instruction, moves into the small oblong of a kitchen, in which are squashed the basic units of a DIY nature, including a pair of overhead cabinets.*

INT. CRYOGENIC LAB. DAY
In reverse, watching the faces as though from the living wall, it is clear that EMMA, FYODOR, LUANDA, TONY *and* BLINDA *are fascinated, puzzled, entranced and certainly gripped by the strangeness of all that time ago.*

328

MRS HAYNES: (*Off, on living wall*) No! The other one! For
    Christ's sake.
    (*As they watch – smiles of anticipation already beginning –*)

INT. KITCHEN. DAY
*Worcestershire sauce, Bovril, mustard jar, Marmite, HP sauce, a
folded-down half packet of sugar, a salt drum, some biscuits, a loose
box of tea bags and about four packets of crisps come cascading down
from the top of the two shelves within the cabinet.*

INT. CRYOGENIC LAB. DAY
*The five watchers break into laughter as they look at the hugely
dominating living wall, where the spilled objects crack, bounce, bump
and roll on to the metal sink, and into it, and on to the floor, with a
lot of mess.*

INT./EXT. POOLSIDE. CALIFORNIA. DAY
NIGEL *looking even more puzzled and out of it as, inches away from
him,* MARTINA *all but doubles up, laughing within her enclosed
world.*
He touches her leg, but she kicks him off, unceremoniously.

EXTREME CLOSE-UP – MARTINA MASDON
*Almost stops laughing, but a shift in her body shows her attention
caught in a new but equally riveted way.*
Fast dissolve.

INT. LIVING ROOM/KITCHEN. FROM DOORWAY. DAY
MRS HAYNES *roaring with inordinate laughter, amidst scattered
jigsaw pieces, and* DANIEL, *rising from all fours, with a blob of
mustard and a smear of Bovril on his face, and particles of sugar or
salt in his hair and eyebrows.*
SANDRA: What the f——?! (*Then, shrieking at* DANIEL.)
    Whatchewbleedin'doin'ere!

CLOSE-UP – FYODOR. LAB
*He looks at his pre-set digital timer, showing only a few seconds left,
as, on the living wall –*
DANIEL: (*Off*) Sandra. Thank God I've found you. It's

important that I – Don't be alarmed! Please!

INT. LIVING ROOM/KITCHEN. DAY

SANDRA: (*Angry, alarmed*) You're a bloody nutter! And you're frightening the life out of me!

FYODOR: (*Off, during last part*) Three. Two. One. *Zero.*

INT. CRYOGENIC LAB. DAY.

The living wall looming in front of the five watchers suddenly collapsing into blobs, and the blobs oozing apart and breaking into dots.

EMMA: (*To* FYODOR) Well, you've got your peptide measurements down to the nth degree, Fyodor!

LUANDA: (*Impressed*) I'll say. You've worked it –
(*She stops dead, as they all do, at the voice from – it seems – the ceiling, God-like, with a deep resonance for added 'power'.*)

MASDON'S VOICE: Professor Emma Porlock. This is Martina Matilda Masdon at eight-fifty a.m. Los Angeles time, five-fifty p.m. your west Europe time. Register what I have to say.
(*The five look at each other in covert foreboding.*)

EMMA: I am registering, Ms Masdon.

MASDON'S VOICE: First, why do you behave in a way that could lead an uncharitable person to conclude that you are a nasty two-faced, two-timing sewer rat?

EMMA: Which uncharitable person would that be, Ms Masdon? I only know of one such.

MASDON'S VOICE: Don't you hoity with *this* bitch, bitch!

EMMA: What am I supposed to have done?

MASDON'S VOICE: At eleven fifty-nine your time this morning you went to elaborate lengths to make a so-say secret audio call while walking to and fro to no purpose *outside* the laboratory. Am I right?

EMMA: My business is my business, Ms Masdon.

MASDON'S VOICE: On the contrary, dear. Your business is my business. (*Sudden, sharp shift.*) Were you calling David Siltz?
(EMMA *shoots a quick glance at* FYODOR, *almost in panic, but he shakes his head vigorously.*)

EMMA: Who?
(*Silence.*)
MASDON'S VOICE: Never mind.
EMMA: Who do you mean? The – (*Laughs*) Muck Merchant – *that* Siltz? Is that who? –
MASDON'S VOICE: (*Sharp cut in*) I said *never mind*! Now – get ready to crack your chops into a *smile*, Professor. If you can still do such a thing.
EMMA: I can, especially when I think of how wide the gap can be.
(EMMA, *glint back in her eye, waits eagerly for* MASDON *to fall into it.*)
MASDON'S VOICE: What gap?
EMMA: That between genuine wit and banter and loutish verbal thuggery.
(MASDON, *however, cackles, then coughs. It sounds nasty coming down the line.*)
MASDON'S VOICE: I bring thee good tidings of great joy, Emma.
(EMMA *looks at* FYODOR *again.*)
Your budget will be maintained.
EMMA: Thank you – but – um –
MASDON'S VOICE: But? Do I hear *but*?
EMMA: It's not big enough.
(*Silence. Then, genuine anger.*)
MASDON'S VOICE: You graceless, ungrateful cow!
(*And the* VOICE *disappears, a light at the same time going off on Emma's autocube. They all look at each other.*)
TONY: (*Quietly*) Wow.
LUANDA: And wow *encore*. Don't you think you – (*This to* EMMA) No, I suppose you know – But if we *can* continue even at only five, six minutes full out each day -- My God, Emma, you played it very cool. I suppose you know what you're doing.
(*Tiny pause.* EMMA *doesn't look happy.*)
EMMA: I hope so.

INT. CIRCULAR CORRIDOR A. DAY
Through the glass doors comes an obvious senior state policeman, weaponed with side-arms, and a peacock uniform. He comes to a

particular door, stops, looks at it, taps. The door has the sign:
ANDREW Q. MILTON, DIRECTOR OF PUBLIC AFFAIRS. *He goes in without waiting for an answer.*

INT. MILTON'S OFFICE. DAY
Three men, not in police uniforms, are at drawers, cabinets and letter racks, whatever, obviously searching the place inch by inch. They scarcely look up.
POLICE CHIEF: Anything?
FIRST SEARCHER: Zero. Zero. Zero.
SECOND SEARCHER: Everything's apple pie.
     (*The third, dropping to his hands and knees to peer under the desk and tap the bottom drawers from below, says nothing.*)
POLICE CHIEF: (*Sighs*) You look as though you've been through everything.
THIRD: (*Emerging*) We have.
POLICE CHIEF: OK. Let's call it a day. The man disappears. So people disappear. But while we're here – yes, why not? Call in our Lab A agent. Nobody here knows that Milton has vanished, do they?
FIRST SEARCHER: Not yet they don't.
     (*He is already tapping out message from pad on Milton's desk.*)

CLOSE-UP – 'MESSAGE' WALL. LAB
     ANDREW Q. MILTON (PUBLIC AFFAIRS) WISHES TO SEE BLINDA GEORGE IN HIS OFFICE THIS FLOOR ASAP.

INT. CRYOGENIC LAB. DAY
BLINDA *and* TONY, *feeding what starts as a spool of tape through a tubular and circular adaptor and comes out capillary-fine in shining threads, leading towards the 'feed' rack.* LUANDA, *at the rack, is topping up one of the neuropeptides.* FYODOR *is doing something genuinely antique: grinding up hard bits of a chemical with a pestle and mortar.* EMMA, *her face inscrutable, has stooped, hands on knees, to peer at the ominous black box which holds Daniel's head. Each turns to look as the message concludes with a tiny ping!*
BLINDA: Public affairs? *Me?*
TONY: What you been up to?

LUANDA: Ask him for some of his coffee, Blinda, it's a real treat
to –
BLINDA: But why me?
EMMA: (*Briskly*) You'll have to find out, won't you, dear?
(*Looking puzzled,* BLINDA *leaves.*)

FLASH: TWO-SHOT. LAB
A quick exchange of glances between FYODOR *and* EMMA.

FLASH. TWO-SHOT. LAB
A quick exchange of glances between TONY *and* LUANDA,
immediately after the above.

INT. CRYOGENIC LAB. DAY
*A small, oddly tense silence, in which each 'couple' feels they have
been observed. Then – almost as a plea –*
LUANDA: Look. Somebody say something.
(*There is a strange little pause, in which at least two of the
others goes to speak and then doesn't. Then, almost tearful*)
There's something going on, Tony. You know it too! I just
saw it on your face –
TONY: Yes. We're not a –well, I was going to say 'a team', but
it's not that. We never were, particularly.
EMMA: I think I know what you mean, but – OK. Elimination.
There have been times when I've been on the brink of
saying something and – well, pulled back.
FYODOR: (*Suddenly*) Because of Blinda.
(*They all look at him. He shrugs and turns his back, hands
clasped behind him. Rather strange, yet somehow honest and
dignified.*)
TONY: But I meant – um – Fuck. This is awkward.
(*Looks at* LUANDA. *For help.*)
LUANDA: (*To* EMMA) We meant *you two*.
(FYODOR *turns around, as abruptly again.*)
FYODOR: Which two?
EMMA: (*To* FYODOR) You and me. (*To* LUANDA) Well. Yes.
You're right. We've got ourselves tangled up with things.
One of which is that, after talking to Fyodor –

333

CLOSE-UP – EMMA

She eyes the ceiling and lip-moves the words to LUANDA.

EMMA: Yes – to – Siltz.

INT. CRYOGENIC LAB. DAY

She turns and lip-moves to TONY.

EMMA:Yes – to – Siltz.

> (LUANDA *has already clapped and done a single jump, as* TONY *gasps. Then, simultaneously, they each have an awful thought.*)

TONY/LUANDA: (*Virtually together*) Does it include – (*They stop and laugh awkwardly.*)

EMMA: (*Beams*) The whole team.

> (*Big smiles. But – in a way that makes them all stop and turn to him –*)

FYODOR: (*Grimly*) Except Blinda.

INT. MILTON'S OFFICE. DAY

The POLICE CHIEF *is very indignant, addressing* BLINDA.

POLICE CHIEF: I really don't understand why you are making such a fadolo about it –

BLINDA: (*Angry*) Think about it! What would Milton want with a laboratory assistant! What am *I* to do with public relations! And what if he suddenly turns up and someone –

FIRST SEARCHER: He *has* turned up.

SECOND: Dead.

> (BLINDA, *despite her youth, is obviously a highly ranked officer – as her manner shows.*)

BLINDA: Where? When?

SECOND: In a bin-liner outside a bakery in Notting Hill. Blunt instrument. Fully clothed. No prints. No unmatching body fluids. No nothing.

THIRD: And he'd left no note as to where he was going or whom he was seeing. Nothing.

POLICE CHIEF: (*Still smarting*) In fact, apart from *your* dossier, Blinda, we have almost damn all to connect him with the RONs.

> (BLINDA *gestures around the book-lined office, with its fine paintings, old woods, etc.*)

BLINDA: He was one of them OK. Everything here tells me.
And I know, I *know* he was up to something, as surely as I
know that Fyodor Glazunov is either a covert supporter or
an active member.

POLICE CHIEF: Then why don't we pick him up?

(BLINDA *looks at him with something that is cousin to
contempt.*)

BLINDA: And lose the chance to nab one of the big ones?
Someone – *I* think – who is very close. To him and to me.
(*Tiniest pause, then, almost inaudible.*) The wicked old bitch.

INT. SILTZ'S SUITE. HOTEL. DAY/DUSK

*A fairly big screen is in position which shows Emma's living room.
On the screen,* EMMA *is with* FYODOR, TONY *and* LUANDA. *She
has brought them all along – except* BLINDA.

SILTZ, *in an excited and excitable mood, is moving around like a
caged animal. A lugubrious, skinny-looking, monk-like man is with
him – a* DR RAWL. *And* HARRY SCHUMPET, *the pessimist.*

SILTZ: I don't want you to worry your head about it one little
jot, Professor. OK? You keep whomsoever of *your* lot –
natch! – and I throw in Dr Rawl here. Say hello, Doc.

DR RAWL: Good evening, Professor Porlock. (*His voice sounds
almost comically cadaverous. And he sits so very primly, knees
drawn high together, arms clasping a small briefcase on his lap.*)

EMMA: (*On screen*) Good evening, Dr Rawl. What is your
particular field, may I ask?

DR RAWL: (*Cadaverous*) Sex.

EMMA: (*On screen*) I beg your pardon?

DR RAWL: I am especially interested in sexual arousal,
Professor. And erectile tissue.

(HARRY *runs his hand down his face, then folds his arms,
trying to sit still. He needs to be allowed just one long explosion
of laughter – but he can't be so indulged.*)

INT. EMMA'S LIVING ROOM. DAY

*Neat, not quite spartan, not particularly feminine – and about a
tenth the size of Siltz's 'sitting room'. Her telephone screen is only
about the size of a contemporary television set, so the four are seated
in a semi-circle around it.*

TONY: (*With difficulty*) Excuse me one moment. (*He leaves quickly, like one in urgent need of medical attention.*)
SILTZ: (*On screen*) I'm sure that when you have talked together a while, Dr Rawl will –

INT. HALL. OFF EMMA'S LIVING ROOM. DAY/DUSK
TONY *lets out the explosion that* HARRY *so badly needed to make. In fact, he howls the laughter and bangs his head against the wall.*

INT. SILTZ'S. DAY/DUSK
SILTZ: – member of your team. I think we need his particular expertise with the biowhatyouwants that he has specialized in. *Anyway*, be that as it may, I have already got a place for you to work. The ICB labs have rented me an entire two floors of their complex at – Where is it?
HARRY: Hampstead.
SILTZ: So you get all the facilities. They make some of the stuff you buy in, anyway. Isn't that true?
EMMA: (*Off screen*) Yes. It's true.
   (TONY *can be seen re-entering the room, with a suitably solemn look.*)

INT. EMMAS'S. DAY/DUSK
As TONY *sits, he exchanges a glance with* FYODOR *which nearly starts him off again. But the Slav will have none of it.*
DR RAWL: (*On screen*) Anything. Everything. All on tap. I can outmatch that old witch cent by cent, dime by dime.

INT. SILTZ'S. DAY
SILTZ *is still pacing, the doctor still sitting as primly as a monk on a lavatory seat, and Harry's eyes follow every inch of Siltz's movements.*
SILTZ: Now. What I reee-quire is, is – (*Claps his hands once, with sheer pleasure*) for one of your team, a guy on your squad, sent around here to my Kubla Khan's stately you know, ASAP. For why? Because we need a navigator who doesn't steer the ship into the fucking rocks – You with me? We got to mo-o-o-ove that box with that magic lump of grey stuff in it without making what's left of the

336

poor guy feel that his fucking face is falling off. Am I right?

FYODOR: (*On screen*) I'll go.

(SILTZ, *too eager, peers at the screen, but* FYODOR *has not instantly stood up.*)

SILTZ: Hey, come on then! Move your feet, fella.

INT. EMMA'S. DUSK

EMMA *sits bolt upright, a Victorian not amused.*

EMMA: Do not address my distinguished colleague Dr
    Glazunov in such an outrageously vulgar manner, Mr Siltz.

HARRY: (*Helplessly, on screen*) Whooo!

SILTZ: (*Blinking, on screen*) Hey. *Hey.* We're family, right?

EMMA: *If* so, let us conduct ourselves accordingly.

TWO-SHOT: TONY/FYODOR. AT EMMA'S. DUSK

FYODOR, *indeed 'moving his feet', passes in front of* TONY. *As he does, he gives* TONY *a wink – which rather astonishes him.*

INT. SILTZ'S. DUSK

SILTZ: (*Pacing*) And then what the rest of you folks do is what
    the rest of you folks *normally* do after you've swallowed
    your juice, cleaned your teeth and emptied your bowels,
    right? You go to work. You turn up all bright and shining,
    as ignorant as bliss. 'Whatchewmean the Head's gone?
    How can *a Head* take a walk?' All that stuff, eh?

EMMA: (*On screen*) And how long do we keep *that* particular
    farce going?

HARRY: (*Interrupting*) As long as it takes!

SILTZ: (*Annoyed*) What? Harry? Keep out of it. But he's right –
    as long as it takes for you all to sit around, tap your feet,
    pick your noses and say hey-*wey*, no head, no point, ta-ta,
    toodle-oo, good-bye-ee. I resign!

EMMA: (*On screen*) And what if Martina Masdon *doesn't* cut our
    budget? What if –

SILTZ: (*Interrupting*) Ha! Thinking of two-timing, are we? Well,
    let me tell you this, upright and honest Professor. Guess
    who called me this afternoon? She's got three names, all
    beginning with 'M' – as does the French word for 'shit', I
    believe. She called *you* first. Right?

INT. EMMA'S. DUSK/NIGHT
EMMA *looks sidelong at* TONY *and* LUANDA, *and then simply nods at the screen.*
EMMA: Correct.

INT. SILTZ'S. NIGHT
SILTZ: (*Gleeful*) And then she calls me, this bombed-out kootchy-koo. 'Let's do a deal,' she quacks through strawberry lips. Yuk almighty. Deal? The deal is, I get *access* to your guy's shrivelled bonce for half an hour a week, one billion unidollars a week. She pays *me* that, the skinny cow. And she takes the commercials! The *risk*, she called it. 'I take the risk,' the weird old hag says. Jee-sus. So you see, Professor, your defrosted lump of gristle is going to be plugged into *everybody's* TV and VR helmet no matter what!

EXT. MASDON SCIENCE CENTER. NIGHT
The golf-ball buildings loom beyond the powerful floodlights into blackness. All round the high perimeter fences flash-flash. Somewhere, off, a guard dog barks. All desolate, alien, seemingly empty.
And then, as though by magic, a nightingale starts to sing, liquid gold, splashing into the poisoned darkness. Hold before the dissolve into —

INT. CRYOGENIC LAB. NIGHT
Unoccupied. Softly lit by its night-light only. Its various machines hum quietly, little red lights aglow. And the living wall is in its minimalist, passive mode: myriad 'dots' on the move, constantly, but not multicoloured, only grey or black-and-grey. Moving across to the opposite wall, and reversing to find -

CLOSE-UP – BLACK BOX
Floating in its liquid nitrogen, and yet seemingly whole, gleaming with its odd luminescence, in the 'shut-down' condition of a sort of repose, there is a faint twitch of eyelid and face muscle beginning.

CLOSE-UP – CAPILLARY LEADS FROM BLACK BOX

The hair-likes traces of all but transparent wisps lead away from the 'feed rack' on the other side – follow them along, slowly, carefully, as though examining a diagram with a rostrum camera, towards a junction about the size of a cigarette packet, from which a single, slightly thicker tube – more opaque – leads across the wall towards the electronic neurotransmitter, like a videocassette.

INT. CRYOGENIC LAB. NIGHT

A sudden ray-like flash omits from the neurotransmitters: it is as though we have slowly followed the twitch of the eyelid through to its expression, thrown in one swift, thin flash or beam across the lab, ending on –

INT. LIVING WALL AND LAB. NIGHT

The constantly moving grey and grey-black dots ignite.

THE SCREEN

Vivid, suddenly, with multicoloured *dots, as in its pre-active state. And then, oozing together, seeking each other, excitingly, the dots make blobs and the blobs struggle into semblances of shapes, and the shapes – with a soft, but unmistakable PLOP-P! are all at once a picture.*

EXT. RIVER BANK. DAY

Beside a small and winding, hill-fringed, clean river like the Wye, as it fringes the forest up-river from Tintern Abbey, a young couple are seen in long shot, sitting on the sloping grass, two bicycles propped against an old tree. They are too far for genuine recognition. They seem alone in the world; or, rather, that the world is just for them. Summer woodland and river sounds: wood pigeons, blackbirds, the gentle murmur of water, the faint breeze through the trees.

CLOSE-UP – BETH. RIVER BANK

As seen from the point of view of her companion, who must be DANIEL *– that is, it includes part of his own body, hands, and the piece of long grass he takes now and then from his mouth as they half-sit, half-sprawl on the soft grass near the river's edge.*
BETH: (*Soft West Country*, not *dialect*) I don't feel – I mean, I'm not ashamed or anything like that – but I don't feel *nice*

about writing to him in the way I did. I mean, doing that damn National Service in Germany and all – but, Daniel, Dan, he'd always taken too much for granted. You know, he'd say. 'This is Beth. She's my girlfriend', and he'd say it like – like – Oh, I don't know –

DANIEL: (*Off screen*) 'Hands off' is the way he said it. And you can't really blame him. Not from where *I'm* sitting.

(BETH *smiles, goes to speak, then leans slightly forward and touches his hand instead.*)

BETH: People say you're a bit – strange.

DANIEL: (*Half-amused, off screen*) Do they? In what way?

BETH: Keep yourself to yourself.

DANIEL: (*Off screen*) Not any more. There's room for one other. Just the one.

(*She laughs, then goes solemn.*)

BETH: (*Hesitant*) Your brother . . .

DANIEL: (*Off screen, change of tone, sharper*) What about him?

BETH: You being identical twins and all –

DANIEL: (*Off screen*) On the outside, only.

(*Pause. She looks at him, shyly. She studies him, less shyly.*)

BETH: Will they ever let him out?

DANIEL: (*Off screen*) Look, he had a –

BETH: (*Quick flurry*) Oh, don't get angry! Please!

(*Tiny pause. His voice softens. His hand goes to the lobe of her ear, her neck, her hair.*)

DANIEL: They called it a nervous breakdown. They said he was more dangerous to himself than others. He's got a brilliant mind – no, I *mean* brilliant – all on the sciences, maths, all the academic subjects I most hate – ! He's taking a degree from where he is. He's happy. I see him sometimes.

BETH: Do you?

(*He takes her hand down from her.*)

DANIEL: (*Off screen*) Not as much as I should.

BETH: (*Moved*) Oh, Dan. You sound so – sad. Don't be, my love. (*And then she suddenly reaches forward.*)

EXTREME CLOSE-UP – BETH
A dazzle of eyes and lips and hair, becoming an enfolding blur as she goes to kiss him.

EXT. MASDON SCIENCE CENTER. NIGHT
The golfballs (so to speak) seen from a long way off.

EXT. ROAD TO THE CENTER. NIGHT
*A line of twenty-fourth-century 'trucks' – five or six of them – which
have something of the near-universal bubble shape all vehicles seem
to have had in this future world, cladding (not too obviously!) what
would be armoured cars in our terms.*
*They are parked. Their lights are off, making them bubble silhouettes
in the transient moonlight. The men are all out of their vehicles,
talking together in small groups, inaudible from this distance, but
undoubtedly menacing.*

EXT. GROUP AT FRONT. NIGHT
*They are all in police uniforms under what look like updated riot
helmets. They still cannot be heard. Narrowing down to –*

EXTREME CLOSE-UP – FYODOR
*Dressed as the others are – and therefore these police uniforms are
spurious. Just recognizable through the protective helmet now that its
visor is in the up position.*
A COMMANDER: (*Off screen*) And when in the actual laboratory
    A you will follow the precise instructions of *this man.*
    Clear?
MUMBLED VOICES: (*Off screen*) Clear!

EXT. GROUP AT FRONT. NIGHT
*Click! Clack! Clack! Click! Click! Clack! as the visors go down, one
by one. And the laser guns are hoisted up on to shoulders.*

EXT. ROAD TO THE CENTER. NIGHT
*The sounds are repeated down the line, and then all the 'police' get
into the menacing darkened vehicles.*
*Flash! Flash! Flash! The lights come on, one after the other. The
engines roar, and the small column moves off, cutting beams of light
like swathes in the darkness.*

EXT. APPROACHES TO MASDON CENTER. NIGHT
The line of 'police' armoured bubbles throbs to a near-halt as the

*golfball buildings tower up, illuminated, and two puzzled, sleepy
sentries at the gate step out, weapons half-raised. The perimeter fence
flash-flashes all around.*

The FIRST SENTRY *has to shout above the roar of the armoured
vehicles.*

FIRST SENTRY: What's all this then? What do you want?

'POLICE' COMMANDER: (*Aggressively*) What's it look like? And
   what do you mean, 'What do we want?' Open the gates
   Quick about it! (*His helmeted head disappearing beneath the
   gun turret.*)

SECOND SENTRY: We can't just – Hey! We want to see your –
   (*The armoured bubbles all re-rev-up again, all at the same
   time, drowning out the words.*)

EXT. 'GATE'. MASDON CENTER. NIGHT

*The sentries look at each other, worried but helpless, But they stand
their ground and actually further raise their laser guns – ludicrously
so.*

CLOSE-UP – FRONT ARMOURED BUBBLE.

*The lid on the turret raises again, briefly. An ominous helmet
appears, the voice amplified from within.*

'POLICE' COMMANDER: I shall count to five. This is a matter of
   state security. There is to be a RON raid here within the
   hour. Open the gates or we smash them down and arrest
   both of you as co-conspirators. (*And disappears, down the
   turret. But the counting begins, at loudspeaker amplification,
   booming into the night, off screen.*) One – two – three – !!

EXT. 'GATE' AREA. MASDON CENTER. NIGHT

*The sentries, looking at each other, suddenly snap, and rush back to
their control box, as the countdown continues.*

COMMANDER: (*Off screen, over*) Four – !!!
   (*The gates slide slowly open.*)
   Five – !!!!
   (*The armoured bubbles, roaring energy, stream in line through a
   gap that – the gates still sliding open – is only just wide enough
   to give them access.*)

EXT. WITHIN MASDON CENTER. NIGHT
As they thunder through in line, the armoured bubbles suddenly turn on their sirens, making a curdling whooooop-whooo whooooop-whooo, much more alarming than the anaemic equivalents of earlier centuries.
All but one of the vehicles deploy in a semi-circle just within the perimeter, their guns pointing outwards towards the gate and the flash-flashing wire.

EXT. CRYOGENIC LAB 'A' BUILDING. NIGHT
The leading armoured vehicle does not take part in the deployment of the others, but roars on along the criss-cross of paths before snarling to a growling halt at the now familiar entrance to 'our' lab complex. Four of the 'police' plus the similarly garbed FYODOR *leap out, armed. As* FYODOR *smart-cards entry into the seamless stalk of the building, two of the others pull out a stretcher-like, shelved, rubber-wheeled trolley.*

INT. CIRCULAR CORRIDOR. NIGHT
The five move in haste – if not flat-out running – along the corridor with the trolley.
FYODOR: Which one is the neurotransmitter guy? I've lost sight
     of you in this stuff.
ONE OF FOUR: Me, Doc.
FYODOR: We ought to be able to disconnect ten leads or
     capillaries in each quarter of a hour.
ONE OF FOUR: Which gives us?
     (FYODOR *again using his 'smart card' for access as they reach* –)

INT. CRYOGENIC LAB. NIGHT
The living wall has stopped relaying brain/memory activity from Daniel's boxed head. It is in the neutral mode: myriad black or grey-and-black dots in a perpetual swirl.
FYODOR: Which gives us an hour and a quarter.

INT. 'BOX' WALL. LAB. NIGHT
FYODOR *goes over to the box. His tone changes. He speaks at the box, gently, as though indeed to a person.*
FYODOR: I'm sorry. We are about to move you, Mr Feeld.

(*Turns to his immediate colleague.*) This primary feed – (*Taps it*) – must be the last one of all.

ONE OF FOUR: With you.

INT. 'LIVING WALL'. LAB. NIGHT

One of the others has taken a paint-spray gun from the lower part of the trolley. He positions himself in front of the myriad-dotted wall. And begins to spray in vivid scarlet, and in very large size, the words REALITY OR NOTHING.

SCREEN

Myriad black and grey-and-black dots in perpetual swirl, with the completed three words splashed vividly across them.

PART FOUR

EXT. THE MASDON HOUSE. CALIFORNIA. NIGHT
Floodlit model shot – and the lighting revels in the curlicues and rococo extravaganzas, as well as all the turrets and towers and security bristles.

INT. MASDON'S BEDROOM. NIGHT
Something has gone wrong. MARTINA MATILDA *lies partially covered in a frou-frou nightie, showing enough scraggy flesh and more than enough sullen pout. She picks at the end of the pillow with a bright-green fingernail.*
MASDON: You're just a bum. Period.
  (*Sitting on the edge of the bed, his back to her charms, a third muscular Adonis – this one is called* BILL *– is pulling on his boots, and he is full of chagrin.*)
BILL: All I can do, all I can beg is – forgive me this once, just this once, Martina –
MASDON: *Hah!*
BILL: It's the first time I ever – well – (*Half-turns, half-laughs.*) First time I haven't risen to the occasion, my darling.
MASDON: Don't you darling me, you jerk!
BILL: But that's what you are. To me, that's what you are. My darling.
MASDON: If there's anything worse than a dickhead, it's a *limp* dickhead. Just get yourself outa here. Prontolo.
BILL: Perhaps if you'd let me try later – or –
MASDON: (Slightly *softer tone*) Later? It's climbing towards midnight already, Bill.
BILL: Yeah, but that's – phoo – Who cares about time – ?
MASDON: How the hell do you think I stay slender and svelte and sparky-eyed as well as run a trillion-unidollar business at one and the same time? Not by missing my beauty sleep, that's for sure!
  (*He stands up, stamping down his boots, as though they were brand new – they are – and he wanted to make sure of the fit. Then he stops, and looks down at her, acting his head off, all*

345

forgotten-James-Dean shy charm.)

BILL: (*Hesitant*) Sometimes it's hard to – to – I don't know if –

MASDON: (*Cackling*) *Sometimes* it's *hard*! Oh, great! Let off the fireworks!

(*He hangs his head, like one deeply hurt.*)

BILL: I don't know whether you'll ever understand this, someone as sophisticated and as self-confident and self-assured as you are, but I –

MASDON: Limp dick. Limp words.

BILL: (*Doggedly, continuous*) but I *know* that sometimes what I really, really feel gets in the way. I mean, my emotions for you, they just sort of sort of – overwhelm me. I don't think of myself as a stud or a – I'm not macho – I get all tangled up in my feelings – and I don't *understand*.

(*He can see her attention genuinely shift back to him, her expression yukkily softening, and is sufficiently encouraged to sit on the bed again, but this time turning so that he is facing her. She suddenly reaches out and puts her hand on his, as it rests on the bedclothing.*)

MASDON: (*Different tones*) Try. Try and talk it through, Bill. And maybe – yes, I *might* begin to see what you –

(*A long, loud buzz-zz-zzzz-zzzzz! stops her short and a laser-like beam of red light darts across the high ceiling.*)

God damn and shit on it!

BILL: (*Startled*) Martina – ? What . . .?

MASDON: A-one em-er-gen-cy. Stay where you are! (*She is already swinging her legs out of bed, toe-stretching for her platform-type multicoloured shoes, then, holding a flap of flimsy nightie around her, storms across the room to – *)

INT. CONSOLE. BEDROOM. NIGHT

MASDON *grabs hold of a control pad and presses the flashing red button which has sent up the beam and sent out the loud noise. Instantly –*

INT. WALL OPPOSITE WINDOWS. BEDROOM. NIGHT

The whole wall, give or take a few square feet, becomes (rather like a lab wall, but not on such a scale) a picture of the London Masdon Science Center.

BILL: (*Off*) Wow-eee.

INT. MASDON BEDROOM. NIGHT

MARTINA, *retreating back to the edge of the bed, sits and watches as the words 'NECESSARY INTERRUPTION: VITAL' snake across the wall screen, as the external (mode) shot of the floodlit center and its golf-ball buildings dissolves into the cryogenic lab, with the bulky* INSPECTOR-GENERAL CHALLENDER *addressing her. He is huge – either extraordinarily fat or extraordinarily big – judged by the* POLICE CHIEF *previously seen in Milton's office.*

At first CHALLENDER *is looking away from camera, at someone off screen.*

CHALLENDER: (*On screen*) We have contact? You sure?

VOICE: (*Off, on screen*) We're there, General.

CHALLENDER: (*On screen*) It's seven a.m. western Europe time, Ms Masdon, which must make it late enough at night for you. (MARTINA *presses another button on the headboard of her bed, and, high in the corner of the room, a small videocam swivels to find her.*)

MASDON: (*Hisses to* BILL) Get out of shot. Lie on the floor, other side of the bed. Now!
(*Ludicrously,* BILL *drops down out of our sight, and the videocam's too.*)

MASDON: (*To wall*) Who are you? And what are you doing in my laboratories?

CHALLENDER: (*On screen*) I am Inspector-General Challender and I –

INT. CRYOGENIC LAB. DAWN/DAY

CHALLENDER *can see* MASDON, *sitting on the bed, tugging some of the bedclothes around herself, by the screen on what has been referred to as the 'message wall'.*

MASDON: (*On screen*) *The* Challender. Are you really Colin Challender?

CHALLENDER: (*Slight indignation*) Certainly I am.

MASDON: (*To screen*) Well, I'm really glad to have the chance to speak with a man who almost single-handedly smashed a whole cell of RONs – forty-two of them, wasn't it?

CHALLENDER: No. I can't boast. It was only forty-one – and I doubt very much whether you'll be quite so glad when you hear what I have to say.

CLOSE-UP – MASDON. HER BED
She half-shutters her painted eyelids in dread.
MASDON: (*Between her teeth*) Go on. Give it me straight.

INT. CRYOGENIC LAB. DAY
CHALLENDER: Between one fifteen a.m. and three-forty-five
    a.m. this morning, our time, the Reality or Nothing
    organization, dressed as police, raided your cryogenic lab
    A – and only this lab – sprayed 'Reality or Nothing' on the
    living wall and escaped without injury or apprehension
    with the – (*Stops dead, jaw sags.*) *Madam! You have an*
    intruder!

CLOSE-UP – SCREEN ON 'MESSAGE WALL'. LAB. DAY
Bill's backside has heaved up into shot – just a little – above the far
side of the bed. It looks ludicrously comical.

INT. MASDON BEDROOM. CALIFORNIA. NIGHT
MARTINA *swivels around with a spit-like hiss of venom.*
MASDON: *Keep your butt down, you dickhead!* (*Turns back,*
    dreadful simper.) It's OK, General. It's a new biochemical
    experiment. I'm trying to put some *brains* into a man's *arse*.
    Forget it.

CLOSE-UP – SCREEN ON 'MESSAGE WALL'. LAB. DAY
Bill's backside disappearing again.

INT. CRYOGENIC LAB. DAY
The POLICE CHIEF *has to turn away from the camera, allegedly in*
a fit of coughing.
CHALLENDER: (*Straight-faced*) You don't seem to have
    succeeded as yet. But so long as you are all right –
MASDON: (*On screen*) I'm OK! Shoot, for Christolo!
CHALLENDER: Stop coughing, Chief.
POLICE CHIEF: (*Gasping*) I – ah – yes – Excuse me one moment
    – hooo!
    (*He has to leave.* CHALLENDER'*s face twitches, but then he*
    carries on.)

CHALLENDER: The long and the short of it is, they've taken the head. I'm sorry. But it's not in its biobox!

INT. MASDON BEDROOM. CALIFORNIA. NIGHT
MARTINA *lets out a long half-scream, half-wail.*
MASDON: The head! My he-ea-ea-ead! No-o-o-o-o-o! (*And she punches one of or several of the pillows in absolute rage and violence.*)

INT. CRYOGENIC LAB. DAY
CHALLENDER *waits for the rage to subside, as depicted on the message-wall screen. In other parts of the room,* THREE DETECTIVES *– out of view from* MASDON *– stand in a sort of appalled trance, watching the old woman beat the shit out of a pillow. They are the same three seen as 'searchers' in Milton's office.*
On the screen, Masdon's rage subsides.
MASDON: (*On screen*) A million bucks for anyone who brings it back. Ten million for anyone who brings it back and kills the fuckers who took it!
CHALLENDER: (*Twitches*) Is that a contract, ma'am?

CLOSE-UP – MARTINA MASDON. BEDROOM
MASDON: (*Yells*) You bet your life it is! Signed and sealed! Get that head back, General. Get it back!
CHALLENDER: (*On screen*) We'll do our damnedest, Ms Masdon. I think the final entry –

INT. CRYOGENIC LAB. DAY
CHALLENDER: (*Continuous*) into *this* room could only have been made by staff 'smart card' or cards. That's where I'll start –
MASDON: (*Yells, on screen*) The bastards!
CHALLENDER: I'll soon find out which one of those who regularly work in this room is most vulnerable to pressure. There's always *one* in any given group of colleagues. – And when I find *that person*, madam, I can assure you here and now – *that person will crack.*
(*Dissolve.*)

EXT. APARTMENT BLOCK. STREET. DAY

Early morning in a generally shabby street, residential. An apartment block stands out as better than all around it. It has old stone steps and the semblance of an awning, leading to the rutted and filthy threads of pavement.

INT./EXT. FYODOR'S 'BUBBLE' CAR. DAY

The car is parked not quite opposite the block but down street a little on the other side. FYODOR *peers tensely across at the block, obviously waiting. There seems to be very little traffic movement and – again, rather eerily – no one is walking, except a tramp carrying his own bed-roll.*

FYODOR *stiffens, suddenly extra alert. His point of view.*

EXT. APARTMENT BLOCK FROM CAR. DAY

BLINDA *emerges from under the awning, carrying a small briefcase, looking about. She waits on the last but one stone step. She turns, speaks to someone – and angrily it seems.*

INT./EXT. AWNING. APARTMENT BLOCK. DAY

Behind her, an armed guard appears, in a hurry.

BLINDA: Why aren't you at your post?

APARTMENT GUARD: Sorry. I got caught short. My guts is like Vesuvius this morning – and the *two*-guard roster doesn't start until eight-thirty a.m., ma'am.

BLINDA: You shouldn't leave your post! It's not safe out there!

APARTMENT GUARD: (*Fed up*) Well, if you don't mind stepping in some fresh shit, lady –

EXT. APARTMENT BLOCK FROM CAR. DAY

FYODOR, *all wired up with tension, watches as, eventually, after what seem to be further angry exchanges, Blinda's 'bubble' car pulls up at the pavement, opposite the descending steps. He sees her get in.*

EXT. RESIDENTIAL STREET. DAY

Blinda's bubble moving off under its verbal instruction. Fyodor's bubble, after a brief pause, moves off, following it. The street has about 200 yards before it reaches the main tangle of highway at a

*junction which looks like stale cooked spaghetti splashed with various
filths rather than sauces.*

INT./EXT. FYODOR'S BUBBLE, STREET. DAY
Tenser by the second, FYODOR *gives his vehicle its instructions.*
FYODOR: FG 170535. Move up alongside – alongside – alongside
    the car left – left. The blue and black with MSC insignia.
CAR VOICE: Oh, it's a stablemate. Will do.

EXT. RESIDENTIAL STREET. DAY
*Just before it comes into the tangle of road and the stream of vehicles
up ahead, Fyodor's 'bubble' draws up wheel to wheel alongside*
BLINDA. *She doesn't at first seem to notice, reading something from
her small briefcase.*

INT./EXT. FYODOR'S BUBBLE. DAY
He buttons down his window and makes big hand gestures, grinning.
FYODOR: Blinda!

INT./EXT. BLINDA'S BUBBLE. DAY
*Her attention eventually caught, she looks up sharply, frowns, then
'puts on' a smile, buttoning down her own window.
Phlopp! Almost silently, a hole appears in her forehead and she
slumps sidelong.*

EXT. RESIDENTIAL STREET. DAY
*Fyodor's car moves away from Blinda's, which nevertheless
continues, and will continue, its journey to the Masdon Science
Center.*

EXT. GATE. MASDON SCIENCE CENTER. DAY
Stream of 'bubbles' awaiting access. Find FYODOR *in the queue, two
back. Carry on, find* BLINDA, *another five or six vehicles back,
slumped dead in such a way that she looks as though she is napping,
using her briefcase as a makeshift pillow.
Fast fade.*

INT. LONG CORRIDOR. CRYOGENIC LAB BUILDING. DAY
TONY, *tunelessly whistling, rolls along happily until he comes to the*

*door of Laboratory A – 'our' lab – rather overdoing the nonchalant,
all-is-just-another-day bit.*

INT. DOOR TO LAB A. DAY
TONY *stops, stares, seeing an MSC* COP *at the door.*
TONY: What's going on? What are you doing here?
   (*The* COP *stares back at him, insolently, chewing gum as
   though his mouth were a kitchen-mixer. He holds a clipboard.*)
DOOR COP: Who's asking?
   (*This seems to be standard police/public relationship.*)
TONY: I am. Unless – (*Looks over shoulder.*) No. Must have been
   me. (*Slowly, as to a child*) What-are-you-doing-here?
   (*A guaranteed, stupid provocation, to which he adds by pushing
   imperiously at the door. But the* DOOR COP *grabs at his
   arm.*)
DOOR COP: Name, smart arse.
TONY: No. It isn't, actually. It's Dr Anthony Watson. And I
   work in there.
   (*The* DOOR COP, *chewing all the time, looks down his little list,
   watched with a sardonically raised eyebrow by* TONY. *Then,
   with a sniff of disdain, the* COP *simply turns away a little,
   enough to allow* TONY, *with an up-you smirk, to go on into –*)

INT. CRYOGENIC LAB. DAY
TONY *stops dead, open-mouthed. He is perilously close to overdoing
it as so many eyes switch to him as he steps through the door:* EMMA,
FYODOR, LUANDA, *the* POLICE CHIEF, *the* THREE SEARCHERS
(*detectives*) *and, not at first noticed by* TONY, *the very large or very
fat man sitting on an autocube in the far corner pretending to be
Sydney Greenstreet in* The Maltese Falcon, COLIN CHALLENDER,
Head of All-Corporate Security.
TONY: What the . . . What – ? (*Eyes flick to living wall.*)

LIVING WALL
*No dots aswirl, only REALITY OR NOTHING in a vivid, large
scrawl.*

INT. CRYOGENIC LAB. DAY
EMMA: Yes – there was a RON raid last night. Chief – this is Dr

Tony Watson, my direct personal assistant in biogenic cryology.

TONY: (*Would-be relaxed*) Oh, I wondered exactly what I was. (*He doesn't pick up* EMMA's *little frown. Is he 'the most vulnerable' of the group?*)

POLICE CHIEF: This is the first you know about any of this?

TONY: Yes. It is. Holy Moseolo! But what in God's name have they –

EMMA: (*Chips in, as though warningly*) They've taken the head, Tony.

POLICE CHIEF: Do you *mind*, Professor?

EMMA: Sorry. I thought –

TONY: (*Stupefied*) They've *what*?

POLICE CHIEF: You heard.

(*Almost derisory remark, because* TONY *overdoes his reaction, plunging his hand into his hair. He slumps down into the nearest vacant autocube.*)

TONY: But what in thundering blazolo would they want with a – Oh, I see. Yes.

CHALLENDER: (*Suddenly*) What do you see, Doctor?

FLASH: CLOSE-UP – FYODOR
A glint of warning in his eyes. But –

INT. CRYOGENIC LAB. DAY
TONY *looks across the length of the room at* CHALLENDER, *with an 'And now who's this?' sort of irritation. Then he seems to catch* FYODOR's *glint and check himself.*

TONY: Ransom money. It must be.

(CHALLENDER *slowly hauls himself up out of his autocube, looking as though a hydraulic crane would do the job better. But then he stands still, taking not a single step forward.*)

CLOSE-UP – CHALLENDER
CHALLENDER: *Must* be? Why? Why *must*?

INT. CRYOGENIC LAB. DAY
TONY, *greatly overplaying his hand, looks at* EMMA.

TONY: (*To* EMMA) Professor. I don't know to whom I – (*But he gets only a blaze of warning back.*)

CHALLENDER: (*Sudden shout*) Why *must* be?

(*Silence. The shout was unexpected.* TONY *suddenly feels endangered – far too late.*)

TONY: Oh – on, um, on the principle of Occam's Razor – Where you – ah – cut away all the most improbable things and – um – what you are left with is the bare-faced or, so to speak, *probable* answer. Something like that.

CLOSE-UP – FYODOR

A sudden flash to show or catch at FYODOR'*s inner shudder of apprehension.*

CLOSE-UP – CHALLENDER

Satisfied, now, that he has found the most nervous one and so maybe the most vulnerable one of them all, CHALLENDER *beams, benevolently.*

CHALLENDER: Occam. Mmm. You refer to the antique monk, yes?

INT. CRYOGENIC LAB. DAY

TONY: Y-yes.

(*He looks at* EMMA, *as though for help.*)

CHALLENDER: All right, youngish man. Give me an improbable explanation for – (*Waves a hand*) all this.

TONY: *Im*probable? Oh, but –

CHALLENDER: Come. You said you had cut away all the improbabilities in order to expose the probable. What did you cut away?

TONY: Oh, but isn't this rather – Well, it's a bit silly, surely?

CHALLENDER: Come, come. Humour me.

(*Everyone is silent.* TONY *feels all eyes are upon himself – as, indeed, they are – and he doesn't like it one bit.*)

TONY: (*Eventually*) Well – it could have, it could have been a protest – a meaningless stupid protest about the way we treat our own species –

CHALLENDER: (*Nods*) Um. Huh.

TONY: (*Marginally more confident*) Or it could equally well have been, um, a rival – yes! A commercial rival like Chemicure or – or – you know, seeing what we're up to. Those sort of things.

CHALLENDER: Did you ever want to be an actor, Dr Watson?

TONY: An actor? W-what do you mean – ?

CHALLENDER: Oh, now. What do I mean? Surely you know what an *ac-tor* is? What an *ac-tor* does?

TONY: Of course I do! But why on earth should I want to be an actor – ?

CHALLENDER: Well. It was a wise choice, in any event.

CLOSE-UP – CHALLENDER
Suddenly, CHALLENDER is moving forward from his static position, like a huge beast bearing down on something small and helpless, as Tony, off screen, tries an uncomfortable little laugh.

INT. CRYOGENIC LAB. DAY
TONY: I don't know whether to be pleased or offended by that!

CHALLENDER: (*Reaching him*) My name is Challender, by the way. Inspector-General Challender. I am Head of All-Corporate Security. So if it should turn out to be a case of inter-company rivalry, I should be considerably embarrassed. (*Suddenly, no break, no change of tone*) Do you think, then, that you are not a *good* actor?
(TONY *takes a startled beat.*)

TONY: I don't think about it at all, thank you very much.
(CHALLENDER *smiles and turns away.*)

CHALLENDER: Thank you, ladies and gentlemen. I'm so sorry that *all this* – (*Flaps his hand again*) should have been awaiting you. I'm quite sure you have been as helpful as you intended to be. Chief. Chaps. I think you and I are done here for the present.

FLASH: CLOSE-UP – TONY
Sudden flood of relief on his features, quickly suppressed. Quickly enough?

INT. CRYOGENIC LAB. DAY
CHALLENDER *turns to* EMMA.
CHALLENDER: This place has been fingerprinted, fluid-printed,

gene-laundered, hydrocycled, odorometered. All in the wee small hours. So *if* you have any meaningful work left here, Professor, you and your staff may proceed with it unhindered. Forgive us our interruption.

EMMA: Thank you, Inspector-General.

CHALLENDER: (*Murmurs*) Not at all.

(*He is leading his men away, towards the door. They watch him go, almost eagerly. The door shuts.*)

INT. CORRIDOR. DAY

Outside the lab door, the DOOR COP *stiffens from his lax lounge to some sort of attention.* CHALLENDER *puts his finger to his lips, with a hard look at his eyes, and a twist of a smile beneath. He seems to count – one – and – two – and – three. And then he opens the cryogenic lab door again.*

INT. CRYOGENIC LAB. DAY

The very large man half-emerges from behind the opening door.

CHALLENDER: I'm so sorry. But there is just one more little thing. Would you be kind enough to accompany us, Dr Watson?

TONY: *Me?* I mean – where to? What for?

CHALLENDER: (*Amused*) I would like to find out just how *sharp* an instrument Occam's Razor might actually be. Come along, Doctor.

(TONY *looks at the others, who try to remain blank, then goes to the door, consternation all over him. The door shuts. Silence. Immobility.*)

CLOSE-UP – EMMA

Sharing the fear, the astonishment of the others, she scribbles quickly on a pad.

EXTREME CLOSE-UP – NOTEPAD

EMMA *writing:*

SAY NOTHING. BUGGED? MEET RELAX ROOM $\frac{1}{2} - \frac{3}{4}$ HOUR.

INT. CRYOGENIC LAB. DAY

As EMMA *speaks, she holds out the pad to each of them in turn,*
receiving answering nods.

EMMA: Poor old Tony. He's the least shifty character I've ever
    met. (*Laughs.*) There must be something about him that
    irritates.

FYODOR: (*Laughs, for effect, nods*) All that whatsname's Razor
    stuff! Why does he do that?

LUANDA: (*Nods*) Oh, they'll soon see he's a babe in the woods.
    (*Looks around.*) Christ. Where do we start – and what do
    we do?

EMMA: Not much we *can* do. If they've taken the head, those
    bastards, they're sure to have damaged it beyond anything
    we can repair.

FYODOR: It's an absolute disgrace! A total, total disaster. I just
    want to throw up.

EMMA: Well, don't do it in here! There's enough mess for us to
    clear up already. And where the hell is Blinda, for a start!
    (*Fast fade.*)

EXT. FOREST OF NEAD COTTAGE. DAY

Late 1950s or so. Some bedraggled forest sheep mooching around.
Trees almost up to the garden of a small but pretty house. It is day
but the curtains at an upstairs window are closed.
In the distance, church bells are ringing, off.

INT. A BEDROOM. THE FOREST HOUSE. DAY

BETH, *her back turned away from the bed, laughs shyly as she*
unhooks her bra. She is seen from the point of view of the young man
sitting unclothed on the edge of the bed, in such a position that he can
see his own bare legs – or part of them – and feet.

BETH: Well, the bells are ringing for us, Daniel.

DANIEL: (*Off screen*) I think they always will, Beth. I *hope* they
    always will.
    (*Stand up with him, so to speak, as* BETH *turns, presenting*
    herself, tenderly, shyly.)

BETH: (*Whispers*) I'm – I feel shy. Isn't that silly?
    (DANIEL, *off screen, has his hands on her shoulders, and we*
    look at her adoringly.)

DANIEL: (*Near whisper*) So do I. And, no, it isn't.
(*She laughs, coming in closer to him, then –*)

BLACK SCREEN
Nothing to be seen. Nothing to be heard.

INT. SECOND CRYOGENIC LAB. DAY
Finding SILTZ, HARRY *and cadaverous* DR RAWL.
SILTZ: (*Furious*) Is that it? Is that the best you can do?
(DR RAWL *spreads his hands in the way an undertaker's mute might.*)
RAWL: I'm afraid so. Alas, yes.
(*His melancholy manner and phrasing only increase Siltz's indignant anger.*)
SILTZ: Just when they were really about to get down to it!
HARRY: Nice tits, too.
SILTZ: Harry! Do you have to be so fucking *vulgar* all the time?
HARRY: OK, OK, so you're in a bad mood. Don't take it out on me.
DR RAWL: I am not experienced in the ratio of those new neuropeptides. That is not my particular field. You need that Slav fellow and the black woman – *and* the old lady. I would have thought you would have been pleased, Mr Siltz.
SILTZ: Pleased!
DR RAWL: We've shown that the head is capable of quote working unquote, so it has survived its – um – its –
HARRY: Kidnap.
DR RAWL: It has survived. And the very first time I stimulate the particular area of the neocortex, which *is* my field, Mr Siltz, lo and behold you have given unto you a proud pair of knockers.
(SILTZ *and* HARRY *both look at him, open-mouthed. The skinny, cadaverous doctor did not change his melancholy appearance nor prissy mode of delivery by one jot or tittle. And then* SILTZ *and* HARRY *look at each other – and, virtually simultaneously, they both start to laugh, long and loud enough to double them up.*)

358

CLOSE-UP — DR RAWL

With no change of expression.

DR RAWL: I fail to see what is so devastatingly amusing when I
choose to descend occasionally into what I believe is the
vernacular.

(*Which, of course, sets them off again.*)

SILTZ: OK. OK. Enough. Enough. I'm damaging something
inside. Felt it go twang! OK – We'll have to wait for the
real team – the 'A' side – (*Digs* RAWL *in the ribs.*) You
miserable old sod. (*Then digs* HARRY, *suddenly in a good
mood.*) A goldmine, Harry. We're talking of a goose
which'll lay a golden egg whenever we want!

HARRY: Yeah – or a lot of feathers.

(*But* SILTZ *has whooped himself up into his manic-enthusiast
mode.*)

SILTZ: Just think of it! Spilling out everything that's locked
away in there! Who'd want made-up stories from a bunch
of lazy overpaid hacks when you can mainline into the *real
thing.* This Daniel Feeld fella is – Christolo –he's *immortal.*

HARRY: Immoral too. We hope.

RAWL: (*Sniffs*) Oh, there's a good chance. It is a characteristic
of the male of the species.

HARRY: What?

(SILTZ *is not listening, off on some dream cruise.*)

CLOSE-UP — SILTZ

SILTZ: We'll plug that brain into everybody else's! What's his is
ours! What he has tucked away, all his secrets, his
behaviour, everything – it's ours. At last privacy has a true
market value. Zillions! Harry – Harry, boy –

INT. SECOND CRYOGENIC LAB. DAY

HARRY: Yes, massa.

SILTZ: Haven't we always tried to get *inside* people's heads?
Isn't that what the game is all about, showbiz and that part
of it we call politics? *Owning* people. But – and this has
been the drag – but we've never been able to get right
inside, to *own* the tiniest little fragment of the inside of a
person's head. Now we have the chance!

INT. SECOND CRYOGENIC LAB. BLACK BOX
In its new position, higher from the floor than it was back in the Masdon lab, so that the various electrodes, neurotransmitters and 'feed' capillaries lead up to rather than down into it. Daniel's head, severed, half-luminous in its ghastly silvery sheen of damaged flesh and bone, seems to flutter a little at the eyelids.

CLOSE-UP – SILTZ. THE BOX
In reverse, SILTZ's *face looms, to peer closely at the severed head, his mouth all but wet with greedy anticipation.*
SILTZ: (*Quietly*) And David Sylvester Siltz is just the man to do it.

INT. LONG CORRIDOR. MASDON SCIENCE CENTER. DAY
LUANDA, *leaving a group of excitedly talking women, comes to double doors marked RELAX ROOM in very large letters, with the smaller subtext (readable) which announces:*
> NO VID OR AUDPHONE. NO RECORDING DEVICES.
> GUARANTEED ARTICLE 16 SECTION 312
> WESTEUROPA SUPREME COURT. 2349.

She goes through the doors into –

INT. RELAX ROOM. MASDON SCIENCE CENTER. DAY
Laid out like a twentieth-century brasserie – or their idea of one. A scatter of staff at various tables. Self-service machines in rows for food, drinks.
LUANDA *looks around, sees* EMMA *and* FYODOR *tête-à-tête in a far corner. She seems agitated.*

INT. CORNER RELAX ROOM. DAY
EMMA *and* FYODOR *in mid-conversation.*
FYODOR: – but what is even more interesting to me is that those cops didn't wait for her to come. They tried all their sniff-sniff stuff with all of us, and Tony so stupidly fell for it. But, no, they weren't interested in *her*. I'm sure she's a snoop for them. I'd eliminate her if I had half the chance.
EMMA: And when does the killing stop?
FYODOR: (*Bleakly*) When it has to. (*Then*) Luanda. Where've you been? What's wrong?

(LUANDA *sits, shaking her head.*)

LUANDA: There's a hell of a kerfuffle going on down the corridor
– and it's full of cops again. It seems Blinda's turned up.
(EMMA, *looking at her closely, leans across and touches
Luanda's hand.*)

EMMA: What's happened, Luanda?

LUANDA: (*Upset*) She's dead. They found her in her bubble.
Somebody'd shot her in the head after she'd given her
journey instructions. My God. What *is* going on? And what
is Tony going to do, or to say? (*Pause.*) I feel scared. I wish
we'd never gotten into any of this.

FYODOR: Tony may be foolish, but I don't *think* he's a coward –
(*The doubt hangs in the air.*)

EMMA: (*Sadly*) Oh, the silly boy.
(*Silence.*)

FYODOR: We've got to get out of this place. Out of the whole
Masdon thing. I don't care what it looks like, but I'm
going formally to resign. (*Standing up.*) I'm going
downstairs and I'm going to do it now. The sooner we can
move to the ICB labs the better. God knows if that head
will survive all this.

EMMA: It will look bad.

FYODOR: I don't care. Tony might crack at any moment anyway.
We're already under suspicion. I've got nothing to lose now.
And neither have you. (*He waits for their responses.*)

EMMA: What will you say?

FYODOR: I'll say our budget is under continual threat, down,
up, down, we don't know where we are. And *harassment* –
first from the dear sweet old lady who thinks she owns us,
and now from the inter-corporate police. We've no head to
work on, and I'm not prepared to put up with any more of
it. That's what I shall say.

EMMA: (*Rising*) Sounds reasonable.

EXT. PRISON. DAY

*Model shot. What looks like a small concrete fortress, towered with
gun turrets, formidably functional and bristling with weird-looking
security devices. No windows.*

(*Dissolve.*)

361

INT. A CELL. PRISON. DAY
Spartan or simple, like a battery unit. A table, two straight-backed chairs, a single bed, shower and wash-basin, lavatory. Food dispenser, so marked. Water dispenser, so marked. No window. But one entire wall is given over to ever-changing pictorial scenes with syrup of accompanying, low-level background music.
TONY, *lying in a depressed manner on the bed, stares almost vacantly at the wall of pictures, presently showing an erupting volcano and soon to show sailing ships on the sea, then sheep in a meadow, with the lambs gambolling. The music (our equivalent, perhaps, would be non-stop Mantovani) is a soft wash of background irritation.*

EXTREME CLOSE-UP – TONY
TONY: (*Muttering to self*) Be strong. Be strong.
    (*A sound, off. He jerks up.*)

INT. TONY'S CELL. DAY
Way off, it seems, and all the more distressing because so, someone beginning to scream.
TONY, *getting off his bed, goes to the seamless wall and puts an ear against it. The scream continues. He begins to shake and tremble.*

EXT. SILTZ'S HOTEL. DAY
The Pleasure Dome of Kubla Khan, 2368 equivalent.

INT. TOP END HUGE DINING ROOM. DAY
SILTZ, *at the top end of the big table in enormous room, rising to await the thump-thump heavy tread of a visitor, all smiles.*

INT. DINING ROOM. DAY
INSPECTOR-GENERAL CHALLENDER *has almost completed the same long journey across the room that* EMMA *had had to make. He takes* SILTZ'*s proffered hand with a hearty shake.*
SILTZ: Glad you could make it, Colin.
CHALLENDER: What? Miss one of your renowned lunches, Dave? No fear of that!
    (*They sit.*)
SILTZ: Ah. But you get no pick of menu. It has to be what *I* like.

CHALLENDER: I prefer the simpler choices in life. Yes and yes,
 preferably.
SILTZ: Yes is a nice word.
CHALLENDER: Yes *can* be a profitable word.
SILTZ: What will you do with him?
CHALLENDER: No one has laid a finger on him. No one has said
 a word to him. But he's not made of much. He weeps at
 night, every night, and he listens to our scream machine in
 the afternoon, every afternoon. And each time the door
 opens, he wets himself.
 (SILTZ *pulls a face.*)
SILTZ: Poor creature. How long have you had him now – six
 days, seven?
CHALLENDER: Six. We still have another eight under the Anti-
 Terrorist Charter. But – (*Shrugs.*) He's well and ready for
 you now, if you want him to eat out of your hand. Or any
 other equivalent.
 (*At which point, the same kind of soup* EMMA *was served is
 brought to the table.*)
SILTZ: I'll take your word.
CHALLENDER: Ah! Lovely smell. Lovely colour.
SILTZ: (*Pleased with himself*) That's the cherries. Of which life is
 supposed to be a bowl of.
CHALLENDER: (*Pleased with himself*) That, or a bowl of dog
 biscuits.
SILTZ: Equally fine for a pair of cunning old hounds, eh?
 (*And they chuckle, contentedly.*)

EXT. POOLSIDE, MASDON'S. CALIFORNIA. DAY
NAT, *the first Adonis, is evidently back in favour, for he is gently or
even sensuously rubbing sticky sun-tan lotion the scrawny length of
Martina Matilda Masdon's old legs.*
*She is stretched out in an unflattering bathing costume on a gaudily
parasoled lounger, next to the high-tech, rubber-pad table, upon
whose top two glasses make the chunks of ice glow in their strangely
coloured liquids. She is speaking vidphone: there is a face of someone
called* KARL (*whose voice was heard talking to* EMMA *in Part One*)
hovering eerily at the edge of the water. MARTINA *is in shot from a
tiny lens clipped to the parasol, its red light on.*

MASDON: (*Bad-tempered*) OK, Karl. OK, OK, OK! Let the cheapskates go. And good fucking riddance, say I! Anyone in the biochemical business who is stupid enough to *resign* from Martina Matilda Masdon is taking a long walk without water out into the wilderness.

KARL: (*On screen*) Yes, ma'am. Too damned right.

MASDON: (*Near scream*) The wilderness!

(*She furiously jabs a button on the table, and the screen slides down – back into the pool, it seems. The red light also goes off on the parasol.*

NAT, utterly expressionless, greases, greases and greases in ever-smaller circles, climbing the leg. She looks at him, fierce-eyed. He acts unaware of the scrutiny, very shrewdly. Her expression softens.)

MASDON: (*Eventually*) Fidelity.

NAT: (*As one puzzled*) Martina – ?

MASDON: It's a wonderful word for a wonderful wonderful concept, Nat.

(*He looks up at her, very solemn and earnest.*)

NAT: Yes. It is. It really is.

EXT. THE PRISON. NIGHT
Model shot. The weird but functional and indisputably menacing building lit by powerful floodlights so that it dazzles against the pitch black.

INT. TONY'S CELL. NIGHT
As the door swings outwards from the seamless wall, a shadowed TONY *backs off into the far corner. It is dark in the room, and the opening door sends a widening expanse of light.*

EXTREME CLOSE-UP – TONY
Hand up to face against the sudden, overpowering light. But it is clear, chiaroscuro, that he is something of a nervous wreck.

GUARD VOICE: Stand to attention!

TONY: (*Quivering*) Yes, sir.

(*He does, or tries to. The* GUARD *comes into the light, into the cell.*)

GUARD: You got a visitor.

TONY: Oh, I – I – didn't kn–

GUARD: Did I say speak?

TONY: N-no, sir.

GUARD: Then shut your mouth. Sit down at the table.

TONY: (*With alacrity*) Yessir. (*Which he does. The door shuts again. The* GUARD *is not there.* TONY *sits as a dark hump in the darkness. He whispers to himself.*) *What's going on?*
　　Then, very gradually, and not from some central point, the cell begins to lighten through from dark grey to a soft, neutral lightness. And the door opens again. Closes.)

SILTZ: Good evening, Dr Watson.

TONY: (*Astonished*) Mr – Mr Siltz – ! But . . .

SILTZ: But what am *I* doing here? Is that what you mean? May I sit down?

TONY: Oh – um – (*Goes to stand.*) Yes. Of course.

SILTZ: You seem a bit edgy, boy.
　　(TONY *sits properly again.*)

TONY: Edgy? You can say that again.

SILTZ: These are not nice places.

TONY: No. They – (*Gulps.*) My God. There are some terrible screams here sometimes. I can't imagine what it is they are doing to the poor devil. But it – it – (*Tries to control himself.*) It plays on the nerves. And the worst thing – (*He stops, looks.*) Why are *you* here?

SILTZ: We've only met via vidphone. But I liked your sense of humour when I introduced Dr Rawl, the sexologist.
　　(TONY *delivers a wan little smile.*)

TONY: Oh. Him. Yes.

SILTZ: Part of my team.

TONY: Yes – I didn't mean to be rude.

SILTZ: Listen. The guy makes me laugh, too. Jeezolo. I wouldn't want him anywhere near *my* erectile tissue, if that's what he calls it! He should marry that Masdon cow. Wouldn't they make a terrific couple? But he *is* family. That's how I think of my team. Family. And as of tomorrow morning, bright as a cockerel or whatever it is in the morning sky, your Professor Porlock, Dr Glazunov and Dr Luanda Partington will be on team, too.

TONY: (*Wistful*) Oh, that's nice. They've escaped the Masdon clutches, then?

SILTZ: Not much she can do, is there? Except scream green murder. Green for envy. Envy. Anyway, I've been looking into things. I want you on the side too.

TONY: Oh, Christ. I wish. Oh, how I wish!

SILTZ: I been checking on you. Family. Friends. Right back to school. Every nook and cranny, and I've prodded at every little pimple, blackhead or bogey. And there's not enough dirt on you to grow a mustard seed.

TONY: Thank you.

SILTZ: I can't understand why they want to execute you.

(TONY *stands up as though an electric rod had been pushed into his anus and his chair falls back with a clatter.*)

TONY: (*Croaks*) *They what –* ?

SILTZ: (*Calmly*) Well, when they think they've got one of the top RONs, that's what they always go for. The big needle and no noise. You never hear much about it, but I know for a fact that that's what they're up to. Safety first, they call it. (*Looks at him.*) Hey. C'mon. Sit down. Let's deal here.

(*Quivering* TONY *rights the chair.*)

TONY: D-deal – ?

SILTZ: Sure.

(TONY *sits and stares hungrily at* SILTZ.)

TONY: Please. Tell me. What sort of deal? What can I do? I mean – if there's anything – anything at all!

(SILTZ *just looks at him for a long beat, as though considering something.* TONY *trembles with the stirring of hope.*)

(*Again, croaks*) Please, Mr Siltz. I'm your man.

(*Fade.*

Fade in.)

INT. KARAOKE CLUB. BAR. 1994. NIGHT

An attractive hostess with routine in place comes up to an ill DANIEL, *clenched a little at the bar. The hostess is* SANDRA.

SANDRA: (*Fixed smile*) Hi! I was looking at you when you came in and I fought, he's the kind of – (*Her voice trailing off. She's sure she's seen him before and that his stare is too set on her.*)

DANIEL: (*Quickly*) You'd like a drink? Please?

(*But she cannot hold back.*)

SANDRA: You were staring at me, weren't you? In that café place.

DANIEL: I – yes.

SANDRA: And you followed me in here, didn'tya?

DANIEL: (*Intense*) Yes. I did.

SANDRA: What you want? What you playing at?

DANIEL: (*Urgently*) Please. What is your name?

SANDRA: (*Half-unwillingly*) Beth.

(*He sucks in his breath, in a way that startles her.*)
What's the matter?

DANIEL: And the man you were with. He was called Christopher, wasn't he? Chris.

SANDRA: Yeah. But – what's that got to do with you? You know him, or what?

DANIEL: Christopher. Chris. My twin. *Me.*

SANDRA: You. Whatchewmean *you*?

(*He looks at her imploringly. He hesitates, unable to explain. When he speaks, it is almost with a stutter.*)

DANIEL: I – I'm a writer.

INT. SECOND CRYOGENIC LAB. DAY

With its own living wall, showing the above scene, which is curiously and revealingly warping out of true, as the memory of other pain as well as of the physical pain at that time bites into his head.

Watching the gigantic living wall: EMMA, LUANDA, FYODOR, DR RAWL *and two lab assistants. Then, for some sensible reason slightly apart, find* TONY, *with (so to speak) a little 'bump of surprise'. All are staring at the huge screen, which dwarfs them.*

INT. KARAOKE CLUB BAR. NIGHT

Played continuously with penultimate scene through the above.

DANIEL: I – put words into other people's mouths. And at the moment – (*Terrible spasm of pain.*) At the moment, I – oh, God! My stomach! (*Gabbles*) It's all coming true in front of me. The reason I'm ill. Sick. I'm not fit for this world. I'm – worthless. (*Winces with pain.*) Listen. I said I put words into people's mouths. Well, now I want to I can't get them out of my own –

INT. SECOND CRYOGENIC LAB. DAY
In reverse, so we see them from front on, looking at the living wall somewhere behind us.

INT. KARAOKE BAR. NIGHT
DANIEL: (*Continuous*) My brother, oh, it's years, years – they let
    him come home for a trial week when he passed this
    degree in – this degree in physics, cryophysics – Are you
    getting any of this? Can you understand *at all?*
    (*So urgently that he grabs at her arm. She pulls away and looks
    around.*)
SANDRA: Hey. Steady on, Romeo.
DANIEL: (*Sobs*) He drove straight at her. Says – says he didn't
    know she was there. But that's what he said about the first
    one. The boy. Straight at her! And he is me. I am him. I
    feel it – him – I feel in my bones I'm not fit to – fit to – I
    should be put away! Put away!
    (*Under the enormously urgent pressure of what he is saying,
    DANIEL seems to be crumpling up, sinking down, and at the
    same time, for support, and in earnest plea, clutching at first
    her arms and then her waist as he crumples – and 'Why Must
    I be a Teenager in Love?' starts up on the karaoke
    machinery.*)
SANDRA: (*Yelling*) Hey! Somebody quick!

EXTREME CLOSE-UP – DANIEL
*As he disintegrates, so to speak, physically and emotionally, falling,
failing this time to clutch at her retreating legs, which go off screen, he
screams with an open mouth but no sound.*

INT. KARAOKE CLUB. AT THE SOUND. NIGHT
*Exactly where the Japanese businessmen stood, and to exactly the
same pictures on all the little karaoke screens they sing to, the
PREACHER from the chapel, dressed exactly as he was in the chapel
scene, holds the karaoke mike.*
PREACHER: Brothers and sisters, children in Jesus, today has
    been a special day in our chapel because the band has
    marched through the street carrying our banner –
    (*But everyone in the club is running now towards DANIEL, who*

is curled up in a ball of pained fear and degradation, just as he was in the chapel aisle.)

INT. SECOND CRYOGENIC LAB. DAY
Reverse from living wall, looking front on at the watchers, who are showing a few signs of bewilderment or consternation, especially DR RAWL, *the newcomer. No wonder, for –*

INT. KARAOKE CLUB. NIGHT
The place is now filled with bandsmen (in uniforms) and children from the chapel. Daniel's FATHER *is rushing from one of the booths, in his brass-band outfit.*
DANIEL'S FATHER: Daniel! Oh, Danny! Danny! My Dan!

TWO-SHOT: FYODOR/LUANDA. LAB
LUANDA, *seeking* FYODOR's *eye, receives a nod of instruction and she gets up immediately.*

INT. KARAOKE CLUB. NIGHT
At the end of the booth (where the 'hostesses' had been sitting), rising with the children, open-mouthed, eyes wide with concern and fear, CHRISTOPHER, *the twin – and of course the boy who had played young* DANIEL *in the woods.*
CHRIS: (*Shouting*) It's Daniel, not me. It's Daniel, not Christopher! Not me! I didn't do it!

INT. BAR. KARAOKE CLUB. NIGHT
A whole throng of bandsmen and children now around DANIEL, *who has stopped crawling.*
DANIEL'S FATHER: Give him some air, oot! Dan. Dan o'butty! Oh, Dan – What's happened – ?
(*Going in closer, closer to* DANIEL.)

CLOSE-UP – DR RAWL. LAB. DAY
Getting up out of his autocube in great alarm as – reversing –

INT. LAB AND LIVING WALL. DAY
The huge, dominating screen wall is now entirely filled with Daniel's face, and the face (as once before, in trauma) is going into rubbery,

DENNIS POTTER

flexible, hideously stretched and warped distortions, before –

BLACK SCREEN
No sound. No sight. Pulling back –

INT. SECOND CRYOGENIC LAB. DAY
The watchers against the wholly black screen –
EMMA: (*To* RAWL) This has happened once before. It comes at
     a particular trauma, and it follows a great deal of displaced
     memory and visual distortion –
     (*Meanwhile –*)

CLOSE-UP – 'FEED' RACK. BELOW BLACK BOX
*Below in this lab, whereas it was above in the first one – but
essentially the same design and with the same purpose.* LUANDA *is
turning off the particular hair-fine loop of capillary coiling up to the
black box, marked alpha-neuropeptide 1042. The male lab assistant,*
GEORGE, *has gone across with her and nods as she shows him what
she is doing.*

INT. SECOND CRYOGENIC LAB. DAY
*The blackness yields to a few grey dots, and then a swirl of grey dots
and then a much faster swirl of multicoloured dots.*
RAWL: (*Interested*) And the distortion, the trauma – breakdown,
     if you like – is connected directly or indirectly with sexual
     activity. Yes?
EMMA: Probably.
TONY: You will have to update yourself on the material we've
     gathered so far, Dr Rawl. But that scene mixed up his
     meeting with a girl who was at his deathbed with the girl he
     had been due to marry, and with a homosexual assault
     Daniel had endured as a boy while alone with his dog in
     the woods.
FYODOR: (*With conviction*) And with what seems to *me* to be a
     lot of self-hatred – or certainly a sense of unworthiness. He
     must have been difficult to know or to like if that is what he
     felt about himself.
LUANDA: And of course he was disguising his own condition
     from himself by the fact that he was a writer.

370

EMMA: (*Smug*) As I tried to point out some time ago.

RAWL: Meaning?

LUANDA: Well, he is then by nature adept at what most of us do rather more awkwardly – make a *shape* out of our own lives, murmur comforting consolations about what we have or have not done – *rewrite* the past, in effect.

RAWL: But now that he has reached this traumatic state, how do you begin again, how do you – ?

TONY: Kick-start him with a memory of some public event during his life that he might have seen or remembered or – We feed him archive stuff, and wait and see.

EMMA: Maybe *this* time – (*Thinks.*) Yes. Why not? If we feed back to him one of his *own* recollections – instead of an old newsreel or whatever – ? What you think?

FYODOR: There's quite a bit of material recorded by now. I haven't even seen all of it myself.

TONY: (*Too quickly*) Has Mr Siltz got this stuff?

(FYODOR *looks at him.*)

FYODOR: Tony. Why are you *always* so concerned about Siltz's interests?

TONY: (*Hotly*) Because he's been fair to us. We owe him.

FYODOR: (*Sardonic smile*) *I* don't.

TONY: (*Passionately*) Well, you should!

(*Then he realizes he's been* too *passionate, and tries to adjust.*)

I mean, I just think, that – (*Lamely*) Fair's fair. That's all.

EMMA: All the material recorded goes automatically to Siltz. It's in the contract. So you needn't worry about that. Worry instead about what he's going to do with it.

(*The other of the two lab assistants, a young woman,* VALERIE, *sees this as a chance to bring up something that has been troubling her.*)

VALERIE: Excuse me, Professor.

EMMA: Yes? Valerie, isn't it? That your name?

VALERIE: Yes, Professor. I wanted –

EMMA: (*Overriding*) And – George, isn't it?

GEORGE: That's right, Professor.

EMMA: Well, it can't have been easy for you two, taking over from nowhere, so to speak, but our two lab assistants *both* had terrible endings, and I hope *you* will not be prone to any disasters.

FLASH: TWO-SHOT – GEORGE AND VALERIE. LAB
Flashing each other looks of potentially comic potential alarm. Then
VALERIE *turns, to try again.*

INT. SECOND CRYOGENIC LAB. DAY
VALERIE: But there *is* one thing that troubled us – isn't there, George?
GEORGE: It's a bit *odd*.
EMMA: What is it?
VALERIE: I took over – whatwashername – ? *Blinda's* log – and there's a difference in footage between the amount of tape actually recorded and the amount entered each day in the log.
(FYODOR *is quickly on to some possible implications. He is very sharp, as, now, is his tone.*)
FYODOR: Difference plus or minus?
VALERIE: More was recorded than was entered.
EMMA: How very strange.
FYODOR: Much more? And every day?
VALERIE: *Nearly* every day. And the differences varied between twenty-two seconds and one minute fifteen seconds.
LUANDA: She was very meticulous about those sorts of things. Why did she make *that* sort of mistake? Over so many days.
FYODOR: If it was once or twice – a mistake, maybe. But this must be by design, or by something she didn't know.
(*Quickly, to* GEORGE) Do you record the amount of time we are in the lab – or anyone, come to that – and the head is, so to speak, switched on?
GEORGE: To the second. It's also done automatically – (*Nods at digital counter at the top of the message wall.*) And they always match.
FYODOR: So – yesterday, for instance, we had the head on, to the best of my recollection, for six different spells of about, give or take a few seconds, eight minutes.

CLOSE-UP – VALERIE
VALERIE *looks at her belt-attached read-out notebook and presses a digit.*
VALERIE: That's it. Forty-seven minutes. 54.3268 seconds.

CLOSE-UP – FYODOR
A blaze of thought flares in his eyes. A beat.
FYODOR: Now – do you *then* measure the length of tape? *Do you?*

INT. SECOND CRYOGENIC LAB. DAY
GEORGE *and* VALERIE *make quick glances at each other.*
VALERIE: Well – no.
FYODOR: (*Snaps*) *Why not?*
GEORGE: Because we know we cannot take more tape than the
time we took making it. I mean, they are obviously the
same thing, sir, the length of tape and the length of time.
LUANDA: Unless *someone else* is coming in here after we've gone
– and managing, somehow, to get the head to – No. That's
utter nonsense.
TONY: Especially for such short times. I mean, the longest was
– what? – a minute and fifteen seconds.

CLOSE-UP – FYODOR
Brooding hard, and hard thoughts which are leading him to misery.
EMMA: (*Off screen*) No, I agree. Nobody would set up such an
elaborate mechanism for so little reward. And then leave
the tape, anyway. How did you come to notice the
mismatch?

INT. SECOND CRYOGENIC LAB. DAY
FYODOR *still broodily abstracted.*
VALERIE: It was just because we were taking over. We had to
record the lengths of tape for Mr Siltz, and it was only later
that I noticed the difference between –
FYODOR: (*Suddenly*) *He did it himself.*
(*Silence. They all look at him. Then –*)
TONY: Come on. That's bloody cretolo!
FYODOR: (*Fiercely*) Cretolo, is it? Cretolo? You think I'm that
stupid, do you?

373

TONY: Hey. I wasn't trying to be personal, or –

FYODOR: (*Interrupts*) I am telling you what is the only logical deduction. We have always soothed ourselves with what I am beginning to think is an anodyne lie. Yes?

EMMA: (*Disturbed*) What lie, Fyodor?

FYODOR: The lie that Daniel Feeld does not in any meaningful sense know that he is in this half-dead, half-alive state. The lie that his memories are to him in this condition as dreams are to a sleeper who is asleep. The lie that Daniel Feeld has no *volition*.
(*Silence.*
LUANDA *is the first to speak, and her voice has thickened with emotion.*)

LUANDA: You mean, you mean that Daniel has been transmitting his memories when we're not here and he's in that neutral, just ticking-over state that – (*Nods at the living wall*) he is in now.
(*The wall, of course, is one continual swirl of incomprehensible, multicoloured dots.*)

FYODOR: That's exactly what I mean.
(*Luanda's hands go to her face and her words are almost a sob.*)

LUANDA: *Oh, the poor creature –*

EMMA: (*Sudden, decisive, to* VALERIE) What day was the first day where there was more tape than there is time recorded for making that tape?
(VALERIE *attends to her read-out electronic notemaker again. They wait.*)

VALERIE: Actually, it was day one. Very first day.

EMMA: And how long is it? The extra.

VALERIE: Twenty-eight seconds.
(EMMA *jabs at something on her autocube, urgently.*)

EMMA: (*To someone beyond*) We want Lazarus Project, Daniel Feeld, Day One. Final twenty-eight seconds. Punch it through quickly.

FYODOR: It might not have been at the end, after we'd gone. Could have been any time we weren't here – lunch, for instance.

EMMA: Could be. But this is the most likely.

374

(*A long, soft bleeeeeep, and they all turn as one to look at the screen on the message wall. It is not as gigantically overpowering as the living wall, but it is still a very large screen indeed.*)

MESSAGE WALL SCREEN
The Siltz logo followed by: TAPE DAY ONE. DANIEL FEELD: FINAL 28 SECONDS. *Then, narrowing down to the screen only, it begins.*

INT. DANIEL'S HOSPITAL ROOM. 1994. DAY
Daniel's lips have just been moistened by SANDRA, *and* BEN *is speaking to* DANIEL *as one might to an injured or fretful child.*
BEN: Better? Eh?
DANIEL: (*Off screen, urgent croak*) Ben. Ben, I – listen.
  (*But he stops. They are all desperately attentive. They wait –
  Then –*)
BEN: Daniel. Say it. Say it, old lad.
  (*Sounds of struggling noises in Daniel's throat.*)
DANIEL: (*Off screen*) No biog-g-gah.
  (*Not really comprehensible.*)

EXTREME CLOSE-UP – BEN. LOOMING IN
BEN: What? No what?
  (*Sounds, off screen, from* DANIEL, *of final struggle and
  eventually a released near-shout.*
DANIEL: (*Off screen, loud*) Ben!

INT. DANIEL'S HOSPITAL ROOM. DAY
All around the bed frozen as though in the still-life of terror *in the face of actual death.*
A gurgle, off screen, and then the very last heave of the last two words the mortal DANIEL *will ever speak.*
DANIEL: (*Off screen, near-scream*) No biography!
  (*Blackness. Then words form.*)

INT. SECOND CRYOGENIC LAB. DAY
They stare at the black screen with the words: END OF TAPE DAY ONE. *Complete with the Siltz logo.*
EMMA/LUANDA: (*Almost same time*) But we saw that –

TONY: The extra must come from elsewhere.

FYODOR: (*Savagely*) Must it? Must it?

(*They all look at him. He is quivering.*)

EMMA: Dr Glazunov –

FYODOR: I don't believe you'll find those twenty-eight seconds anywhere else on Day One Tape. I think he was deliberately summoning up *that* memory.

(LUANDA *lets the implications sink in.*)

LUANDA: And he cut it short, too.

FYODOR: Exactly. Now, correct me if I'm wrong, but didn't the memory *we* saw go up on to the – um – what did you call it, Luanda? The out-of-body experience.

LUANDA: Yes. It did.

EMMA: (*To* RAWL) He saw himself on his own deathbed, as though from the ceiling.

RAWL: (*Comically lugubrious*) That has also been known to happen during a particular energetic copulation.

LUANDA: (*Helplessly*) Has it?

RAWL: (*Prissily, slowly spoken*) Oh, certainly. When enough energy has been *spent*, so to speak, the oxygen supply can get rather limited, and what is then alleged to be the ecstasy of ejaculation is at times accompanied by the out-of-body descriptions associated with the narratives of those who have been brought back from the very point of death. (*To* VALERIE) If I may say so, this is especially true in the descriptions subsequently given by young ladies of their carnal activities, more particularly when they experienced multiple orgasms. Have you ever found that to be so?

VALERIE: (*Flustered*) Me?

LUANDA: (*Laughs*) Yeah – Why aren't you looking at me, Doctor?

(*But her slightly forced laugh dies at the continued expression on* FYODOR'*s face. He has no time for* RAWL'*s diversions.*)

FYODOR: (*Between his teeth*) The point is – the point *surely* is – that he chose to cut off the out-of-body experience and the tunnel experience in order to leave it precisely at his final two mortal words.

EMMA: No biography.

(*Pause.* FYODOR *turns away, as though in self-disgust.*)

FYODOR: We are his torturers.

EXT. SILTZ HOTEL. DAY
The extravaganza as extravaganzaed as ever.

INT./EXT. A POLICE 'BUBBLE'. STREETS. DAY
INSPECTOR-GENERAL COLIN CHALLENDER *in one of the larger 'bubbles' that are the standard vehicles of the time. He is alone, but speaking audphone only.*
CHALLENDER: Of course I don't want to interrupt Mr Siltz unnecessarily. But if you could give him this message –
VOICE WITHIN CAR: Will do.
CHALLENDER: Tell him Inspector-General Challender is on his way to the hotel via the Central Station, and that I will be there in about forty-five minutes if he could speak to me. Tell him it is sensitive.
VOICE WITHIN CAR: Will do.
CHALLENDER: Operation Lazarus sensitive. Repeat.
VOICE WITHIN CAR: Operation Lazarus sensitive. Will do.

INT. MASSAGE ROOM. SILTZ'S SUITE. DAY
The marbled and slabbed palace we have seen before, where the same TWO MASSEUSES *are pummelling and greasing the president of the corporation for which they work.*
SILTZ: (*Self-parody glee*) More. More. Yet more. I want to slither like an eel!
THE GIRLS: (*In unison*) Yes, Mr President!
(*All the screens in the big, marbled room are occupied, without sound, by a continuous loop of all the material Daniel's head has recorded in the four episodes to date.*)
SILTZ: Atta girls!
(SILTZ *just likes savouring the pictures. He keeps looking across at them as they slap, slap, rub, ooze, slap their fleshly cacophony.*)
SILTZ: (*Eventually*) Great stuff, isn't it? The pictures.
THE GIRLS: (*Almost in unison*) Yes, Mr President.
SILTZ: (*Grunts*) Turn me over.
(*And they do as he asks, with a big slithering splosh as his not ungenerous frame slides belly-down on the massage table.*

*There is a ding-dong! ding-dong! followed by a female voice,
from some speaker somewhere in the marble-echoey depths of the
room.)*

VOICE: Inspector-General Challender would like to see you
briefly in about forty-four minutes, Mr President.

SILTZ: *(Mildly)* Tell him to fuck off. I've got the hag-hour
coming up, with that batty old professor.

VOICE: Certainly, sir. But he says its quote sensitive unquote.

SILTZ: *(Sighs)* Still tell him to fuck off. Dealing with the dame is
enough to spoil one evening.

VOICE: Quote Operation Lazarus sensitive unquote, sir.

(SILTZ totally changes. His face sets.)

SILTZ: Then tell him the fuck *hurry up!* Come on, girls. Get me
sitting up. I've got to see an old lady. And then *another* old
lady. Who'd be me? Who'd be me!

INT. LEISURE ROOM. ICB LABORATORIES. DAY

EMMA, LUANDA *and* FYODOR *having a drink, or a snack.* EMMA,
*as though to break into some discussion that is getting tedious, is
looking around.*

EMMA: Well, it's no worse than the relax room at the other
place. And I *suppose* we can trust the no-bugging notices.

FYODOR: Which is supposing a great deal.

EMMA: You really *are* cynical, Fyodor. But you know that, don't
you?

FYODOR: No. I don't.

*(LUANDA laughs at this trenchancy. The dislike she had very
early on – Part One – shown to him has considerably toned
down since then.)*

LUANDA: At least you know where you are with him, Emma.

EMMA: *(Sighs)* Yes. Which is not always where you would wish
to be.

FYODOR: All I'm saying – No, listen, Emma – all I'm saying is
that from now on, everything we do to or about that head
has a moral dimension we too easily persuaded ourselves
was not actually there.

INT. ENTRANCE TO LEISURE ROOM. DAY

TONY, *coming in, looks around and then, with a slight frown of*

irritation, sees the three over at the far end of the room, talking earnestly.
He wends across towards them. They do not seem to have noticed his arrival.

INT. EMMA'S TABLE. REST ROOM. DAY
LUANDA: No, Fyodor, that's not what I'm saying at all. I'm not
 justifying the unjustifiable. It's simply, and I think fairly,
 that I want to be absolutely sure about this 'volition'
 business.
EMMA: And so do I.
 (TONY, *approaching, has still not been noticed because of the
 very serious nature of their conversation. He is coming in at an
 angle, partly obscured by the large potted plant.*)

INT. REST ROOM. PLANT. DAY
TONY *comes to a stop as –*
FYODOR: (*Off*) Well, I *am* sure. I am absolutely sure. And I'm
 sick to my stomach with the thought of it. Daniel Feeld has
 to be put out of whatever misery we are inflicting upon
 him –

CLOSE-UP – TONY. POTTED PLANT
*Deliberately cautious now, and not proceeding forward to join them,
he slightly adjusts his position so that the large potted plant more fully
obscures him from view.*
FYODOR: (*Off*) And I tell you this. If and when I get the chance,
 I'm willing to do it myself. Destroy the head.

INT. EMMA'S TABLE. DAY
Some slight shoulder or leg movement catches her eye. Then she sees
TONY, *walking quietly away from them.*
She frowns, but says nothing. FYODOR *mistakes her expression for
one of serious doubt.*
FYODOR: Isn't that *right*? Emma?
EMMA: You're both right.
FYODOR: (*Splutters*) We can't be!
EMMA: Oh, yes, you can. I agree with you, Fyodor, that we
 should not allow ourselves to become torturers –

FYODOR: (*Interrupts*) Particularly in the name of mass entertainment!
(*But* EMMA *holds up a hand to indicate that she has not finished.*)

EMMA: But it should not be impossible for the three of us together to devise a very specific response test which will establish for sure that, A, he has volition and, B, he is aware of his own condition.
(*Pause.*)

FYODOR: Fair enough. I accept that.
(*Pause.*)

LUANDA: And I accept the need to release him from bondage if that really is what he is in.
(*They all shake hands, in a duly solemn vow.*)

EMMA: (*With a half-laugh*) If Siltz finds out, we shall be hunted down for the rest of our given days. There will be nowhere to hide, you can be sure of that.

INT. 'LIVING ROOM'. SILTZ'S HOTEL. DAY
The warehouse-sized room seen before when vidphone conversation took place between EMMA *and* SILTZ.
SILTZ, *in a post-massage robe, is insisting that* CHALLENDER *do something with him that* CHALLENDER *doesn't seem too keen on.*

SILTZ: Come on, don't be prissy piss-arse English – it's one of the oldest games known to mankind. And good for the spirit, too.

CHALLENDER: Fine. If you know what you're doing. But I don't! (*He is being led through into – *)

INT. 'BILLIARD' OR POOL ROOM. SILTZ'S. DAY
Comparatively modest in scale when taken against the size and luxury of what else we have seen on this sky-high penthouse floor – made up like a typical American pool room of the 1920s and 1930s. A pool table, one only, with the necessary space around it, cue racks, a stocked bar with bar stools. A few communication gadgets, but otherwise nothing abnormal.

SILTZ: Sharpens up your sense of perspective. Get the right angle on things. And maybe win a little on the sidolo, eh?

CHALLENDER: (*Groans*) We *have* to wager?

SILTZ: We have to wager. What's a game if there's no winner? Christ, just a *hobby*, that's what. Hey, c'mon. We'll play for –

CHALLENDER: Fifty.

SILTZ: (*Taking cue*) A hundred.

CHALLENDER: (*Groans*) OK. But I get to start.

SILTZ: (*Wolfish gleam*) You get to start.

(*The balls on table, numbered, are already set up for play.* CHALLENDER *makes a big deal out of chalking his cue. It can be seen that both men very much want to win.*)

CHALLENDER: (*Chalking*) We at Central think that one of your Lazarus team is a RON.

(SILTZ *stiffens.* CHALLENDER *smirks, bends, pots.*)

INT. POOL TABLE TOP. DAY

A good shot. He gets to keep going, potting one straight off. Click!

CLOSE-UP – SILTZ

Tense, eyes narrowing, watching CHALLENDER. *Click! of balls, off, but* CHALLENDER *has not sunk one.*

INT. POOL ROOM. DAY

SILTZ *is slow about coming to the table.*

SILTZ: I don't want my team disturbed. This is a very, very delicate process. A team is a team is a team.

(*He bends. As he is about to pot.*)

CHALLENDER: A RON is a RON is a RON. To be eliminated.

(SILTZ *cues, click!, but no sink in pocket.* CHALLENDER *smirks.*)

SILTZ: (*Angrily*) So who is it? And whatcha grinning about?

(CHALLENDER *takes care to adjust his face.*)

CHALLENDER: Nothing. Nothing. I simply have amiable features, Dave, old man. Who? I don't think you'll be *totally* knocked off your horse. Glazunov. Fyodor Glazunov, the Slav.

(*He bends to pot – not easy for a man of his size.*)

SILTZ: Evidence?

(CHALLENDER *sinks another.*)

CHALLENDER: (*Smirks, again*) What you say?

SILTZ: (*Roars*) What's your fucking evidence!
> (CHALLENDER *adjusts his face again, realizing that he had better tread more carefully. He fails to pot next ball.*)

CHALLENDER: Principally – at first, that is – the notes given in by our agent in the lab, Blinda. An accumulation of small details.
> (SILTZ *bends to pot.*)

INT. POOL TABLE TOP. DAY
SILTZ *sinks a numbered ball with a satisfying click! and thump! into the pocket.*

INT. POOL ROOM. DAY
SILTZ *is suddenly a happier man.*
SILTZ: *Small* details. Itsy-bitsy, eh? Scraps. Little lumps of frog shit. That what you mean?
> (CHALLENDER *frowns as* SILTZ, *with a gleeful little suddenly-full-of-himself chuckle, walks around the table to take a profitable new position.*)

CHALLENDER: All pointing to *something*. And then this morning we recovered a scrap of paper from a man called Milton, who was a senior RON, which has the name Glazu- G-l-a-z-u – the rest incomplete, but it tells us something.
> (SILTZ *eyes up the cue ball, straightens, looks straight at* CHALLENDER.)

SILTZ: Glazuchevsky. Glazukon. Glazudyen. Glazupoff. Shall I go on?
CHALLENDER: No. But it's –
> (SILTZ *leaves table-side, comes up very close –*)

CLOSE-UP – SILTZ AND CHALLENDER
Cold eyes, jaw thrust, inches close, as face to face as their heights allow.
SILTZ: Nobody disturbs my team. Got it? I don't care if he's a fucking leper or a hermaphrodite, not if he's on my team. (*Deadly little pause.*) As you are. (*Deadly little pause.*) Tick one box. Yes. No.
CHALLENDER: Yes. As I am.

INT. POOL ROOM. DAY
SILTZ, *all beam and twinkle suddenly, slaps* CHALLENDER *hard on back or arm before resuming his stance, and his bend, at the table. He pots.*

INT. POOL TABLE TOP. DAY
Satisfyingly, a numbered ball traverses two-thirds of the length of the table before, almost out of length, it slowly hesitates (almost) on the brink of the pocket, then drops.

INT. POOL ROOM. DAY
CHALLENDER *looks pretty fed up about everything.*
SILTZ: (*Exuberantly*) Hey! Weigh! Hey-ey! (*Looks slyly across at* CHALLENDER.) Wonder if we could get that batty old dame to play? She ought to be hot-shit at working out angles.
CHALLENDER: (*Sullen*) Which old dame?
(SILTZ *eyes up the cue ball again.*)
SILTZ: The Professor. I have a drink with her in twenty minutes. Contractual. She hates me, but she can't escape. (*Chuckles.*) I rub her toffee-nose in the toffee-paper wrapping, and make her blow into it. Hee-hee.
(*Bends to pot.*)

INT. TABLE TOP. DAY
Click-click! Clunk into pocket.

INT. POOL ROOM. DAY
As pleased as a small boy, SILTZ *pretends a concern.*
SILTZ: Twenty minutes. Think that's too soon? With this game and all?

INT. TONY WATSON'S APARTMENT. DAY
Another comfortable, even luxurious, space, brimming with all the 2368 communications technology. But TONY *does not seem to be at his ease. In fact, he is walking up and down, up and down, in diminishing lengths, wrestling with some problem, or his conscience.*

CLOSE-UP – EMMA
With as much disdain as she can muster.

EMMA: Thank you, no. I'll stick to good, plain mineral water.
No ice.

INT. BAR CORNER. SILTZ'S 'LIVING ROOM'. DUSK
EMMA *is sitting bolt upright on a bar stool, her back all but up
against the wall, as though she were as far away as she can get. But,
in all this vast space,* SILTZ *insists on crowding her.*
SILTZ: Hey, come on. You never let your hair down, do you?
EMMA: You know nothing whatsoever about me, Mr Siltz. So
please do not make such categorical statements.
(SILTZ *moves back an inch or two and squats on a stool, his
hands making a gesture of mock surrender.*)
SILTZ: OK. OK. I won't keep you long. There's some pretty
damn good stuff coming out to my editors. When we
launch this thing, it'll knock everyone's head off. Rumour
is already blowing up a storm for us, and if the first –
FEMALE VOICE: Audcall from Anthony Watson for you, Mr
President. Want to take?
SILTZ: Not at the – (*Then*) Sure. Why the hell not? (*To* EMMA)
We're all colleagues, right? (*Leans over bar, presses a button
on an array of them.*) How's you doing, Tony?
TONY'S VOICE: May I ask if you are alone, Mr Siltz?
(SILTZ *eyes* EMMA *with a malicious little chuckle.*)
SILTZ: You may. The answer is No. I'm having a great time
with a dame. She's a real flyer!
TONY'S VOICE: S-sorry, sir – but – there's something you really
ought to know. Eff why ee oh.
SILTZ: What's that mean? You lose your teeth, what?
TONY'S VOICE: (*Abashed*) Um. For your ears only.
(*Siltz's grin half-dies. He looks at* EMMA, *considering.*)
SILTZ: Well, I don't suppose it would bother the lady I'm with,
Tony – but, Jeezolo, if you're going to go all spooky on me
I guess I'd better hitch a lift to another room. Stay on hold.
(*To* EMMA) Excuse me, ma'am.
(*She simply inclines her head in response to his half-mocking,
formal little bow. He waddles out of the room. She goes to sip
her water, with a slight frown, then suddenly freezes.*)

CLOSE-UP – EMMA
*A look of sick foreboding. An image, a sound, flies up at her, starting
with the sound only.*
FYODOR: (*Over*) – *if and when I get the chance. I'm willing to do it
    myself. Destroy the head.*

INT. POTTED PLANT. REST ROOM. DAY
As from Emma's point of view: the image of TONY, *walking quietly
away from them.*

CLOSE-UP – EMMA. THE BAR
A slow sigh of fear or doubt.
EMMA: (*Softly*) I wonder.

INT. BAR CORNER, SILTZ'S 'LIVING ROOM'. DUSK/NIGHT
Suddenly, she moves. She scuttles along the bar to the row of buttons
SILTZ *had just used. She leans over the bar, as he did.*

CLOSE-UP – VID/AUDPHONE ARRAY OF BUTTONS
*One of them – the engaged one – glows red. She runs her finger
along the row, finds a similarly shaped one as the glowing one,
presses.*

INT. BAR CORNER. DUSK/NIGHT
EMMA *sounds hasty and furtive, one eye on the door.*
EMMA: 009896102. Fyodor. I think they're on to you. Get out
    now. Get out in case. Message ends.
    (*She resumes her place, sips her water.*
        *After a few seconds more, and he has not returned, she leans
    over to look at the glowing button. It goes off. As she is about
    to relax back again, the same button glows again. A fresh
    call.*)

INT. STUDY/LIBRARY. SILTZ'S SUITE. DUSK/NIGHT
*Books bought by the yard. Library steps. Desk. High-tech
accoutrements. Screens. On one of which –*

INT. SCREEN. STUDY. DUSK/NIGHT
CHALLENDER *in his underclothing.*

CHALLENDER: (*On screen*) – into the tub, Dave. So this had better be – and I'm not, repeat not, playing pool again. OK. Shoot.

INT. STUDY. DUSK/NIGHT
SILTZ: I made a mistake, Colin. You're right. A RON is a RON is a RON. What's the world coming to! Go get him, Colin. And syringe the bastard to death.

INT./EXT. FYODOR'S BUBBLE. STREETS. NIGHT
Passing through a particularly desolate area of 'old London', beyond the abandoned warehouse once called the Albert Hall, FYODOR *stares out with a grim sigh.*
FYODOR: (*To self*) Oh, brave new world. (*Then he buttons in his messages. They begin with a whirr and a bleep.*)
FIRST VOICE: Fyodor. John. I'd like to arrange a meeting with you to discuss your equities. My advice is if you buy an extra tranche in Rothman bubble you'll, A, make a small profit and, B, qualify as a full voter in state elections because you will then have shares beyond the thirty-corporation equity barrier. Can you try Wednesday, six p.m.? Bleep!
FYODOR: (*To self*) No.
SECOND VOICE: Bleep! Fyodor. I think they're on to you. Get out now. Get out in case. Message ends. Bleep! (*Fyodor's expression does not change. Then, calmly, taking out and checking his small gun.*) FG 170535. Return to the ICB laboratories. Turn around and go back.
CAR VOICE: Registered.

CLOSE-UP – EMMA. BAR
Flustered, but firm.
EMMA: The point I'm *trying* to make Mr Siltz, *if you would please stop screaming and shouting –*

INT. CORNER OF BAR. SILTZ'S. NIGHT
SILTZ: (*Yells*) You stupid stupid stupid old cow! Don't tell *me* what to do!
(*It looks as though he is going to hit her. She stands up, pushes*

him away with the palm of her hand against his chest,
astounding him.)

EMMA: The point is that that head may well be aware of its own
condition. And *if* that is indeed the case, it'll be a moral
outrage for us to proceed further.
(*She is already walking away. Rigid with anger, his hands*
clenched, he bellows after her.)

SILTZ: For *you* to, yes! You won't get the fucking chance, you
prim old bag! I'll put in a new team by the time it takes you
to widdle yourself!

INT. CORRIDOR. ICB LABS. NIGHT
FYODOR *is running down the corridor. A curious employee from*
another department looks at him, with a would-be sardonic raise of
eyebrow.
EMPLOYEE: Work can always wait, mate!
(FYODOR *reaches his lab, and in.*)

INT. SECOND CRYOGENIC LAB. NIGHT
FYODOR *immediately begins to drag, heave, push, carry and stack*
as many of the high-tech black boxes, cubes, devices and as much
furniture as he can high and hard up against the lab door, panting
now as the effort increases.
On the living wall, the same myriad dots, multicoloured and in
perpetual swirl, showing that Daniel's head is in 'neutral'.

INT. THE BLACK BOX. OPPOSITE LIVING WALL. NIGHT
Looking straight at Daniel's ghastly severed head, gleaming silvery.
There seems, again, to be a twitch of sorts at eyelid or mouth or both.

INT. SECOND CRYOGENIC LAB. NIGHT
Almost done stacking, FYODOR *stops dead at a change in the light*
flickering from the living wall. He turns, slowly, and watches,
paralysed, as –

INT. LAB AND LIVING WALL. NIGHT
The dots, blobs, bigger blobs yielding up the picture of DANIEL *at his*
desk in his apartment, 1994, exactly as it was last seen in Karaoke.
He is scribbling, urgently.

Then the face turns, and DANIEL *seems to indicate his pad. He holds it up. Go in to –*

CLOSE-UP – A4 WRITING PAD
DANIEL *has written in capital letters: LET ME GO!*

INT. SECOND CRYOGENIC LAB. NIGHT
FYODOR *bursts into tears and puts his hands to his face, with the now incontrovertible truth that* DANIEL *has volition and knows his own condition.*
He goes to the box, tears streaming, and looks straight in.
FYODOR: Forgive. Forgive us. Forgive me. (*Then*) Can you hear me? Can you? Is there any –

INT. BLACK BOX. NIGHT
DANIEL'*s eyelid twitches once, and then his face goes into what has* (*stretching the word*) *been called 'composed'.*

INT. SECOND CRYOGENIC LAB. NIGHT
FYODOR: No. Of course you can't.
    (*He turns and looks at the living wall. The Daniel-at-desk image is sliding apart into long blobs, then shorter ones, then fragmenting totally into the swirl of dots.*)

INT. FYODOR'S APARTMENT. NIGHT
The doors have been smashed in and everything turned upside-down by rampaging MILITIA POLICE, *heavily armed and in severe protective gear. One of them, helmet cocked as he listens, eye-shutters open, holds up an arm to still the rest.*
MILITIAMAN: Got you. OK. They've scrawled through his vehicle instructions. The bubble was told to return to the ICB laboratories. Let's go it!

INT. SECOND CRYOGENIC LAB. NIGHT
FYODOR, *with a good 'blunt instrument' – some hunk of wood or metal from the lab – is systematically smashing up the laboratory.*

INT. CORRIDOR. ICB BUILDING. NIGHT
Heavily armed militia-style police come running, at least ten of them.

CLOSE-UP – 'FEED' RACK. CRYOGENIC LAB. NIGHT
Smash! Crash! Smash! as FYODOR *lays waste all the rows of liquid seeping out from the fractured phials.*

INT. SECOND CRYOGENIC LAB. NIGHT
Out of breath, FYODOR *pulls his gun as he hears the approaching thunder of feet. They stop. The door is pushed, but does not, of course, yield.*

INT. CORRIDOR OUTSIDE LAB. NIGHT
MILITIAMAN: He knows. He's barricaded. (*Shrugs.*) We've got to wait anyway. Switch on the address system and give me the lead.
(*They wait, in a menacing row, laser guns cradled ready.*)

INT. SECOND CRYOGENIC LAB. NIGHT
By climbing up some of the impedimenta he has put in place all along the door wall, FYODOR *can reach a small vent. He looks around and, identifying this possible firing position, calculates it in relationship to the head box.*
Then he climbs. But as he does so –
LOUDSPEAKER VOICE: Fyodor Glazunov. We know you are in there, and *you* know you have no chance of escape. There is no need for violence. Come out now and you will be treated properly. Come out now, before it is too late.
FYODOR: (*Panting to self*) Arsehole. (*He has got himself into position to look through the vent, down into the corridor. He turns his head, aims his gun at the box and sees that he can indeed do what he intends to do from this position. He turns back to the vent.*)

INT. CORRIDOR. VENT-VIEW. NIGHT
The small oblong view just above the head of the MILITIAMAN *who spoke. The* MILITIAMAN *is turning.*
MILITIAMAN: (*Off, just audible*) He's here, sir. But he's barricaded. That's no problem to us, but I understand there are areas you want undamaged –

INT. CORRIDOR. NIGHT
SILTZ *seizes hold of the loudspeaker lead.*
SILTZ: Listen. Fyodor. You've got yourself in a jam, my boy.
Now, I'm here to help you. I *know* I can help you. All I
want – and you have my guarantee on this, my personal ga-
aaaaaaaa – (*Ending so as a bullet hits him in the throat. He
falls, hands going up to his throat, but he'll be dead by the time
he hits the floor.*)

INT. SECOND CRYOGENIC LAB. NIGHT
With a ferocious grin, FYODOR *pulls the gun away from how he had
rested it on or at the vent, and turns to look down at the box.*
FYODOR: Personal guarantee, Daniel. (*He fires straight at the box,
just as the firing begins in the corridor outside, blasting at the
shored-up defences.*)

INT. BLACK BOX. LAB. NIGHT
*The bullet hits, fracturing the front casing, and the whole box, with
Daniel's head floating in liquid nitrogen, explodes like a massive
bomb in a tremendous orange flash and reverberating noise.*
FYODOR *falls, dead. The door wall blows out.*

INT. CORRIDOR OUTSIDE. NIGHT
*The front rank of militia lie dead and wounded from the force of the
blast, and flames gush out of the lab, making a fireball as they scorch
along the corridor, devastating everything in sight.*
(*Dissolve.*)

BLACK SCREEN
*With just a tiny flicker of white at its very centre, like a remnant of
flame.*

WITHIN SWIRLING TUNNEL
*The flame pulses, brighter and larger at far end of suddenly swirling
black. A tinkle of syncopated music, and on the first 'Hush' of the
vocal.*

INT. SMALL BEDROOM. NIGHT
Boy DANIEL *pulling the bedsheet up over his nose and mouth.*

SINGER:
> – hush, hush, here comes the bogey man,
> **Don't let him get too close to you,**
> **He'll catch you if he can!**

DANIEL: Chris!
> (*Great crowd roar as, within the swirl, the images fade and change.*)

EXT. TWICKENHAM. DAY
A dazzling England try. Fading as light at centre pulses, grows.

X-RAY MONITOR SCREEN
A digestive system at work, within the 'tunnel', instantly succeeded by –

EXT. TREE TOP
Young DANIEL *clings to the top of an oak tree, fade, flicking to –*

MAX WALL ON STAGE DOING HIS 'FUNNY WALK'

INT. CHAPEL. DAY
SINGING CHILDREN:
> **Will there be any stars, any stars in my crown –**
> (*Taking on richer resonances, the light getting bigger –*)

INT. BEDROOM
BETH *undoes her bra-strap from the back, then turns shyly.*
> **When at evening the sun goes down?**
> **When I wake –**

EXT. NEW COLLEGE LANE, OXFORD
Young man on bicycle – from back – whoopees!, spreading his arms, crashing.
> **– with the blest**
> **In the mansion of rest**
> **Will there –**

CLOSE-UP – DANIEL. WINE BAR. 1994. NIGHT
Draining red wine with deliberately vulgar little burp, and cackling a

glee of a challenge to someone mostly off screen.
– be any stars in my crown?

SWIRLING TUNNEL. BRIGHT LIGHT
Tropical bird flutters briefly, and the beat of its wing the last remnant of the swirl as we seem to plunge headlong into the very bright light – and briefly, comically, movingly an amplified fragment of Ronnie Ronalde whistling 'Birdsong at Eventide' with Robert Farnon and his Orchestra completing the plunge into –

BRILLIANT WHITE SCREEN
Scarcely discernible hint of child's image of angel wings and cherubs, white on white.
DANIEL: (*Over, triumphant cry, repeated in increasing joy*)
    Ye-e-e-e-e-es! Ye-e-e-e-es! Ye-e-e-e-e-es! Ye-e-e-e-e-es!